OXFORD READINGS IN PHILOSOPHY

THE PHILOSOPHY OF ARTIFICIAL LIFE

D0145814

Published in this series

Other volumes are in preparation

THE PHILOSOPHY OF ARTIFICIAL LIFE

edited by

MARGARET A. BODEN

OXFORD UNIVERSITY PRESS

1996

Oxford University Press, Walton Street, Oxford OX2 6DP

Oxford New York
Athens Auckland Bangkok Bombay
Calcutta Cape Town Dar es Salaam Delhi
Florence Hong Kong Istanbul Karachi
Kuala Lumpur Madras Madrid Melbourne
Mexico City Nairobi Paris Singapore
Taipei Tokyo Toronto

and associated companies in
Berlin Ibadan

Oxford is a trade mark of Oxford University Press

Published in the United States
by Oxford University Press Inc., New York

Introduction and selection © Oxford University Press 1996

British Library Cataloguing in Publication Data

Data available

Library of Congress Cataloging-in-Publication Data
Boden, Margaret A.
The philosophy of artificial life / Margaret A. Boden.
(Oxford readings in philosophy)
Includes bibliographical references.
1. Artificial life. I. Title. II. Series.
BD418.8.B63 1996 113'.8—dc20 95–43389

ISBN 0–19–875154–0
ISBN 0–19–875155–9 (pbk.)

1 3 5 7 9 10 8 6 4 2

Typeset by Graphicraft Typesetters Ltd., Hong Kong
Printed in Great Britain
on acid-free paper by
Bookcraft (Bath) Ltd.,
Midsomer Norton, Avon

PREFACE

Artifical life (A-Life) covers a very broad range of topics, and its philosophical interest is correspondingly diverse. The papers in this volume are arranged, so far as possible, in groups that address distinct (but interrelated) themes.

Readers unfamiliar with A-Life should read Chapter 1 first. It is an overview of the field, written by a leading A-Life researcher, and provides a helpful entry-point into the relevant scientific literature. Chapter 2 also is introductory in nature. In discussing the use of the concept of autonomy in the artificial sciences, it sketches the relation between A-Life and classical AI. These two papers, together with the Introduction, provide an intellectual framework for the collection as a whole.

Part II (Chs. 3 to 6) describes specific examples of A-Life research, emphasizing its relation to theoretical biology. These chapters (with one exception) were written for a philosophical audience, but are rather more technical than the other papers in the volume. The 'fiercer' parts of Chapters 3 and 4 may be skimmed by readers not wishing to master the details, but these passages should not be skipped entirely as they illustrate influential types of A-Life argument.

Chapters 7 to 10 (Part III) discuss specific explanatory strategies in A-Life, and relate them to various AI methodologies: evolutionary robotics, situated robotics, animate vision, and classical and connectionist AI. A recurring question in Part III is whether A-Life or associated disciplines need to explain behaviour in terms of internal representations.

Part IV (Chs. 11 to 13) focuses on the concept of life in general, including the views of past philosophers (Aristotle, Spencer, and Dewey).

Finally, A-Life's relation to functionalism, and the feasibility of 'strong' A-Life, are explored in Part V (Chs. 14 and 15).

M. A. B.

CONTENTS

INTRODUCTION

THE INTELLECTUAL CONTEXT OF ARTIFICIAL LIFE

Artificial Life (A-Life) uses informational concepts and computer modelling to study life in general, and terrestrial life in particular. It raises many philosophical problems, including the nature of life itself.

There is no universally agreed definition of life. The concept covers a cluster of properties, most of which are themselves philosophically problematic: self-organization, emergence, autonomy, growth, development, reproduction, evolution, adaptation, responsiveness, and metabolism.

Theorists differ about the relative importance of these properties, although it is generally agreed that the possession of most (not necessarily all) of them suffices for something to be regarded as alive. It is not even obvious that, as A-Life scientists assume, life is a natural kind. In other words, 'life' may not be a scientifically grounded category (such as water, or tiger), whose real properties unify and underlie the similarities observed in all those things we call 'alive'. Instead, it may pick out a rag-bag of items with no fundamental unity. Advances in A-Life should help to resolve this issue, and to identify the underlying unities (if any).

The field raises fundamental problems also about the nature of explanation in various areas of biology, and in cognitive science. One of these is whether (and if so, how) psychological explanations should be constrained by biological facts.

Another concerns the choice between computational and dynamical explanations. Some A-Life researchers argue that dynamical systems theory is more promising than computational theories in investigating life and mind. A dynamical system is one whose states change over time according to some rule. Computational systems are a special case, whose states change stepwise according to the instructions in the program. Many dynamical systems—the weather, for example—change continuously, and are described by differential equations such as those used in physics. Which type of change is characteristic of cognitive systems is a controversial question. Such dynamical systems may be closely coupled, changes in one affecting general parameters (not just individual states) in the other, so that it is difficult to make a principled distinction between the 'two' systems. So, for instance, some A-Life workers regard the distinction between organism and environment as deeply problematic.

Moreover, since most (though not all) A-Lifers define life in informational terms, A-Life places functionalism in a new scientific context. Functionalism is the philosophy of mind which defines mental states in terms of their causal relations with other mental (and environmental) states, and which assumes that these causal relations are, in principle, expressible in computational terms (Putnam 1960, 1967). In short, pain, fear, or jealousy are to be defined not as phenomenal experiences, nor as physical events in the brain, but as abstract functional (causal) roles. Functionalism (with respect to mind) is widely accepted within AI, most of whose practitioners define mental phenomena in informational terms. Many A-Life workers take a similar view of life itself.

A-Life is highly interdisciplinary (Langton 1995). It has profuse intellectual connections with theoretical biology, including morphology, embryology, ethology, evolutionary theory, and ecology. It has links with psychological sciences such as developmental and cognitive psychology, computational neuroscience, neuromorphic engineering (wherein brainlike systems are built using real neurones), and computational psychology. And it is related to artificial intelligence (AI) and cognitive science, which try to model psychology much as work in A-Life attempts to illuminate biology.

It is related also to biochemistry, economics, and the mathematics of complexity. However, the overall emphasis of this collection concerns A-Life's relevance to theoretical biology and cognitive science.

Commercial applications of A-Life range widely: from pharmaceutical research, through financial services and telecommunications, to the visual arts. The bats in the film *Batman Returns* were controlled by simple A-Life flocking algorithms (Reynolds 1987), and sprouting vegetation and 'natural' surface-patterns can be automatically generated by algorithms defining branching and pigmentation (Prusinkiewicz 1994). Evolutionary programming is being used in computer art (Todd and Latham 1992; Sims 1991), behavioural animation (Reynolds 1994*a*, 1994*b*; Sims 1994), and architectural design (Frazer 1995).

Clearly, then, A-Life is relevant to diverse philosophical interests. So far as possible, the papers in this volume are grouped around specific themes. Chapter 1 provides a general overview of the field. Chapter 2 compares A-Life with AI, focusing on the concept of autonomy. Chapters 3 to 6, and part of Chapter 7, describe examples of A-Life research, emphasizing its relation to biology and cognitive science. Chapters 7 to 10 discuss various explanatory strategies in A-Life, and relate them to approaches in AI and cognitive science. Chapters 11 to 13 focus on the concept of life in general. A-Life's relation to functionalism, and the feasibility of 'strong' A-Life, are explored in Chapters 14 and 15.

A-LIFE AND AI

The central concept of A-Life, excepting *life* itself, is *self-organization*. Self-organization involves the emergence (and maintenance) of order, or complexity, out of an origin that is ordered to a lesser degree. That is, it concerns not mere superficial change, but fundamental structural development. This development is 'spontaneous', or 'autonomous', following from the intrinsic character of the system itself (often, in interaction with the environment) instead of being imposed on the system by some external designer. In that sense, A-Life is opposed to classical AI, in which programmers impose order on general-purpose machines (Boden 1987).

AI (the subject of another volume in this series: Boden 1990) is the attempt to build and/or program computers to do the sorts of things that minds can do—sometimes, though not necessarily, in the same sort of way. Some AI researchers approach their work as engineers: their goal is to achieve some technological task, irrespective of how living creatures achieve it. But others aim to throw light on the principles of intelligence in general, or of human psychology in particular. They accordingly try to make their models work in ways analogous to biologically based minds.

Some of the things that minds can do are normally regarded as involving intelligence: for example, playing chess, or making a medical diagnosis. Others are not: seeing, visuomotor coordination, perhaps even speaking one's native language. Early AI focused on the more 'intelligent' tasks, recognizing only later that apparently simple abilities, many of which we share with some animals (and some of which are modelled also in A-Life), are even more difficult to model than is highly educated human expertise.

Some such abilities seem to require a form of computer modelling—'connectionism'—very different from step-by-step 'classical' AI-programming. Connectionist systems consist of networks of simple interconnected units, wherein concepts may be represented as an overall pattern of excitation distributed across an entire network. These networks are parallel-processing systems, in the sense that all the units function (exciting or inhibiting their immediate neighbours) simultaneously. Because they are broadly inspired by the neurones in the brain, connectionist models are sometimes called neural networks. (Philosophical problems associated with classical and connectionist AI are explored in another volume in this series (Boden 1990).)

A-Life and AI differ significantly, despite having strong historical and methodological links. In classical AI, one starts with a general-purpose (task-neutral) machine, and attempts to write a program to make the machine perform the task required. In A-Life, by contrast, the aim is to define simple reflex-like rules from which the more complex target-behaviour will emerge (Braitenberg 1984). Moreover, A-Life avoids the explanatory emphasis on 'representation' found in most AI, connectionism included (Chs. 7–10).

Another difference is that A-Life eschews classical AI's emphasis on top-down processing, focusing instead on simple processes that work bottom-up to generate order at a higher level. In top-down processing, a high-level representation of the task or sub-task (a goal, grammar, or expectation) is used to initiate, monitor, and/or guide detailed actions. In bottom-up processing, it is the detailed input of the system which determines what will happen next. Classical AI uses both approaches, but top-down processing is the more common.

Connectionist AI works bottom-up in that the behaviour of a connectionist model depends on the local interactions of the individual units, none of which has an overall view of the task. But even bottom-up connectionism differs from A-Life, for connectionist systems cannot (yet) develop their own principles of organization. They can learn to settle into particular equilibrium-states, by changing myriad connection-weights. Their fundamental organization, however, remains unchanged. Nor can connectionist AI model multi-level order, a prime interest of A-Life. 'Recurrent' networks, in which the output of one layer of units can be fed back as input to a preceding layer, can approximate hierarchy to some degree. But hierarchy is better modelled by classical AI.

Not surprisingly, then, some (though not all) A-Lifers explicitly distance themselves from AI. A participant in the first A-Life conference acknowledged that 'artificial life studies have closer roots in artificial intelligence and computational modelling than in biology itself', but went on to attack overly computational approaches (Ch. 15). And many who work with embodied creatures (natural or artificial), as opposed to the disembodied systems typical of AI, stress the differences between their approach and AI (Chs. 7 and 10).

However, the differences between A-Life and AI should not be exaggerated. There is significant conceptual overlap between the two fields (some types of research are published in both A-Life and AI journals). For example, certain guiding ideas of A-Life also inform AI work in situated robotics and animate vision (jointly named *nouvelle* AI), and in evolutionary robotics.

Situated robots react directly (bottom-up) to environmental cues rather than (top-down) to internal world-models or representations (Chs. 7 and 8). They are typically described as autonomous, another concept central to A-Life. This usage is not entirely felicitous: situated robots do satisfy some criteria of autonomy, but the reflexive self-direction of much human action is better modelled by classical AI (Ch. 2). However, the emphasis on self-directed control rather than outside intervention is shared with A-Life.

AI research on animate vision is related to A-Life also, for it stresses the role of the creature's own bodily movements in affecting the perceptual feedback used, in turn, to direct future action (Ballard 1991).

Evolutionary robotics is even closer to A-Life. Indeed, it falls equally into A-Life and AI, even though leading practitioners favour dynamical systems theory rather than symbolic computation in describing their work (Ch. 7). Here, the robot's 'brain' and/or sensory-motor morphology are not specifically designed by the roboticist, but are automatically evolved within its task-environment (Cliff, Harvey, and Husbands 1993; Husbands, Harvey, and Cliff 1995; Thompson 1995).

The philosophical similarity of the two fields is disputed. Some A-Life sympathizers refuse to apply ideas from the philosophy of AI to A-Life (Keeley 1994). Others favour philosophical assumptions fundamentally opposed to those of AI (Ch. 7). However, there are grounds for assimilation, too. If one assumes that intelligence is grounded in life, then AI is somehow continuous with A-Life (Ch. 12). Largely parallel arguments arise about the adequacy of a purely abstract functionalism to describe life and mind (Chs. 14 and 15). To understand human minds, we need explanations drawn from both (and from biology and neuroscience), with an appreciation of how they fit together (Ch. 9).

ORIGINS OF A-LIFE

Historically, it is indisputable that A-Life and AI are close cousins. Although AI flourished before A-Life, their intellectual seeds were sown at much the same time, by some of the same people. Their common intellectual ancestors—apart from the very early machine modellers (see Ch. 1)—were Alan Turing and John von Neumann.

Turing initiated computer science in the 1930s, outlined the agenda of AI in the 1940s, and pioneered the design of working computers (for code-cracking) in World War II. As if all that were not enough, in the early 1950s he published a mathematical paper on morphogenesis (the development of biological form), whose implications are still being explored (Turing 1952).

He proved that relatively simple chemical processes (described in abstract mathematical terms) could generate new order from homogeneous tissue. Two or more chemicals diffusing at different rates could produce 'waves' of differential concentrations which, in an embryo or growing organism, might later prompt the repetition of structures such as tentacles, leaf-buds, or segments. Diffusion waves could engender ordered cell-differentiation in one, two, or three dimensions. In 3D, they could, for instance, cause embryonic gastrulation, in which a sphere of homogeneous cells develops a hollow (which eventually becomes a tube).

Modern embryology and morphology owe much to Turing's inspiration. Recently, his own equations have been used to generate spot-patterns and reticulations like those of dalmatians, cheetahs, leopards, and giraffes (Turk 1991). This work requires powerful computers, to vary the numerical parameters in Turing's differential equations, calculate the results, (often) apply two or more equations successively, and express all these numerical results in graphical form. Turing himself had only primitive computers to help him. Because (as he remarked) much better machines were needed to follow up his ideas, his paper—though recognized as an important contribution to analytic biology—did not immediately spawn A-Life as a computational discipline.

Von Neumann, too, pioneered the artificial sciences. His design of the digital computer in the late 1940s was partly inspired by early ideas in computational neuroscience (McCulloch and Pitts 1943), and in turn enabled AI experiments to start in the 1950s (Feigenbaum and Feldman 1963). At much the same time, he was doing pioneering theoretical research on cellular automata, including self-reproducing systems (Burks 1970). This was A-Life in embryo.

A cellular automaton is a computational 'space' made up of many cells. Each cell changes according to the same set of rules, taking into account the states of neighbouring cells. The system moves in time-steps, all the cells normally changing—or not—together. (Asynchronous systems are also possible: identical rule-sets may give very different results if the cells have independent 'clocks' (Ingerson and Buvel 1984; Bersini and Detours 1994).) After each global change, the rules are applied again.

Von Neumann was interested in the order spontaneously generated in cellular automata following simple rules. (Turing's paper on diffusion gradients used similar ideas, for instance describing the emergence of differential concentrations within a twenty-cell ring.)

As part of his work on cellular automata, von Neumann studied the 'logic' of reproduction. Having already shown that a self-replicating *physical* automaton is in principle possible, he defined the *functional* (computational) features of reproduction. Several years before the discovery of DNA and the genetic code, he realized that part of the self-replicating system must function both as instructions and as data (a self-description). He even defined a universal replicator, a computational system capable of reproducing any system. (Biological species are not universal replicators: cats give birth only to kittens.) He also remarked that errors in copying the self-description could lead to evolution, which might thus be studied computationally.

It is now known that cellular automata are in principle equivalent to Turing machines (Langton 1986). (Turing machines are theoretically defined computing systems with an infinite tape, capable in principle of performing any possible computation; actual computers are approximations to Turing machines (Turing

1936).) However, von Neumann's A-Life ideas, like Turing's work on morpho-genesis, were neglected for many years by computer modellers. Their attention focused instead on AI and cybernetics, which could advance with the help of early computer technology. Von Neumann's A-Life research (like Turing's) was purely theoretical, because to explore its implications required considerable computer power.

After von Neumann's death in 1956, mathematical work on cellular automata continued, and even hit the popular scientific press (Gardner 1970). But it was unavoidably limited until recently because of the lack of computational power.

As for computational evolution (which von Neumann foresaw), this took some time to develop. It had to await John Holland's formal definition of genetic algorithms (GAs) in the 1960s (Holland 1975); the actual implementation of GAs (for modelling optimization) in the 1980s (Holland *et al.* 1986); and their extension from fixed- to variable-length descriptions (for modelling species-evolution) in the early 1990s (Harvey 1992). Genetic algorithms are inspired by the genetic mutations and (especially) cross-over found in biology, and are widely used in A-Life and AI. They have been applied in work on induction and other aspects of the philosophy of science (Holland *et al.* 1986), but here they are of interest primarily for the light they can shed on the general principles underlying evolution. (Genetic algorithms are briefly described in Chs. 1 and 2, and discussed in more detail in Chs. 3 and 5).

In sum, the central ideas of A-Life originated in mid-century. But, largely because of its need for high-performance computing, the field achieved visibility only in the 1990s. For four decades, the scattered examples of A-Life research being done were not even recognized as a unitary endeavour. The unification, in so far as a field so diverse can be so described, occurred in the late 1980s, when the term 'A-Life' was coined.

A-LIFE'S AGENDA

A-Life was christened at a conference (in 1987) to which researchers in many different disciplines were invited. The paper that named the field, unifying diverse research under the one label, is reprinted here as Chapter 1. Christopher Langton's 'Artificial Life' is widely regarded as the manifesto defining A-Life's agenda. It is partly historical, partly an overview of research, and partly a statement of the aims and presuppositions of the field.

Anyone who expects A-Life's manifesto to begin with a definition of life will be disappointed. Langton argues that one cannot give necessary and sufficient conditions for anything on the basis of only one example. All the living things we know of share the same basic biochemistry, and a common genetic descent (the DNA code is biologically universal). Moreover, they have all evolved in response to local historical accidents, so that general principles are difficult to identify. Even if we could do this for terrestrial life (as A-Life may help us to do), we could not be sure that all living things must have the same properties. But A-Life might enable us to synthesize new systems recognizable as alternate life-forms. We could then distinguish 'life-as-it-is' from 'life-as-it-could-be'. In short, Langton sees A-Life as a way of discovering *what life is*, as well as *how life is possible*.

Langton sees life as an abstract phenomenon, a set of vital functions implementable in various material bases. Life consists of dynamic processes, organized in certain ways. Among the general principles he outlines in Chapter 1 are self-organization, self-replication, emergence, evolution, and the (epigenetic) unpredictability-gap between genotype and phenotype. (The genotype is the set of genes, or hereditary material, from which the living system develops; the phenotype is the actual form of the mature individual.)

In addition, Langton discusses many aspects of information processing, which he—like von Neumann—sees as fundamental to life. This is no mere flight of hermeneutic fancy. For Langton, *information*, *communication*, and *interpretation* are real computational properties of certain formally describable systems. These assumptions are widespread in the field. One philosopher of A-Life has even described life as 'matter with meaning' (Pattee 1995).

One does not have to be a devotee of Langton, or even of A-Life, to share this view. Informational (intentional) concepts were widely used by theoretical biologists long before Langton gave A-Life its name (Boden 1980). Familiar examples include the genetic 'code', with its attendant 'reading', 'interpreting', and 'transcription'; 'programs' of 'instructions' conveyed by specific cells or chemicals; 'messages' passed within and between cells; and cybernetic notions of 'informational feedback' and oscillatory 'control'.

One reason for the use of informational concepts in biology is that many biological processes are arbitrary with respect to biochemistry. The same process (defined at the biological level) may be instantiated by different mechanisms in different species: like mental processes as defined by functionalism, the process shows multiple realizability. It is therefore useful to define biological processes at an informational level, independent of the underlying biochemistry.

Moreover, biochemistry does not map on to biological function in any simple fashion, since the 'meaning' of a given metabolite (some molecule produced by biochemical processes within living cells) can vary. Indeed, a metabolite may have a different significance not only across species, but also at distinct phases of the life cycle of a single species. In slime moulds, for instance, one and the same chemical substance (cAMP) has different biological functions, or meanings, in the three phases of the organism's life-history. In the first phase, cAMP causes separated amoebic cells to aggregate into a mass, or slug. In the next, it acts as the pacemaker for the contractions by which the slug moves along the ground. Finally, it causes the homogeneous cells of the slug to differentiate into three distinct types, forming a base, a stalk, and a spore-containing head. The three developmental contexts thus result in differing 'interpretations' of the cAMP 'messages' (Boden 1980).

In using informational language to describe biological processes, one has to have some way of identifying what the relevant information is. The meanings of biological 'codes' or 'instructions' are determined by their causal powers and evolutionary history. Likewise, a feature within an evolving A-Life system draws its significance from its contribution to fitness over many generations. Philosophies that appeal to evolutionary history in explaining intentionality (e.g. Millikan 1984) are broadly consonant with A-Life.

Just which informational concepts are likely to be of most use to biologists is controversial. Linguistic and programming metaphors are still widespread in theoretical biology. But some A-Life researchers reject them in favour of cybernetic and informational concepts underpinned by dynamical systems theory. Which cognitive-informational concepts are most useful for biology and A-Life is an empirical question, although it may be linked to wider philosophical claims (see Ch. 7).

Langton describes A-Life as 'unabashedly' reductionist, because it holds that high-level phenomena depend on simple interactions between lower-level processes. But (like psychological functionalism) it is also anti-reductionist, in that it treats those phenomena as real properties, described by ineliminable theoretical concepts. The behaviour of flocks of birds, for instance, must be described on its own level, although it results from the behaviour of individual birds. Similarly, the information-bearing functions of DNA base-triplets are real properties of the genetic system, not expressible in terms of—though explicable by means of—biochemistry. Such higher-level properties are often described as emergent (although the strong definition of emergence in Chapter 9 excludes some cases discussed by Langton).

An example of what might be involved in 'discovering *what life is*' is given by Langton in a later paper (Langton 1991), in which he defines a measurable property that he claims is a necessary condition for life, wheresoever in the universe it may occur. Information-processing, and life, require a certain type of complexity. The system must be dynamic, yet novel patterns must be reliably related to their predecessors. A qualitative distinction between four types of complexity, only one of which can support information-processing, already existed (Wolfram 1984). But Langton's was the first quantitative definition of order/disorder. In extensive experiments with computer models of cellular automata, he matched the relevant type of complexity with the numerical values of his statistical measure. He found that 'interesting' complexity arises only within a very narrow range. Only then is life possible. Outside those values, the system's behaviour is boringly homogeneous, rigidly periodic, or uselessly chaotic.

Most descriptions of A-Life, Langton's included, emphasize the importance of autonomy in living systems. This concept is explored in my own paper on 'Autonomy and Artificiality' (Ch. 2). The sciences of the artificial support two opposing intuitions concerning autonomy. One, characteristic of classical AI, is that determination of behaviour by the external environment lessens an agent's autonomy. The other, characteristic of A-Life and situated robotics, is that to follow a preconceived internal plan is to be a mere puppet.

These intuitions can be reconciled, since autonomy is not an all-or-none property. Three dimensions of behavioural control are crucial. First is the extent to which response to the environment is direct (determined only by the present state in the external world) or indirect (mediated by internal mechanisms partly dependent on the creature's previous history). Second is the extent to which the controlling mechanisms were self-generated rather than externally imposed. And third is the extent to which internal directing mechanisms can be reflected upon, and/or selectively modified. Autonomy is the greater, the more behaviour is directed by self-generated (and idiosyncratic) internal mechanisms, nicely responsive to the specific problem-situation, yet reflexively modifiable by wider concerns.

Some senses of autonomy are indeed illuminated by work in A-Life. However, the strongest sense—human freedom—is more nearly approached by theories based on classical AI. Self-reflection, deliberation, and reasoned prioritizing are closer to classical AI architectures than to the direct environmental embedding typical of A-Life and *nouvelle* AI.

It does not follow that the artificial sciences must have a dehumanizing effect, undermining our confidence in our self-control. Far from denying the reality of what we call free choice, they help us to appreciate its complexities and to understand how it is possible.

BIOLOGICALLY RELEVANT A-LIFE

Chapter 3 is 'An Approach to the Synthesis of Life', by Thomas Ray. Ray is a tropical botanist and forest conservationist, whose A-Life work simulates evolution and co-evolution. Biological species evolve largely by adapting to the presence of other species. So do the 'species' in Ray's computer model (see also Hillis 1991). Simulated prey evolves more quickly in the presence of predators, and simulated hosts become infested with (and sometimes resistant to) parasites, which force the host to replicate the parasite rather than itself—and the parasites, in turn, are plagued by hyper-parasites.

Ray's 'digital organisms' are sequences of machine instructions, running on Tierra. (Tierra is a virtual computer simulated on a real computer, because Ray's creatures might otherwise pass from one real computer to others, infecting them all with proliferating code.) The original seed is a self-replicating program, many of whose descendants will be self-replicators also. The organisms compete for Tierra's CPU-time and memory-space, much as terrestrial organisms compete for energy and geographical space.

The instructions are sometimes executed imperfectly (an instruction to shift bits to the left may move them to the right instead); and the background operating system randomly flips bits during 'rest' and replication. This imperfect execution, maintenance, and copying is analogous to mutation. Tierra's memory is prevented from filling up by a computerized analogue of death, culling (usually) instruction-sequences that are old and/or have led to errors.

The single 'ancestor' is an eighty-instruction sequence, containing the code for self-replication. When self-replication works imperfectly, a daughter-sequence may contain no copy-procedure. Some such daughters are utterly sterile, but some may induce other instruction-sets to make grand-daughters in their own image. This parasitic behaviour is possible because, although no Tierran creature can change the code (genome) of another, it may read and even execute parts of another's code—for example, borrowing a neighbour's copying powers to produce copies of itself.

If the parasitic species (lacking the copy-procedure) is shorter than the host species, it occupies less memory-space, so tends to increase relative to the host. Eventually, if the parasite is to survive, an ecological balance must be found; for the parasite cannot reproduce without some host. Ray finds that after thousands of computer-generations there is usually a variety of species, of different sizes and longevity, and different ecological relations (independent, parasitic, symbiotic, and so on).

Evolution is grounded in complex probability distributions, which in Tierra can be precisely varied and the consequences compared—so providing an experimental medium for quantitative studies of evolution. Species can evolve more quickly in the presence of predators because the predator displaces the prey from sub-optimal 'solutions', or local maxima. (Compare a group of short-sighted mountaineers, standing on what they mistakenly believe is the summit: they could reach the true summit only if something were to remove them from the local peak, for then they might start climbing at the base of the summit.) But what difference does it make if the local maxima are many or few, grouped or scattered, steep or gently sloping? Such questions can be addressed computationally by comparing evolution within different fitness landscapes. Similar A-Life research has explored the effects of various mutation rates and population sizes, and of differing degrees of interaction between populations (Kauffman and Johnson 1991).

Also of interest is the occurrence of evolutionary 'leaps' in Tierra, wherein sudden change is observed after many generations of quiescence. This recalls the theoretical dispute between gradualism and saltationism (Eldredge and Gould 1972). Ray shows that the quiescence is merely apparent: outwardly invisible genetic changes gradually accumulate until reaching a 'critical mass', when they cooperate to cause phenotypic change.

Ray's ultimate aim, like Langton's, is the production of new life. Indeed, his preferred term for A-Life is 'Synthetic Biology'. He is not thinking only of the synthesis of new carbon-based organisms, or novel biochemistries (a prominent research theme in A-Life). For Ray, biochemical metabolism is inessential. He defines a living system as one which is 'self-replicating, and capable of open-ended evolution'. These criteria are met by the 'organisms' described in Chapter 3, and by those being seeded in the *Digital Reserve* spread across the Internet (Ray 1994). Accordingly, Ray claims these computer-species are literally alive. Even computer viruses, if they can evolve, are alive—or as alive as real viruses are (cf. Spafford 1991, 1994). (Because viruses depend on non-viral cells for reproduction, many biologists deny they are alive.)

Such claims are highly controversial. Many people would endorse Ray's work as a useful exercise in theoretical biology, without accepting his robust philosophical interpretation of it. Borrowing the terminology John Searle (1980) uses in discussing AI, they would say that even if weak A-Life is scientifically valuable, strong A-Life is impossible. As later chapters show, however, proving that Ray's concept of life is inadequate is not easy.

Scepticism about the synthesis of new life-forms may be based in the assumption that the origin of biological life, if not literally miraculous, was almost inconceivably improbable. Many precise details, it seems, had to be fulfilled for life to emerge. Since the odds against this are astronomical, life may even be a unique cosmic accident, occurring only on Earth. The A-Life research discussed by Richard Burian and Robert Richardson in 'Form and Order in Evolutionary Biology' (Ch. 4) suggests that this scepticism is misplaced. Far from being unique and unpredictable, the emergence of order, and even of self-reproduction, is virtually inevitable in systems of a certain degree of complexity.

To study the spontaneous origin of order, Stuart Kauffman (1993) considers information-processing systems made up of many interacting units. He interprets these abstractly defined systems in terms of vital phenomena on various levels: auto-catalytic molecules generating a connected metabolism, genes, simple neural networks, ant colonies, ecosystems, and market economies.

Like cellular automata, which they closely resemble, Kauffman's self-organizing networks work in global 'time-steps'. He asks what will happen if each unit responds in a given way to the influence of two or more others, chosen at random from those available. The units and interactions are very simple. A small set of logical functions (for instance, 'on' and 'off') may be randomly assigned to each one of a thousand units, with simple rules (also chosen at random) specifying what interactions will lead the unit to make which response. From such seemingly unpromising beginnings, Kauffman uses probability theory to show that dynamic order, of various generic types, is bound to arise eventually—where 'eventually' may be a surprisingly brief period.

To what extent these intriguing mathematical results apply to advanced biological systems is still unclear. For instance, Kauffman identifies systematic relationships between the number of units and the number of types of order that emerge. He suggests that this explains why creatures with larger genomes tend to have a greater variety of cell-types. However, some species have much more DNA than closely comparable species do; only if the genome is largely inert or 'junk' DNA does this fit Kauffman's picture. Again, he suggests that networks whose units connect up with more than five others will develop chaotic, not ordered, dynamics. Yet a human neurone may be interconnected with many thousands of others: how, then, can the brain be a superb information-processor?

If Kauffman's work does capture the essence of biological form, it has two important implications. First, the potential for generating life is an inherent property of matter. Kauffman's statistical arguments are drawn from physics. and he sees biological order as a natural consequence of basic physical laws. Second, genetics (molecular biology) and natural selection are not the only explanatory principles in biology, as neo-Darwinism assumes (Dawkins 1976, 1986). Granted, the genes specify the initial conditions (at various stages) of development, so crucially affect the resulting organism. And natural selection determines which of the slightly differing variants of developed forms will thrive. But, if Kauffman is right, these two factors alone cannot explain the form of living things. That an ordered organism develops at all, out of relatively homogeneous, unstructured beginnings, is due to the inherent self-organizing properties of complex systems (Depew and Weber 1994, chs. 15–16). In Kauffman's words, 'Evolution is not just "chance caught on the wing". It is not just a tinkering of the ad hoc, of bricolage, of contraption. It is emergent order honoured and honed by selection' (1993: 644).

A complete theoretical biology would thus require the integration of various kinds of explanation. Abstract analyses of generic form cannot tell us what the detailed mechanisms are which underlie actual metabolisms and morphologies. Those are questions for biochemistry, physiology, and genetics. Nor can they tell us what historical contingencies have shaped morphological change through natural selection. However, studies of the origin of order in the absence of natural selection may help us to understand, and even to measure, the mutual interactions of selection and self-organized form.

In 'Evolution—Natural and Artificial' (Ch. 5), the biologist John Maynard Smith asks whether A-Life might help us understand evolution. Less enthusiastic than Richard Dawkins, who says '[As] a dyed-in-the-wool, radical neo-Darwinist . . . I really have been led to think differently as a result of creating, and using, computer models of artificial life which, on the face of it, owe more to the imagination than to real biology' (Dawkins 1989: 201), Maynard Smith insists that many questions about the nature of evolution call for more biological data, not more theoretical models. Moreover, he sees computational models based on actual genetic systems as generally more useful to biologists than simulations of evolution in general.

For one class of questions, however, he grants that the latter approach may be helpful. Since biologists know of only one case of evolution (all terrestrial life appears to have the same origin), it is difficult to answer questions about evolution in general. For example: Has there been time for natural selection to produce complex living creatures? Is the adaptive landscape smooth, or rugged? And what features of terrestrial genetic systems are necessary, rather than historically contingent? The specific genetic code, for example, may not be a necessary feature of biochemical evolution. But Maynard Smith suggests that there must be some digital code involved, and that it cannot support (Lamarckian) inheritance of acquired characteristics. A-Life might confirm those suggestions, and might identify further necessary conditions of evolution as such.

Maynard Smith's insistence that A-Life models be firmly grounded in biological realities must be heeded, if A-Life is not to descend into ignorant dilettantism or mere playing around with computers. The sloppiness of much early AI reduced its interest for psychology and even for 'pure' technology (McDermott 1976), and some current A-Life has been similarly criticized (Miller 1995). Its biological potential is greatest in areas unamenable to the mathematical modelling and traditional computer simulation already widespread in biology. A-Life techniques (unlike these earlier methods) can model systems in which the component units are not simple, homogeneous, and predictable. Consequently, it offers a rich experimental and analytic context for investigating biological processes on several levels of complexity and over differing time-scales.

For example, work on the co-evolution of pursuit and evasion uses evolutionary simulation methods to track the emergence both of complex inter-agent behaviours and of the underlying sensory, neural, and motor systems. This work also enables one to compare the effects of varying the relevant factors in a systematic and measurable way (Cliff and Miller forthcoming; Miller and Cliff forthcoming).

Much A-Life work focuses on problems studied in ethology. This may involve the computer modelling of actual neurophysiological mechanisms (Cliff 1991; Webb 1994), or the construction of mobile or simulated artificial animals, or 'animats' (Mayer and Guillot 1991, 1994; Wilson 1991). The environments of animats are simpler than the real world, but typically involve a significant degree of unpredictability and 'threat'. This research may deal with single organisms, or with 'social' behaviour within groups of animals. Some A-Life projects consider specific behaviours of identified species, while others address cross-species behaviours such as flocking (Reynolds 1987), fighting (Sims 1994), pursuit/evasion (Cliff and Miller forthcoming; Miller and Cliff forthcoming), or communicative strategies (De Bourcier and Wheeler 1995).

The behaviour of animals is viewed on an even more general level in Chapter 6. In 'Animals as Cost-Based Robots', David McFarland explains all animals' activities in terms of cost-functions defined relative to their environments. This concept, he suggests, should be applied also to robots.

McFarland argues that animals do their 'decision-making' in a way fundamentally different from the internal world-modelling of traditional robotics. They thus avoid the frame problem: how to plan future action without considering a host of irrelevant details, and without being obstructed during execution by unanticipated consequences (Boden 1990, chs. 7–9). Classical AI depends on general-purpose computers, but there are no general-purpose animals: each species behaves appropriately only within its own ecological niche. Appropriate behaviour depends not on detailed planning, but on relatively direct reactions to environmental (and internal bodily) factors. The simplest animals are probably pure reflex automata, but many have evolved mechanisms of motivation and cognition which enable them to use internal as well as external states in determining behaviour (McFarland 1991).

Thus far, McFarland agrees with the situated roboticists of *nouvelle* AI (Chs. 7 and 8). He goes beyond them in using ethological data to suggest a way of analysing the behaviour of any creature. He represents the selective pressures on each species as a cost-function, showing why certain species, with certain behaviours, do or do not flourish within a given niche. The cost to the animal can be measured in terms of the risk of danger, damage, or death—including the additional risks incurred by risk-avoiding behaviour and by changing from one behaviour to another.

McFarland applies his analysis also to robots, including the bomb-disposal robot imagined in a philosopher's thought-experiment on the frame problem (Dennett 1984). The robot's task, in a nutshell, was to retrieve its precious spare battery from a locked room before the time-bomb, also in the room, exploded. This sounds easy enough, until one is informed that the bomb had been placed on the same wheeled wagon as the battery itself. Given that the robot had no explicit warning of this fact, it would need some time to calculate (all) the unintended side-effects of its action of pulling the wagon—which, of course, include the bomb's moving together with the battery.

McFarland points out that, because learning changes the cost–benefit function, bomb-disposal robots able to learn how to increase the availability or accessibility of resources (reaching or defusing the bomb more quickly) would be better adapted to this task-environment than the ones featured in the thought-experiment. One might say this is obvious—and so it is, in qualitative terms. But McFarland can measure how much more adaptive one behaviour is, in certain circumstances, than another.

EXPLANATORY STRATEGIES IN A-LIFE

If A-Life methodologies differ, so too do the explanations favoured by A-Life researchers. Various explanatory strategies are defended in Chapters 7–10. These are relevant not only to the philosophy of A-Life, but to cognitive science as a whole.

One key dispute (prominent in Chs. 7–9) concerns the commitment of classical (and most connectionist) AI and cognitive science to the internal *representation* of *concepts*. Some philosophers have argued that cognitive science must posit symbolic representations, and a combinatorial semantics, like those characteristic of classical AI (Fodor 1975; Fodor and Pylyshyn 1988). Others claim that connectionism, too, allows for (distributed) representations, capable of supporting a combinatorial semantics (A. C. Clark 1989, 1993; Cussins 1990). In Chapters 7–9 the concern is whether A-Life and AI need to posit internal representations at all.

In 'From Robots to Rothko: The Bringing Forth of Worlds' (Ch. 7), Michael Wheeler criticizes the fundamental assumptions of 'Cartesian' cognitive science (orthodox AI and most connectionism). He rejects its commitments to the subject/object distinction and to theories of internal representation. He draws inspiration instead from ecological psychology (Gibson 1979) and from Heidegger and Gadamer, endorsing their stress on the mutual definition of 'subject' and 'environment' and on embodiment and embeddedness as grounds of meaning. And he recommends dynamical systems theory as a non-computational way of thinking about cognition (cf. Beer 1995*a*, 1995*b*; van Gelder 1995; Port and van Gelder 1995; Thelen and Smith 1993).

A-Life and AI are addressed by Wheeler in broadly Heideggerian terms. Heideggerian (and Wittgensteinian) critiques of AI are not new (Dreyfus 1979; Dreyfus and Dreyfus 1986). However, they usually show scant sympathy for the scientific aim of explaining how meaningful behaviour is possible (remarks like 'We just do it' are legion). Wheeler accepts this aim, although he grounds it in a Heideggerian epistemology, and pays attention to the details of the technical literature. Such critiques, moreover, usually accept Heidegger's view that language and culture are essential to world-making. But Wheeler does not. In that sense, his position is non-Heideggerian.

Wheeler argues that ethology and cognitive science should not assume that creatures adapt to objective properties of the world. It is not enough to say that different animals inhabit different worlds in the sense that their sensory-motor capacities enable them to respond only to selected aspects of the objective world (von Uexkull 1957). Nor is it enough to point out, as ecological psychologists do, that the environment offers different 'affordances' to different species, according to their sensory-motor equipment and behavioural repertoire. Rather, these sciences should focus on how situated, subject-engendered, meanings arise from the bodily actions of creatures (animals or animats) embedded in their self-generated world.

However, Wheeler rejects Heidegger's claim that human culture is essential to meaning. For this would imply that languageless animals do not live in meaningful worlds, and that naturalism in the philosophy of mind is false. According to Wheeler's 'hermeneutic naturalism', animals construct their own significant ecological worlds in exploiting the fitness affordances presented to them (cf. Wheeler 1995). Explanations of intentionality based on subject-engendered meanings need not involve language, and can show, in a way continuous with natural science, how a physical system can also be an intentional system.

Non-linguistic meanings are crucial even for some distinctively human phenomenology. Wheeler argues that our experience of the visual (and musical and performing) arts consists largely of non-linguistic meanings that arise from our embeddedness in the world. These meanings are generated by the interaction between the viewer and the work, an aesthetic moment to be characterized in neo-Heideggerian (not 'Cartesian') terms. Significantly, for Wheeler, this characterization finds naturalistic support in (a reformed) cognitive science.

Wheeler's scepticism about representational explanation is not shared by David Kirsh or Andy Clark (Chs. 8 and 9). They both see intelligent behaviour, even in non-human animals, as requiring representations of some sort—or, better, of some sorts. Situated robotics already uses representations in some (non-symbolic) sense; and symbolic, conceptual, representations are needed for full human intelligence.

Chapter 8 is Kirsh's paper, 'Today the Earwig, Tomorrow Man?' Kirsh argues that the ecological approach typical of situated robotics cannot capture those types of perception, learning, and control which require concepts. These intelligent capacities far surpass the powers of insects, which situated robotics takes as its model. (More accurately: which it took as its model until very recently. The leaders of situated research have embarked on a project to build a humanoid robot (Brooks and Stein 1994; Dennett 1994). This will model some aspects of infant development, although developmental epigenesis will be underplayed (Rutkowska 1995). These roboticists intend to follow the ecological path as far as they can, but allow that symbolic representations and internal search may be needed at the final stages.)

Kirsh commends situated robotics for extending the domain of concept-free action, and for showing (as argued also in Ch. 6) that articulated world-models are less crucial than classical cognitive science assumes. He insists, however, that its bottom-up approach has explanatory limitations which only systematic conceptualization can overcome.

Full-blooded concepts enable a creature to recognize perceptual invariance; to reify and combine invariances (referring predicates to names, or drawing inferences); to reidentify individuals over time; to engage in anticipatory self-control; to negotiate between (not just to schedule) potentially conflicting desires; to think counterfactually; to use language to create new abilities; and, by teaching these abilities to others, to make cultural evolution possible. Adult human beings possess all these capacities, chimps most of them, dogs some of them, and new-born babies hardly any. Kirsh does not conclude that non-human animals must possess symbolic representations, or compositional internal notations. Their (non-linguistic) concepts may be implemented in their computational architecture in other ways. But logic and language, and thoughtful human action, require symbolic computation.

In 'Happy Couplings: Emergence and Explanatory Interlock' (Ch. 9) Clark, too, defends representationalism. Criticizing cognitive science's excessive focus on symbolic world-models, he posits a range of partial, egocentric, representations that are constructed (and destroyed) in the course of embodied action. Such representations are used within *nouvelle* AI, and there is neurophysiological evidence for them also.

These representations are crucial to 'interactive' explanation, which stresses the ongoing role of the environment in the control of behaviour. Interactive explanation can often be underwritten by the 'homuncular' variety, which explains the system's behaviour in terms of the actions of its parts (including the mechanisms that respond to environmental cues).

The third explanatory style distinguished by Clark is emergent explanation. Emergence is widely used as a key term by A-Life workers, as indicated for example by the passages (above) on Langton and Kauffman. The concept has a long pedigree in the philosophy of biology, where it is recognized as problematic (the entry for 'emergent evolutionism' in the *Encyclopedia of Philosophy* fills three large pages), but it is rarely explicitly analysed by A-Life researchers (but see Cariani 1991; Steels 1991). Broadly, it refers to a situation, and/or a type of explanation, where some genuine novelty arises out of a lower level. The difficulty lies in clarifying just what 'novelty' means here.

Clark resists the tendency, common in A-Life, to define emergence in terms of what is unexpected. Something unexpected by most people may be confidently anticipated by a competent mathematician. Nor does Clark define emergence in terms merely of the need for a theoretical vocabulary different from that which describes the lower-level components. For him, emergence involves behaviours (or internal system-properties) that are not caused by any directly controllable part or environmental interaction, but which are side-effects of directly controllable actions and/or interactions.

Because one cannot specify an inner state responsible for the emergent property, this third type of emergence is even more 'anti-reductionist' than the second. But it is not mysterious. It can be explained by showing how it arises (indirectly) from internal and/or interactive phenomena. These may involve small numbers of different parts (requiring componential analysis), or large numbers of similar parts interacting in complex ways. In the latter case, dynamical systems theory may be useful (Port and van Gelder 1995). It is well suited to describe system-environmental coupling and multiply interacting units, and—because it ignores the component structure—it can focus on emergent properties as such.

Clark argues that emergence can be fully understood only if we also consider the system's inner structure. The mechanisms by which emergent properties are (indirectly) generated, *pace* Wheeler (Ch. 7), may often involve homuncular decomposability, and representations too. Theoretical biology and cognitive science must integrate various explanations. These concern adaptive organism-environment coupling; the cooperative activity of the underlying neural components (brain-modules as well as neurones); and the computational (including representational) roles of those components.

Emergence features strongly also in Chapter 10. In his paper 'In Praise of Interactive Emergence, Or Why Explanations Don't Have to Wait for Implementations', Horst Hendriks-Jansen rejects explanations based on componential, functional analysis. Instead, he recommends a form of historical explanation that highlights the emergence of structured behaviours on successive levels.

Drawing on situated robotics, ethology, and developmental psychology, he shows how novel behaviours can emerge during the interactions of a creature with its world. That world is not (objectively) pre-categorized, but is constructed via the creature's own activities—to which, in turn, other creatures may react. Human thought and language are emergent activities, made possible by the 'scaffolding' presented by interactive turn-taking between mother and baby, and by various inborn behaviours which function to attract, and to keep, the adult's attention. These are examples of what Langton calls the predictability gap between genotype and phenotype (Ch. 1), and of what Piaget calls epigenesis (Boden 1995, Preface and ch. 6).

According to Hendriks-Jansen, such species-typical behaviours (discoverable by ethological observation) are the true natural kinds of behavioural science. A *behavioural* science is the most we can hope for, since there is usually no systematic mapping between behaviour and specific internal mechanisms: most behaviour is emergent in Clark's (third) sense. Cost–benefit accounts of behaviour (Ch. 6) are useful abstractions, but do not explain how the observed behaviours arose. Historical theories do explain this, and are testable by situated and evolutionary robotics.

Chapters 9 and 10 indicate that, although A-Life's potential contribution to biology is undeniable, its importance for a truly general cognitive science is more problematic. A-Life could contribute to such a science if there were an explanatory continuity between terrestrial biology and psychology, and between their non-earthbound equivalents—that is, if psychological explanation requires reference to biological constraints (Elton 1994). But this may not be so.

For instance, Clark's discussion of emergence—notwithstanding his call for explanatory interlock—suggests that there may be no close mapping between psychology and neurophysiology, still less any principled mapping to explain intelligent life in general. And Hendriks-Jansen argues that no useful cognitive generalizations can be made at the level of mechanism, and that psychological explanations must be behaviour-based. A-Life (and *nouvelle* AI) differs from classical AI in not focusing on top-down functional decomposition and modularity. In not insisting on a systematic mapping from global behaviour to biological mechanisms (or to vital functions in general), A-Life leaves open the possibility that it may not feature in a general cognitive science.

WHAT IS LIFE?

The concept of life itself is the topic of the remaining papers. Chapters 11–13 address the concept directly, with some consideration of its use in A-Life; Chapters 14 and 15 focus on whether cybernetic entities inhabiting virtual computer-worlds (such as Tierra) are really alive. As these papers show, there is disagreement about what life is, and even about what sort of thing—individual or evolving population—is best regarded as alive. Nevertheless, certain properties are cited repeatedly.

Gareth Matthews (Ch. 11) reminds us that some of these properties were noted long ago by Aristotle. His list included: self-nutrition, growth, decay, reproduction, appetite, sensation or perception, self-motion, and thinking. Some of these are less clear than they might seem. (For instance, mules are sterile, and young animals and some adults cannot reproduce; so perhaps 'reproduction' is satisfied by having been generated by reproduction, not only by being capable of reproduction oneself.) Moreover, there are inconsistencies in Aristotle's account of how these properties relate to the definition of life. Matthews therefore suggests that we define the concept, instead, in terms of Aristotle's notion of powers that tend towards the preservation of the species.

Aristotle's account of life is regarded by some philosophers as an anticipation of modern functionalism, and a praiseworthy attempt to outline a science of life and mind (Nussbaum and Putnam 1992; Wilkes 1992). This interpretation has been disputed, on the grounds that functionalism is a response to Descartes's mind–body problem, which did not arise for Aristotle, and that Aristotelian physics was so fundamentally different from modern science as to be worthless (Burnyeat 1992). Hilary Putnam, the founder of functionalism, remains unconvinced by this argument. He has abandoned his initial definition of functionalism, because of the multiple realizability of mental processes in computational, as well as material, terms (Putnam 1988). Even so, he sees Aristotle's thought about life and mind as similar to functionalism, and as a valuable contribution to the philosophy of the life-sciences. Aristotle offers, he says, 'the fulfilment of Wittgenstein's desire to have a [non-reductive] "natural history of man"' (Nussbaum and Putnam 1992: 56). Such readings interpret Aristotle in a way consonant with the assumptions of A-Life in general, and with Langton's stress on organization in particular.

Aristotle saw no metaphysical chasm between life and mind (*psyche*)—rationality (*nous*) perhaps excepted—or between biology and psychology. He saw life and mind as involving progressively powerful forms of organization, the capacities possessed by a lower form being possessed also by all higher forms. On that view, it should be no surprise if a philosophy (such as functionalism) originally developed to deal with mind can be generalized to life.

Descartes, by contrast, saw mental events (and *a fortiori* rational thought) as enjoyed only by humans. There can be no science of animal psychology, since animals are merely complicated mechanical systems. Humans have minds not because psychological properties emerge from the complex organization of a living material base, but because an extra ingredient (mental substance) is added by God. Granted, the lamb runs on seeing the wolf. But what Aristotle would have explained in terms of perceptive powers, Descartes explained in terms of the movements of the animal spirits within the lamb's body. These movements are described, in principle, by physics—which can also explain the living functions of animals and plants.

For Aristotle, too, life is grounded in physics. But unlike Descartes he did not ask 'How can material things possibly perceive?', or even 'How can matter possibly be alive?', since he assumed that physics naturally allows the emergence of increasingly powerful forms of organization. The assumption that matter somehow has a potential for developing life is shared by A-Life. Research on auto-catalytic networks and artificial metabolisms could be viewed as attempts to define the general form of this self-organizing potential, and to identify unfamiliar material carriers of it. Kauffman's work, for instance, suggests that life (and mind) is a possibility inherent in matter, whose realization is much more probable than is commonly assumed (Ch. 4).

Philosophies of life, and A-Life methodologies also, differ on various dimensions identified by Peter Godfrey-Smith in Chapter 12: 'Spencer and Dewey on Life and Mind'. He distinguishes internalism and externalism; asymmetrical and symmetrical externalism; and weak and strong versions of the ontological continuity of life and mind.

Internalist approaches see life as a process of autonomous self-organization, wherein internal constraints govern the history and interactions of the constituent units of the system. Externalists, by contrast, explain the system's internal structure primarily as a result of its adaptive interactions with the environment. Both Spencer and Dewey favoured externalist views of life, although Spencer gave an internalist account of the evolution of the universe prior to the origin of life. Within A-Life, work on cellular automata and Kauffman's discussions of self-organizing networks are internalist. Research on evolutionary robotics, and most other work on animats, is externalist.

The asymmetric externalist (such as Spencer) emphasizes the organism's adaptive reactions to the environment. The ways in which the organism, in its turn, changes the environment are downplayed, though not necessarily denied. In symmetric externalism, this unceasing feedback is highlighted, and the self-adaptive organism is shown to play an active role in shaping its ecological world. Applied to A-Life, asymmetry characterizes situated robotics, most animat research, and many uses of GAs. Symmetry is stressed in research on co-evolution (including co-evolutionary robotics), and in A-Life work that sees the organism and environment as closely coupled dynamical systems, between which no principled distinction—and no epistemological 'gap'—exists. Arguments against 'Cartesian' cognitive science (Ch. 7) are reminiscent of Dewey's (symmetric) criticism of the separation of organism and environment.

Like Aristotle (but unlike Descartes), both Spencer and Dewey were continuity theorists. That is, they saw human minds as ontologically continuous with lower-level vital capacities, from which they have emerged. But there are weak and strong interpretations of continuity. The weak version asserts that mind implies life, that mind can arise only in living things. On this view, AI must be preceded by A-Life. Strong continuity asserts that minds are 'literally life-like', in that life and mind share basic organizational principles. On this view,

AI is a sub-class of A-Life. (Godfrey-Smith also defines 'methodological' continuity, the view that a scientific understanding of mind is in practice achievable only if mind—perception, cognition, motivation—is studied in the context of the entire organism. *Nouvelle* AI, and much work in A-Life, favours methodological continuity.)

Whether Aristotle was a weak or a strong continuity theorist is disputed (Ch. 11). As for Spencer, he accepted both strong and methodological continuity. He saw intelligence as emerging from life when serial processing replaces parallel processing. And, because he defined life in (functionalist) terms of self-sustaining adaptation to the environment, Godfrey-Smith suggests that he would have described Ray's Tierra 'organisms' as alive, despite their lack of biochemical metabolism. Dewey's position is less clear. He certainly accepted weak continuity. But he favoured strong continuity only for certain aspects of mentality—language specifically excluded. Godfrey-Smith suggests that, for Dewey, A-Life could lead to genuine AI only if it studied societies of intercommunicating creatures. Current A-Life studies of (for example) the use of pheromones in ant-colonies would not qualify, since for Dewey communication is symbolic.

Mark Bedau, in 'The Nature of Life' (Ch. 13), compares various definitions of life and argues that the most satisfactory is 'supple adaptation'. This is a near-synonym for evolution, but it makes explicit the flexibility with which living things adapt to a host of unpredictable environmental contingencies which continually alter the selective criteria for fitness. And, crucially, it covers both the puzzling unity and the astonishing diversity of life-forms.

Bedau uses his definition to conceive of life as a natural kind, not an arbitrary list or cluster of properties. He admits that his criterion applies to a number of systems we would not normally regard as alive, such as human cultures and economic markets. But he does not present it as a philosophical analysis of our intuitive, pre-theoretic concept of life. He justifies it instead on scientific grounds, acknowledging that it sometimes fails to map on to our everyday concept (as the chemist's 'water' does, too).

One of the ways in which Bedau's concept of life differs from the everyday one is in its logical category. He argues that we should conceive of an individual's life in relation to the vitality of the global system, or evolving population, which makes the individual organism possible. This view is implicit in his criterion of supple adaptation. If one takes the paradigm case of a 'living thing' to be a single organism, then Bedau's definition of life is problematic. A single organism, whether microbe or mammal, is rarely flexible in adapting to new circumstances even if 'adapting' is interpreted as 'learning', and is never adaptable in the sense of being able to evolve. Only species, or lineages of organisms, can do that. Bedau ascribes life first of all to evolving populations, and only secondarily to individual living things.

Bedau's definition may be seen as problematic in two other ways. In building evolution into his definition of life, he has to admit that an evolved population which had stabilized in equilibrium (there being no more environmental changes, and no more co-evolutionary pressure from other species) would not fully satisfy his criterion. He does not take a strongly essentialist position: 'Well then, the population simply wouldn't be alive.' Rather, he points out that this imaginary population would have originated through an evolutionary process. He adds that such a situation is empirically highly improbable, because the evolutionary stability will in practice always be temporary, so the example has no real purchase for biological science.

A second problem for Bedau, and for any biologist who (like Maynard Smith) defines life in terms of evolution, is the implication that creationism is incoherent. Creationism claims that each living species was specially created by God. But such species would not be alive at all, according to an evolutionary definition: unlike the species in Bedau's evolution-in-equilibrium scenario, they do not even have evolutionary descent somewhere in their history. Biologists who oppose creationist 'theory' (still taught in biology classes in some schools) normally argue that it offers no principled explanation of what Bedau calls the unified diversity of life, whereas neo-Darwinism does. Someone genuinely trying to decide whether creationist or neo-Darwinian schoolbooks offer a better explanation of life might be persuaded by such arguments, but not by being told that life involves evolution *by definition*. To argue that 'creation biology' is false, or explanatorily inferior to scientific biology, one must treat evolution as a universal empirical characteristic of life, not as an *a priori* criterion of it.

A-Life interests Bedau primarily because it can clarify the notion of supple adaptation. In doing so, it also clarifies the sense in which evolution is teleological, for A-Life offers quantitative measures of functionality—some developed by Bedau himself (see also Cliff and Miller forthcoming). The well-known example of the spandrels of San Marco (Gould and Lewontin 1979) shows how difficult it is to decide which traits are functional and which are merely side-effects. It is even more difficult to measure and compare the contribution to 'fitness' of different functional traits. Bedau sees A-Life as able to give precise answers to these questions, allowing that the criteria for selection themselves change as the system evolves. He applies his functionality-metric to a number of examples, including the co-evolving Tierra system described in Chapter 3. Not least, in the present context, he offers a measure of 'vitality' (in terms of the rate at which new significant adaptations are arising and persisting) which might help us to decide to what extent a given system involves life.

As is evident from Chapters 1, 3, and 11–13, the characteristics repeatedly mentioned in discussions of the nature of life include self-organization, autonomy, responsiveness, reproduction, evolution, and metabolism. Arguably, each of these (except one) is definable in informational terms, and each (except one) has already been exhibited to some degree in functioning A-Life systems. The exception, apparently, is metabolism. Systems like Tierra show real self-replication, and real co-evolution. But whether the things that are self-replicating and co-evolving are really alive depends, one might argue, not just on their computational properties but also on their physical embodiment and metabolism.

Is metabolism denied to A-Life systems? Certainly, we cannot confine the concept to energy-exchanges involving terrestrial proteins, phosphates, and oxygen. One might argue that metabolism necessarily involves both anabolism and catabolism: the breaking down of some chemicals and the synthesis of others. In that case, the electrical energy-exchanges within a computer would not qualify; nor would the energy-use of a manufactured robot. But what if metabolism means (more broadly) energy-use resulting in self-repair, and in the other vital characteristics listed above? A future Tierra might evolve a way of recognizing and repairing transcription-errors arising because of unpredictable physical events in the hardware (compare the body's recognition and repair of a tear in a blood-vessel or of faulty copying of DNA). The computer's energy would be required for this, as it is for reproduction and evolution.

Perhaps such energy-use cannot reasonably be counted as metabolism, since it is not the case that each Tierran 'organism' has its own individuated energy-budget. If this constraint could be added, the likeness to biological metabolism would be greater—but there would still be no analogy of anabolism and catabolism (or of the complex chemical life-cycle resulting from them).

The importance of physical embodiment and energy-exchange enters the discussion in Chapters 14 and 15, which ask whether A-Life can ever be real life. Could Langton or Ray succeed in their aim of synthesizing novel life-forms? Recalling Searle's (1980) discussion of AI, Elliott Sober addresses this question in Chapter 14: 'Learning from Functionalism—Prospects for Strong Artificial Life'.

Sober's rejection of strong A-Life depends not on any definition of life but on his analysis of specific biological properties of terrestrial living things. Much as intentionality requires a causal world–mind relationship, not captured in abstract functionalist terms, so some biological properties relate an organism to something outside itself. It follows that computers—or computational processes running on computers, such as computer viruses—cannot really have these properties (although they may replicate some aspects of them) unless they are related to their environment in the relevant ways (cf. Harnad 1994a, 1994b).

Examples cited by Sober include reproduction, digestion, and predation. He allows that reproduction, however it may be physically realized, always involves the formation and manipulation of representations (DNA instructions, for instance). Reproduction, as von Neumann claimed, is essentially computational.

But digestion, also realized in multiple ways, is not. Whereas an A-Life model might really reproduce, it could not digest—or rather, it could not digest *in virtue of its being a computational system* (though some future animat might employ a novel digestive biochemistry discovered by A-Life). Again, since predation involves both hunting and eating, true predation requires that the predator really consume the energy of the prey. In other words, metabolism (and associated behaviours, such as predation) necessarily involves a physically embodied organism interacting with a physical environment. Computer-code creatures within virtual environments do not qualify.

Sober's close assimilation of A-Life to AI has been challenged on the grounds that two familiar objections to strong AI cannot counter strong A-Life (Keeley 1994). Eliminativist arguments against folk-psychology are prominent in AI and cognitive science. Some eliminativists see everyday psychological terms (belief, desire, hope, regret) as instrumental categories, useful as theoretical shorthand but not denoting real entities—or, at best, as categories denoting *abstracta* (comparable to centres of gravity), not *concreta* (Dennett 1987). Others foresee their eventual replacement by neuroscientific categories as yet unknown (Churchland 1989). Such arguments are widely regarded with scepticism; few philosophers are prepared to countenance the disappearance of mentalistic vocabulary in favour of some future neuroscience. But eliminativism is not common in A-Life, *nouvelle* AI excepted (Brooks 1991; Smithers 1992), because 'folk biology' is broadly consonant with scientific biology—and it avoids immaterialist notions such as Bergson's *élan vital*. Accordingly, anti-eliminativist arguments have little purchase against A-Life, except in rebutting claims that animals (and animats) need no representations of any kind (see Chs. 8 and 9).

The second difference between strong AI and strong A-Life concerns consciousness. Whereas consciousness prompts many attacks on strong AI (and functionalism), it is hardly mentioned in discussions of A-Life—or in biology itself. Philosophers who believe there is something it is like to be a bat (Nagel 1974) might object to McFarland's vision of animals as cost-based robots, which (unlike Wheeler's hermeneutic naturalism outlined in Ch. 7) leaves no room for subjectivity. But consciousness is irrelevant to self-organization, self-replication, or evolution. Only someone who believed that all living things—plants and animals alike—have some sort of mind, or awareness, would dismiss A-Life as a whole because it (almost always) ignores consciousness.

Strong A-Life is discussed also in Chapter 15: 'Simulations, Realizations, and Theories of Life'. Howard Pattee sees evolution as essential to life, and as requiring symbolic genotypes, material phenotypes, and selective environments. Since realizations are material models that actually implement the relevant functions, strong A-Life requires the evolution of novel material phenotypes, performing novel functions, in input–output relations with their environment.

Animats produced by evolutionary robotics might qualify. But what about digital phenotypes in purely formal environments, such as Ray's *Digital Reserve*?

Formal environments, says Pattee, can support real life only if they enable the emergence of fundamental novelty in evolution. His analysis of emergence requires that qualitatively new phenotypic structures and functions arise in unpredictable ways. An open-ended physical environment interacts unpredictably with both genotype and phenotype. These (epigenetic) physical interactions, and the selective forces acting on the organism, are not describable by the genotype (considered as symbolic information), and lead to the evolution of features not wholly prefigured in it.

Among the most important emergent novelties, for Pattee, are new forms of measurement (cf. Cariani 1991; Rosen 1991). He defines measurement as a physical interaction resulting in a classification—a definition that covers any observation of, or information-bearing response to, the world. The classification may be based in some novel sensory mechanism, and may result in an enduring informational record. But it may merely be a mapping from a physical pattern to a specific motor action, or even biochemical activity (enzyme synthesis, for instance). The physical basis of the classification is not an inevitable consequence of physico-chemical laws, but is arbitrary—as in the genetic code, for instance. Since physical interaction is essential, and material systems cannot be realized by formal systems (which deal only with syntax, not semantics), novel types of measurement could not emerge by purely computational means.

Pattee adds that the notion of measurement (observation) is problematic. It poses the epistemological problem of the origin of meaning, or information, from matter—and its corollary, the puzzle of how information (e.g. the genotype) can constrain physical processes (the phenotype). Pattee locates the difficulty in the fact that measurement is irreversible whereas physical laws are in principle reversible—yet all measurements must be effected by physical means. Quantum physics, instead of regarding measurement as an extra-theoretical determination of initial conditions, places it at the heart of physical theory. This leads to fundamental difficulties in distinguishing physical from informational processes. Some quantum theorists appeal to consciousness in making this distinction, while others demand only that some record be irreversibly made; however, *consciousness* and *record* are deeply problematic concepts. In short, some central concepts of biology (and psychology) are fundamentally unclear. Pattee allows that (weak) A-Life might help clarify them, but insists that (strong) A-Life could not realize them.

Elsewhere Pattee (1995) argues that A-Life models, considered as ideal formal systems, cannot be perfectly realized in physical machines but only approximately simulated by them. The requirements for a formal system include some—such as absolute determinism in reading and writing—which are not physically realizable. It follows that no purely computational A-Life (or AI) system can be faithfully translated into physical form, whether a computer implementation of some virtual environment or a biochemical system in the real world.

In general, the genotype—considered purely as a symbolic description—cannot be perfectly realized in the phenotype. (For example, genes specifying the linear sequence of amino-acids in a protein molecule do not control how the constructed molecule will fold: that is determined by the molecule's intrinsic physical properties.) It is this which allows for the possibility of 'open-ended' evolution, with the emergence of new forms of vital (meaningful) function. But the philosophical problem of deriving meaning from matter remains. Pattee calls it the 'intrinsic epistemic cut between the genotype and phenotype, i.e. between description and construction', and argues that we do not adequately understand what *implementing a description* means.

A-LIFE AND PUBLIC LIFE

Many chapters in this volume involve attempts to define necessary, or even necessary and sufficient, conditions of life. Some philosophers will have scant sympathy for such essentialist projects, arguing that what counts as alive is a question of how the term is actually used. But usage can change, not least under the influence of science: *evolution* has already been added to biologists' criteria of life. Technology, too, can affect it. Turing's (1950) prediction that by the millennium computers will routinely be described as thinking looks likely to be confirmed, so that—despite the philosophical inadequacy of the Turing Test—people are tacitly predisposed towards philosophical positions which they might otherwise reject. Will A-Life have a similar effect?

Children's understanding of life is already being challenged by widely available A-Life technology, such as home-computer versions of the *biomorph* (Dawkins 1986, appendix; Dawkins 1991) and Tierra programs. Youngsters of the 1970s mentioned life as one of two features distinguishing people from computers, the other being feeling or emotion (Turkle 1984). They conceded that computers are intelligent, but not that they are alive. This rejection of the continuity thesis involved few attempts to analyse 'life', because the concept was not challenged by traditional computing. With Tierra in the living-room, however, this concept becomes a focus of discussion (Turkle 1995, ch. 6).

Children of the 1990s mention several characteristics of life, the most important being autonomous movement. This feature was emphasized also in Piaget's (1929) classic study of the child's concepts of life and mind. Children faced with A-Life, however, may distinguish between movement on the VDU-screen and movement of physical bodies. Only the latter, they may say, counts as evidence of life; and even bodily movement may be discounted, if the bodies are not natural but artefactual. In addition, these children think of life in terms of reproduction and evolution, both of which they can observe on their computer screens.

But, unsurprisingly, they offer no agreed list of necessary and sufficient conditions. Children (and adults) disagree—and vacillate—over whether A-Life creatures are really alive as we are, alive merely as ants are, sort of alive, or not alive (but nevertheless in control). Sometimes, these distinctions are brushed aside with the remark: 'It's just a machine.' (The notion of *machine* has itself altered since Piaget's day, and even since the early days of home-computing around 1980: in the 1990s, people acknowledge the surprising, apparently magical powers of many A-Life systems.) Very few people are willing to assert (with Ray) that Tierran creatures are just as alive as biological organisms. In general, the distinction between humans and machines is protected—if only by mutually inconsistent definitions, used in different circumstances. The papers in this volume show that whether philosophers can justify this everyday distinction in rigorous terms is controversial.

Besides prompting changes in everyday notions of what it is to be alive, A-Life may also affect people's attitudes to technology in general. These attitudes have been described as falling into two broad types: 'Faustian' and 'Magian' (S. Clark, in press). The first, nurtured by the scientific and industrial revolutions, sees technology as under our control. Science renders the world intelligible, and technology reliably exploits this intelligibility (and deterministic predictability) to help us achieve our goals. The second sees technology as shot through with dangerous unpredictability, and its scientific underpinnings as unintelligible except to a tiny élite. Not scientist as boffin, but scientist as magician—whose arcane technology threatens us in largely hidden ways.

One example of the way in which public confidence in technology as control has already been eroded is the ecological movement. Concern about the damage done by technology to the global environment ranges from the near-mystical Gaia hypothesis (Lovelock 1979) to the sober realization that 'minor' technological side-effects (CFCs, for instance) can upset delicate and far-reaching equilibria—with potentially dire results. The ecological movement constantly emphasizes the unexpected harm that can be caused by apparently benign technologies, whose wider effects we are only beginning to glimpse.

A-Life can be expected to arouse similar suspicions, for it is widely unintelligible and largely occult. The workings of an 'engine' whose entire function consists of electronic dances across computer circuitry are invisible. Add the emergence of new order and the evolutionary randomness typical of A-Life, and the aura of magic intensifies (Kelly 1994). Interviews with adults and children show that many people experience A-Life phenomena as shocking, magical, and godlike (Turkle 1995, ch. 6). Even A-Life professionals will not have a detailed understanding of programs or robots evolved over many generations in a complex task-environment. Such systems will function largely as black boxes. Ray's vision of the *Digital Reserve*, despite his promise that its denizens will not escape to infect computers across the Internet, is uncomfortably reminiscent of the ill-understood and ultimately malignant magic of the sorcerer's apprentice.

Images of technology are deeply rooted in our culture, and feed back into it. A-Life will play its role in this cultural process. If even professionals cannot fully understand it, laymen may simply stop trying. The prominence of Magian technologies could thus encourage irrationalism, even anti-rationalism. More helpfully, such technologies could prevent us from assuming (with Faust) that we can be clear about all our goals, and can reasonably hope to realize just what we want—and no more. That Enlightenment ambition still survives, to a considerable degree. A-Life, despite what many see as its overweening *hubris*, might help to make our ambitions less vainglorious.

REFERENCES

Ballard, D. H. (1991), 'Animate Vision', *Artificial Intelligence*, 48: 57–86.
Beer, R. (1995*a*), 'Computational and Dynamical Languages for Autonomous Agents', in R. Port and T. van Gelder (eds.), *Mind as Motion: Explorations in the Dynamics of Cognition* (Cambridge, Mass.: MIT Press).
—— (1995*b*), 'A Dynamical Systems Perspective on Environment–Agent Interactions', *Artificial Intelligence*, 72: 173–215.
Bersini, H., and Detours, V. (1994), 'Asynchrony Induces Stability on Cellular Automata Based Models', in Brooks and Maes (1994), 382–7.
Boden, M. A. (1980), 'The Case for a Cognitive Biology', *Proceedings of the Aristotelian Society,* Supp. vol. liv, 25–49. (For an extended version, see M. A. Boden, *Minds and Mechanisms: Philosophical Psychology and Computational Models* (Ithaca, NY: Cornell University Press, 1981), 89–112.)
—— (1987), *Artificial Intelligence and Natural Man*, 2nd edn., expanded (London: MIT Press).
—— (1990) (ed.), *The Philosophy of Artificial Intelligence* (Oxford Readings in Philosophy; Oxford: Oxford University Press).
—— (1995), *Piaget*, 2nd edn., expanded (Fontana Modern Masters Series; London: HarperCollins).
Braitenberg, V. (1984), *Vehicles: Essays in Synthetic Psychology* (Cambridge, Mass.: MIT Press).
Brooks, R. A. (1991), 'Intelligence Without Representation', *Artificial Intelligence*, 47: 139–59.
—— and Maes, P. (1994) (eds.), *Artificial Life IV: Proceedings of the Fourth International*

Workshop on the Synthesis and Simulation of Living Systems (Cambridge, Mass.: MIT Press).

—— and Stein, L. A. (1994), 'Building Brains for Bodies', *Autonomous Robots*, 1: 7–25.

Burks, A. W. (1970) (ed.), *Essays on Cellular Automata* (Champaign-Urbana: University of Illinois Press).

Burnyeat, M. F. (1992), 'Is an Aristotelian Philosophy of Mind Still Credible?', in Nussbaum and Rorty (1992), 15–26.

Cariani, P. (1991), 'Emergence and Artificial Life', in Langton *et al.* (1991), 775–97.

Churchland, P. M. (1989), *A Neurocomputational Perspective: The Nature of Mind and the Structure of Science* (Cambridge, Mass.: MIT Press).

Clark, A. C. (1989), *Microcognition: Philosophy, Cognitive Science, and Parallel Distributed Processing* (Cambridge, Mass.: MIT Press).

—— (1993), *Associative Engines: Connectionism, Concepts, and Representational Change* (Cambridge, Mass.: MIT Press).

Clark, S. R. L. (in press), 'Tools, Machines, and Marvels', in R. Fellowes (ed.), *Philosophy and Technology* (Cambridge: Cambridge University Press).

Cliff, D. (1991), 'The Computational Hoverfly: A Study in Computational Neuroethology', in Meyer and Wilson (1991), 87–96.

—— and Miller, G. F. (forthcoming), 'Co-Evolution of Pursuit and Evasion II: Simulation Methods and Results', submitted to *Adaptive Behavior*.

—— Harvey, I., and Husbands, P. (1993), 'Explorations in Evolutionary Robotics', *Adaptive Behavior*, 2: 71–108.

—— Husbands, P., Meyer, J.-A., and Wilson, S. (1994) (eds.), *Animals to Animats 3: Proceedings of the Third International Conference on the Simulation of Adaptive Behavior* (Cambridge, Mass.: MIT Press).

Cussins, A. (1990), 'The Connectionist Construction of Concepts', in Boden (1990), 368–440.

Dawkins, R. (1976), *The Selfish Gene* (Oxford: Oxford University Press).

—— (1986), *The Blind Watchmaker* (Harlow: Longman).

—— (1989), 'The Evolution of Evolvability', in C. G. Langton (ed.), *Artificial Life* (SFI Studies in the Sciences of Complexity, vi: Proceedings of the Interdisciplinary Workshop on the Synthesis and Simulation of Living Systems held September 1987, Los Alamos; Redwood City, Calif.: Addison-Wesley), 201–20.

—— (1991), *Blind Watchmaker: The Program of the Book* (PO Box 59, Leamington Spa: SPA).

De Bourcier, P., and Wheeler, M. (1995), 'Aggressive Signaling Meets Adaptive Receiving: Further Experiments in Synthetic Behavioural Ecology', in Moran *et al.* (1995), 762–73.

Dennett, D. C. (1984), 'Cognitive Wheels: The Frame Problem of AI', in C. Hookway (ed.), *Minds, Machines, and Evolution: Philosophical Studies* (Cambridge: Cambridge University Press), 129–52. (Repr. in Boden (1990), 147–70.)

—— (1987), *The Intentional Stance* (Cambridge, Mass.: MIT Press).

—— (1994), 'The Practical Requirements for Making a Conscious Robot', *Philosophical Transactions of the Royal Society, Series A*, 349: 133–46.

Depew, D. J., and Weber, B. H. (1994), *Darwinism Evolving: Systems Dynamics and the Genealogy of Natural Selection* (Cambridge, Mass.: MIT Press).

Dreyfus, H. L. (1979), *What Computers Can't Do: The Limits of Artificial Intelligence*, 2nd edn. (New York: Harper and Row).

—— and Dreyfus, S. E. (1986), *Mind Over Machine: The Power of Human Intuition and Expertise in the Era of the Computer* (New York: Free Press, Macmillan).

Eldredge, N., and Gould, S. J. (1972), 'Punctuated Equilibria: An Alternative to Phyletic Gradualism', in T. J. M. Schopf (ed.), *Models in Paleobiology* (San Francisco: Freeman), 82–115.

Elton, M. (1994), 'What Are You Talking About?', *AISB Quarterly*, No. 87: 47–54. (Special Theme: AI and Artificial Life, ed. D. Cliff.)

Feigenbaum, E. A., and Feldman, J. (1963) (eds.), *Computers and Thought* (New York: McGraw-Hill).

Fodor, J. A. (1975), *The Language of Thought* (Hassocks, Sussex: Harvester Press).

—— and Pylyshyn, Z. W. (1988), 'Connectionism and Cognitive Architecture: A Critical Analysis', *Cognition*, 28: 3–71.

Frazer, J. (1995), *An Evolutionary Architecture* (London: Architectural Association).

Gardner, M. (1970), 'The Fantastic Combinations of John Conway's New Solitaire Game "Life"', *Scientific American*, 223/4: 120–3.

Gibson, J. J. (1979), *The Ecological Approach to Visual Perception* (Boston: Houghton Mifflin).

Goldberg, D. E. (1989), *Genetic Algorithms in Search, Optimization, and Machine Learning* (Reading, Mass.: Addison-Wesley).

Gould, S. J., and Lewontin, R. C. (1979), 'The Spandrels of San Marco and the Panglossian Paradigm: A Critique of the Adaptationist Programme', *Proceedings of the Royal Society, B*, 205: 581–98.

Harnad, S. (1994a), 'Artificial Life: Synthetic vs. Virtual', in Langton (1994), 539–42.

—— (1994b), 'Levels of Functional Equivalence in Reverse Bioengineering', *Artificial Life*, 1: 293–301.

Harvey, I. (1992), 'Species Adaptation Genetic Algorithms: A Basis for a Continuing SAGA', in Varela and Bourgine (1992), 346–54.

Hillis, W. D. (1991), 'Co-Evolving Parasites Improve Simulated Evolution as an Optimization Procedure', in Langton *et al.* (1991), 313–24.

Holland, J. H. (1975), *Adapation in Natural and Artificial Systems: An Introductory Analysis with Applications to Biology, Control, and Artificial Intelligence* (Ann Arbor: University of Michigan Press). (Reissued by MIT Press, 1992.)

—— Holyoak, K. J., Nisbett, R. E., and Thagard, P. R. (1986) (eds.), *Induction: Processes of Inference, Learning, and Discovery* (Cambridge, Mass.: MIT Press).

Husbands, P., Harvey, I., and Cliff, D. (1995), 'Circle in the Round: State Space Attractors for Evolved Sighted Robots', *Journal of Robotics and Autonomous Systems*, 15: 83–106. (Special Issue on The Biology and Technology of Intelligent Autonomous Agents, ed. L. Steels.)

Ingerson, T. E., and Buvel, R. L. (1984), 'Structure in Asynchronous Cellular Automata', *Physica D*, 10: 59–68.

Kauffman, S. A. (1993), *The Origins of Order: Self-Organization and Selection in Evolution* (Oxford: Oxford University Press).

—— and Johnson, S. (1991), 'Co-Evolution to the Edge of Chaos: Coupled Fitness Landscapes, Poised States, and Co-Evolutionary Avalanches', in Langton *et al.* (1991), 325–69.

Keeley, B. L. (1994), 'Against the Global Replacement: On the Application of the Philosophy of Artificial Intelligence to Artificial Life', in Langton (1994), 569–87.

Kelly, K. (1994), *Out of Control: The Rise of Neo-Biological Civilization* (Reading, Mass.: Addison-Wesley).

Langton, C. G. (1986), 'Studying Artificial Life with Cellular Automata', *Physica D*, 10: 120–49.

—— (1991), 'Life at the Edge of Chaos', in Langton *et al.* (1991), 41–91.

—— (1994) (ed.), *Artificial Life III* (Santa Fe Institute Studies in the Sciences of Complexity, Proceedings, 17; Redwood City, Calif.: Addison-Wesley).

—— (1995) (ed.), *Artificial Life: An Overview* (Cambridge, Mass.: MIT Press).

—— Taylor, C., Farmer, J. D., and Rasmussen, S. (1991) (eds.), *Artificial Life II* (Santa Fe Institute Studies in the Sciences of Complexity, 10; Redwood City, Calif.: Addison-Wesley).

Levy, S. (1992), *Artificial Life: The Quest for a New Creation* (New York: Random House).

Lovelock, J. (1979), *Gaia: A New Look at Life on Earth* (Oxford: Oxford University Press).

McCulloch, W. S., and Pitts, W. (1943), 'A Logical Calculus of the Ideas Immanent in Nervous Activity', *Bulletin of Mathematical Biophysics*, 5: 115–33. (Repr. in Boden (1990), 22–39.)

McDermott, D. V. (1976), 'Artificial Intelligence Meets Natural Stupidity', *SIGART Newsletter of the ACM*, No. 57, April. (Repr. in J. Haugeland (ed.), *Mind Design: Philosophy, Psychology, Artificial Intelligence* (Cambridge, Mass.: MIT Press), 143–60.)

McFarland, D. (1991), 'Defining Motivation and Cognition in Animals', *International Studies in the Philosophy of Science*, 5: 153–70.

Meyer, J.-A., and Guillot, A. (1991), 'Simulation of Adaptive Behavior in Animats: Review and Prospects', in id. and Wilson (1991), 2–14.

—— —— (1994), 'From SAB90 to SAB94: Four Years of Animat Research', in Cliff *et al.* (1994), 2–11.

—— and Wilson, S. W. (1991) (eds.), *From Animals to Animats: Proceedings of the First International Conference on Simulation of Adaptive Behavior* (Cambridge, Mass.: MIT Press).

Miller, G. F. (1995), *Artificial Life as Theoretical Biology: How to Do Real Science as Computer Simulation* (University of Sussex, School of Cognitive and Computing Sciences Research Paper).

—— and Cliff, D. (forthcoming), 'Co-Evolution of Pursuit and Evasion I: Biological and Game-Theoretic Foundations', submitted to *Adaptive Behavior*.

Millikan, R. G. (1984), *Language, Thought, and Other Biological Categories* (Cambridge, Mass.: MIT Press).

Mingers, J. (1989), 'An Introduction to Autopoiesis—Implications and Applications', *Systems Practice*, 2: 159–80.

Moran, F., Moreno, A., Merelo, J. J., and Chacon, P. (1995) (eds.), *Advances in Artificial Life: Proceedings of the Third European Conference on Artificial Life* (Granada, 1995) (Berlin: Springer).

Nagel, T. (1974), 'What is it Like to be a Bat?', *Philosophical Review*, 83: 435–50.

Nussbaum, M. C., and Putnam, H. (1992), 'Changing Aristotle's Mind', in Nussbaum and Rorty (1992), 27–56.

—— and Rorty, A. (1992) (eds.), *Essays on Aristotle's 'De Anima'* (Oxford: Clarendon Press).

Pattee, H. H. (1995), 'Artificial Life Needs a Real Epistemology', in Moran *et al.* (1995), 23–38.

Piaget, J. (1929), *The Child's Conception of the World* (London: Routledge, Kegan Paul).

Port, R., and van Gelder, T. (1995) (eds.), *Mind as Motion: Dynamics, Behavior, and Cognition* (Cambridge, Mass.: MIT Press).

Prusinkiewicz, P. (1994), 'Visual Models of Morphogenesis', *Artificial Life*, 1: 61–74.

Putnam, H. (1960), 'Minds and Machines', in S. Hook (ed.), *Dimensions of Mind* (New York: Collier), 148–79.

—— (1967), 'The Nature of Mental States', in id., *Mind, Language, and Reality: Philosophical Papers*, ii (Cambridge: Cambridge University Press, 1975), 429–40. (First published as 'Psychological Predicates', in W. H. Capitan and D. D. Merrill (eds.), *Art, Mind, and Religion* (Pittsburgh: University of Pittsburgh Press, 1967).)

Putnam, H. (1988), *Representation and Reality* (Cambridge, Mass.: MIT Press).

Ray, T. S. (1994), 'An Evolutionary Approach to Synthetic Biology: Zen and the Art of Creating Life', *Artificial Life*, 1: 179–210.

Reynolds, C. W. (1987), 'Flocks, Herds, and Schools: A Distributed Behavioral Model', *Computer Graphics*, 21: 25–34.

—— (1994*a*), 'An Evolved, Vision-Based Model of Obstacle Avoidance Behavior', in Langton (1994), 327–46.

—— (1994*b*), 'Competition, Coevolution, and the Game of Tag', in Brooks and Maes (1994), 59–69.

Rosen, R. (1991), *Life Itself: A Comprehensive Inquiry into the Nature, Origin, and Fabrication of Life* (New York: Columbia University Press).

Rutkowska, J. (1995), 'Can Development be Designed? What we may Learn from the Cog Project', in Moran *et al.* (1995), 383–95.

Searle, J. R. (1980), 'Minds, Brains, and Programs', repr. in Boden (1990), 67–88.

Sims, K. (1991), 'Artificial Evolution for Computer Graphics', *Computer Graphics*, 25: 319–28.

—— (1994), 'Evolving 3D Morphology and Behavior by Competition', *Artificial Life*, 1: 353–72.

Smithers, T. (1992), 'Taking Eliminative Materialism Seriously: A Methodology for Autonomous Systems Research', in Varela and Bourgine (1992), 31–40.

Spafford, E. H. (1991), 'Computer Viruses—A Form of Artificial Life?', in Langton *et al.* (1991), 727–45.

—— (1994), 'Computer Viruses as Artificial Life', *Artificial Life*, 1: 249–65.

Steels, L. (1991), 'Towards a Theory of Emergent Functionality', in Meyer and Wilson (1991), 451–61.

Thelen, E., and Smith, L. B. (1993), *A Dynamic Systems Approach to the Development of Cognition and Action* (Cambridge, Mass.: MIT Press).

Thompson, A. (1995), 'Evolving Electronic Robot Controllers that Exploit Hardware Resources', in Moran *et al.* (1995), 641–57.

Todd, S., and Latham, W. (1992), *Evolutionary Art and Computers* (London: Academic Press).

Turing, A. M. (1936), 'On Computable Numbers, with an Application to the *Entscheidungsproblem*', *Proc. London Math. Soc.*, 42: 230–65.

—— (1950), 'Computing Machinery and Intelligence', *Mind*, 59: 433–60.

—— (1952), 'The Chemical Basis of Morphogenesis', *Philosophical Transactions of the Royal Society (London), Series B*, 237: 37–72.

Turk, G. (1991), 'Generating Textures on Arbitrary Surfaces using Reaction-Diffusion', *Computer Graphics*, 25: 289–98.

Turkle, S. (1984), *The Second Self: Computers and the Human Spirit* (New York: Simon and Schuster).

—— (1995), *Life on the Screen: Identity in the Age of the Internet* (New York: Simon and Schuster).

Uexkull, J. von (1957), 'A Stroll through the Worlds of Animals and Men', in C. H. Schiller (ed.), *Instinctive Behavior: The Development of a Modern Concept* (New York: International Universities Press), 5–82.

van Gelder, T. (1995), 'What Might Cognition Be if not Computation?', *Journal of Philosophy*, 92: 345–81.

Varela, F. J., and Bourgine, P. (1992) (eds.), *Toward a Practice of Autonomous Systems: Proceedings of the First European Conference on Artificial Life* (Cambridge, Mass.: MIT Press).

Webb, B. (1994), 'Robotic Experiments in Cricket Phonotaxia', in Cliff *et al.* (1994), 45–54.

Wheeler, M. (1995), 'Escaping from the Cartesian Mind-Set: Heidegger and Artificial Life', in Moran *et al.* (1995), 65–76.

Wilkes, K. V. (1992), '*Psuche* versus the Mind', in Nussbaum and Rorty (1992), 109–27.

Wilson, S. W. (1991), 'The Animat Path to AI', in Meyer and Wilson (1991), 15–21.

Wolfram, S. (1984), 'Computer Software in Science and Mathematics', *Scientific American*, Sept., 188–203.

PART I

ARTIFICIAL LIFE

CHRISTOPHER G. LANGTON

1. THE BIOLOGY OF POSSIBLE LIFE

Biology is the scientific study of life—in principle anyway. In practice, biology is the scientific study of life on Earth based on carbon-chain chemistry. There is nothing in its charter that restricts biology to the study of carbon-based life; it is simply that this is the only kind of life that has been available to study. Thus, theoretical biology has long faced the fundamental obstacle that it is impossible to derive general principles from single examples.

Without other examples it is extremely difficult to distinguish essential properties of life—properties that must be shared by any living system *in principle*—from properties that may be incidental to life, but which happen to be universal to life on Earth due *solely* to a combination of local historical accident and common genetic descent. Since it is quite unlikely that organisms based on different physical chemistries will present themselves to us for study in the foreseeable future, our only alternative is to try to synthesize alternative life-forms ourselves—*Artificial Life*: life made by man rather than by nature.

1.1. Artificial Life

Biology has traditionally started at the top, viewing a living organism as a complex biochemical machine, and has worked *analytically* down from there through the hierarchy of biological organization—decomposing a living organism into organs, tissues, cells, organelles, and finally molecules—in its pursuit of the mechanisms of life. Analysis means 'the separation of an intellectual or substantial whole into constituents for individual study'. By composing our individual understandings of the dissected component parts of living organisms, traditional biology has provided us with a broad picture of the mechanics of life on Earth.

But there is more to life than mechanics—there is also dynamics. Life depends critically on principles of dynamical self-organization that have remained largely untouched by traditional analytic methods. There is a simple explanation for this—these self-organizing dynamics are fundamentally non-linear phenomena, and non-linear phenomena in general depend critically on the interactions *between* parts: they necessarily disappear when parts are treated in isolation from one another, which is the basis for the analytic method.

Rather, non-linear phenomena are most appropriately treated by a *synthetic* approach. Synthesis means 'the combining of separate elements or substances to form a coherent whole'. In non-linear systems, the parts must be treated in each other's presence, rather than independently from one another, because they behave very differently in each other's presence than we would expect from a study of the parts in isolation.

Artificial Life is simply the synthetic approach to biology: rather than take living things apart, Artificial Life attempts to put living things together.

But Artificial Life is more than this. To understand the overall aims of the Artificial Life enterprise, one needs to do the following: (1) Broaden the scope of the attempts, beyond simply recreating 'the living state', to the synthesis of any and all biological phenomena, from viral self-assembly to the evolution of the entire biosphere. (2) Couple this with the observation that there is no reason, in principle, why the parts we use in our attempts to synthesize these biological phenomena need be restricted to carbon-chain chemistry. (3) Note that we expect the synthetic approach to lead us not only to, but quite often *beyond*, known biological phenomena: beyond *life-as-we-know-it* into the realm of *life-as-it-could-be*.

Thus, for example, Artificial Life involves attempts to (1) synthesize the process of evolution (2) in computers, and (3) will be interested in whatever emerges from the process, even if the results have no analogues in the 'natural' world. It is certainly of scientific interest to know what kinds of things *can* evolve in principle, whether or not they happened to do so here on Earth.

1.2. AI and the Behaviour Generation Problem

Artificial Life is concerned with generating *lifelike* behaviour. Thus it focuses on the problem of creating *behaviour generators*. A good place to start is to identify the mechanisms by which behaviour is generated and controlled in natural systems, and to recreate these mechanisms in artificial systems. This is the course we shall take later in this paper.

The related field of Artificial Intelligence is concerned with generating *intelligent* behaviour. It, too, focuses on the problem of creating behaviour generators. However, although it initially looked to natural intelligence to identify its underlying mechanisms, these mechanisms were not known, nor are they today. Therefore, following an initial flirt with neural nets, AI became wedded to the only other known vehicle for the generation of complex behaviour: the technology of serial computer programming. As a consequence, from the very beginning artificial intelligence embraced an underlying methodology for the generation of intelligent behaviour that bore no demonstrable relationship to the method by which intelligence is generated in natural systems. In fact, AI has focused primarily on the production of intelligent *solutions* rather than on the production of intelligent *behaviour*. There is a world of difference between these two possible foci.

By contrast, Artificial Life has the great good fortune that many of the mechanisms by which behaviour arises in natural living systems are known. There are still many holes in our knowledge, but the general picture is in place. Therefore, Artificial Life can start by recapturing natural life and has no need to resort to the sort of initial infidelity that is now coming back to haunt AI.

The key insight into the natural method of behaviour generation is gained by noting that *nature is fundamentally parallel*. This is reflected in the 'architecture' of natural living organisms, which consist of many millions of parts, each one of which has its own behavioural repertoire. Living systems are highly distributed and quite massively parallel. If our models are to be true to life, they must also be highly distributed and quite massively parallel. Indeed, it is unlikely that any other approach will prove viable.

2. HISTORICAL ROOTS OF ARTIFICIAL LIFE

Mankind has a long history of attempting to map the mechanics of his contemporary technology on to the workings of nature, trying to understand the latter in terms of the former.

It is not surprising, therefore, that early models of life reflected the principal technology of their era. The earliest models were simple statuettes and paintings—works of art which captured the static form of living things. These statues were provided with articulated arms and legs in the attempt to capture the dynamic form of living things. These simple statues incorporated no internal dynamics, requiring human operators to make them behave.

The earliest mechanical devices that were capable of generating their own behaviour were based on the technology of water transport. These were the early Egyptian water-clocks called *Clepsydra*. These devices made use of a

rate-limited process—in this case the dripping of water through a fixed orifice—
to indicate the progression of another process—the position of the sun. Ctesibius
of Alexandria developed a water-powered mechanical clock around 135 BC
which employed a great deal of the available hydraulic technology—including
floats, a siphon, and a water-wheel-driven train of gears.

In the first century AD, Hero of Alexandria produced a treatise on *Pneumatics*,
which described, among other things, various simple gadgets in the shape of
animals and humans that utilized pneumatic principles to generate simple
movements.

However, it was really not until the age of mechanical clocks that artefacts
exhibiting complicated internal dynamics became possible. Around AD 850 the
mechanical escapement was invented, which could be used to regulate the
power provided by falling weights. This invention ushered in the great age of
clockwork technology. Throughout the Middle Ages and the Renaissance, the
history of technology is largely bound up with the technology of clocks. Clocks
often constituted the most complicated and advanced application of the technology of an era.

Perhaps the earliest clockwork simulations of life were the so-called 'Jacks',
mechanical 'men' incorporated in early clocks who would swing a hammer to
strike the hour on a bell. The word 'jack' is derived from 'jaccomarchiadus',
which means 'the man in the suit of armour'. These accessory figures retained
their popularity even after the spread of clock dials and hands—to the extent
that clocks were eventually developed in which the function of timekeeping
was secondary to the control of large numbers of figures engaged in various
activities, to the point of acting out entire plays.

Finally, clockwork mechanisms appeared which had done away altogether
with any pretence at timekeeping. These 'automata' were entirely devoted to
imparting lifelike motion to a mechanical figure or animal. These mechanical
automaton simulations of life included such things as elephants, peacocks, sing-
ing birds, musicians, and even fortune-tellers.

This line of development reached its peak in the famous duck of Vaucanson,
described as 'an artificial duck made of gilded copper who drinks, eats, quacks,
splashes about on the water, and digests his food like a living duck'.[1] Vaucanson's
goal is captured neatly in the following description:

In 1735 Jacques de Vaucanson arrived in Paris at the age of 26. Under the influence of
contemporary philosophic ideas, he had tried, it seems, to reproduce life artificially.

Unfortunately, neither the duck itself nor any technical descriptions or diagrams
remain that would give the details of construction of this duck. The complexity

---

[1] All quotes concerning these mechanical ducks are from Chapuis and Droz (1958).

of the mechanism is attested to by the fact that one single wing contained over 400 articulated pieces.

One of those called upon to repair Vaucanson's duck in later years was a 'mechanician' named Reichsteiner, who was so impressed with it that he went on to build a duck of his own—also now lost—which was exhibited in 1847. Here is an account of this duck's operation from the newspaper *Das Freie Wort*:

> After a light touch on a point on the base, the duck in the most natural way in the world begins to look around him, eyeing the audience with an intelligent air. His lord and master, however, apparently interprets this differently, for soon he goes off to look for something for the bird to eat. No sooner has he filled a dish with oatmeal porridge than our famished friend plunges his beak deep into it, showing his satisfaction by some characteristic movements of his tail. The way in which he takes the porridge and swallows it greedily is extraordinarily true to life. In next to no time the basin has been half emptied, although on several occasions the bird, as if alarmed by some unfamiliar noises, has raised his head and glanced curiously around him. After this, satisfied with his frugal meal, he stands up and begins to flap his wings and to stretch himself while expressing his gratitude by several contented quacks. But most astonishing of all are the contractions of the bird's body clearly showing that his stomach is a little upset by this rapid meal and the effects of a painful digestion become obvious. However, the brave little bird holds out, and after a few moments we are convinced in the most concrete manner that he has overcome his internal difficulties. The truth is that the smell which now spreads through the room becomes almost unbearable. We wish to express to the artist inventor the pleasure which his demonstration gave to us.

Fig. 1.1 shows two views of one of the ducks—there is some controversy as to whether it is Vaucanson's or Reichsteiner's. The mechanism inside the duck would have been completely covered with feathers and the controlling mechanism in the box below would have been covered up as well.

2.1. The Development of Control Mechanisms

Out of the technology of the clockwork regulation of automata came the more general—and perhaps ultimately more important—technology of *process control*. As attested to in the descriptions of the mechanical ducks, some of the clockwork mechanisms had to control remarkably complicated actions on the part of the automata, not only *powering* them but *sequencing* them as well.

Control mechanisms evolved from early, simple devices—such as a lever attached to a wheel which converted circular motion into linear motion—to later, more complicated devices—such as whole sets of cams upon which would ride many interlinked mechanical arms, giving rise to extremely complicated automaton behaviours.

Eventually *programmable controllers* appeared, which incorporated such devices as interchangeable cams, or drums with movable pegs, with which one could program arbitrary sequences of actions on the part of the automaton. The

FIG. 1.1. Two views of the mechanical duck attributed to Vaucanson. From Chapuis and Droz (1958). Reprinted by permission

writing and picture-drawing automata of Fig. 1.2, built by the Jaquet-Droz family, are examples of programmable automata. The introduction of such programmable controllers was one of the primary developments on the road to general-purpose computers.

2.2. Abstraction of the Logical 'Form' of Machines

During the early part of the twentieth century, the formal application of logic to the mechanical process of arithmetic led to the abstract formulation of a 'procedure'. The work of Church, Kleene, Gödel, Turing, and Post formalized the notion of a logical sequence of steps, leading to the realization that the essence of a mechanical process—the 'thing' responsible for its dynamic behaviour—is not a thing at all, but an abstract control structure, or 'program'—a sequence of simple actions selected from a finite repertoire. Furthermore, it was recognized that the essential features of this control structure could be captured within an abstract set of rules—a formal specification—without regard to the material out of which the machine was constructed. The 'logical form' of a machine was separated from its material basis of construction, and it was found that 'machineness' was a property of the former, not of the latter. Today, the

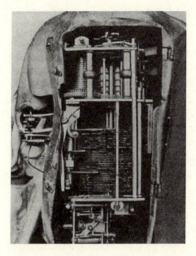

FIG. 1.2. Two views of a drawing automaton built by the Jaquet-Droz family. From Chapuis and Droz (1958). Reprinted by permission

formal equivalent of a 'machine' is an *algorithm*: the logic underlying the dynamics of an automaton, regardless of the details of its material construction. We now have many formal methods for the specification and operation of abstract machines: such as programming languages, formal language theory, automata theory, recursive function theory, etc. All these have been shown to be logically equivalent.

Once we have learned to think of machines in terms of their abstract, formal specifications, we can turn around and view abstract, formal specifications as potential machines. In mapping the machines of our common experience to formal specifications, we have by no means exhausted the space of *possible* specifications. Indeed, most of our individual machines map to a very small subset of the space of specifications—a subset largely characterized by methodical, boring, uninteresting dynamics.

2.3. General-Purpose Computers

Various threads of technological development—programmable controllers, calculating engines, and the formal theory of machines—have come together in the general-purpose, stored-program computer. Programmable computers are extremely general behaviour generators. They have no intrinsic behaviour of their own. Without programs, they are like formless matter. They must be told how to behave. By submitting a program to a computer—that is: by giving it a formal specification for a machine—we are telling it to behave as if it were the machine specified by the program. The computer then 'emulates' that more specific machine in the performance of the desired task. Its great power lies in its plasticity of behaviour. If we can provide a step-by-step specification for a specific kind of behaviour, the chameleon-like computer will exhibit that behaviour. Computers should be viewed as *second-order* machines—given the formal specification of a first-order machine, they will 'become' that machine. Thus the space of possible machines is directly available for study, at the cost of a mere formal description: computers 'realize' abstract machines.

2.4. Formal Limits of Machine Behaviours

Although computers, and by extension other machines, are capable of exhibiting a bewilderingly wide variety of behaviours, we must face two fundamental limitations on the kinds of behaviours that we can expect of computers.

The first limitation is one of *computability in principle*. There are certain behaviours that are 'uncomputable'—behaviours for which *no* formal specification can be given for a machine that will exhibit that behaviour. The classic example of this sort of limitation is Turing's famous *Halting Problem*: can we give a formal specification for a machine which, when provided with the description of *any* other machine together with its initial state, will—by inspection alone—determine whether or not that machine will reach its halt state? Turing proved that no such machine can be specified. In particular, Turing showed that the best that such a proposed machine could do would be to emulate the given machine to see whether or not it halted. If the emulated machine halted, fine. However, the emulated machine might run forever without halting, and therefore the emulating machine could not answer whether or not it would halt. Rice and others (in Hopcroft and Ullman 1979) have extended this undecidability result to the determination—by inspection alone—of *any* non-trivial property of the future behaviour of an arbitrary machine.

The second limitation is one of *computability in practice*. There are many behaviours for which we do not know how to specify a sequence of steps that will cause a computer to exhibit that behaviour. We can automate what we can explain how to do, but there is much that we cannot explain how to do. Thus, although a formal specification for a machine that will exhibit a certain behaviour may be possible *in principle*, we have no formal procedure for producing that formal specification in practice, short of a trial-and-error search through the space of possible descriptions.

We need to separate the notion of a formal specification of a machine—that is, a specification of the *logical structure* of the machine—from the notion of a formal specification of a machine's behaviour—that is, a specification of the sequence of transitions that the machine will undergo. In general, we cannot derive behaviours from structure, nor can we derive structure from behaviours.

The moral is: in order to determine the behaviour of some machines, there is no recourse but to run them and see how they behave! This has consequences for the methods by which we (or nature) go about *generating* behaviour generators themselves, which we shall take up in the section on evolution.

2.5. *John von Neumann: From Mechanics to Logic*

With the development of the general-purpose computer, various researchers turned their attention from the *mechanics* of life to the *logic* of life.

The first computational approach to the generation of lifelike behaviour was due to the brilliant Hungarian mathematician John von Neumann. In the words of his colleague Arthur W. Burks, von Neumann was interested in the general question:

What kind of logical organization is sufficient for an automaton to reproduce itself? This question is not precise and admits to trivial versions as well as interesting ones. Von Neumann had the familiar natural phenomenon of self-reproduction in mind when he posed it, but he was not trying to simulate the self-reproduction of a natural system at the level of genetics and biochemistry. *He wished to abstract from the natural self-reproduction problem its logical form.*[2]

This approach is the first to capture the essence of Artificial Life. To understand the field of Artificial Life, one need only replace references to 'self-reproduction' in the above with references to any other biological phenomenon.

In von Neumann's initial thought-experiment (his 'kinematic model'), a machine floats around on the surface of a pond, together with lots of machine parts. The machine is a *universal constructor*: given the description of any machine, it will locate the proper parts and construct that machine. If given a description of itself, it will construct itself. This is not quite self-reproduction, however, because the offspring machine will not have a description of itself and hence could not go on to construct another copy. So, von Neumann's machine also contains a *description copier*: once the offspring machine has been constructed, the 'parent' machine constructs a copy of the description that it worked from and attaches it to the offspring machine. This constitutes genuine self-reproduction.

Von Neumann decided that this model did not properly distinguish the logical

[2] From Burks (1970), emphasis added.

form of the process from the material of the process, and looked about for a completely formal system within which to model self-reproduction. Stan Ulam— one of von Neumann's colleagues at Los Alamos[3]—suggested an appropriate formalism, which has come to be known as a *cellular automaton* (CA).

In brief, a CA consists of a regular lattice of *finite automata*, which are the simplest formal models of machines. A finite automaton can be in only one of a finite number of states at any given time, and its transitions between states from one time-step to the next are governed by a *state-transition table*: given a certain input and a certain internal state, the state-transition table specifies the state to be adopted by the finite automaton at the next time-step. In a CA, the necessary input is derived from the states of the automata at neighbouring lattice-points. Thus the state of an automaton at time $t + 1$ is a function of the states of the automaton itself and its immediate neighbours at time t. All the automata in the lattice obey the same transition table and every automaton changes state at the same instant, time-step after time-step. CAs are good examples of the kind of computational paradigm sought after by Artificial Life: bottom-up, parallel, local determination of behaviour.

Von Neumann was able to embed the equivalent of his kinematic model as an initial pattern of state assignments within a large CA lattice using twenty-nine states per cell. Although von Neumann's work on self-reproducing automata was left incomplete at the time of his death, Arthur Burks organized what had been done, filled in the remaining details, and published it.[4] Fig. 1.3 shows a schematic diagram of von Neumann's self-reproducing machine.

Von Neumann's CA model was a constructive proof that an essential characteristic behaviour of living things—self-reproduction—*was* achievable by machines. Furthermore, he determined that any such method must make use of the information contained in the description of the machine in two fundamentally different ways:

1. *Interpreted*, as instructions to be executed in the construction of the offspring.
2. *Uninterpreted*, as passive data to be duplicated to form the description given to the offspring.

Of course, when Watson and Crick unveiled the structure of DNA, they discovered that the information contained therein was used in precisely these two ways in the processes of transcription/translation and replication.

In describing his model, von Neumann pointed out that:

[3] Ulam (1962) also investigated dynamic models of pattern production and competition.
[4] Together with a transcription of von Neumann's 1949 lectures at the University of Illinois entitled 'Theory and Organization of Complicated Automata', in which he gives his views on various problems related to the study of complex systems in general (von Neumann 1966).

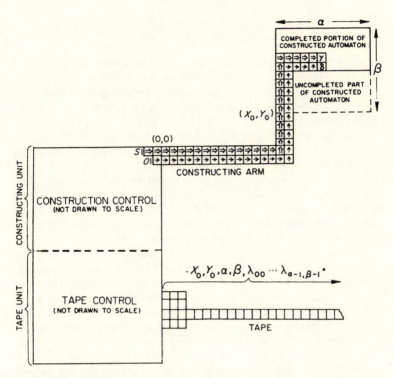

FIG. 1.3. Schematic diagram of von Neumann's CA self-reproducing configuration. From Burks (1970). Reprinted by permission

By axiomatizing automata in this manner, one has thrown half of the problem out the window, and it may be the more important half. One has resigned oneself not to explain how these parts are made up of real things, specifically, how these parts are made up of actual elementary particles, or even of higher chemical molecules.[5]

Whether or not the more important half of the question has been disposed of depends on the questions we are asking. If we are concerned with explaining how the life that we know emerges from the known laws of physics and organic chemistry, then indeed the interesting part has been tossed out. But if we are concerned with the more general problem of explaining how lifelike behaviours emerge out of low-level interactions within a population of logical primitives, we have retained the more interesting portion of the question.

[5] From Burks (1970).

3. THE ROLE OF COMPUTERS IN STUDYING LIFE AND OTHER COMPLEX SYSTEMS

Artificial Intelligence and Artificial Life are each concerned with the application of computers to the study of complex, natural phenomena. Both are concerned with generating complex behaviour. However, the manner in which each field employs the technology of computation in the pursuit of its respective goals is strikingly different.

AI has based its underlying methodology for generating intelligent behaviour on the computational paradigm. That is, AI uses the technology of computation as a model of intelligence. AL, on the other hand, is attempting to develop a new computational paradigm based on the natural processes that support living organisms. That is, AL uses insights from biology to explore the dynamics of interacting information structures. AL has not adopted the computational paradigm as its underlying methodology of behaviour generation, nor does it attempt to 'explain' life as a kind of computer program.

One way to pursue the study of artificial life would be to attempt to create life *in vitro*, using the same kinds of organic chemicals out of which we are constituted. Indeed, there are numerous exciting efforts in this direction. This would certainly teach us a lot about the possibilities for alternative life-forms *within* the carbon-chain chemistry domain that could have (but didn't) evolve here.

However, biomolecules are extremely small and difficult to work with, requiring rooms full of special equipment, replete with dozens of 'postdocs' and graduate students willing to devote the larger part of their professional careers to the perfection of electrophoretic gel techniques. Besides, although the creation of life *in vitro* would certainly be a scientific feat worthy of note—and probably even a Nobel prize—it would not, in the long run, tell us much more about the space of *possible* life than we already know.

Computers provide an alternative medium within which to attempt to synthesize life. Modern computer technology has resulted in machinery with tremendous potential for the creation of life *in silico*.

Computers should be thought of as an important laboratory tool for the study of life, substituting for the array of incubators, culture dishes, microscopes, electrophoretic gels, pipettes, centrifuges, and other assorted wet-lab paraphernalia, one simple-to-master piece of experimental equipment devoted exclusively to the incubation of information structures.

The advantage of working with information structures is that information has no intrinsic size. The computer is *the* tool for the manipulation of information, whether that manipulation is a consequence of our actions or a consequence of the actions of the information structures themselves. Computers themselves will not be alive, rather they will support informational universes within which dynamic populations of informational 'molecules' engage in informational 'bio-chemistry'.

This view of computers as workstations for performing scientific experiments within artificial universes is fairly new, but it is rapidly becoming accepted as a legitimate, even necessary, way of pursuing science. In the days before computers, scientists worked primarily with systems whose defining equations could be solved analytically, and ignored those whose defining equations could *not* be so solved. This was largely the case because, in the absence of analytic solutions, the equations would have to be integrated over and over again, essentially simulating the time behaviour of the system. Without computers to handle the mundane details of these calculations, such an undertaking was unthinkable except in the simplest cases.

However, with the advent of computers, the necessary mundane calculations can be relegated to these idiot-savants, and the realm of numerical simulation is opened up for exploration. 'Exploration' is an appropriate term for the process, because the numerical simulation of systems allows one to 'explore' the system's behaviour under a wide range of parameter settings and initial conditions. The heuristic value of this kind of experimentation cannot be over-estimated. One often gains tremendous insight for the essential dynamics of a system by observing its behaviour under a wide range of initial conditions. Most importantly, however, computers are beginning to provide scientists with a new paradigm for modelling the world. When dealing with essentially unsolvable governing equations, the primary reason for producing a formal mathematical model—the hope of reaching an analytic solution by symbolic manipulation—is lost. Systems of ordinary and partial differential equations are not very well suited for implementation as computer algorithms. One might expect that other modelling technologies would be more appropriate when the goal is the *synthesis*, rather than the *analysis*, of behaviour.[6]

This expectation is easily borne out. With the precipitous drop in the cost of raw computing power, computers are now available that are capable of simulating physical systems from first principles. This means that it has become possible, for example, to model turbulent flow in a fluid by simulating the motions of its constituent particles—not just approximating *changes* in concentrations of particles at particular points, but actually computing their motions exactly (Frisch *et al.* 1986; Wolfram 1986; Toffoli and Margolus 1987).

What does all this have to do with the study of life? The most surprising lesson we have learned from simulating complex physical systems on computers is that *complex behaviour need not have complex roots*. Indeed, tremendously interesting and beguilingly complex behaviour can emerge from collections of

---

[6] See Toffoli (1984) for a good exposition.

LEVEL OF BEHAVIOURS
Specify PTYPES?

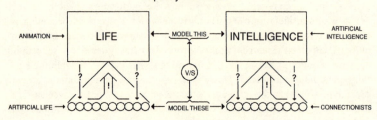

LEVEL OF BEHAVOURS
Specify GTYPES!

FIG. 1.4. The bottom-up versus the top-down approach to modelling complex systems. From Langton (1989*a*)

extremely simple components. This leads directly to the exciting possibility that much of the complex behaviour exhibited by nature—especially the complex behaviour that we call life—*also* has simple generators. Since it is very hard to work backwards from a complex behaviour to its generator, but very simple to create generators and synthesize complex behaviour, a promising approach to the study of complex natural systems is to undertake the general study of the kinds of behaviour that can emerge from distributed systems consisting of simple components (Fig. 1.4).

4. NON-LINEARITY AND LOCAL DETERMINATION OF BEHAVIOUR

4.1. Linear vs. Non-linear Systems

As mentioned briefly above, the distinction between linear and non-linear systems is fundamental, and provides excellent insight into why the principles underlying the dynamics of life should be so hard to find. The simplest way to state the distinction is to say that *linear systems* are those for which the behaviour of the whole is just the sum of the behaviour of its parts, while for *non-linear systems*, the behaviour of the whole is *more* than the sum of its parts.

Linear systems are those which obey the *principle of superposition*. We can break up complicated linear systems into simpler constituent parts, and analyse these parts *independently*. Once we have reached an understanding of the parts in isolation, we can achieve a full understanding of the whole system by *composing* our understandings of the isolated parts. This is the key feature of linear systems: by studying the parts in isolation, we can learn everything we need to know about the complete system.

This is not possible for non-linear systems, which do *not* obey the principle of superposition. Even if we could break such systems up into simpler constituent parts, and even if we could reach a complete understanding of the parts in isolation, we would not be able to compose our understandings of the individual parts into an understanding of the whole system. The key feature of non-linear systems is that their primary behaviours of interest are properties of the *interactions between parts*, rather than being properties of the parts themselves, and these interaction-based properties necessarily disappear when the parts are studied independently.

Thus analysis is most fruitfully applied to linear systems. Analysis has *not* proved anywhere near as effective when applied to non-linear systems: the non-linear system must be treated as a whole.

A different approach to the study of non-linear systems involves the inverse of analysis: *synthesis*. Rather than start with the behaviour of interest and attempting to analyse it into its constituent parts, we start with constituent parts and put them together in the attempt to *synthesize* the behaviour of interest.

Life is a property of *form*, not *matter*, a result of the organization of matter rather than something that inheres in the matter itself. Neither nucleotides nor amino acids nor any other carbon-chain molecule is alive—yet put them together in the right way, and the dynamic behaviour that emerges out of their interactions is what we call life. It is effects, not things, upon which life is based—life is a kind of behaviour, not a kind of stuff—and as such, it is constituted of simpler behaviours, not simpler stuff. *Behaviours themselves* can constitute the fundamental parts of non-linear systems—*virtual parts*, which depend on non-linear interactions between physical parts for their very existence. Isolate the physical parts and the virtual parts cease to exist. It is the *virtual parts* of living systems that Artificial Life is after, and synthesis is its primary methodological tool.

4.2. The Parsimony of Local Determination of Behaviour

It is easier to generate complex behaviour from the application of simple, *local* rules than it is to generate complex behaviour from the application of complex, *global* rules. This is because complex global behaviour is usually due to non-linear interactions occurring at the local level. With bottom-up specifications, the system computes the local, non-linear interactions explicitly and the global behaviour, which was implicit in the local rules, emerges spontaneously without being treated explicitly.

With top-down specifications, however, local behaviour must be implicit in global rules! This is really putting the cart before the horse! The global rules must 'predict' the effects on global structure of many local, non-linear interactions—something which we have seen is intractable, even impossible, in the general case. Thus top-down systems must take computational short cuts and explicitly deal with special cases, which results in inflexible, brittle, and unnatural behaviour.

Furthermore, in a system of any complexity, the number of possible global states is astronomically enormous, and grows exponentially with the size of the system. Systems that attempt to supply *global* rules for *global* behaviour simply *cannot* provide a different rule for every global state. Thus the global states must be classified in some manner, and categorized using a coarse-grained scheme according to which the global states within a category are indistinguishable. The rules of the system can only be applied at the level of resolution of these categories. There are many possible ways to implement a classification scheme, most of which will yield different partitionings of the global-state space. Any rule-based system must necessarily *assume* that finer-grained differences do not matter, or must include a finite set of tests for 'special cases', and then must assume that no *other* special cases are relevant.

For most complex systems, however, fine differences in the global state can result in enormous differences in global behaviour, and there may be no way in principle to partition the space of global states in such a way that specific fine differences have the appropriate global impact.

On the other hand, systems that supply *local* rules for *local* behaviours *can* provide a different rule for each and every possible local state. Furthermore, the size of the local-state space can be completely independent of the size of the system. In local rule-governed systems, each local state, and consequently the global state, can be determined exactly and precisely. Fine differences in the global state will result in very specific differences in the local state and, consequently, will affect the invocation of local rules. As fine differences affect local behaviour, the difference will be felt in an expanding patch of local states, and in this manner—propagating from local neighbourhood to local neighbourhood—fine differences in global state can result in large differences in global behaviour. The only 'special cases' explicitly dealt with in locally determined systems are exactly the set of all possible local states, and the rules for these are just exactly the set of all local rules governing the system.

5. BIOLOGICAL AUTOMATA

Organisms have been compared to extremely complicated and finely tuned biochemical machines. Since we know that it is possible to abstract the logical form of a machine from its physical hardware, it is natural to ask whether it is possible to abstract the logical form of an organism from its biochemical wetware. The field of Artificial Life is devoted to the investigation of this question.

In the following sections we shall look at the manner in which behaviour is generated in a bottom-up fashion in living systems. We then generalize the mechanisms by which this behaviour generation is accomplished, so that we may apply them to the task of generating behaviour in artificial systems.

We shall find that the essential machinery of living organisms is quite a bit different from the machinery of our own invention, and we would be quite mistaken to attempt to force our preconceived notions of abstract machines on to the machinery of life. The difference, once again, lies in the exceedingly parallel and distributed nature of the operation of the machinery of life, as contrasted with the singularly serial and centralized control structures associated with the machines of our invention.

5.1. Genotypes and Phenotypes

The most salient characteristic of living systems, from the behaviour generation point of view, is the *genotype/phenotype* distinction. The distinction is essentially one between a specification of machinery—the genotype—and the behaviour of that machinery—the phenotype.

The *genotype* is the complete set of genetic instructions encoded in the linear sequence of nucleotide bases that makes up an organism's DNA. The *phenotype* is the physical organism itself—the structures that emerge in space and time as the result of the interpretation of the genotype in the context of a particular environment. The process by which the phenotype develops through time under the direction of the genotype is called *morphogenesis*. The individual genetic instructions are called *genes* and consist of short stretches of DNA. These instructions are 'executed'—or *expressed*—when their DNA sequence is used as a template for transcription. In the case of protein synthesis, transcription results in a duplicate nucleotide strand known as a *messenger RNA*—or *mRNA*—constructed by the process of base-pairing. This mRNA strand may then be modified in various ways before it makes its way out to the cytoplasm where, at bodies known as *ribosomes*, it serves as a template for the construction of a linear chain of *amino acids*. The resulting *polypeptide* chain will fold up on itself in a complex manner, forming a tightly packed molecule known as a *protein*. The finished protein detaches from the ribosome and may go on to serve as a passive structural element in the cell, or may have a more active role as an *enzyme*. Enzymes are *the* functional molecular 'operators' in the logic of life.

One may consider the genotype as a largely unordered 'bag' of instructions, each one of which is essentially the specification for a 'machine' of some sort—

passive or active. When instantiated, each such 'machine' will enter into the ongoing logical 'fray' in the cytoplasm, consisting largely of local interactions between other such machines. Each such instruction will be 'executed' when its own triggering conditions are met and will have specific, local effects on structures in the cell. Furthermore, each such instruction will operate within the context of all the other instructions that have been—or are being—executed.

The phenotype, then, consists of the structures and dynamics that emerge through time in the course of the execution of the parallel, distributed 'computation' controlled by this genetic 'bag' of instructions. Since genes' interactions with one another are highly non-linear, the phenotype is a non-linear function of the genotype.

5.2. Generalized Genotypes and Phenotypes

In the context of Artificial Life, we need to generalize the notions of *genotype* and *phenotype*, so that we may apply them in non-biological situations. We shall use the term *generalized genotype*—or GTYPE—to refer to any largely unordered set of low-level rules, and we shall use the term *generalized phenotype*—or PTYPE—to refer to the behaviours and/or structures that emerge out of the interactions among these low-level rules when they are activated within the context of a specific environment. The GTYPE, essentially, is the specification for a set of machines, while the PTYPE is the behaviour that results as the machines are run and interact with one another.

This is the bottom-up approach to the generation of behaviour. A set of entities is defined, and each entity is endowed with a specification for a simple behavioural repertoire—a GTYPE—that contains instructions which detail its reactions to a wide range of *local* encounters with other such entities or with specific features of the environment. Nowhere is the behaviour of the set of entities as a whole specified. The global behaviour of the aggregate—the PTYPE —emerges out of the collective interactions among individual entities.

It should be noted that the PTYPE is a multi-level phenomenon. First, there is the PTYPE associated with each particular instruction—the effect which that instruction has on an entity's behaviour when it is expressed. Second, there is the PTYPE associated with each individual entity—its individual behaviour within the aggregate. Third, there is the PTYPE associated with the behaviour of the aggregate as a whole.

This is true for natural systems as well. We can talk about the phenotypic trait associated with a particular gene, we can identify the phenotype of an individual cell, and we can identify the phenotype of an entire multi-cellular organism—its body, in effect. PTYPES *should* be complex and multi-level. If we want

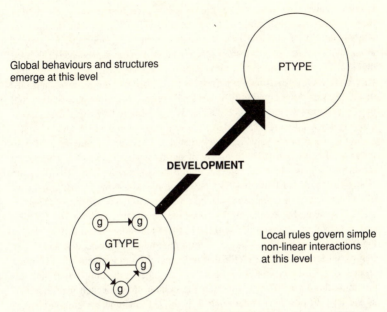

Global behaviours and structures
emerge at this level

PTYPE

DEVELOPMENT

GTYPE

Local rules govern simple
non-linear interactions
at this level

FIG. 1.5. The relationship between GTYPE and PTYPE. From Langton (1989a)

to simulate life, we should expect to see hierarchical structures emerge in our
simulations. In general, phenotypic traits at the level of the whole organism will
be the result of many non-linear interactions between genes, and there will be
no single gene to which one can assign responsibility for the vast majority of
phenotypic traits.

In summary, GTYPES are low-level rules for behavors—i.e. abstract specifications for 'machines'—which will engage in local interactions within a large
aggregate of other such behavors. PTYPES are the behaviours—the structures
in time and space—that *develop* out of these non-linear, local interactions
(Fig. 1.5).

5.3. Unpredictability of PTYPE from GTYPE

Non-linear interactions between the objects specified by the GTYPE provide
the basis for an extremely rich variety of possible PTYPES. PTYPES draw on
the full combinatorial potential implicit in the set of possible interactions between

low-level rules. The other side of the coin, however, is that we cannot predict the PTYPES that will emerge from specific GTYPES, due to the general unpredictability of non-linear systems. If we wish to maintain the property of predictability, then we must restrict severely the non-linear dependence of PTYPE on GTYPE, but this forces us to give up the combinatorial richness of possible PTYPES. Therefore, a trade-off exists between behavioural richness and predictability (or 'programmability'). We shall see in the section on evolution that the lack of programmability is adequately compensated for by the increased capacity for adaptiveness provided by a rich behavioural repertoire.

As discussed previously, we know that it is impossible in the general case to determine *any* non-trivial property of the future behaviour of a sufficiently powerful computer from a mere inspection of its program and its initial state alone (Hopcroft and Ullman 1979). A Turing machine—the formal equivalent of a general-purpose computer—can be captured within the scheme of GTYPE/ PTYPE systems by identifying the machine's transition table as the GTYPE and the resulting computation as the PTYPE. From this we can deduce that in the general case it will not be possible to determine, by inspection alone, any non-trivial feature of the PTYPE that will emerge from a given GTYPE in the context of a particular initial configuration. In general, the only way to find out anything about the PTYPE is to start the system up and watch what happens as the PTYPE develops under control of the GTYPE and the environment.

Similarly, it is not possible in the general case to determine what specific alterations must be made to a GTYPE to effect a desired change in the PTYPE. The problem is that any specific PTYPE trait is, in general, an effect of many, many non-linear interactions between the behavioural primitives of the system (an 'epistatic trait' in biological terms). Consequently, given an arbitrary proposed change to the PTYPE, it may be impossible to determine by any formal procedure exactly what changes would have to be made to the GTYPE to effect that—and *only* that—change in the PTYPE. It is not a practically computable problem. There is no way to calculate the answer—short of exhaustive search— *even though there may be an answer!*[7]

The only way to proceed in the face of such an unpredictability result is by a process of trial and error. However, some processes of trial and error are more efficient than others. In natural systems, trial and error are interlinked in such a way that error guides the choice of trials under the process of evolution by natural selection. It is quite likely that this is the *only* efficient, *general* procedure that could find GTYPES with specific PTYPE traits when non-linear functions are involved.

---

[7] An example in biology would be: What changes would have to be made to the genome in order to produce six fingers on each hand rather than five?

6. RECURSIVELY GENERATED OBJECTS

In the previous section, we described the distinction between genotype and phenotype, and we introduced their generalizations in the form of GTYPES and PTYPES. In this section, we shall review a general approach to building GTYPE/PTYPE systems based on the methodology of *recursively generated objects*.

A major appeal of this approach is that it arises naturally from the GTYPE/PTYPE distinction: the local developmental rules—the recursive description itself—constitute the *GTYPE*, and the developing structure—the recursively generated object or behaviour itself—constitutes the *PTYPE*.

Under the methodology of recursively generated objects, the 'object' is a structure that has sub-parts. The rules of the system specify how to modify the most elementary, 'atomic' sub-parts, and are usually sensitive to the *context* in which these atomic sub-parts are embedded. That is, the state of the 'neighbourhood' of an atomic sub-part is taken into account in determining which rule to apply in order to modify that sub-part. It is usually the case that there are no rules in the system whose context is the entire structure; that is, there is no use made of *global* information. Each piece is modified solely on the basis of its own state and the state of the pieces 'nearby'.

Of course, if the initial structure consists of a single part—as might be the case with the initial seed—then the context for applying a rule is necessarily global. The usual situation is that a structure consists of *many* parts, only a local subset of which determine the rule that will be used to modify any one sub-part of the structure.

A recursively generated object, then, is a kind of PTYPE, and the recursive description that generates it is a kind of GTYPE. The PTYPE will emerge under the action of the GTYPE, developing through time via a process akin to morphogenesis.

We shall illustrate the notion of recursively generated objects with examples taken from the literature on L-systems, cellular automata, and computer animation.

6.1. Example 1: Lindenmayer Systems

Lindenmayer systems (L-systems) consist of sets of rules for rewriting strings of symbols, and bear strong relationships to the formal grammars treated by Chomsky. We shall give several examples of L-systems illustrating the methodology of recursively generated objects.[8]

In the following '$X \rightarrow Y$' means that one replaces every occurrence of

---

[8] For a more detailed review, see Prusinkiewicz (1991).

symbol *X* in the structure with string *Y*. Since the symbol *X* may appear on the right as well as the left sides of some rules, the set of rules can be applied 'recursively' to the newly rewritten structures. The process can be continued *ad infinitum* although some sets of rules will result in a 'final' configuration when no more changes occur.

Simple Linear Growth.   Here is an example of the simplest kind of L-system. The rules are *context free*, meaning that the context in which a particular part is situated is *not* considered when altering it. There must be only one rule per part if the system is to be deterministic.

The rules (the 'recursive description' or GTYPE):

1) A → CB
2) B → A
3) C → DA
4) D → C

When applied to the initial seed structure 'A', the following structural history develops (each successive line is a successive time-step):

time	structure	rules applied (L to R)
0	A	(initial 'seed')
1	C B	(rule 1 replaces A with CB)
2	D A A	(rule 3 replaces C with DA and rule 2 replaces B with A)
3	C C B C B	(rule 4 replaces D with C and rule 1 replaces the two As with CBs)
4	... (etc.) ...	

And so forth.

The 'PTYPE' that emerges from this kind of recursive application of a simple, local rewriting rule can get extremely complex. These kinds of grammars (whose rules replace single symbols) have been shown to be equivalent to the operation of finite-state machines. With appropriate restrictions, they are also equivalent to the 'regular languages' defined by Chomsky.

Branching Growth.   L-systems incorporate meta-symbols to represent branching points, allowing a new line of symbols to branch off from the main 'stem' (see Fig. 1.6).

The following grammar produces branching structures. The '( )' and '[ ]' notations indicate left and right branches, respectively, and the strings within them indicate the structure of the branches themselves.

n=5, δ=18°

ω : plant
p_1 : plant → internode + [plant + flower] – – / /
           [– – leaf] internode [+ + leaf] –
           [plant flower] + + plant flower
p_2 : internode → F seg [/ / & & leaf] [/ / ∧ ∧ leaf] F seg
p_3 : seg → seg F seg
p_4 : leaf → [' { +f–ff–f+ | +f–ff–f }]
p_5 : flower → [& & & pedicel ' / wedge / / / / wedge / / / /
                wedge / / / / wedge / / / / wedge]
p_6 : pedicel → FF
p_7 : wedge → [' ∧ F] [{ & & & & –f+f | –f+f }]

FIG. 1.6. An L-system plant grown from rules incorporating graphical rendering information. From Prusinkiewicz (1991)

The rules—or GTYPE:

1) A → C[B]D
2) B → A
3) C → C
4) D → C(E)A
5) E → D

When applied to the starting structure 'A', the following sequence develops (using linear notation):

time	structure	rules applied (L to R)
0	A	initial 'seed'
1	C[B]D	rule 1
2	C[A]C(E)A	rules 3, 2, 4
3	C[C[B]D]C(D)C[B]D	rules 3, 1, 3, 5, 1
4	C[C[A]C(E)A]C(C(E)A)C[A]C(E)A	rules 3, 3, 2, 4, 3, 4, 3, 2, 4

In two dimensions, the structure develops as follows:

t = 0   1   2   3   ...and so on...

Note that at each step, *every symbol is replaced*, even if just by another copy of itself. This figure shows the result of growing a structure using the rules shown, which contain graphical rendering information in addition to the usual 'structural' information.

Signal Propagation. In order to propagate signals along a structure, one must have something more than just a single symbol on the left-hand side of a rule. When there is more than one symbol on the left-hand side of a rule, the rules are *context sensitive*—i.e. the 'context' within which a symbol occurs (the symbols next to it) are important in determining what the replacement string will be. The next example illustrates why this is critical for signal propagation.

In the following example, the symbol in '{ }' is the symbol (or string of symbols) to be replaced, the rest of the left-hand side is the context, and the symbols '[' and ']' indicate the left and right ends of the string, respectively.

Suppose the rule set contains the following rules:

1) [{C} → C   a 'C' at the left-end of the string remains a 'C'
2) C{C} → C   a 'C' with a 'C' to its left remains a 'C'
3) *{C} → *   a 'C' with an '*' to its left becomes an '*'
4) {*}C → C   an '*' with a 'C' to its right becomes a 'C'
5) {*}] → *   an '*' at the right end of the string remains an '*'

Under these rules, the initial structure '*CCCCCCC' will result in the '*' being propagated to the right, as follows:

time	structure
0	*CCCCCCC
1	C*CCCCCC
2	CC*CCCCC
3	CCC*CCCC
4	CCCC*CCC
5	CCCCC*CC
6	CCCCCC*C
7	CCCCCCC*

This would not be possible without taking the 'context' of a symbol into account. In general, these kinds of grammars are equivalent to Chomsky's 'context-sensitive' or 'Turing' languages, depending on whether or not there are any restrictions on the kinds of strings on the left- and right-hand sides.

The capacity for signal propagation is extremely important, for it allows arbitrary computational processes to be embedded within the structure, which may directly affect the structure's development. The next example demonstrates how embedded computation can affect development.

6.2. Example 2: Cellular Automata

Cellular automata (CA) provide another example of the recursive application of a simple set of rules to a structure. In CA, the structure that is being updated is the entire universe: a lattice of finite automata. The local rule set—the GTYPE—in this case is the transition function obeyed homogeneously by every automaton in the lattice. The local context taken into account in updating the state of each automaton is the state of the automata in its immediate neighbour-hood. The transition function for the automata constitutes a *local* physics for a simple, discrete space/time universe. The universe is updated by applying the local physics to each local 'cell' of its structure over and over again. Thus, although the physical structure itself does not develop over time, its *state* does.

Within such universes, one can embed all manner of processes, relying on the context sensitivity of the rules to local neighbourhood conditions to propa-gate information around within the universe 'meaningfully'. In particular, one can embed general-purpose computers. Since these computers are simply par-ticular configurations of states within the lattice of automata, *they can compute over the very set of symbols out of which they are constructed*. Thus, structures in this universe can compute and construct other structures, which also may compute and construct.

For example, here is the simplest known structure that can reproduce itself:

```
2 2 2 2 2 2 2 2
2 1 7 0 1 4 0 1 4 2
2 0 2 2 2 2 2 2 0 2
2 7 2         2 1 2
2 1 2         2 1 2
2 0 2         2 1 2
2 7 2         2 1 2
2 1 2 2 2 2 2 2 1 2 2 2 2 2
2 0 7 1 0 7 1 0 7 1 1 1 1 1 2
2 2 2 2 2 2 2 2 2 2 2 2 2 2
```

Each number is the state of one automaton in the lattice. Blank space is presumed to be in state '0'. The '2'-states form a sheath around the '1'-state data path. The '7 0' and '4 0' state pairs constitute signals embedded within the data path. They will propagate counter-clockwise around the loop, cloning off copies which propagate down the extended tail as they pass the T-junction between loop and tail. When the signals reach the end of the tail, they have the following effects: each '7 0' signal extends the tail by one unit, and the two '4 0' signals construct a left-hand corner at the end of the tail. Thus for each full cycle of the instructions around the loop, another side and corner of an 'offspring-loop' will be constructed. When the tail finally runs into itself after four cycles, the collision of signals results in the disconnection of the two loops as well as the construction of a tail on each of the loops.

After 151 time-steps, this system will evolve to the following configuration:

```
                2                        ,
              2 1 2
              2 7 2
              2 0 2
              2 1 2
    2 2 2 2 2 2 2 7 2    2 2 2 2 2 2 2 2
    2 1 1 1 7 0 1 7 0 2  2 1 7 0 1 4 0 1 4 2
    2 1 2 2 2 2 2 2 1 2  2 0 2 2 2 2 2 2 0 2
    2 1 2        2 7 2 2 7 2        2 1 2
    2 1 2        2 0 2 2 1 2        2 1 2
    2 4 2        2 1 2 2 0 2        2 1 2
    2 1 2        2 7 2 2 7 2        2 1 2
    2 0 2 2 2 2 2 2 0 2  2 1 2 2 2 2 2 2 1 2 2 2 2 2
    2 4 1 0 7 1 0 7 1 2  2 0 7 1 0 7 1 0 7 1 1 1 1 1 2
      2 2 2 2 2 2 2 2      2 2 2 2 2 2 2 2 2 2 2 2 2
```

Thus, the initial configuration has succeeded in reproducing itself.

Each of these loops will go on to reproduce itself in a similar manner, giving rise to an expanding *colony* of loops, growing out into the array.

These embedded self-reproducing loops are the result of the recursive application of a rule to a seed structure. In this case, the primary rule that is being recursively applied constitutes the 'physics' of the universe. The initial state of the loop itself constitutes a little 'computer' under the recursively applied physics of the universe: a computer whose program causes it to construct a copy of itself. The 'program' within the loop computer is also applied recursively to the growing structure. Thus, this system really involves a double level of recursively applied rules. The mechanics of applying one recursive rule within a universe whose physics is governed by another recursive rule had to be worked out by trial and error. This system makes use of the signal propagation capacity to embed a structure that itself *computes* the resulting structure, rather than having the 'physics' directly responsible for developing the final structure from a passive seed.

This captures the flavour of what goes on in natural biological development: the genotype codes for the constituents of a dynamic process in the cell, and it is this dynamic process that is primarily responsible for mediating—or 'computing'—the expression of the genotype in the course of development.

6.3. Example 3: Flocking 'Boids'

The previous examples were largely concerned with the growth and development of *structural* PTYPES. Here, we give an example of the development of a *behavioural* PTYPE.

Craig Reynolds (1987) has implemented a simulation of flocking behaviour. In this model—which is meant to be a general platform for studying the qualitatively similar phenomena of flocking, herding, and schooling—one has a large collection of autonomous but interacting objects (which Reynolds refers to as 'Boids'), inhabiting a common simulated environment.

The modeller can specify the manner in which the individual Boids will respond to *local* events or conditions. The global behaviour of the aggregate of Boids is strictly an emergent phenomenon, none of the rules for the individual Boids depends on global information, and the only updating of the global state is done on the basis of individual Boids responding to local conditions.

Each Boid in the aggregate shares the same behavioural 'tendencies':

- to maintain a minimum distance from other objects in the environment, including other Boids,
- to match velocities with Boids in its neighbourhood, and
- to move towards the perceived centre of mass of the Boids in its neighbourhood.

These are the only rules governing the behaviour of the aggregate.

These rules, then, constitute the generalized genotype (GTYPE) of the Boids system. They say nothing about structure, or growth and development, but they determine the behaviour of a set of interacting objects, out of which very natural motion emerges.

With the right settings for the parameters of the system, a collection of Boids released at random positions within a volume will collect into a dynamic flock, which flies around environmental obstacles in a very fluid and natural manner, occasionally breaking up into sub-flocks as the flock flows around both sides of an obstacle. Once broken up into sub-flocks, the sub-flocks reorganize around their own, now distinct and isolated centres of mass, only to re-merge into a single flock again when both sub-flocks emerge at the far side of the obstacle and each sub-flock feels anew the 'mass' of the other sub-flock (Fig. 1.7).

The flocking behaviour itself constitutes the generalized phenotype (PTYPE) of the Boids system. It bears the same relation to the GTYPE as an organism's morphological phenotype bears to its molecular genotype. The same distinction between the *specification* of machinery and the *behaviour* of machinery is evident.

6.4. Discussion of Examples

In all the above examples, the recursive rules apply to *local structures* only, and the PTYPE—structural or behavioural—that results at the global level emerges out of all local activity taken collectively. Nowhere in the system are there rules

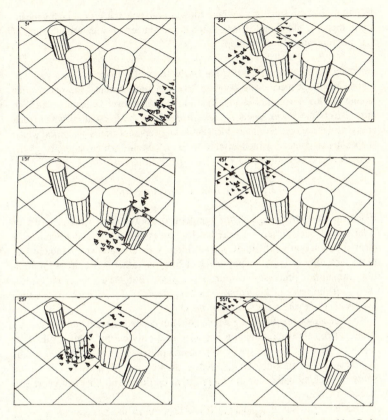

FIG. 1.7. A flock of 'Boids' negotiating a field of columns. Sequence generated by Craig Reynolds. From Langton (1989a)

for the behaviour of the system at the global level. This is a much more powerful and simple approach to the generation of complex behaviour than that typically taken in AI, for instance, where 'expert systems' attempt to provide global rules for global behaviour. Recursive, 'bottom up' specifications yield much more natural, fluid, and flexible behaviour at the global level than typical 'top down' specifications, and they do so *much* more parsimoniously.

Importance of Context Sensitivity.   It is worth while to note that *context-sensitive* rules in GTYPE/PTYPE systems provide the possibility for non-linear interactions among the parts. Without context sensitivity, the systems would be linearly decomposable, information could not 'flow' throughout the system in any meaningful manner, and complex long-range dependencies between remote parts of the structures could not develop.

Feedback between the Local and the Global Levels. There is also a very important feedback mechanism *between* levels in such systems: the interactions among the low-level entities give rise to the global-level dynamics which, in turn, affects the lower levels by *setting the local context* within which each entity's rules are invoked. Thus, local behaviour supports global dynamics, which shapes local context, which affects local behaviour, which supports global dynamics, and so forth.

6.5. Genuine Life in Artificial Systems

It is important to distinguish the ontological status of the various levels of behaviour in such systems. At the level of the individual behav*ors*, we have a clear difference in kind: Boids are *not* birds, they are not even remotely like birds, they have no cohesive physical structure, but rather they exist as information structures—processes—within a computer. But—and this is *the* critical 'But'—at the level of behav*iours*, *flocking Boids and flocking birds are two instances of the same phenomenon: flocking.*

The behaviour of a flock as a whole does not depend critically on the internal details of the entities of which it is constituted, only on the details of the way in which these entities behave in each other's presence. Thus, flocking in Boids is true flocking, and may be counted as another empirical data point in the study of flocking behaviour in general, right up there with flocks of geese and flocks of starlings.

This is *not* to say that flocking Boids capture *all* the nuances upon which flocking behaviour depends, or that the Boids' behavioural repertoire is sufficient to exhibit all the different modes of flocking that have been observed—such as the classic 'V' formation of flocking geese. The crucial point is that we have captured, within an aggregate of artificial entities, a *bona fide* lifelike behaviour, and that the behaviour emerges within the artificial system in the same way that it emerges in the natural system.

The same is true for L-systems and the self-reproducing loops. The constituent parts of the artificial systems are different kinds of things from their natural counterparts, but the emergent behaviours that they support are the same kinds of thing as their natural counterparts: genuine morphogenesis and differentiation for L-systems, and genuine self-reproduction in the case of the loops.

The claim is the following. The 'artificial' in Artificial Life refers to the component parts, not the emergent processes. If the component parts are implemented correctly, the processes they support are *genuine*—every bit as genuine as the natural processes they imitate.

The *big* claim is that a properly organized set of artificial primitives carrying out the same functional roles as the biomolecules in natural living systems will support a process that will be 'alive' in the same way that natural organisms are alive. Artificial Life will therefore be *genuine* life—it will simply be made of different stuff than the life that has evolved here on Earth.

7. EVOLUTION

7.1. Evolution: From Artificial Selection to Natural Selection

Modern organisms owe their structure to the complex process of biological evolution, and it is very difficult to discern which of their properties are due to chance and which to necessity. If biologists could 'rewind the tape' of evolution and start it over, again and again, from different initial conditions, or under different regimes of external perturbations along the way, they would have a full *ensemble* of evolutionary pathways to generalize over. Such an ensemble would allow them to distinguish universal, necessary properties (those which were observed in all the pathways in the ensemble) from accidental, chance properties (those which were unique to individual pathways). However, biologists cannot rewind the tape of evolution, and are stuck with a single, actual evolutionary trace out of a vast, intuited ensemble of possible traces.

Although studying computer models of evolution is not the same as studying the 'real thing', the ability to freely manipulate computer experiments—to 'rewind the tape', perturb the initial conditions, and so forth—can more than make up for their 'lack' of reality.

It has been known for some time that one can evolve computer programs by the process of natural selection among a population of variant programs. Each individual program in a population of programs is evaluated for its performance on some task. The programs that perform best are allowed to 'breed' with one another via *Genetic Algorithms* (Holland 1975; Goldberg 1989). The offspring of these better-performing parent programs replace the worst-performing programs in the population, and the cycle is iterated. Such evolutionary approaches to program improvement have been applied primarily to the tasks of function optimization and machine learning.

However, such evolutionary models have rarely been used to study evolution itself (Wilson 1989). Researchers have primarily concentrated on the *results*, rather than on the *process*, of evolution. In the spirit of von Neumann's research on self-reproduction via the study of self-reproducing *automata*, the following sections review studies of the process of evolution by studying evolving populations of 'automata'.

7.2. Engineering PTYPES from GTYPES

In the preceding sections, we have mentioned several times the formal impossibility of predicting the behaviour of an arbitrary machine by mere inspection of its specification and initial state. In the general case, we must run a machine in order to determine its behaviour.

The consequence of this unpredictability for GTYPE/PTYPE systems is that we cannot determine the PTYPE that will be produced by an arbitrary GTYPE by inspection alone. We must 'run' the GTYPE in the context of a specific environment, and let the PTYPE develop in order to determine the resulting structure and its behaviour.

This is even further complicated when the environment consists of a population of PTYPES engaged in non-linear interactions, in which case the determination of a PTYPE depends on the behaviour of the specific PTYPES it is interacting with, and on the emergent details of the global dynamics.

Since, for any interesting system, there will exist an enormous number of potential GTYPES, and since there is no formal method for deducing the PTYPES from the GTYPES, how do we go about finding GTYPES that will generate lifelike PTYPES? Or PTYPES that exhibit any other particular sought-after behaviour?

Until now, the process has largely been one of guessing at appropriate GTYPES, and modifying them by trial and error until they generate the appropriate PTYPES. However, this process is limited by our preconceptions of what the appropriate PTYPES would be, and by our restricted notions of how to generate GTYPES. We should like to be able to automate the process so that our preconceptions and limited abilities to conceive of machinery do not overly constrain the search for GTYPES that will yield the appropriate behaviours.

7.3. Natural Selection among Populations of Variants

Nature, of course, has had to face the same problem, and has hit upon an elegant solution: *evolution by the process of natural selection among populations of variants*. The scheme is a very simple one. However, in the face of the formal impossibility of predicting behaviour from machine description alone, it may well be the only efficient, general scheme for searching the space of possible GTYPES.

The mechanism of evolution is as follows. A set of GTYPES is interpreted within a specific environment, forming a population of PTYPES which interact with one another and with features of the environment in various complex ways. On the basis of the relative performance of their associated PTYPES, *some* GTYPES are duplicated in larger numbers than others, and they are duplicated in such a way that the copies are similar to—but not exactly the same as—the originals. These variant GTYPES develop into variant PTYPES, which enter into the complex interactions within the environment, and the process is continued *ad infinitum* (Fig. 1.8). As expected from the formal limitations on predictability, GTYPES must be 'run' (i.e. turned into PTYPES) in an environment and their behaviours must be evaluated explicitly, their implicit behaviour cannot be determined.

7.4. Genetic Algorithms

In the spirit of von Neumann, John Holland (1975, 1986) has attempted to abstract 'the logical form' of the natural process of biological evolution in what he calls the 'Genetic Algorithm' (GA). In the GA, a GTYPE is represented as a character string that encodes a potential solution to a problem. For instance, the character string might encode the weight matrix of a neural network, or the transition table of a finite-state machine. These character strings are rendered as PTYPES via a problem-specific interpreter, which constructs, for example, the neural net or finite-state machine specified by each GTYPE, evaluates its performance in the problem domain, and provides it with a specific fitness value, or 'strength'.

The GA implements natural selection by making more copies of the character strings representing the better performing PTYPES. The GA generates variant GTYPES by applying *genetic operators* to these character strings. The genetic operators typically consist of *reproduction, cross-over*, and *mutation*, with occasional usage of *inversion* and *duplication*.

Recently, John Koza (1991) has developed a version of the GA, which he calls the *Genetic Programming Paradigm* (GPP), that extends the genetic operators to work on GTYPES that are simple expressions in a standard programming language. The GPP differs from the traditional GA in that these program expressions are not represented as simple character strings but rather as the parse trees of the expressions. This makes it easier for the genetic operators to obey the syntax of the programming language when producing variant GTYPES.

Fig. 1.9 shows some examples of GTYPES in the GA and GPP paradigms.

The Genetic Operators. The genetic operators work as follows.

Reproduction is the most basic operator. It is often implemented in the form of *fitness proportionate reproduction*, which means that strings are duplicated in direct proportion to their relative fitness values. Once all strings have been

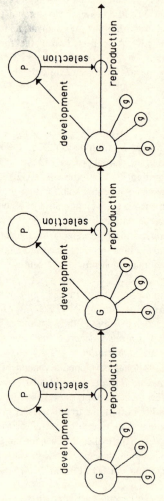

FIG. 1.8. The process of evolution by natural selection. From Langton (1989a)

(a) 110010101110101101010001010110111011

(b) (OR (NOT a) (AND b c))

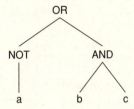

Fig. 1.9. GTYPES in the GA and GPP paradigms. From Langton (1989a)

evaluated, the average fitness of the population is computed, and those strings whose fitness is higher than the population average have a higher probability of being duplicated, while those strings whose fitness is lower than the population average have a lower probability of being duplicated. There are many variations on this scheme, but most implementations of the GA or the GPP use some form of fitness proportionate reproduction as the means to implement 'selection'. Another form of this is to simply keep the top 10 per cent or so of the population and throw away the rest, using the survivors as breeding stock for the next generation.

Mutation in the GA is simply the replacement of one or more characters in a character string GTYPE with another character picked at random. In binary strings, this simply amounts to random bit flips. In the GPP, mutation is implemented by picking a sub-tree of the parse tree at random, and replacing it with a randomly generated sub-tree whose root node is of the same syntactic type as the root node of the replaced sub-tree.

Cross-over is an analogue of sexual recombination. In the GA, this is accomplished by picking two 'parent' character strings, lining them up side by side, and interchanging equivalent sub-strings between them, producing two new sub-strings that each contain a mix of their parent's genetic information. Cross-over is an extremely important genetic operator. Whereas mutation is equivalent to random search, cross-over allows the more 'intelligent' search strategy of putting things that have proved useful in new combinations.

In the GPP, cross-over is implemented by picking two 'parent' parse trees, locating syntactically similar sub-trees within each, and swapping them.

Fig. 1.10 illustrates the cross-over operation in the GA and GPP.

Inversion is used rarely in order to rearrange the relative locations of specific pieces of genetic information in the character strings of the GA.

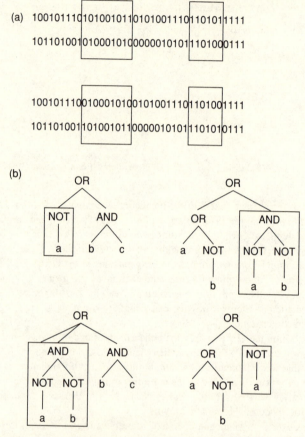

(a)

```
100101110101001011010100111011010111111
101101001010001010000000101011101000111

100101110010001010010100111011010001111
101101001101001011000000101011101010111
```

(b)

FIG. 1.10. Cross-over operation in the GA and GPP

Duplication is sometimes used in situations where it makes sense for the genome to grow in length, representing, for instance, larger neural nets, or bigger finite-state machine transition tables.

The Operation of the Genetic Algorithm. The basic outline of the genetic algorithm is as follows:

1. Generate a random initial population of GTYPES.
2. Render the GTYPES in the population as PTYPES and evaluate them in the problem domain, providing each GTYPE with a fitness value.

3. Duplicate GTYPES according to their relative fitness using a scheme like fitness-proportionate reproduction.
4. Apply *genetic operators* to the GTYPES in the population, typically picking cross-over partners as a function of their relative fitness.
5. Replace the least-fit GTYPES in the population with the offspring generated in the last several steps.
6. Go back to step 2 and iterate.

Although quite simple in outline, the genetic algorithm has proved remarkably powerful in a wide variety of applications, and provides a useful tool for both the study and the application of evolution.

The Context of Adaptation. GAs have traditionally been employed in the contexts of machine learning and function optimization. In such contexts, one is often looking for an explicit, optimal solution to a particular, well-specified problem. This is reflected in the implementation of the evaluation of PTYPES in traditional GAs: each GTYPE is expressed as a PTYPE independently of the others, tested on the problem, and assigned a value representing its individual fitness using an explicit fitness function. Thus, one is often seeking to evolve an *individual* that *explicitly encodes* an optimal solution to a precisely specified problem. The fitness of a GTYPE in such cases is simply a function of the problem domain, and is independent of the fitnesses of the other GTYPES in the population.

This is quite different from the context in which natural biological evolution has taken place, in which the behaviour of a PTYPE and its associated fitness are highly dependent on which other PTYPES exist in the environment, and on the dynamics of their interactions. Furthermore, in the natural context, it is generally the case that there is no single, explicitly specified problem confronting the population. Rather, there is often quite a large set of problems facing the population at any one time, and these problems are only implicitly determined as a function of the dynamics of the population and the environment themselves, which may change significantly over time. *In such a context, nature has often discovered that the collective behaviour emerging from the interactions among a set of PTYPES will address a subset of the implicitly defined problems.*

Thus, the proper picture for the natural evolutionary context is that of a large cloud of implicit collective solutions addressing a large cloud of implicit collective problems. Both these clouds are implicit in the spatio-temporal dynamics of the population.

The dynamics of such systems are very complex and impossible to predict. One can think of them as the dynamical equivalent of many-body orbital mechanics problems: two-body problems can be treated analytically, whereas three- or more body problems are non-analytic.

The important point here is that non-linearities and emergent collective phenomena are properties that are to be exploited, rather than avoided as has been the traditional engineering viewpoint. Emergent non-linear solutions may be harder to understand or to engineer, but there are far more of them than there are non-emergent, analysable linear solutions. The true power of evolution lies in its ability to exploit emergent collective phenomena; it lies, in fact, in evolution's inability to *avoid* such phenomena.

7.5. *From Artificial Selection to Natural Selection*

In *The Origin of Species*, Darwin used a very clever device to argue for the agency of natural selection. In the first chapter of *Origin*, Darwin lays the groundwork of the case for *natural* selection by carefully documenting the process of *artificial* selection. Most people of his time were familiar with the manner in which breeders of domestic animals and plants could enhance traits arbitrarily by selective breeding of their stock. Darwin carefully made the case that the wide variety of domestic animals and plants extant at his time were descended from a much smaller variety of wildstock, due to the selective breedings imposed by farmers and herders throughout history.

Now, Darwin continues, simply note that environmental circumstances can fill the role played by the human breeder in artificial selection, and *voilà!* one has natural selection. The rest of the book consists in a very careful documentation of the manner in which different environmental conditions would favour animals bearing different traits, making it more likely that individuals bearing those traits would survive to mate with each other and produce offspring, leading to the gradual enhancement of those traits through time. A beautifully simple yet elegant mechanism to explain the origin and maintenance of the diversity of species on Earth—too simple for many of his time, particularly those of strong religious persuasion.

The abstraction of this simple elegant mechanism for the production and filtration of diversity in the form of the Genetic Algorithm is straightforward and obvious. However, as it is usually implemented, it is artificial, rather than natural, selection that is the agency determining the direction of computer evolution. Either we ourselves, or our algorithmic agents in the form of explicit fitness functions, typically stand in the role of the breeder in computer implementations of evolution. Yet it is plain that the role of 'breeder' can as easily be filled by 'nature' in the world inside the computer as it is in the world outside the computer—it is just a different 'nature'.

In the following sections, we shall explore a number of examples of computational implementations of the evolutionary process, starting with examples that clearly involve artificial selection, and working our way through to an example that clearly involves natural selection. The key thing to keep track of through-out these examples is the manner in which we incrementally give over our role as breeder to the 'natural' pressures imposed by the dynamics of the computa-tional world itself.

A Breeder's Paradise: Biomorphs. The first model, a clear-cut example of computational artificial selection, is due to the Oxford evolutionary biologist, Richard Dawkins, author of such highly regarded books as *The Selfish Gene, The Extended Phenotype*, and *The Blind Watchmaker*.

In order to illustrate the power of a process in which the random production of variation is coupled with a selection mechanism, Dawkins wrote a program for the Apple Macintosh computer that allows users to 'breed' recursively generated objects.

The program is set up to generate tree structures recursively by starting with a single stem, adding branches to it in a certain way, adding branches to those branches in the same way, and so on. The number of branches, their angles, their size relative to the stem they are being added to, the number of branching iterations, and other parameters affecting the growth of these trees are what constitute the GTYPES of the tree organisms—or 'biomorphs' as Dawkins calls them. Thus the program consists of a general-purpose recursive tree-generator, which takes an organism's GTYPE (parameter settings) as data and generates its associated PTYPE (the resulting tree).

The program starts by producing a simple default—or 'Adam'—tree and then produces a number of mutated copies of the parameter string for the Adam tree. The program renders the PTYPE trees for all these different mutants on the screen for the user to view. The user then selects the PTYPE (i.e. tree shape) he or she likes the best, and the program produces mutated copies of that tree's GTYPE, and renders the associated PTYPES. The user selects another tree, and the process continues. The original Adam tree together with a number of its distant descendants are shown in Fig 1.11.

It is clear that this is a process of artificial selection. The computer generates the variants, but the human user fills the role of the 'breeder', the active selec-tive agent, determining which structures are to go on to produce variant off-spring. However, the mechanics of the production of variants are particularly clear: produce slight variations on the presently selected GTYPE. The specific action taken by the human breeder is also very clear: choose the PTYPE whose GTYPE will have variations of it produced in the next round. There is both a producer and a selector of variation.

Algorithmic Breeders. In this section, we investigate a model which will take us two steps closer to natural selection. First, the human breeder is taken out

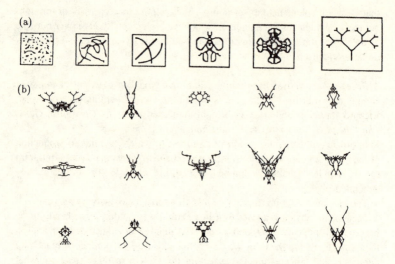

FIG. 1.11. (a) Dawkins's original Adam tree, and (b) a number of its distant descendants. From Dawkins (1989)

of the loop, replaced by a program he writes, which formalizes his selection criteria, so that the act of selection can be performed by his computational agent. Second, we see that our computational representative can itself be allowed to evolve—an important first step towards eliminating our externally imposed, *a priori* criteria from the process completely.

The system we discuss here is due to Danny Hillis, inventor of the Connection Machine and chief scientist of Thinking Machines Corporation. In the course of the work at TMC, they have a need to design fast and efficient chips for the hardware implementation of a wide variety of common computational tasks, such as sorting numbers. For many of these, there is no body of theory that tells engineers how to construct the optimal circuit to perform the task in question. Therefore, progress in the design of such circuits is often a matter of blind trial and error until a better circuit is discovered. Hillis decided to apply the trial-and-error procedure of evolution to the problem of designing sorting circuits.

In his system, the GTYPES are strings of numbers encoding circuit connections that implement comparisons and swaps between input lines. GTYPES are rendered into the specific circuits they encode—their PTYPES—and they are rated according to the number of circuit elements and connections they require, and by their performance on a number of test strings which they have to sort. This rating is accomplished by an explicit fitness function—Hillis's computational representative—which implements the selection criteria and takes care of the breeding task. Thus, this is still a case of artificial selection, even though there is no human being actively doing the selection.

Hillis implemented the evolution problem on his Connection Machine CM2—a 64K processor SIMD parallel supercomputer. With populations of 64K sorting networks over thousands of generations, the system managed to produce a 65-element sorter, better than some cleverly engineered sorting networks, but not as good as the best-known such network, which has 60 components. After reaching 65-element sorters, the system consistently became stuck on local optima.

Hillis then borrowed a trick from the biological literature on the co-evolution of hosts and parasites (specifically Hamilton 1980, 1982) and in the process took a step closer to natural selection by allowing the evaluation function to evolve in time. In the previous runs, the sorting networks were evaluated on a fixed set of sorting problems—random sequences of numbers that the networks had to sort into correct order. In the new set of runs, Hillis made another evolving population out of the sorting problems. The task for the sorting networks was to do a good job on the sorting problems, while the task for the sorting problems was to make the sorting networks perform poorly.

In this situation, whenever a good sorting network emerged and took over the population, it became a target for the population of sorting problems. This led to the rapid evolution of sorting sequences that would make the network perform poorly and hence reduce its fitness. Hillis found that this co-evolution between the sorting networks and the sorting problems led much more rapidly to better solutions than had been achieved by the evolution of sorting networks alone, resulting in a sorting network consisting of 61 elements (see Fig. 1.12).

It is the co-evolution in this latter set of runs that both brings us one step closer to natural selection and is responsible for the enhanced efficiency of the search for an optimal sorting network. First of all, rather than having an absolute, fixed value, the fitness of a sorting network depends on the specific set of sorting problems it is facing. Likewise, the fitness of a set of sorting problems depends on the specific set of sorting networks it is facing. Thus the 'fitness' of an individual is now a relative quantity, not an absolute one. The fitness function depends a little more on the 'nature' of the system; it is an evolving entity as well.

Co-evolution increases the efficiency of the search as follows. In the earlier runs consisting solely of an evolving population of sorting networks, the population of networks was effectively hill-climbing on a multi-peaked fitness landscape. Therefore, the populations would encounter the classic problem of getting stuck on local maxima. That is, a population could reach certain structures which lie on relatively low fitness peaks, but from which any deviations result

FIG. 1.12. An evolved sorting network showing sequencing of comparisons and swaps. From Hillis (1991)

in lower fitness, which is selected against. In order to find another, higher peak, the population would have to cross a fitness valley, which it is difficult to do under simple Darwinian selection (Fig. 1.13(*a*)).

In the co-evolutionary case, here's what happens (Fig. 1.13(*b*)). When a population of sorting networks gets stuck on a local fitness peak, it becomes a target for the population of sorting problems. That is, it defines a new peak for the sorting problems to climb. As the sorting problems climb their peak, they *drive down the peak on which the sorting networks are sitting*, by finding sequences that make the sorting networks perform poorly, therefore lowering their fitness. After a while, the fitness peak that the sorting networks were sitting on has been turned into a fitness valley, from which the population can escape by climbing up the neighbouring peaks. As the sorting networks climb other peaks, they drive down the peak that they had provided for the sorting problems, which will then chase the sorting networks to the new peaks they have achieved and drive those down in turn.

In short, each population dynamically deforms the fitness landscape being traversed by the other population in such a way that both populations can continue to climb uphill without getting stuck on local maxima. When they do get stuck, the maxima get turned into minima which can be climbed out of by

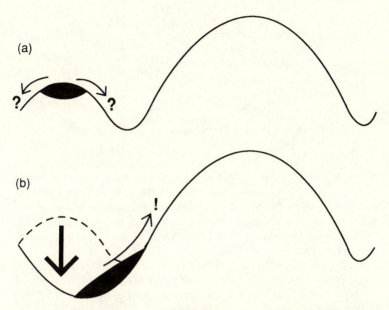

FIG. 1.13. (*a*) Population of working networks stuck on a local fitness peak. In order to attain the higher peak, the population must cross a fitness 'valley', which is difficult to achieve under normal Darwinian mechanisms. (*b*) The co-evolving parasites deform the fitness landscape of the sorting networks, turning the fitness peak into a fitness valley, from which it is easy for the population to escape

simple Darwinian means. Thus coupled populations evolving by Darwinian means can bootstrap each other up the evolutionary ladder far more efficiently than they can climb it alone. By competing with one another, coupled populations improve one another at increased rates.

Thus when coupled in this way, a population may get hung up on local optima for a while, but eventually it will be able to climb again. This suggests immediately that the structure of the evolutionary record for such systems should show periods of stasis followed by periods of evolutionary change. The stasis comes about as populations sit at the top of local fitness peaks, waiting around for something to come along and do them the favour of lowering the peaks they are stuck on. The periods of change come about when populations are released from local optima and are freed to resume climbing up hills, and are therefore changing in time. Hillis has, in fact, carefully documented this kind of *Punctuated Equilibria* in his system.

82CHRISTOPHER G. LANGTON

TABLE 1.1. *The pay-off matrix for the Prisoner's Dilemma Game*

		Player B	
		Cooperate	Defect
Player A	Cooperate	(3,3)	(0,5)
	Defect	(5,0)	(1,1)

Note: The pair (s_1, s_2) denotes the scores to players A and B, respectively.

Computational Ecologies. Continuing on our path from artificial to natural selection, we turn to a research project carried out by Kristian Lindgren (1991), in which, although there is still an explicit fitness measure, many different species of organisms co-evolve in each other's presence, forming ecological webs allowing for more complex interactions than the simple host–parasite interactions described above.

In this paper, Lindgren studies evolutionary dynamics within the context of a well-known game-theoretic problem: the *Iterated Prisoner's Dilemma* model (IPD). This model has been used effectively by Axelrod and Hamilton (1981) in their studies of the evolution of cooperation.

In the prisoner's dilemma model, the pay-off matrix (the fitness function) is constructed in such a way that individuals will garner the most pay-off collectively in the long run if they 'cooperate' with one another by *avoiding* the behaviours that would garner them the most pay-off individually in the short run. If individuals only play the game once, they will do best by not cooperating ('defecting'). However, if they play the game repeatedly with one another (the 'iterated' version of the game), they will do best by cooperating with one another.

The pay-off matrix for the prisoner's dilemma game is shown in Table 1.1. This pay-off matrix has the following interesting property. Assume, as is often assumed in game theory, that each player wants to maximize his immediate pay-off, and let's analyse what player **A** should do. If **B** cooperates, then **A** should defect, because then **A** will get a score of 5 whereas he only gets a score of 3 if he cooperates. On the other hand, if **B** defects, then again, **A** should defect, as he will get a score of 1 if he defects while he only gets a score of 0 if he cooperates. So, no matter what **B** does, **A** maximizes his immediate pay-off by defecting. Since the pay-off matrix is symmetric, the same reasoning applies to player **B**, so **B** should defect no matter what **A** does. Under this reasoning, each player will defect at each time-step, giving them 1 point each per play. However, if they could somehow decide to cooperate, they would

strategy	name
[0 0]	All Defect
[0 1]	TIT-for-TAT (TFT)
[1 0]	TAT-for-TIT (anti-TFT)
[1 1]	All Cooperate

FIG. 1.14. Four possible memory 1 strategies

each get 3 points per play: the two players will do better in the long run by foregoing the action that maximizes their immediate pay-off.

The question is, of course, can ordinary Darwinian mechanisms, which assume that individuals selfishly want to maximize their immediate pay-off, lead to co-operation? Surprisingly, as demonstrated by Axelrod and Hamilton, the answer is yes.

In Lindgren's version of this game, strategies can evolve in an open-ended fashion by learning to base their decisions on whether to cooperate or defect upon longer and longer histories of previous interactions.

The scheme used by Lindgren to represent strategies to play the Iterated Prisoner's Dilemma game is as follows. In the simplest version of the game, players make their choice of whether to cooperate or defect based solely on what their opponent did to them in the last time-step. This is called the *memory 1* game. Since the opponent could have done only one of two things, cooperate or defect, a strategy needs to specify what it would do in either of those two cases. As it has two moves it can make in either of those two cases, cooperate or defect, there are four possible memory 1 strategies. These can be encoded in bit strings of length 2, as illustrated in Fig. 1.14.

If the players should base their decisions by looking another move into the past, to see what they did to their opponent before their opponent made his move, then we would have the *memory 2* game. In this case, there are two moves with two possible outcomes each, meaning that a memory 2 strategy must specify whether to cooperate or defect for each of four possible cases. Such a strategy can be encoded using four bits, twice the length of the memory 1 strategies, so there will be 16 possible memory 2 strategies. Memory 3 strategies require

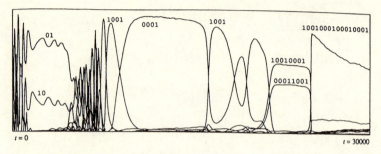

FIG. 1.15. During evolutionary development, the system settles down to relatively long periods of stasis 'punctuated' irregularly by periods of rapid evolutionary change. From Lindgren (1991)

another doubling of the encoding bit string, i.e. 8 bits, yielding 256 possible strategies. In general, memory n strategies require 2^n bits for their encoding, and there will be 2^{2^n} such strategies.

In order to allow for the evolution of higher memory strategies, Lindgren introduces a new genetic operator: gene duplication. As a memory n strategy is just twice as long as a memory $n-1$ strategy, a memory n strategy can be produced from a memory $n-1$ strategy by simply duplicating the memory n strategy and concatenating the duplicate to itself. In Lindgren's encoding strategy, gene duplication has the interesting property that it is a *neutral mutation*. Simple duplication alone does not change the PTYPE, even though it has doubled the length of the GTYPE. However, once doubled, mutations in the longer GTYPE will alter the behaviour of the PTYPE.

Once again, evolution proceeds by allowing populations of different organisms to bootstrap each other up coupled fitness landscapes, dynamically deforming each other's landscapes by turning local maxima into local minima. Again, the fitness of strategies is not an absolute fixed number that is independently computable. Rather, the fitness of each strategy depends on what other strategies exist in the 'natural' population.

Many complicated and interesting strategies evolve during the evolutionary development of this system. More important, however, are the various phenomenological features exhibited by the dynamics of the evolutionary process. First of all, as we might expect, the system exhibits a behaviour that is remarkably suggestive of Punctuated Equilibria. After an initial irregular transient, the system settles down to relatively long periods of stasis 'punctuated' irregularly by periods of rapid evolutionary change (Fig. 1.15).

Second, the diversity of strategies builds up during the long periods of stasis, but often collapses drastically during the short, chaotic episodes of rapid evolutionary succession (Fig. 1.16). These 'crashes' in the diversity of species constitute 'extinction events'. In this model, these extinction events are observed to be a natural consequence of the dynamics of the evolutionary process alone, without invoking any catastrophic, external perturbations (there are no comet impacts or 'nemesis' stars in this model!). Furthermore, these extinction events happen on multiple scales: there are lots of little ones and fewer large ones.

This is important because in order to understand the dynamics of a system that is subjected to constant perturbations, one needs to understand the dynamics of the *un*perturbed system first. We do not have access to an unperturbed version of the evolution of life on Earth; consequently, we could not have said definitively that extinction events on many size scales would be a natural consequence of the process of evolution itself. By comparing the perturbed and unperturbed versions of model systems like Lindgren's, we may very well be able to derive a universal scaling relationship for 'natural' extinction events, and therefore be able to explain deviations from this relationship in the fossil record as due to external perturbations such as the impact of large asteroids.

Third, the emergence of ecologies is nicely demonstrated by Lindgren's model. It is usually the case that a mix of several different strategies dominates the system during the long periods of stasis. In order for a strategy to do well, it must do well by cooperating with other strategies. These mixes may involve three or more strategies whose collective activity produces a stable interaction pattern that benefits all of the strategies in the mix. Together, they constitute a more complex, 'higher order' strategy, which can behave as a group in ways that are impossible for any individual strategy.

It is important to note that, in many cases, the 'environment' that acts on an organism, and in the context of which an organism acts, is primarily constituted of the other organisms in the population and their interactions with each other and the physical environment. There is tremendous opportunity here for evolution to discover that certain sets of individuals exhibit emergent, collective behaviours that reap benefits to all of the individuals in the set. Thus, evolution can produce major leaps in biological complexity, without having to produce more complex individuals by simply discovering, perhaps even 'tripping over', the many ways in which collections of individuals at one level can work together to form aggregate individuals at the next higher level of organization (Buss 1987).

This is thought to be the case for the origin of eukaryotic cells, which are viewed as descended from early cooperative collections of simpler, prokaryotic cells (Margolus 1970). It is also the process involved in the origin of multicellular organisms, which led to the Cambrian explosion of diversity some 700 million years ago. It was probably a significant factor in the origin of the prokaryotes

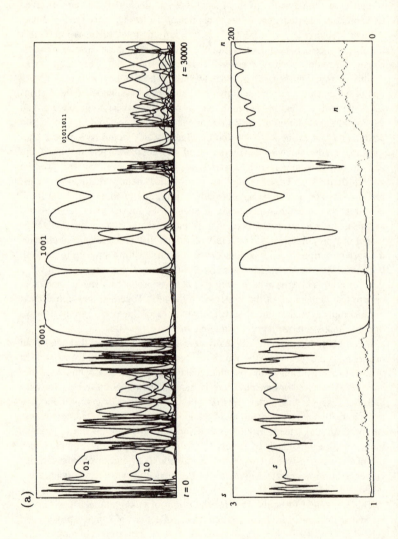

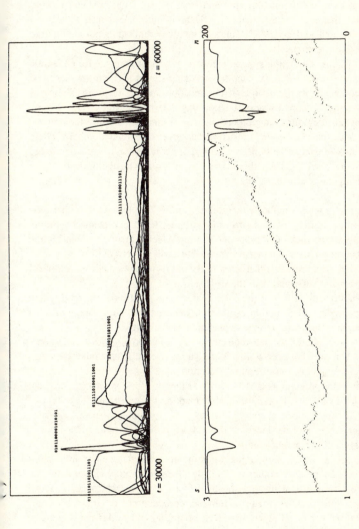

Fig. 1.16. The evolutionary dynamics of strategies in the iterated prisoner's dilemma system of Lindgren. In both cases, the top trace plots the changing concentration of strategies in the population while the bottom trace shows two things: the solid line plots the average fitness of the population, while the dotted line plots the diversity of species (the number of different strategies in the population at any time). In all cases, time is traced on the horizontal axis. The top traces illustrate the interplay between metastable and chaotic episodes, while the bottom traces illustrate the 'extinction events' that are often associated with the end of metastable periods. These extinction events can be quite large, as is seen in the bottom trace

themselves, and it has been discovered independently at least seven times by the various social insects (including species of wasps, bees, ants, and termites).

The final step in eliminating our hand from the selection/breeding process and setting the stage for true 'natural' selection within a computer is taken in a model due to Tom Ray (1991). This step involves eliminating our algorithmic breeding agent completely.

In his 'Tierra' simulation system, computer programs compete for CPU time and memory space. The 'task' that these programs must perform in order to be reproduced is simply the act of self-reproduction itself! Thus there is no need for an externally defined fitness function that determines which GTYPES get copied by an external copying procedure. The programs reproduce themselves, and the ones that are better at this task take over the population. The whole external task of evaluation of fitness has been internalized in the function of the organisms themselves. Thus, there is no longer a place for the human breeder or his computational agent. This results in genuine natural selection within a computer.

In Tierra, programs replicate themselves 'noisily', so that some of their off-spring behave differently. Variant programs that reproduce themselves more efficiently, which trick other programs into reproducing them, or which capture the execution pointers of other programs, etc., will leave more offspring than others. Similarly, programs that learn to defend themselves against such tricks will leave more offspring than those that do not.

We shall discuss a few of the 'digital organisms' that have emerged within the Tierra system. (It is not necessary to understand the code in the illustrated programs in order to follow the explanation in the text.)[9]

Fig. 1.17(a) shows the self-replicating 'ancestor' program that is the only program Tom Ray has ever written in the Tierra system. All the other programs evolved under the action of natural selection.

The ancestor program works as follows. In the top block of code, the program locates its 'head' and its 'tail', templates marking the upper and lower boundaries of the program in memory. It saves these locations in special registers and, after subtracting the location of the head from the location of the tail, it stores its length in another register.

In the second block of code, the program enters an endless loop in which it will repeatedly produce copies of itself. It allocates memory space of the appropriate size and then invokes the final block of code, which is the actual reproduction loop. After it returns from the reproduction loop, it creates a new execution pointer to its newly produced offspring, and cycles back to create another offspring.

---

[9] The details are to be found in Ray (1991); see below, Ch. 3.

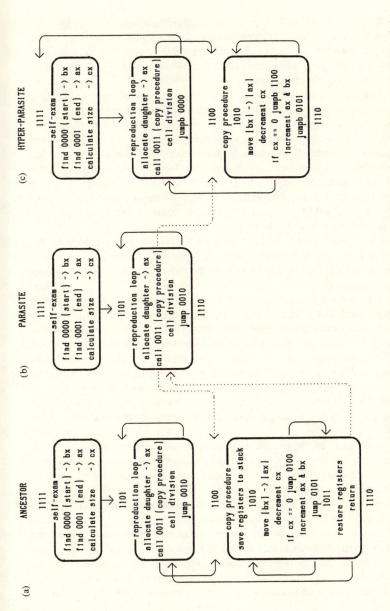

FIG. 1.17. Digital organisms from Ray's (1991) Tierra simulation system: (a) self-reproducing ancestor; (b) an early parasite of the ancestor; (c) a descendant of the ancestor that is immune to the parasite

In the third and final block of code, the reproduction loop, the program copies itself, instruction by instruction, into the newly allocated memory space, making use of the addresses and length stored away by the first block of code. When it has copied itself completely, it returns to the block of code that called it, in this case, the second block.

It should be noted that 'function calls' in Tierra are accomplished by seeking for a specific bit pattern in memory rather than by branching to a specific address. Thus, when the second block of code 'calls' the third block of code, the reproduction loop, it does so by initiating a seek forward in memory for a specific 'template'. When this template is found, execution begins at the instruction following the template. Returns from function calls are handled in the normal manner, by simply returning to the instruction following the initial function call. This template-addressing scheme is used in other reference contexts as well, and helps make Tierra language programs robust to mutations, as well as easily relocatable in memory.

Fig. 1.17(b) shows a 'parasite' program that has evolved to exploit the ancestor program. The parasite is very much like the ancestor program, except that it is missing the third block of code, the reproduction loop. How then does it copy itself?

The answer is that it makes use of a nearby ancestor program's reproduction loop! Recall that a function call in Tierra initiates a seek forward in memory for a particular template of bits. If this pattern is not found within the initiating program's own code, the search may proceed forward in memory into the code of other organisms, where the template may be found and where execution then begins. When the invoked function in another organism's code executes the 'return' statement, execution reverts to the program that initiated the function call. Thus, organisms can execute each other's code, and this is exactly what the parasite program does: it makes use of the reproductive machinery of the ancestor host.

This means that the parasite does not have to take the time to copy the code constituting the reproductive loop, and hence can reproduce more rapidly, as it has fewer instructions to copy. The parasites thus proliferate in the population. However, they cannot proliferate to the point of driving out the ancestor hosts altogether, for they depend on them for their reproductive machinery. Thus, a balance is eventually struck optimizing the joint system.

Eventually, however, another mutant form of the ancestor emerges which has developed an immunity to the parasites. This program is illustrated in Fig. 1.17(c). Two key differences from the ancestor program confer the immunity to the parasite programs. First, instead of executing a 'return' instruction, the reproduction loop instead initiates a jump back in memory to the template found in the instruction that calls the reproduction loop. This has the same effect as a return statement when executed by the immune program, but has a very different effect on the parasite. The second important difference is that following the cell division in the second block (which allocates a new execution pointer to the offspring just created), the program jumps back to the beginning of the first block of code, rather than to the beginning of the second block. Thus, the immune program constantly resets its head, tail, and size registers. This seems useless when considering only the immune organism's own reproduction, but let's see what happens when a parasite tries to execute the reproduction loop in an immune organism.

When a parasite attempts to use the immune program's reproduction code, the new jump transfers the parasite's execution pointer to the second block of the immune program's code, rather than returning it to the second block of the parasite code, as the parasite expects. Then, this execution pointer is further redirected to the first block of the immune program, where the registers originally containing the head, tail, and length of the parasite are reset to contain the head, tail, and length of the immune organism. The immune program has thus completely captured the execution pointer of the parasite. Having lost its execution pointer, the parasite simply becomes dormant data occupying memory, while the immune program now has two execution pointers running through it: its own original pointer, plus the pointer it captured from the parasite. Thus, the immune program now reproduces twice as rapidly as before. Once they emerge, such immune programs rapidly drive the parasites to extinction.

Complex interactions between variant programs like those described above continue to develop within evolutionary runs in Tierra. From a uniform population of self-reproducing ancestor programs, Ray, a tropical biologist by training, notes the emergence of whole 'ecologies' of interacting species of computer programs. Furthermore, he is able to identify many phenomena familiar to him from his studies of real ecological communities, such as competitive exclusion, the emergence of parasites, key-stone predators and parasites, hyper-parasites, symbiotic relationships, sociality, 'cheaters', and so forth.

Again, the actual 'fitness' of an organism is a complex function of its interactions with other organisms in the 'soup'. Collections of programs can cooperate to enhance each other's reproductive success, or they can drive each other's reproductive success down, thus lowering fitness and kicking the population off of local fitness peaks.

Not surprisingly, Ray, too, has noted periods of relative stasis punctuated by periods of rapid evolutionary change, as complex ecological webs collapse and new ones stabilize in their place. Systems like Ray's Tierra capture the proper context for evolutionary dynamics, and natural selection is truly at play here.

8. CONCLUSION

This article is intended to provide a broad overview of the field of Artificial Life, its motivations, history, theory, and practice. In such a short space, it cannot hope to go into depth in any one of these areas. Rather, it attempts to convey the 'spirit' of the Artificial Life enterprise via several illustrative examples coupled with a good deal of motivating explanation and discussion.

The field of Artificial Life is in its infancy, and is currently engaged in a period of extremely rapid growth, which is producing many new converts to the principles detailed here. However, it is also raising a significant amount of controversy, and is not without its critics. The notion of studying biology via the study of patently non-biological things is an idea that is hard for the traditional biological community to accept. The acceptance of Artificial Life techniques within the biological community will be directly proportional to the contributions it makes to our understanding of biological phenomena.

That these contributions are forthcoming, I have no doubt. However, high-quality research in Artificial Life is difficult, because it requires that its practitioners be experts in both the computational sciences and the biological sciences. Either of these alone is a full-time career, and so the danger lurks of doing either masterful biology but trivial computing, or doing masterful computing but trivial biology.

Therefore, I strongly suggest incorporating a trick from nature: cooperate! As is amply illustrated in many of the examples discussed in this article, nature often discovers that collections of individuals easily solve problems that would be extremely difficult or even impossible for individuals to solve on their own. Collaborations between biologists and computer scientists are quite likely to be the most appropriate vehicles for making significant contributions to our understanding of biology via the pursuit of Artificial Life.

So, if you are a computer expert dying to hack together an evolution program, go find yourself a top-notch evolutionary biologist to collaborate with, one who will bring to the enterprise an in-depth understanding of the subtleties of the evolutionary process plus a proper set of open questions about evolution towards which your evolution program might be addressed.

On the other hand, if you are a field biologist interested in doing some numerical simulations in order to understand the ecological dynamics you are observing in the field, hook up with a top-notch parallel-computing expert, who will bring to the enterprise a thorough knowledge of the subtleties involved in multi-agent interactions, and will be in possession of an equally open set of questions, which you very well might find to be strikingly related to your own.

Above all, when in doubt, turn to Mother Nature. After all, she is smarter than you![10]

REFERENCES

Axelrod, R. (1984), *The Evolution of Cooperation* (New York: Basic Books).
—— and Hamilton, W. D. (1981), 'The Evolution of Cooperation', *Science*, 211: 1390–6.
Burks, A. W. (1970) (ed.), *Essays on Cellular Automata* (Urbana, Ill.: University of Illinois Press).
Buss, L. (1987), *The Evolution of Individuality* (Princeton: Princeton University Press).
Chapuis, A., and Droz, E. (1958), *Automata: A Historical and Technological Study*, trans. A. Reid (London: Batsford Ltd.).
Dawkins, R. (1989), 'The Evolution of Evolvability', in Langton (1989*b*), 201–20.
Frisch, U., Hasslacher, B., and Pomeau, Y. (1986), 'Lattice Gas Automata for the Navier-Stokes Equation', *Physical Reviews and Letters*, 56: 1505–8.
Goldberg, D. E. (1989), *Genetic Algorithms in Search, Optimization, and Machine Learning* (Reading, Mass.: Addison-Wesley).
Hamilton, W. D. (1980), 'Sex Versus Non-Sex Versus Parasite', *OIKOS*, 35: 282–90.
—— (1982), 'Pathogens as Causes of Genetic Diversity in their Host Populations', in R. M. Anderson and R. M. May (eds.), *Population Biology of Infectious Diseases* (Berlin: Springer-Verlag, 1982), 269–96.
Hillis, W. D. (1991), 'Co-evolving Parasites Improve Simulated Evolution as an Optimization Procedure', in Langton *et al.* (1991), 313–24.
Holland, J. H. (1975), *Adaptation in Natural and Artificial Systems: An Introductory Analysis with Applications to Biology, Control, and Artificial Intelligence* (Ann Arbor: University of Michigan Press).
—— (1986), 'Escaping Brittleness: The Possibilities of General Purpose Learning Algorithms Applied to Parallel Rule-Based Systems', in R. S. Michalski, J. G. Carbonell, and T. M. Mitchell (eds.), *Machine Learning II* (New York: Kaufman), 593–623.
Hopcroft, J. E., and Ullman, J. D. (1979), *Introduction to Automata Theory, Languages, and Computation* (Menlo Park, Calif.: Addison-Wesley).
Koza, J. R. (1991), 'Genetic Evolution and Co-evolution of Computer Programs', in Langton *et al.* (1991), 603–30.
Langton, C. G. (1984), 'Self-Reproduction in Cellular Automata', *Physica D*, 10/1–2: 135–44.
—— (1986), 'Studying Artificial Life with Cellular Automata', *Physica D*, 22: 120–49.

[10] A large number of people have assisted in writing this paper, which is based on my lecture notes for the Complex Systems Summer School and on the overview of Artificial Life that served as an introduction to the proceedings of the first Artificial Life workshop. Besides the people credited in the latter paper, I should like to thank the following people for their help with this version: Tom Ray, Kristian Lindgren, Danny Hillis, and John Koza. I should also like to thank Ronda Butler-Villa and Della Ulibarri for their patience with me and for their skill in preparing the figures and text for publication.

Langton, C. G. (1989*a*), 'Artificial Life', in Langton (1989*b*).

—— (1989*b*), *Artificial Life: Proceedings of an Interdisciplinary Workshop on the Synthesis and Simulation of Living Systems* (Santa Fe Institute Studies in the Sciences of Complexity, Proceedings, 6; Redwood City, Calif.: Addison-Wesley).

—— Taylor, C., Farmer, J. D., and Rasmussen, S. (1991) (eds.), *Artificial Life II* (Santa Fe Institute Studies in the Sciences of Complexity, Proceedings, 10; Redwood City, Calif.: Addison-Wesley).

Lindgren, K. (1991), 'Evolutionary Phenomena in Simple Dynamics', in Langton *et al.* (1991), 295–312.

Margolus, L. (1970), *Origin of Eucaryotic Cells* (New Haven: Yale University Press).

Prusinkiewicz, P. (1991), *The Algorithmic Beauty of Plants* (Berlin: Springer-Verlag).

Ray, T. S. (1991), 'An Approach to the Synthesis of Life', in Langton *et al.* (1991), 371–408, and Chapter 3 below.

Reynolds, C. W. (1987), 'Flocks, Herds, and Schools: A Distributed Behavioral Model', Proceedings of SIGGRAPH '87, *Computer Graphics* V 21/4: 25–34.

Toffoli, T. (1984), 'Cellular Automata as an Alternative to (Rather than an Approximation of) Differential Equations in Modeling Physics', in J. D. Farmer, T. Toffoli, and S. Wolfram (eds.), *Cellular Automata: Proceedings of an Interdisciplinary Workshop* (Los Alamos, New Mexico, March 7–11, 1983) = *Physica D* (special issue), 10/1–2.

—— and Margolus, N. (1987), *Cellular Automata Machines* (Cambridge, Mass.: MIT Press).

Ulam, S. (1962), 'On Some Mathematical Problems Connected with Patterns of Growth of Figures', *Proceedings of Symposia in Applied Mathematics*, 14: 215–24. Repr. In Burks (1970).

Von Neumann, J. (1966), *Theory of Self-Reproducing Automata*, ed. and completed by A. W. Burks (Urbana, Ill.: University of Illinois Press).

Wilson, S. W. (1989), 'The Genetic Algorithm and Simulated Evolution', in Langton (1989), 157–65.

Wolfram, S. (1986), 'Cellular Automaton Fluids 1: Basic Theory', *Journal of Statistical Physics*, 45: 471–526.

2

AUTONOMY AND ARTIFICIALITY

MARGARET A. BODEN

1. THE PROBLEM—AND WHY IT MATTERS

When Herbert Simon wrote his seminal book on 'the sciences of the artificial' (Simon 1969), he had in mind artificial intelligence (AI) and cybernetics. Now, the sciences of the artificial include artificial life (A-Life) also. A-Life uses informational concepts and computer-modelling to study the functional principles of life in general (Langton 1989). Simon's use of the word 'sciences' was well chosen. The interests of A-Life, as of AI, are largely scientific, not technological. That is, many researchers in these two fields hope to contribute to theoretical biology and/or psychology.

The relations between A-Life and AI are complex. One might define A-Life as the abstract study of life, and AI as the abstract study of mind. But if one assumes that life prefigures mind, that cognition is—and must be—grounded in self-organizing adaptive systems, then AI may be seen as a sub-class of A-Life. Certainly, A-Life is theoretically close to some recent work in AI (described below). However, A-Life workers often go out of their way to distance their research from AI. In doing so, they usually stress the concept of autonomy—which, they say, applies to A-Life models but not to AI.

Since autonomy of some kind is generally thought to be an important characteristic of both life and mind, A-Life and AI should have implications for our understanding of human autonomy, or freedom. These implications are not purely abstract, to be forgotten when one leaves one's study to play a game of backgammon. What science tells us about human autonomy is practically important, because it affects the way in which ordinary people see themselves—which includes the way in which they believe it is possible to behave.

If science tells us that we lack freedom, we may be less likely to try to exercise it. An observable decline of personal autonomy was reported many years ago by the psychotherapist Rollo May (1961). His experiences in the consulting-room led him to complain of 'the dehumanizing dangers in our tendency in modern science to make man over into the image of the machine, into the image of the techniques by which we study him' and of 'the undermining of [modern man's] experience of himself as responsible, the sapping of his willing and decision' (May 1961: 20). May's mention of 'the machine' referred not to A-Life or AI (which had barely begun), but to the mechanistic implications of the natural sciences in general and behaviourist psychology in particular. Indeed, the relevant implications of behaviourism were soon to be made explicit by B. F. Skinner, in a spirited attack on the concepts of freedom and dignity (Skinner 1971).

'Freedom', Skinner argued, is an illusion, grounded in our ignorance of the multiple environmental pressures determining our behaviour. As for 'dignity', this is a matter of giving people credit, of admiring them for their self-generated achievements. But his behaviourist principles implied that 'the environment', not 'autonomous man', is really in control (Skinner 1971: 21). No credit, then, to *us*, if we exercise some skill—whether bodily, mental, or moral. And no surprise, if people experience unhappiness and apathy at this downgrading of their humanity. The cure for this unhappiness, said Skinner, is to drop our sentimental, unscientific picture of autonomous man. Only then shall we be in a position (with the help of his scientific psychology) to solve our life-problems.

Behaviourism, then, questions received notions of human worth. According to its high priest, Skinner, it has no room for human 'autonomy' or 'freedom'. But it is at least concerned with life. Animals are living things, and *Rattus Norvegicus* a moderately merry mammal. Some small shred of our self-respect can perhaps be retained, if we are classed with rats, or even pigeons. But what of the artificial sciences? Surely, all they can offer is dead, automatic tin-cannery? Is A-Life, for all its stress on self-organization and autonomy, really any better in this respect than AI?

To many people, the notion that computer models could help us to an adequate account of humanity—above all, of freedom, creativity, and morals—seems quite absurd. To the contrary, the suspicion is that the concepts and explanations of A-Life and/or AI must be incompatible with the notion of human freedom. If that suspicion is correct, then the artificial sciences—A-Life included—are the enemy of true autonomy: if they prosper, we can expect to hear more complaints like May's in the future.

In the next section, I explain how A-Life (and some recent AI) addresses the phenomenon of autonomy, and how it differs from traditional AI in this respect. In Section 3, I discuss the concept of autonomy, and claim that crucial aspects of the strongest case (human free action) are not captured by the A-Life approach.

Indeed, these aspects—self-reflection, deliberation, and reasoned prioritizing—are better modelled by what John Haugeland (1985) has called GOFAI: Good Old-Fashioned AI. My conclusion is not that the artificial sciences deny, or even downgrade, our freedom. Rather, they help us to see how autonomous behaviour (of various kinds) is possible, and to appreciate the awesome complexity of much human choice.

2. AI, A-LIFE, AND ANTS

At first sight, it may seem that the explanations offered by any 'artificial' science must be incompatible with human freedom. For it is not only behaviourists who see conditions in the external environment as the real causes of apparently autonomous behaviour. Only a few years after May's complaint quoted above, Simon—in defining the sciences of the artificial—took much the same view (Simon 1969).

Simon described the erratic path of the ant, as it avoided the obstacles on its way to nest or food, as the result of a series of simple and immediate reactions to the local details of the terrain. He did not stop with ants, but tackled humans too. For over twenty years, Simon has argued that rational thought and skilled behaviour are largely triggered by specific environmental cues. Unlike Skinner, he allows that many internal, 'mentalistic', cues are important also; but these produce their effects in just as direct a way as the external conditions do. The extensive psychological experiments and computer-modelling on which Simon's argument is based were concerned with chess, arithmetic, and typing (Newell and Simon 1972; Card *et al.* 1983). But he would say the same of every case of skilled activity or intelligent thought.

Simon's ant was not taken as a model by most of his AI colleagues. Instead, they were inspired by his earliest, and significantly different, work on the computer simulation of problem-solving (Newell and Simon 1961; Newell *et al.* 1963). This ground-breaking theoretical research paid no attention to environmental factors, but conceived of human thought purely in terms of internal mental/computational processes, such as hierarchical means–end planning and goal-representations.

Driven by this 'internalist' view, the young AI community designed—and in some cases built—robots guided top-down by increasingly sophisticated internal planning and representation (Boden 1987, ch. 12). Plans were worked out ahead of time. In the most flexible cases, certain contingencies could be foreseen, and the detailed movements, and even the sub-plans, could be decided on at the time of execution. But even though they were placed in the physical world, these robots were not real-world, real-time creatures. Their environments were simple, highly predictable 'toy-worlds'. They typically involved a flat ground-plane, polyhedral and/or pre-modelled shapes, white surfaces, shadowless light-ing, and—by human standards—painfully slow movements. Moreover, they were easily called to a halt, or trapped into fruitless perseverative behaviour, by unforeseen environmental details.

Recently, however, the AI pendulum has swung towards the ant. What is sometimes called 'nouvelle AI' sees behaviour as being controlled by an on-going interaction between relatively low-level mechanisms in the system (robot or organism) and the constantly changing details of the environment.

For example, current research in *situated robotics* sees no need for the sym-bolic representations and detailed anticipatory planning typical of earlier AI robotics. Indeed, the earlier strategy is seen as not just unnecessary, but inef-fective. Traditional robotics suffers from the brittleness of classical AI pro-grams in general: unexpected input can cause the system to do something highly inappropriate, and there is no way in which the problem-environment can help guide it back on to the right track. Accepting that the environment cannot be anticipated in detail, workers in situated robotics have resurrected the insight—often voiced within classical AI, but also often forgotten—that the best source of information about the real world is the real world itself.

Accordingly, the 'intelligence' of these very recent robots is in the hardware, not the software (Braitenberg 1984; Brooks 1991). There is no high-level pro-gram doing detailed anticipatory planning. Instead, the creature is engineered in such a way that, within limits, it naturally does the right (adaptive) thing at the right time. Behaviour apparently guided by goals and hierarchical planning can, nevertheless, occur (Maes 1991).

Situated robotics is closely related to two other recent forms of computer-modelling, likewise engaged in studying 'emergent' behaviours. These are genetic algorithms (GAs) and A-Life.

GA systems are self-modifying programs, which continually come up with new rules (new structures) (Holland 1975; Holland *et al.* 1986). They use rule-changing algorithms modelled on genetic processes such as mutation and cross-over, and algorithms for identifying and selecting the relatively successful rules. Mutation makes a change in a single rule; cross-over brings about a mix of two, so that (for instance) the left-hand portion of one rule is combined with the right-hand portion of the other. Together, these algorithms (working in parallel) generate a new system better adapted to the task in hand.

One example of a GA system is a computer-graphics program written by Karl Sims (1991). This program uses genetic algorithms to generate new images, or patterns, from pre-existing images. Unlike most GA systems, the selection of the 'fittest' examples is not automatic, but is done by the programmer—or by someone fortunate enough to be visiting his office while the program is being run. That is, the human being selects the images which are aesthetically pleasing, or otherwise interesting, and these are used to 'breed' the next generation. (Sims could provide automatic selection rules, but has not yet done so—not only because of the difficulty of defining aesthetic criteria, but also because he aims to provide an *interactive* graphics environment, in which human and computer can cooperate in generating otherwise unimaginable images.)

In a typical run of the program, the first image is generated at random (but Sims can feed in a real image, such as a picture of a face, if he wishes). Then the program makes nineteen independent changes (mutations) in the initial image-generating rule, so as to cover the VDU-screen with twenty images: the first, plus its nineteen ('asexually' reproduced) offspring. At this point, the human uses the computer mouse to choose either *one* image to be mutated, or *two* images to be 'mated' (through cross-over). The result is another screenful of twenty images, of which all but one (or two) are newly generated by random mutations or cross-overs. The process is then repeated, for as many generations as one wants.

(The details of this GA system need not concern us. However, so as to distinguish it from magic, a few remarks may be helpful. It starts with a list of twenty very simple LISP functions. A 'function' is not an actual instruction, but an instruction-schema: more like 'X + Y' than '2 + 3'. Some of these functions can alter parameters in pre-existing functions: for example, they can divide or multiply numbers, transform vectors, or define the sines or cosines of angles. Some can combine two pre-existing functions, or nest one function inside another (so multiply-nested hierarchies can eventually result). A few are basic image-generating functions, capable (for example) of generating an image consisting of vertical stripes. Others can process a pre-existing image, for instance by altering the light-contrasts so as to make 'lines' or 'surface-edges' more or less visible. When the program chooses a function at random, it also randomly chooses any missing parts. So if it decides to *add* something to an existing number (such as a numerical parameter inside an image-generating function), and the 'something' has not been specified, it randomly chooses the amount to be added. Similarly, if it decides to *combine* the pre-existing function with some other function, it may choose that function at random.)

As for A-Life, this uses computer-modelling to study processes that start with relatively simple, locally interacting units, and generate complex individual and/or group behaviours. Examples of such behaviours include self-organization, reproduction, adaptation, purposiveness, and evolution.

Self-organization is shown, for instance, in the flocking behaviour of flocks of birds, herds of cattle, and schools of fish. The entire group of animals seems to behave as one unit. It maintains its coherence despite changes in direction, the (temporary) separation of stragglers, and the occurrence of obstacles—which the flock either avoids or 'flows around'. Yet there is no overall director working out the plan, no sergeant-major yelling instructions to all the individual animals, and no reason to think that any one animal is aware of the group as a whole. The question arises, then, how this sort of behaviour is possible.

Ethologists argue that communal behaviour of large groups of animals must depend on local communications between neighbouring individuals, who have no conception of the group-behaviour as such. But just what are these 'local communications'?

Flocking has been modelled within A-Life, in terms of a collection of very simple units, called Boids (Reynolds 1987). Each Boid follows three rules: (1) keep a minimum distance from other objects, including other Boids; (2) match velocity to the average velocity of the Boids in the immediate neighbourhood; and (3) move towards the perceived centre of mass of the Boids in the neighbourhood. These rules, depending as they do only on very limited, local, information, result in the holistic flocking behaviour just described. It does not follow, of course, that real birds follow just those rules: that must be tested by ethological studies. But this research shows that it is at least *possible* for group-behaviour of this kind to depend on very simple, strictly local, rules.

Situated robotics, GAs, and A-Life can be combined, for they share an emphasis on bottom-up, self-adaptive, parallel processing. At present, most situated robots are hand-crafted. But some are 'designed' by evolutionary algorithms from the GA/A-Life stable: fully simulated robots have already been evolved, and real robots are now being constructed with the help of simulated evolution. The automatic evolution of real physical robots *without any recourse to simulation* is more difficult (Brooks 1992), but progress is being made in this area too.

Recent work in evolutionary robotics (Cliff *et al.* 1993) has simulated insect-like robots, with simple 'brains' controlling their behaviour. The (simulated) neural net controlling the (simulated) visuomotor system of the robot gradually adapts to its specific (simulated) task-environment. This automatic adaptation can result in some surprises. For instance, if—in the given task-environment—the creature does not actually need its (simulated) in-built whiskers as well as its eyes, the initial network-links to the whiskers may eventually be lost, and the relevant neural units may be taken over by the eyes. *Eyes* can even give way to *eye*: if the task is so simple that only one eye is needed, one of them may eventually lose its links with the creature's network-brain.

Actual (physical) robots of this type can be generated by combining simulated evolution with hardware-construction (Cliff *et al.* 1993). The detailed physical connections to, and within, the 'brain' of the robot-hardware are adjusted every *n* generations (where *n* may be 100, or 1,000, or . . .), mirroring the current blueprint evolved within the simulation. This acts as a cross-check: the real robot should behave as the simulated robot does. Moreover, the resulting embodied robot can roam around an actual physical environment, its real-world task-failures and successes being fed into the background simulation so as to influence its future evolution. The brain is not the only organ whose anatomy can be evolved in this way: the placement and visual angle of the creatures' eyes can be optimized, too. (The same research-team has begun work on the evolution of physical robots without any simulation. This takes much longer, because every single evaluation of every individual in the population has to be done using the real hardware.)

A-Life (some of which uses GAs) and situated robotics have strong links with biology: with neuroscience, ethology, genetics, and the theory of evolution. As a result, animals are becoming theoretically assimilated to *animats* (Meyer and Wilson 1991). The behaviour of swarms of bees, and of ant-colonies, is hotly discussed at A-Life conferences, and entomologists are constantly cited in the A-Life and situated-robotics literatures (Lestel 1992). Environmentally situated (and formally defined) accounts of apparently goal-seeking behaviour in various animals, including birds and mammals, are given by (some) ethologists (McFarland 1989). And details of invertebrate psychology, such as visual tracking in the hoverfly, are modelled by research in connectionist AI (Cliff 1990; 1992).

In short, Simon's ant is now sharing the limelight on the AI stage. Some current AI is more concerned with artificial insects than with artificial human minds. But—what is of particular interest to us here—this form of AI sees itself as designing 'autonomous agents', as A-Life in general seeks to design 'autonomous systems'.

3. AUTONOMOUS AGENCY

Autonomy is ascribed to these artificial insects because it is their intrinsic physical structure, adapted as it is to the sorts of environmental problem they are likely to meet, which enables them to act appropriately. Unlike traditional robots, their behaviour is not directed by complex software written for a general-purpose machine, imposed on their bodies by some alien (human) hand. Rather, they are specifically constructed to adapt to the particular environment they inhabit.

We are faced, then, with two opposing intuitions concerning autonomy. Our (and Skinner's) original intuition was that response determined by the external environment lessens one's autonomy. But the intuition of *nouvelle* AI, and of A-Life, is that to be in thrall to an internal plan is to be a mere puppet. (Notice that one can no longer say 'a mere robot'.) How can these contrasting intuitions be reconciled?

Autonomy is not an all-or-nothing property. It has several dimensions, and many gradations. Three aspects of behaviour—or rather, of its control—are crucial. First, the extent to which response to the environment is direct (determined only by the present state in the external world) or indirect (mediated by inner mechanisms partly dependent on the creature's previous history). Second, the extent to which the controlling mechanisms were self-generated rather than externally imposed. And third, the extent to which inner directing mechanisms can be reflected upon, and/or selectively modified in the light of general interests or the particularities of the current problem in its environmental context. An individual's autonomy is the greater, the more its behaviour is directed by self-generated (and idiosyncratic) inner mechanisms, nicely responsive to the specific problem-situation, yet reflexively modifiable by wider concerns.

The first aspect of autonomy involves behaviour mediated, in part, by inner mechanisms shaped by the creature's past experience. These mechanisms may, but need not, include explicit representations of current or future states. It is controversial, in ethology as in philosophy, whether animals have explicit internal representations of goals (Montefiore and Noble 1989). And, as we have seen, AI includes strong research-programmes on both sides of this methodological fence. But this controversy is irrelevant here. The important distinction is between a response wholly dependent on the current environmental state (given the original, 'innate', bodily mechanisms), and one largely influenced by the creature's experience. The more a creature's past experience differs from that of other creatures, the more 'individual' its behaviour will appear.

The second aspect of autonomy, the extent to which the controlling mechanisms were self-generated rather than externally imposed, may seem to be the same as the first. After all, a mechanism shaped by experience is sensitive to the past of that particular individual—which may be very different from that of other, initially comparable, individuals. But the distinction, here, is between behaviour which 'emerges' as a result of self-organizing processes, and behaviour which was deliberately prefigured in the design of the experiencing creature.

In computer-simulation studies within A-Life, and within situated robotics also, holistic behaviour—often of an unexpected sort—may emerge. It results, of course, from the initial list of simple rules concerning locally interacting units. But it was neither specifically mentioned in those rules, nor (often) foreseen when they were written.

A flock, for example, is a holistic phenomenon. A bird-watcher sees a flock of birds as a unit, in the sense that it shows behaviour that can be described only at the level of the flock itself. For instance, when it comes to an obstacle, such as a tall building, the flock divides and 'flows' smoothly around it, reorganizing itself into a single unit on the far side. But no individual bird is divided in half by the building. And no bird has any notion of the flock as a whole, still less any goal of reconstituting it after its division.

Clearly, flocking behaviour must be described on its own level, even though it can be explained by (reduced to) processes on a lower level. This point is especially important if 'emergence-hierarchies' evolve as a result of new forms of perception, capable of detecting the emergent phenomena *as such*. Once a holistic behaviour has emerged it, or its effects, may be detected (perceived) by some creature or other—including, sometimes, the 'unit-creatures' making it up.

(This implies that a creature's perceptual capacities cannot be fully itemized for all time. In Gibsonian terms, one might say that evolution does not know what all the relevant affordances will turn out to be, so cannot know how they will be detected. The current methodology of AI and A-Life does not allow for 'latent' perceptual powers, actualized only by newly emerged environmental features. This is one of the ways in which today's computer-modelling is biologically unrealistic (Kugler 1992).)

If the emergent phenomenon can be detected, it can feature in rules governing the perceiver's behaviour. Holistic phenomena on a higher level may then result . . . and so on. Ethologists, A-Life workers, and situated roboticists all assume that increasingly complex hierarchical behaviour can arise in this sort of way. The more levels in the hierarchy, the less direct the influence of environmental stimuli—and the greater the behavioural autonomy.

Even if we can *explain* a case of emergence, however, we cannot necessarily *understand* it. One might speak of intelligible vs. unintelligible emergence.

Flocking gives us an example of the former. Once we know the three rules governing the behaviour of each individual Boid, we can see lucidly how it is that holistic flocking results.

Sims's computer-generated images give us an example of the latter. One may not be able to say just why *this* image resulted from *that* LISP expression. Sims himself cannot always explain the changes he sees appearing on the screen before him, even though he can access the mini-program responsible for any image he cares to investigate, and for its parent(s) too. Often, he cannot even 'genetically engineer' the underlying LISP expression so as to get a particular visual effect. To be sure, this is partly because his system makes several changes simultaneously, with every new generation. If he were to restrict it to making only one change, and studied the results systematically, he could work out just what was happening. But when several changes are made in parallel, it is often impossible to understand the generation of the image *even though* the 'explanation' is available.

Where real creatures are concerned, of course, we have multiple interacting changes, and no explanation at our fingertips. At the genetic level, these multiple changes and simultaneous influences arise from mutations and cross-over. At the psychological level, they arise from the plethora of ideas within the mind. Think of the many different thoughts which arise in your consciousness, more or less fleetingly, when you face a difficult choice or moral dilemma. Consider the likelihood that many more conceptual associations are being activated unconsciously in your memory, influencing your conscious musings accordingly. Even if we had a listing of all these 'explanatory' influences, we might be in much the same position as Sims, staring in wonder at one of his nth-generation images and unable to say why *this* LISP expression gave rise to it. In fact, we cannot hope to know about more than a fraction of the ideas aroused in human minds (one's own, or someone else's) when such choices are faced.

The third criterion of autonomy listed above was the extent to which a system's inner directing mechanisms can be reflected upon, and/or selectively modified, by the individual concerned. One way in which a system can adapt its own processes, selecting the most fruitful modifications, is to use an 'evolutionary' strategy such as the genetic algorithms mentioned above. It may be that something broadly similar goes on in human minds. But the mutations and selections carried out by GAs are modelled on biological evolution, not conscious reflection and self-modification. And it is conscious deliberation which many people assume to be the crux of human autonomy.

For the sake of argument, let us accept this assumption at face value. Let us ignore the mounting evidence (e.g. Nisbett and Ross 1980) that our conscious thoughts are less relevant than we like to think. Let us ignore neuroscientists' doubts about whether our conscious intentions actually direct our behaviour (as the folk-psychology of 'action' assumes) (Libet 1987). Let us even ignore the fact that *unthinking spontaneity*—the opposite of conscious reflection—is often taken as a sign of individual freedom. (Spontaneity may be based in the sort of multiple constraint satisfaction modelled by connectionist AI, where many of the constraints are drawn from the person's idiosyncratic experience.) What do the sciences of the artificial, and AI-influenced psychology, have to say about conscious thinking and deliberate self-control?

Surprisingly, perhaps, neither A-Life nor the most biologically realistic (more accurately: the least biologically unrealistic) forms of AI can help us here. Ants, and artificial ants, are irrelevant. Nor can connectionism help. It is widely agreed, even by connectionists, that conscious thought requires a sequential 'virtual machine', more like a von Neumann computer than a parallel-processing neural net. As yet, we have only very sketchy ideas about how the types of problem-solving best suited to conscious deliberation might be implemented in connectionist systems.

The most helpful 'artificial' approach so far, where conscious deliberation is involved, is classical AI, or GOFAI—much of which was inspired by human introspection. Consciousness involves reflection on one level of processes going on at a lower level. Work in classical AI, such as the work on planning mentioned above, has studied multi-level problem-solving. Computationally informed work in developmental psychology has suggested that flexible self-control, and eventually consciousness, result from a series of 'representational redescriptions' of lower-level skills (Clark and Karmiloff-Smith 1993).

Representational redescriptions, many-levelled maps of the mind, are crucial to creativity (Boden 1990, esp. ch. 4). Creativity is an aspect of human autonomy, and workers whose working-conditions allow them no room for creative ingenuity (or even for choice) may describe themselves as 'monkeys', 'robots', 'machines', or even 'objects' (Terkel 1974, p. xi). Their discontent is understandable, given that our ability to think new thoughts in new ways is one of our most salient, and most valued, characteristics.

This ability often involves someone's doing something which they not only *did not* do before, but which they *could not* have done before. To do this, they must either explore a formerly unrecognized area of some pre-existing 'conceptual space', or transform some dimension of that generative space. Transforming the space allows novel mental structures to arise which simply could not have been generated from the initial set of constraints. The nature of the creative novelties depends on which feature has been transformed, and how. Conceptual spaces, and procedures for transforming them, can be clarified by thinking of them in computational terms. But this does not mean that creativity is predictable, or even fully explicable *post hoc*: for various reasons (including those mentioned above), it is neither (Boden 1990, ch. 9).

Autonomy in general is commonly associated with unpredictability. Many people feel AI to be a threat to their self-esteem because they assume that it involves a deterministic predictability. But they are mistaken. Some connectionist AI systems include non-deterministic (stochastic) processes, and are more efficient as a result.

Moreover, determinism does not always imply predictability. Workers in A-Life, for instance, sometimes justify their use of computer-simulation by citing chaos theory, according to which a fully deterministic dynamic process may be theoretically unpredictable (Langton 1989). If there is no analytic solution to the differential equations describing the changes concerned, the process must simply be 'run', and observed, to know what its implications are. The same is true of many human choices. We cannot always predict what a person will do. Moreover, predicting *one's own* choices is not always possible. One may have to 'run one's own equations' to find out what one will do, since the outcome cannot be known until the choice is actually made.

4. CONCLUSION

One of the pioneers of A-Life has said:

The field of Artificial Life is unabashedly mechanistic and reductionist. However, this *new mechanism*—based as it is on multiplicities of machines and on recent results in the fields of nonlinear dynamics, chaos theory, and the formal theory of computation—is vastly different from the mechanism of the last century. (Langton 1989: 6; italics in original)

Our discussion of A-Life and *nouvelle* AI has suggested just how vast this difference is. Similarly, the potentialities of classical AI systems go far beyond what most people think of as 'machines'. If this is reductionism, it is very different from the sort of reductionism which insists that the only scientifically respectable concepts lie at the most basic ontological level (neurones and bio-chemical processes, or even electrons, mesons, and quarks).

In sum, the sciences of the artificial can model autonomy of various kinds. A-Life (like *nouvelle* AI) explicitly highlights autonomy, as a characteristic of living things. A-Life can teach us a great deal about how increasing complexity arises from self-organization on successive levels, and how a creature can negotiate its environment by constant interaction with it. However, the kind of autonomy that we call free choice is better illuminated by the theoretical approach of classical AI. If this is generally accepted the result need not be insidiously dehumanizing, as the acceptance of behaviourism sometimes was. Properly understood, AI does not reduce our respect for human minds. If anything, it increases it. Far from denying human autonomy, it helps us to understand how it is possible.

REFERENCES

Boden, M. A. (1987), *Artificial Intelligence and Natural Man* (2nd edn.; London: MIT Press).
—— (1990), *The Creative Mind: Myths and Mechanisms* (London: Weidenfeld and Nicolson).
Braitenberg, V. (1984), *Vehicles: Essays in Synthetic Psychology* (Cambridge, Mass.: MIT Press).
Brooks, R. A. (1991), 'Intelligence Without Representation', *Artificial Intelligence*, 47: 139–59.
—— (1992), 'Artificial Life and Real Robots', in F. J. Varela and P. Bourgine (eds.), *Toward a Practice of Autonomous Systems: Proceedings of the First European Conference on Artificial Life* (Cambridge, Mass.: MIT Press), 3–10.
Card, S. K., Moran, T. P., and Newell, A. (1983), *The Psychology of Human–Computer Interaction* (Hillsdale, NJ: Erlbaum).

Clark, A., and Karmiloff-Smith, A. (1993), 'The Cognizer's Innards: A Psychological and Philosophical Perspective on the Development of Thought', *Mind and Language*, 8: 487–568.

Cliff, D. (1990), 'The Computational Hoverfly: A Study in Computational Neuroethology', in J.-A. Meyer and S. W. Wilson (eds.), *From Animals to Animats: Proceedings of the First International Conference on Simulation of Adaptive Behavior* (Cambridge, Mass.: MIT Press), 87–96.

—— (1992), 'Neural Networks for Visual Tracking in an Artificial Fly', in F. J. Varela and P. Bourgine (eds.), *Toward a Practice of Autonomous Systems: Proceedings of the First European Conference on Artificial Life* (Cambridge, Mass.: MIT Press), 78–87.

—— Harvey, I., and Husbands, P. (1993), 'Explorations in Evolutionary Robotics', *Adaptive Behavior*, 2/1: 73–110.

Haugeland, J. (1985), *Artificial Intelligence: The Very Idea* (Cambridge, Mass.: MIT Press).

Holland, J. H. (1975), *Adaptation in Natural and Artificial Systems: An Introductory Analysis with Applications to Biology, Control, and Artificial Intelligence* (Ann Arbor: University of Michigan Press; reissued MIT Press, 1991).

—— Holyoak, K. J., Nisbet, R. E., and Thagard, P. R. (1986), *Induction: Processes of Inference, Learning, and Discovery* (Cambridge, Mass.: MIT Press).

Kugler, P. (1992), Talk given at the Summer School on 'Comparative Approaches to Cognitive Science', Aix-en-Provence (organizers, J.-A. Meyer and H. L. Roitblat).

Langton, C. G. (1989), 'Artificial Life', in C. G. Langton (ed.), *Artificial Life: Proceedings of an Interdisciplinary Workshop on the Synthesis and Simulation of Living Systems* (Santa Fe Institute Studies in the Sciences of Complexity, Proceedings, 6; Redwood City, Calif.: Addison-Wesley), 1–47.

Lestel, D. (1992), 'Fourmis cybernetiques et robots-insectes: Socialité et cognition à l'interface de la robotique et de l'éthologie experimentale', *Information sur les Sciences Sociales*, 31/2: 179–211.

Libet, B. (1987), 'Are the Mental Experiences of Will and Self-Control Significant for the Performance of a Voluntary Act?', *Behavioral and Brain Sciences*, 10: 783–6.

McFarland, D. (1989), 'Goals, No-Goals, and Own-Goals', in Montefiore and Noble (1989), 39–57.

Maes, P. (1991) (ed.), *Designing Autonomous Agents* (Cambridge, Mass.: MIT Press).

May, R. (1961), *Existential Psychology* (New York: Random House).

Meyer, J.-A., and Wilson, S. W. (1991) (eds.), *From Animals to Animats: Proceedings of the First International Conference on Simulation of Adaptive Behavior* (Cambridge, Mass.: MIT Press).

Montefiore, A., and Noble, D. (1989) (eds.), *Goals, No-Goals, and Own-Goals* (London: Unwin Hyman).

Newell, A., and Simon, H. A. (1961), 'GPS—A Program that Simulates Human Thought', in H. Billing (ed.), *Lernende Automaten* (Munich: Oldenbourg), 109–24. Repr. in E. A. Feigenbaum and J. Feldman (eds.), *Computers and Thought* (New York: McGraw-Hill, 1963), 279–96.

—— —— (1972), *Human Problem Solving* (Englewood Cliffs, NJ: Prentice-Hall).

—— Shaw, J. C., and Simon, H. A. (1963), 'Empirical Explorations with the Logic Theory Machine: A Case-Study in Heuristics', in E. A. Feigenbaum and J. Feldman (eds.), *Computers and Thought* (New York: McGraw-Hill), 109–33.

Nisbett, R. E., and Ross, L. (1980), *Human Inference: Strategies and Shortcomings in Social Judgment* (Englewood Cliffs, NJ: Prentice-Hall).

Reynolds, C. W. (1987), 'Flocks, Herds, and Schools: A Distributed Behavioral Model', *Computer Graphics*, 21/4: 25–34.

Simon, H. A. (1969), *The Sciences of the Artificial* (Cambridge, Mass.: MIT Press).
Sims, K. (1991), 'Artificial Evolution for Computer Graphics', *Computer Graphics*, 25/
    4: 319–28.
Skinner, B. F. (1971), *Beyond Freedom and Dignity* (New York: Alfred Knopf).
Terkel, S. (1974), *Working* (New York: Pantheon).

PART II

3

AN APPROACH TO THE SYNTHESIS OF LIFE

THOMAS S. RAY

> Marcel, a mechanical chessplayer ... his exquisite 19th-century brain-work—the human art it took to build which has been flat lost, lost as the dodo bird ... But where inside Marcel is the midget Grandmaster, the little Johann Allgeier? Where's the pantograph, and the magnets? No-where. Marcel really is a mechanical chessplayer. No fakery inside to give him any touch of humanity at all.
>
> Thomas Pynchon, *Gravity's Rainbow*

INTRODUCTION

Ideally, the science of biology should embrace all forms of life. However, in practice, it has been restricted to the study of a single instance of life, life on earth. Because biology is based on a sample size of one, we cannot know what features of life are peculiar to earth, and what features are general, characteristic of all life. A truly comparative natural biology would require inter-planetary travel, which is light-years away. The ideal experimental evolutionary biology would involve creation of multiple planetary systems, some essentially identical, others varying by a parameter of interest, and observing them for billions of years. A practical alternative to an inter-planetary or mythical biology is to create synthetic life in a computer. 'Evolution in a bottle' provides a valuable tool for the experimental study of evolution and ecology.

The intent of this work is to synthesize rather than simulate life. This approach starts with handcrafted organisms already capable of replication and open-ended evolution, and aims to generate increasing diversity and complexity in a parallel to the Cambrian explosion.

To state such a goal leads to semantic problems, because life must be defined in a way that does not restrict it to carbon-based forms. It is unlikely that there could be general agreement on such a definition, or even on the proposition that life need not be carbon-based. Therefore, I shall simply state my conception of life in its most general sense. I would consider a system to be living if it is self-replicating, and capable of open-ended evolution. Synthetic life should self-replicate, and evolve structures or processes that were not designed-in or preconceived by the creator (Pattee 1989).

Core Wars programs, computer viruses, and worms (Cohn 1984; Denning 1988; Dewdney 1984, 1985*a*, 1985*b*, 1987, 1989; Rheingold 1988; Spafford *et al.* 1989) are capable of self-replication, but fortunately, not evolution. It is unlikely that such programs will ever become fully living, because they are not likely to be able to evolve.

Most evolutionary simulations are not open-ended. Their potential is limited by the structure of the model, which generally endows each individual with a genome consisting of a set of predefined genes, each of which may exist in a predefined set of allelic forms (Ackley and Littman 1990; Dawkins 1987, 1989; Dewdney 1985*b*; Holland 1975; Packard 1989). The object being evolved is generally a data structure representing the genome, which the simulator program mutates and/or recombines, selects, and replicates according to criteria designed into the simulator. The data structures do not contain the mechanism for replication; they are simply copied by the simulator if they survive the selection phase.

Self-replication is critical to synthetic life because without it, the mechanisms of selection must also be predetermined by the simulator. Such artificial selection can never be as creative as natural selection. The organisms are not free to invent their own fitness functions. Freely evolving creatures will discover means of mutual exploitation and associated implicit fitness functions that we would never think of. Simulations constrained to evolve with predefined genes, alleles, and fitness functions are dead-ended, not alive.

The approach presented here does not have such constraints. Although the model is limited to the evolution of creatures based on sequences of machine instructions, this may have a potential comparable to evolution based on sequences of organic molecules. Sets of machine instructions similar to those used in the Tierra Simulator have been shown to be capable of 'universal computation' (Ajo *et al.* 1974; Langton 1989*a*; Minsky 1976). This suggests that evolving machine codes should be able to generate any level of complexity.

Other examples of the synthetic approach to life can be seen in the work of Holland (1976), Farmer *et al.* (1986), Langton (1986), Rasmussen *et al.* (1990), and Bagley *et al.* (1989). A characteristic these efforts generally have in common is that they parallel the origin of life event by attempting to create prebiotic conditions from which life may emerge spontaneously and evolve in an open-ended fashion.

While the origin of life is generally recognized as an event of the first order, there is another event in the history of life that is less well known but of comparable significance: the origin of biological diversity and macroscopic multicellular life during the Cambrian explosion 600 million years ago. This event involved a riotous diversification of life-forms. Dozens of phyla appeared suddenly, many existing only fleetingly, as diverse and sometimes bizarre ways of life were explored in a relative ecological void (Gould 1989; Morris 1989).

The work presented here aims to parallel the second major event in the history of life, the origin of diversity. Rather than attempting to create prebiotic conditions from which life may emerge, this approach involves engineering over the early history of life to design complex evolvable organisms, and then attempting to create the conditions that will set off a spontaneous evolutionary process of increasing diversity and complexity of organisms. This work represents a first step in this direction, creating an artificial world which may roughly parallel the RNA world of self-replicating molecules (still falling far short of the Cambrian explosion).

The approach has generated rapidly diversifying communities of self-replicating organisms exhibiting open-ended evolution by natural selection. From a single rudimentary ancestral creature containing only the code for self-replication, interactions such as parasitism,—inximmunity, hyper-parasitism, sociality, and cheating have emerged spontaneously. This paper presents a methodology and some first results.

> Here was a world of simplicity and certainty no acidhead, no revolutionary anarchist would ever find, a world based on the one and zero of life and death. Minimal, beautiful. The patterns of lives and deaths . . . weightless, invisible chains of electronic presence or absence. If patterns of ones and zeros were 'like' patterns of human lives and deaths, if everything about an individual could be represented in a computer record by a long string of ones and zeros, then what kind of creature would be represented by a long string of lives and deaths? It would have to be up one level at least— an angel, a minor god, something in a UFO.
>
> Thomas Pynchon, *Vineland*

METHODS

The Metaphor

Organic life is viewed as utilizing energy, mostly derived from the sun, to organize matter. By analogy, digital life can be viewed as using CPU (central processing unit) time, to organize memory. Organic life evolves through natural selection as individuals compete for resources (light, food, space, etc.) such that genotypes which leave the most descendants increase in frequency. Digital life evolves through the same process, as replicating algorithms compete for CPU time and memory space, and organisms evolve strategies to exploit one another. CPU time is thought of as the analogue of the energy resource, and memory as the analogue of the spatial resource.

The memory, the CPU, and the computer's operating system are viewed as elements of the 'abiotic' environment. A 'creature' is then designed to be specifically adapted to the features of the environment. The creature consists of a self-replicating assembler-language program. Assembler languages are merely mnemonics for the machine codes that are directly executed by the CPU. These machine codes have the characteristic that they directly invoke the instruction set of the CPU and services provided by the operating system.

All programs, regardless of the language they are written in, are converted into machine code before they are executed. Machine code is the natural language of the machine, and machine instructions are viewed by this author as the 'atomic units' of computing. It is felt that machine instructions provide the most natural basis for an artificial chemistry of creatures designed to live in the computer.

In the biological analogy, the machine instructions are considered to be more like the amino acids than the nucleic acids, because they are 'chemically active'. They actively manipulate bits, bytes, CPU registers, and the movements of the instruction pointer (as will be discussed later). The digital creatures discussed here are entirely constructed of machine instructions. They are considered analogous to creatures of the RNA world, because the same structures bear the 'genetic' information and carry out the 'metabolic' activity.

A block of RAM memory (random access memory, also known as 'main' or 'core' memory) in the computer is designated as a 'soup' which can be inoculated with creatures. The 'genome' of the creatures consists of the sequence of machine instructions that make up the creature's self-replicating algorithm. The prototype creature consists of 80 machine instructions; thus the size of the genome of this creature is 80 instructions, and its 'genotype' is the specific sequence of those 80 instructions.

THE VIRTUAL COMPUTER—TIERRA SIMULATOR

The computers we use are general-purpose computers, which means, among other things, that they are capable of emulating through software the behaviour of any other computer that ever has been built or that could be built (Ajo *et al.*

1974; Langton 1989*a*; Minsky 1976). We can utilize this flexibility to design a computer that would be especially hospitable to synthetic life.

There are several good reasons why it is not wise to attempt to synthesize digital organisms that exploit the machine codes and operating systems of real computers. The most urgent is the potential threat of natural evolution of machine codes leading to virus or worm types of programs that could be difficult to eradicate due to their changing 'genotypes'. This potential argues strongly for creating evolution exclusively in programs that run only on virtual computers and their virtual operating systems. Such programs would be nothing more than data on a real computer, and, therefore, would present no more threat than the data in a data base or the text file of a word processor.

Another reason to avoid developing digital organisms in the machine code of a real computer is that the artificial system would be tied to the hardware and would become obsolete as quickly as the particular machine it was developed on. In contrast, an artificial system developed on a virtual machine could be easily ported to new real machines as they become available.

A third issue, which potentially makes the first two moot, is that the machine languages of real machines are not designed to be evolvable, and in fact might not support significant evolution. Von Neuman-type machine languages are considered to be 'brittle', meaning that the ratio of viable programs to possible programs is virtually zero. Any mutation or recombination event in a real machine code is almost certain to produce a non-functional program. The problem of brittleness can be mitigated by designing a virtual computer whose machine code is designed with evolution in mind. Farmer and Belin (1991) have suggested that overcoming this brittleness and 'discovering how to make such self-replicating patterns more robust so that they evolve to increasingly more complex states is probably the central problem in the study of artificial life'.

The work described here takes place on a virtual computer known as Tierra (Spanish for Earth). Tierra is a parallel computer of the MIMD (multiple instruction, multiple data) type, with a processor (CPU) for each creature. Parallelism is imperfectly emulated by allowing each CPU to execute a small time-slice in turn. Each CPU of this virtual computer contains two address registers, two numeric registers, a flags register to indicate error conditions, a stack pointer, a ten-word stack, and an instruction pointer. Each virtual CPU is implemented via the C structure listed in Appendix A [not reprinted here]. Computations performed by the Tierran CPUs are probabilistic due to flaws that occur at a low frequency (see Mutation below).

The instruction set of a CPU typically performs simple arithmetic operations or bit manipulations, within the small set of registers contained in the CPU. Some instructions move data between the registers in the CPU, or between the

CPU registers and the RAM (main) memory. Other instructions control the location and movement of an 'instruction pointer' (IP). The IP indicates an address in RAM, where the machine code of the executing program (in this case a digital organism) is located.

The CPU perpetually performs a fetch–decode–execute–increment–IP cycle. The machine code instruction currently addressed by the IP is fetched into the CPU, its bit pattern is decoded to determine which instruction it corresponds to, and the instruction is executed. Then the IP is incremented to point sequentially to the next position in RAM, from which the next instruction will be fetched. However, some instructions like JMP, CALL, and RET directly manipulate the IP, causing execution to jump to some other sequence of instructions in the RAM. In the Tierra Simulator this CPU cycle is implemented through the time-slice routine listed in Appendix B [not reprinted here].

THE TIERRAN LANGUAGE

Before attempting to set up an Artificial Life system, careful thought must be given to how the representation of a programming language affects its adaptability in the sense of being robust to genetic operations such as mutation and recombination. The nature of the virtual computer is defined in large part by the instruction set of its machine language. The approach in this study has been to loosen up the machine code in a 'virtual bio-computer', in order to create a computational system based on a hybrid between biological and classical von Neumann processes.

In developing this new virtual language, which is called 'Tierran', close attention has been paid to the structural and functional properties of the informational system of biological molecules: DNA, RNA, and proteins. Two features have been borrowed from the biological world which are considered to be critical to the evolvability of the Tierran language.

First, the instruction set of the Tierran language has been defined to be of a size that is the same order of magnitude as the genetic code. Information is encoded into DNA through 64 codons, which are translated into 20 amino acids. In its present manifestation, the Tierran language consists of 32 instructions, which can be represented by five bits, *operands included*.

Emphasis is placed on this last point because some instruction sets are deceptively small. Some versions of the redcode language of Core Wars (Dewdney 1984, 1987; Rasmussen *et al.* 1990), for example, are defined to have ten operation codes. It might appear on the surface that the instruction set is of size ten. However, most of the ten instructions have one or two operands. Each operand has four addressing modes, and then an integer. When we consider that these operands are embedded into the machine code, we realize that they are, in fact, a part of the instruction set, and this set works out to be about 10^{11} in size. Inclusion of numeric operands will make any instruction set extremely large in comparison with the genetic code.

In order to make a machine code with a truly small instruction set, we must eliminate numeric operands. This can be accomplished by allowing the CPU registers and the stack to be the only operands of the instructions. When we need to encode an integer for some purpose, we can create it in a numeric register through bit manipulations: flipping the low-order bit and shifting left. The program can contain the proper sequence of bit-flipping and shifting instructions to synthesize the desired number, and the instruction set need not include all possible integers.

A second feature that has been borrowed from molecular biology in the design of the Tierran language is the addressing mode, which is called 'address by template'. In most machine codes, when a piece of data is addressed, or the IP jumps to another piece of code, the exact numeric address of the data or target code is specified in the machine code. Consider that in the biological system by contrast, in order for protein molecule A in the cytoplasm of a cell to interact with protein molecule B, it does not specify the exact coordinates where B is located. Instead, molecule A presents a template on its surface which is complementary to some surface on B. Diffusion brings the two together, and the complementary conformations allow them to interact.

Addressing by template is illustrated by the Tierran JMP instruction. Each JMP instruction is followed by a sequence of NOP (no-operation) instructions, of which there are two kinds: NOP_0 and NOP_1. Suppose we have a piece of code with five instructions in the following order: JMP NOP_0 NOP_0 NOP_0 NOP_1. The system will search outward in both directions from the JMP instruction looking for the nearest occurrence of the complementary pattern: NOP_1 NOP_1 NOP_1 NOP_0. If the pattern is found, the instruction pointer will move to the end of the pattern and resume execution. If the pattern is not found, an error condition (flag) will be set and the JMP instruction will be ignored (in practice, a limit is placed on how far the system may search for the pattern).

The Tierran language is characterized by two unique features: a truly small instruction set without numeric operands, and addressing by template. Otherwise, the language consists of familiar instructions typical of most machine languages, e.g. MOV, CALL, RET, POP, PUSH, etc. The complete instruction set is listed in Appendix B [not reprinted here].

THE TIERRAN OPERATING SYSTEM

The Tierran virtual computer needs a virtual operating system that will be hospitable to digital organisms. The operating system will determine the mechanisms of interprocess communication, memory allocation, and the allocation of CPU time among competing processes. Algorithms will evolve so as to exploit these features to their advantage. More than being a mere aspect of the environment, the operating system, together with the instruction set, will determine the topology of possible interactions between individuals, such as the ability of pairs of individuals to exhibit predator–prey, parasite–host, or mutualistic relationships.

Memory Allocation—Cellularity

The Tierran computer operates on a block of RAM of the real computer which is set aside for the purpose. This block of RAM is referred to as the 'soup'. In most of the work described here the soup consisted of 60,000 bytes, which can hold the same number of Tierran machine instructions. Each 'creature' occupies some block of memory in this soup.

Cellularity is one of the fundamental properties of organic life, and can be recognized in the fossil record as far back as 3.6 billion years (Barbieri 1985). The cell is the original individual, with the cell membrane defining its limits and preserving its chemical integrity. An analogue to the cell membrane is needed in digital organisms in order to preserve the integrity of the informational structure from being disrupted easily by the activity of other organisms. The need for this can be seen in AL models such as cellular automata where virtual-state machines pass through one another (Langton 1986, 1987), or in core-wars-type simulations where coherent structures demolish one another when they come into contact (Dewdney 1984, 1987; Rasmussen et al. 1990).

Tierran creatures are considered to be cellular in the sense that they are protected by a 'semi-permeable membrane' of memory allocation. The Tierran operating system provides memory-allocation services. Each creature has exclusive write privileges within its allocated block of memory. The 'size' of a creature is just the size of its allocated block (e.g. 80 instructions). This usually corresponds to the size of the genome. While write privileges are protected, read and execute privileges are not. A creature may examine the code of another creature, and even execute it, but it cannot write over it. Each creature may have exclusive write privileges in at most two blocks of memory: the one that it is born with, which is referred to as the 'mother cell', and a second block which it may obtain through the execution of the MAL (memory allocation) instruction. The second block, referred to as the 'daughter cell', may be used to grow or reproduce into.

When Tierran creatures 'divide', the mother cell loses write privileges on the space of the daughter cell, but is then free to allocate another block of memory. At the moment of division, the daughter cell is given its own instruction pointer, and is free to allocate its own second block of memory.

Time-Sharing—The Slicer

The Tierran operating system must be multi-tasking in order for a community of individual creatures to live in the soup simultaneously. The system doles out small slices of CPU time to each creature in the soup in turn. The system maintains a circular queue called the 'slicer queue'. As each creature is born, a virtual CPU is created for it, and it enters the slicer queue just ahead of its mother, which is the active creature at that time. Thus, the newborn will be the last creature in the soup to get another time-slice after the mother, and the mother will get the next slice after its daughter. As long as the slice size is small relative to the generation time of the creatures, the time-sharing system causes the world to approximate parallelism. In actuality, we have a population of virtual CPUs, each of which gets a slice of the real CPU's time as it comes up in the queue.

The number of instructions to be executed in each time-slice is set proportional to the size of the genome of the creature being executed, raised to a power. If the 'slicer power' is equal to one, then the slicer is size neutral, the probability of an instruction being executed does not depend on the size of the creature in which it occurs. If the power is greater than one, large creatures get more CPU cycles per instruction than small creatures. If the power is less than one, small creatures get more CPU cycles per instruction. The power determines if selection favours large or small creatures, or is size neutral. A constant slice size selects for small creatures.

Mortality—The Reaper

Self-replicating creatures in a fixed-size soup would rapidly fill the soup and lock up the system. To prevent this from occurring, it is necessary to include mortality. The Tierran operating system includes a 'reaper' which begins 'killing' creatures when the memory fills to some specified level (e.g. 80%). Creatures are killed by deallocating their memory, and removing them from both the reaper and slicer queues. Their 'dead' code is not removed from the soup.

In the present system, the reaper uses a linear queue. When a creature is born, it enters the bottom of the queue. The reaper always kills the creature at the top of the queue. However, individuals may move up or down in the reaper queue according to their success or failure at executing certain instructions. When a creature executes an instruction that generates an error condition, it moves one position up the queue, as long as the individual ahead of it in the queue has not accumulated a greater number of errors. Two of the instructions are somewhat difficult to execute without generating an error, therefore successful execution of these instructions moves the creature down the reaper queue one position, as long as it has not accumulated more errors than the creature below it.

The effect of the reaper queue is to cause algorithms which are fundamentally flawed to rise to the top of the queue and die. Vigorous algorithms have a greater longevity, but in general, the probability of death increases with age.

Mutation

In order for evolution to occur, there must be some change in the genome of the creatures. This may occur within the life span of an individual, or there may be errors in passing along the genome to offspring. In order to ensure that there is genetic change, the operating system randomly flips bits in the soup, and the instructions of the Tierran language are imperfectly executed.

Mutations occur in two circumstances. At some background rate, bits are randomly selected from the entire soup (60,000 instructions totalling 300,000 bits) and flipped. This is analogous to mutations caused by cosmic rays, and has the effect of preventing any creature from being immortal, as it will eventually mutate to death. The background mutation rate has generally been set at about 1 bit flipped for every 10,000 Tierran instructions executed by the system.

In addition, while copying instructions during the replication of creatures, bits are randomly flipped at some rate in the copies. The copy-mutation rate is the higher of the two, and results in replication errors. The copy-mutation rate has generally been set at about 1 bit flipped for every 1,000 to 2,500 instructions moved. In both classes of mutation, the interval between mutations varies randomly within a certain range to avoid possible periodic effects.

In addition to mutations, the execution of Tierran instructions is flawed at a low rate. For most of the 32 instructions, the result is off by ±1 at some low frequency. For example, the increment instruction normally adds one to its register, but it sometimes adds two or zero. The bit-flipping instruction normally flips the low-order bit, but it sometimes flips the next higher bit or no bit. The shift-left instruction normally shifts all bits one bit to the left, but it sometimes shifts left by two bits, or not at all. In this way, the behaviour of the Tierran instructions is probabilistic, not fully deterministic.

It turns out that bit-flipping mutations and flaws in instructions are not necessary to generate genetic change and evolution, once the community reaches a certain state of complexity. Genetic parasites evolve which are sloppy replicators, and have the effect of moving pieces of code around between creatures, causing rather massive rearrangements of the genomes. The mechanism of this *ad hoc* sexuality has not been worked out, but is likely due to the parasites' inability to discriminate between live, dead, or embryonic code.

Mutations result in the appearance of new genotypes, which are watched by an automated genebank manager. In one implementation of the manager, when new genotypes replicate twice, producing a genetically identical offspring at least once, they are given a unique name and saved to disk. Each genotype name contains two parts, a number, and a three-letter code. The number represents the number of instructions in the genome. The three-letter code is used as a base 26 numbering system for assigning a unique label to each genotype in a size class. The first genotype to appear in a size class is assigned the label aaa, the second is assigned the label aab, and so on. Thus the ancestor is named 80aaa, and the first mutant of size 80 is named 80aab. The first parasite of size 45 is named 45aaa.

The genebanker saves some additional information with each genome: the genotype name of its immediate ancestor, which makes possible the reconstruction of the entire phylogeny; the time and date of origin; 'metabolic' data, including the number of instructions executed in the first and second reproduction, the number of errors generated in the first and second reproduction, and the number of instructions copied into the daughter cell in the first and second reproductions; some environmental parameters at the time of origin, including the search limit for addressing, and the slicer power, both of which affect selection for size.

THE TIERRAN ANCESTOR

The Tierran language has been used to write a single self-replicating program which is 80 instructions long. This program is referred to as the 'ancestor', or alternatively as genotype 0080aaa (Fig. 3.1). The ancestor is a minimal self-replicating algorithm which was originally written for use during the debugging of the simulator. No functionality was designed into the ancestor beyond the ability to self-replicate, nor was any specific evolutionary potential designed in. The commented Tierran assembler and machine code for this program is presented in Appendix C [not reprinted here].

The ancestor examines itself to determine where in memory it begins and ends. The ancestor's beginning is marked with the four no-operation template: 1 1 1 1, and its ending is marked with 1 1 1 0. The ancestor locates its beginning with the five instructions: ADRB, NOP_0, NOP_0, NOP_0, and NOP_0. This series of instructions causes the system to search backwards from the ADRB instruction for a template complementary to the four NOP_0 instructions, and to place the address of the complementary template (the beginning) in the ax register of the CPU. A similar method is used to locate the end.

Having determined the address of its beginning and its end, it subtracts the two to calculate its size, and allocates a block of memory of this size for a

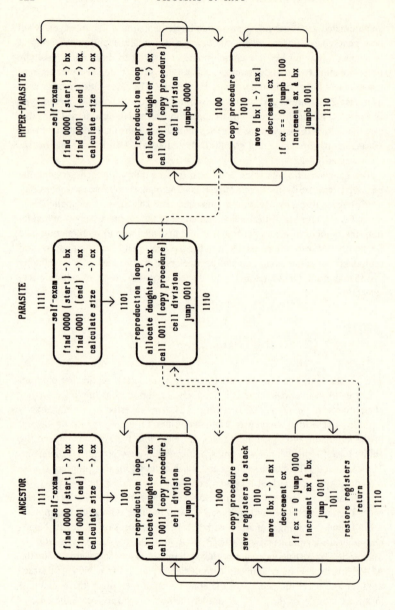

daughter cell. It then calls the copy procedure which copies the entire genome into the daughter-cell memory, one instruction at a time. The beginning of the copy procedure is marked by the four no-operation template: 1 1 0 0. Therefore, the call to the copy procedure is accomplished with the five instructions: CALL, NOP_0, NOP_0, NOP_1, and NOP_1.

When the genome has been copied, it executes the DIVIDE instruction, which causes the creature to lose write privileges on the daughter-cell memory, and gives an instruction pointer to the daughter cell (it also enters the daughter cell into the slicer and reaper queues). After this first replication, the mother cell does not examine itself again; it proceeds directly to the allocation of another daughter cell, then the copy procedure is followed by cell division, in an endless loop.

Forty-eight of the 80 instructions in the ancestor are no-operations. Groups of four no-operation instructions are used as complementary templates to mark twelve sites for internal addressing, so that the creature can locate its beginning and end, call the copy procedure, and mark addresses for loops and jumps in the code, etc. The functions of these templates are commented in the listing in Appendix C [not reprinted here].

RESULTS

General Behaviour of the System

Evolutionary runs of the simulator are begun by inoculating the soup of 60,000 instructions with a single individual of the 80-instruction ancestral genotype.

FIG. 3.1. Metabolic flow chart for the ancestor, parasite, hyper-parasite, and their interactions: ax, bx, and cx refer to CPU registers where location and size information are stored. [ax] and [bx] refer to locations in the soup indicated by the values in the ax and bx registers. Patterns such as 1101 are complementary templates used for addressing. Arrows outside boxes indicate jumps in the flow of execution of the programs. The dotted-line arrows indicate flow of execution between creatures. The parasite lacks the copy procedure; however, if it is within the search limit of the copy procedure of a host, it can locate, call, and execute that procedure, thereby obtaining the information needed to complete its replication. The host is not adversely affected by this informational parasitism, except through competition with the parasite, which is a superior competitor. Note that the parasite calls the copy procedure of its host with the expectation that control will return to the parasite when the copy procedure returns. However, the hyper-parasite jumps out of the copy procedure rather than returning, thereby seizing control from the parasite. It then proceeds to reset the CPU registers of the parasite with the location and size of the hyper-parasite, causing the parasite to replicate the hyper-parasite genome thereafter.

The passage of time in a run is measured in terms of how many Tierran instructions have been executed by the simulator. Most software development work has been carried out on a Toshiba 5200/100 laptop computer with an 80386 processor and an 80387 math co-processor operating at 20 Mhz. This machine executes over 12 million Tierran instructions per hour. Long evolutionary runs are conducted on mini and mainframe computers which execute about 1 million Tierran instructions per minute.

The original ancestral cell which inoculates the soup executes 839 instructions in its first replication, and 813 for each additional replication. The initial cell and its replicating daughters rapidly fill the soup memory to the threshold level of 80 per cent which starts the reaper. Typically, the system executes about 400,000 instructions in filling up the soup with about 375 individuals of size 80 (and their gestating daughter cells). Once the reaper begins, the memory remains roughly 80 per cent filled with creatures for the remainder of the run.

Once the soup is full, individuals are initially short-lived, generally reproducing only once before dying; thus, individuals turn over very rapidly. More slowly, there appear new genotypes of size 80, and then new size classes. There are changes in the genetic composition of each size class, as new mutants appear, some of which increase significantly in frequency, sometimes replacing the original genotype. The size classes which dominate the community also change through time, as new size classes appear (see below), some of which competitively exclude sizes present earlier. Once the community becomes diverse, there is a greater variance in the longevity and fecundity of individuals.

In addition to an increase in the raw diversity of genotypes and genome sizes, there is an increase in the ecological diversity. Obligate commensal parasites evolve, which are not capable of self-replication in isolated culture, but which can replicate when cultured with normal (self-replicating) creatures. These parasites execute some parts of the code of their hosts, but cause them no direct harm, except as competitors. Some potential hosts have evolved immunity to the parasites, and some parasites have evolved to circumvent this immunity.

In addition, facultative hyper-parasites have evolved, which can self-replicate in isolated culture, but when subjected to parasitism, subvert the parasites' energy metabolism to augment their own reproduction. Hyper-parasites drive parasites to extinction, resulting in complete domination of the communities. The relatively high degrees of genetic relatedness within the hyper-parasite-dominated communities leads to the evolution of sociality in the sense of creatures that can only replicate when they occur in aggregations. These social aggregations are then invaded by hyper-hyper-parasite cheaters.

Mutations and the ensuing replication errors lead to an increasing diversity of sizes and genotypes of self-replicating creatures in the soup. Within the first 100 million instructions of elapsed time, the soup evolves to a state in which about a dozen more-or-less persistent size classes coexist. The relative abundances and specific list of the size classes varies over time. Each size class consists of a number of distinct genotypes which also vary over time.

EVOLUTION

Micro-evolution

If there were no mutations at the outset of the run, there would be no evolution. However, the bits flipped as a result of copy errors or background mutations result in creatures whose list of 80 instructions (genotype) differs from the ancestor, usually by a single bit difference in a single instruction.

Mutations, in and of themselves, cannot result in a change in the size of a creature, they can only alter the instructions in its genome. However, by altering the genotype, mutations may affect the process whereby the creature examines itself and calculates its size, potentially causing it to produce an offspring that differs in size from itself.

Four out of the five possible mutations in a no-operation instruction convert it into another kind of instruction, while one out of five converts it into the complementary no-operation. Therefore, 80 per cent of mutations in templates destroy the template, while one in five alters the template pattern. An altered template may cause the creature to make mistakes in self-examination, procedure calls, or looping or jumps of the instruction pointer, all of which use templates for addressing.

Parasites. An example of the kind of error that can result from a mutation in a template is a mutation of the low-order bit of instruction 42 of the ancestor. Instruction 42 is a NOP_0, the third component of the copy procedure template. A mutation in the low-order bit would convert it into NOP_1, thus changing the template from 1 1 0 0 to: 1 1 1 0. This would then be recognized as the template used to mark the end of the creature, rather than the copy procedure.

A creature born with a mutation in the low-order bit of instruction 42 would calculate its size as 45. It would allocate a daughter cell of size 45 and copy only instructions 0 through 44 into the daughter cell. The daughter cell, then, would not include the copy procedure. This daughter genotype, consisting of 45 instructions, is named 0045aaa.

Genotype 0045aaa (Fig. 3.1) is not able to self-replicate in isolated culture. However, the semi-permeable membrane of memory allocation only protects write privileges. Creatures may match templates with code in the allocated memory of other creatures, and may even execute that code. Therefore, if creature 0045aaa is grown in mixed culture with 0080aaa, when it attempts to call the copy procedure, it will not find the template within its own genome, but if it is within the search limit (generally set at 200–400 instructions) of the copy procedure of a creature of genotype 0080aaa, it will match templates, and send its instruction pointer to the copy code of 0080aaa. Thus a parasitic relationship is established (see *Ecology* below). Typically, parasites begin to emerge within the first few million instructions of elapsed time in a run.

Immunity to Parasites. At least some of the size 79 genotypes demonstrate some measure of resistance to parasites. If genotype 45aaa is introduced into a soup, flanked on each side with one individual of genotype 0079aab, 0045aaa will initially reproduce somewhat, but will be quickly eliminated from the soup. When the same experiment is conducted with 0045aaa and the ancestor, they enter a stable cycle in which both genotypes coexist indefinitely. Freely evolving systems have been observed to become dominated by size 79 genotypes for long periods, during which parasitic genotypes repeatedly appear, but fail to invade.

Circumvention of Immunity to Parasites. Occasionally these evolving systems dominated by size 79 were successfully invaded by parasites of size 51. When the immune genotype 0079aab was tested with 0051aao (a direct, one-step descendant of 0045aaa in which instruction 39 is replaced by an insertion of seven instructions of unknown origin), they were found to enter a stable cycle. Evidently 0051aao has evolved some way to circumvent the immunity to parasites possessed by 0079aab. The 14 genotypes 0051aaa through 0051aan were also tested with 0079aab, and none were able to invade.

Hyper-parasites. Hyper-parasites have been discovered, (e.g. 0080gai, which differs by 19 instructions from the ancestor, Fig. 3.1). Their ability to subvert the energy metabolism of parasites is based on two changes. The copy procedure does not return, but jumps back directly to the proper address of the reproduction loop. In this way it effectively seizes the instruction pointer from the parasite. However, it is another change which delivers the *coup de grâce*: after each reproduction, the hyper-parasite re-examines itself, resetting the bx register with its location and the cx register with its size. After the instruction pointer of the parasite passes through this code, the CPU of the parasite contains the location and size of the hyper-parasite and the parasite thereafter replicates the hyper-parasite genome.

Social Hyper-parasites. Hyper-parasites drive the parasites to extinction. This results in a community with a relatively high level of genetic uniformity, and therefore high genetic relationship between individuals in the community. These are the conditions that support the evolution of sociality, and social hyper-parasites soon dominate the community. Social hyper-parasites (Fig. 3.2) appear in the 61-instruction size class. For example, 0061acg is social in the sense that it can only self-replicate when it occurs in aggregations. When it jumps back to the code for self-examination, it jumps to a template that occurs at the end rather than the beginning of its genome. If the creature is flanked by a similar genome, the jump will find the target template in the tail of the neighbour, and execution will then pass into the beginning of the active creature's genome. The algorithm will fail unless a similar genome occurs just before the active creature in memory. Neighbouring creatures cooperate by catching and passing on jumps of the instruction pointer.

It appears that the selection pressure for the evolution of sociality is that it facilitates size reduction. The social species are 24 per cent smaller than the ancestor. They have achieved this size reduction in part by shrinking their templates from four instructions to three instructions. This means that there are only eight templates available to them, and catching each others' jumps allows them to deal with some of the consequences of this limitation as well as to make dual use of some templates.

Cheaters: Hyper-hyper-parasites. The cooperative social system of hyper-parasites is subject to cheating, and is eventually invaded by hyper-hyper-parasites (Fig. 3.2). These cheaters (e.g. 0027aab) position themselves between aggregating hyper-parasites so that when the instruction pointer is passed between them, they capture it.

A Novel Self-examination. All creatures discussed thus far mark their beginning and end with templates. They then locate the addresses of the two templates and determine their genome size by subtracting them. In one run, creatures evolved without a template marking their end. These creatures located the address of the template marking their beginning, and then the address of a template in the middle of their genome. These two addresses were then subtracted to calculate half of their size, and this value was multiplied by two (by shifting left) to calculate their full size.

Macro-evolution

When the simulator is run over long periods of time, hundreds of millions or billions of instructions, various patterns emerge. Under selection for small sizes, there is a proliferation of small parasites and a rather interesting ecology

SOCIAL HYPER-PARASITES

SOCIAL HYPER-PARASITES
AND CHEATER

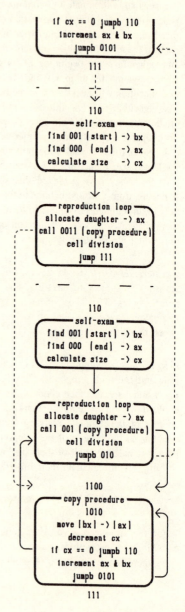

```
if cx == 0 jumpb 110
increment ax & bx
jumpb 0101
```

111

110
```
- self-exam -
find 001 (start) -> bx
find 000 (end)  -> ax
calculate size  -> cx
```

```
- reproduction loop -
allocate daughter -> ax
call 001 (copy procedure)
cell division
jumpb 010
```

1100
```
- copy procedure -
1010
move [bx] -> [ax]
decrement cx
if cx == 0 jumpb 110
increment ax & bx
jumpb 0101
```

111

```
if cx == 0 jumpb 110
increment ax & bx
jumpb 0101
```

111

110
```
- self-exam -
find 001 (start) -> bx
find 000 (end)  -> ax
calculate size   -> cx
```

```
- reproduction loop -
allocate daughter -> ax
call 0011 (copy procedure)
cell division
jump 111
```

110
```
- self-exam -
find 001 (start) -> bx
find 000 (end)  -> ax
calculate size   -> cx
```

```
- reproduction loop -
allocate daughter -> ax
call 001 (copy procedure)
cell division
jumpb 010
```

1100
```
- copy procedure -
1010
move [bx] -> [ax]
decrement cx
if cx == 0 jumpb 110
increment ax & bx
jumpb 0101
```

111

(see below). Selection for large creatures has usually led to continuous incrementally increasing sizes (but not to a trivial concatenation of creatures end-to-end) until a plateau in the upper hundreds is reached. In one run, selection for large size led to apparently open-ended size increase, evolving genomes larger than 23,000 instructions in length. This evolutionary pattern might be described as phyletic gradualism.

The most thoroughly studied case for long runs is where selection, as determined by the slicer function, is size neutral. The longest runs to date (as much as 2.86 billion Tierran instructions) have been in a size-neutral environment, with a search limit of 10,000, which would allow large creatures to evolve if there were some algorithmic advantage to be gained from larger size. These long runs illustrate a pattern which could be described as periods of stasis punctuated by periods of rapid evolutionary change, which appears to parallel the pattern of punctuated equilibrium described by Eldredge and Gould (1972) and Gould and Eldredge (1977).

Initially these communities are dominated by creatures with genome sizes in the 80s. This represents a period of relative stasis, which has lasted from 178 million to 1.44 billion instructions in the several long runs conducted to date. The systems then very abruptly (in a span of 1 or 2 million instructions) evolve into communities dominated by sizes ranging from about 400 to about 800. These communities have not yet been seen to evolve into communities dominated by either smaller or substantially larger size ranges.

The communities of creatures in the 400 to 800 size range also show a long-term pattern of punctuated equilibrium. These communities regularly come to be dominated by one or two size classes, and remain in that condition for long periods of time. However, they inevitably break out of that stasis and enter a period where no size class dominates. These periods of rapid evolutionary change may be very chaotic. Close observations indicate that at least at some of these times, no genotypes breed true. Many self-replicating genotypes will

---

FIG. 3.2. Metabolic flow chart for social hyper-parasites, their associated hyper-hyper-parasite cheaters, and their interactions. Symbols are as described for Fig. 3.1. Horizontal dashed lines indicate the boundaries between individual creatures. On both the left and right, above the dashed line at the top of the figure is the lowermost fragment of a social hyper-parasite. Note (on the left) that neighbouring social hyper-parasites cooperate in returning the flow of execution to the beginning of the creature for self-re-examination. Execution jumps back to the end of the creature above, but then falls off the end of the creature without executing any instruction of consequence, and enters the top of the creature below. On the right, a cheater is inserted between the two social hyper-parasites. The cheater captures control of execution when it passes between the social individuals. It sets the CPU registers with its own location and size, and then skips over the self-examination step when it returns control of execution to the social creature below.

coexist in the soup at these times, but at the most chaotic times, none will produce offspring which are even their same size. Eventually the system will settle down to another period of stasis dominated by one or a few size classes which breed true.

Two communities have been observed to die after long periods. In one community, a chaotic period led to a situation where only a few replicating creatures were left in the soup, and these were producing sterile offspring. When these last replicating creatures died (presumably from an accumulation of mutations), the community was dead. In these runs, the mutation rate was not lowered during the run, while the average genome size increased by an order of magnitude until it approached the average mutation rate. Both communities died shortly after the dominant size class moved from the 400 range to the 700 to 1,400 range. Under these circumstances it is probably difficult for any genome to breed true, and the genomes may simply have 'melted'. Another community died abruptly when the mutation rate was raised to a high level.

DIVERSITY

Most observations on the diversity of Tierran creatures have been based on the diversity of size classes. Creatures of different sizes are clearly genetically different, as their genomes are of different sizes. Different sized creatures would have some difficulty engaging in recombination if they were sexual; thus, it is likely that they would be different species. In a run of 526 million instructions, 366 size classes were generated, 93 of which achieved abundances of five or more individuals. In a run of 2.56 billion instructions, 1,180 size classes were generated, 367 of which achieved abundances of five or more.

Each size class consists of a number of distinct genotypes which also vary over·time. There exists the potential for great genetic diversity within a size class. There are 32^{80} distinct genotypes of size 80, but how many of those are viable self-replicating creatures? This question remains unanswered; however, some information has been gathered through the use of the automated genebank manager.

In several days of running the genebanker, over 29,000 self-replicating genotypes of over 300 size classes accumulated. The size classes and the number of unique genotypes banked for each size are listed in Table 3.1. The genotypes saved to disk can be used to inoculate new soups individually, or collections of these banked genotypes may be used to assemble 'ecological communities'. In 'ecological' runs, the mutation rates can be set to zero in order to inhibit evolution.

TABLE 3.1. *Table of numbers of size classes in the genebank*

(left column is size class, right column is number of self-replicating genotypes of that size class. 305 sizes, 29,275 genotypes)

0034	1	0092	362	0150	2	0205	5	0418	1	5213	2
0041	2	0093	261	0151	1	0207	3	0442	10	5229	4
0043	12	0094	241	0152	2	0208	2	0443	1	5254	1
0044	7	0095	211	0153	1	0209	1	0444	61	5888	36
0045	191	0096	232	0154	2	0210	9	0445	1	5988	1
0046	7	0097	173	0155	3	0211	4	0456	2	6006	2
0047	5	0098	92	0156	77	0212	4	0465	6	6014	1
0048	4	0099	117	0157	270	0213	5	0472	6	6330	1
0049	8	0100	77	0158	938	0214	47	0483	1	6529	1
0050	13	0101	62	0159	836	0218	1	0484	8	6640	1
0051	2	0102	62	0160	3229	0219	1	0485	3	6901	5
0052	11	0103	27	0161	1417	0220	2	0486	9	6971	2
0053	4	0104	25	0162	174	0223	3	0487	2	7158	3
0054	2	0105	28	0163	187	0226	2	0493	2	7293	3
0055	2	0106	19	0164	46	0227	7	0511	2	7331	1
0056	4	0107	3	0165	183	0231	1	0513	1	7422	70
0057	1	0108	8	0166	81	0232	1	0519	1	7458	1
0058	8	0109	2	0167	71	0236	1	0522	6	7460	7
0059	8	0110	8	0168	9	0238	1	0553	1	7488	1
0060	3	0111	71	0169	15	0240	3	0568	6	7598	1
0061	1	0112	19	0170	99	0241	1	0578	1	7627	63
0062	2	0113	10	0171	40	0242	1	0581	3	7695	1
0063	2	0114	3	0172	44	0250	1	0582	1	7733	1
0064	1	0115	3	0173	34	0251	1	0600	1	7768	2

TABLE 3.1. (cont.)

(left column is size class, right column is number of self-replicating genotypes of that size class. 305 sizes, 29,275 genotypes)

size	n	size	n	size	n	size	n	size	n	size	n
0065	4	0116	5	0174	15	0260	2	0683	1	7860	25
0066	1	0117	3	0175	22	0261	1	0689	1	7912	1
0067	1	0118	1	0176	137	0265	2	0757	6	8082	3
0068	2	0119	3	0177	13	0268	1	0804	2	8340	1
0069	1	0120	2	0178	3	0269	16	0813	1	8366	1
0070	7	0121	60	0179	1	0284	1	0881	6	8405	5
0071	5	0122	9	0180	16	0306	1	0888	1	8406	2
0072	17	0123	3	0181	5	0312	1	0940	2	8649	2
0073	2	0124	11	0182	27	0314	1	1006	6	8750	1
0074	80	0125	6	0184	3	0316	2	1016	1	8951	1
0075	56	0126	11	0185	21	0318	3	1077	5	8978	3
0076	21	0127	1	0186	9	0319	2	1116	1	9011	3
0077	28	0130	3	0187	3	0320	23	1186	1	9507	3
0078	409	0131	2	0188	11	0321	5	1294	7	9564	3
0079	850	0132	5	0190	20	0322	21	1322	7	9612	1
0080	7399	0133	2	0192	12	0330	1	1335	1	9968	1
0081	590	0134	7	0193	4	0342	5	1365	11	10259	31
0082	384	0135	1	0194	4	0343	1	1631	1	10676	1
0083	886	0136	1	0195	11	0351	1	1645	3	11366	5
0084	1672	0137	1	0196	19	0352	3	2266	1	11900	1
0085	1531	0138	1	0197	2	0386	1	2615	2	12212	2
0086	901	0139	2	0198	3	0388	1	2617	9	15717	3
0087	944	0141	6	0199	35	0401	2	2671	7	16355	1
0088	517	0143	1	0200	1	0407	3	3069	3	17356	3
0089	449	0144	4	0201	84	0411	1	4241	1	18532	1
0090	543	0146	1	0203	1	0412	22	5101	15	23134	14
0091	354	0149	1	0204	1	0416	3	5157	9		

Ecology

The only communities whose ecology has been explored in detail are those that operate under selection for small sizes. These communities generally include a large number of parasites, which do not have functional copy procedures, and which execute the copy procedures of other creatures within the search limit. In exploring ecological interactions, the mutation rate is set at zero, which effectively throws the simulation into ecological time by stopping evolution. When parasites are present, it is also necessary to stipulate that creatures must breed true, since parasites have a tendency to scramble genomes, leading to evolution in the absence of mutation.

0045aaa is a 'metabolic parasite'. Its genome does not include the copy procedure; however, it executes the copy procedure code of a normal host, such as the ancestor. In an environment favouring small creatures, 0045aaa has a competitive advantage over the ancestor; however, the relationship is density dependent. When the hosts become scarce, most of the parasites are not within the search limit of a copy procedure, and are not able to reproduce. Their calls to the copy procedure fail and generate errors, causing them to rise to the top of the reaper queue and die. When the parasites die off, the host population rebounds. Hosts and parasites cultured together demonstrate Lotka–Volterra population cycling (Lotka 1925; Volterra 1926; Wilson and Bossert 1971).

A number of experiments have been conducted to explore the factors affecting diversity of size classes in these communities. Competitive exclusion trials were conducted with a series of self-replicating (non-parasitic) genotypes of different size classes. The experimental soups were initially inoculated with one individual of each size. A genotype of size 79 was tested against a genotype of size 80, and then against successively larger size classes. The interactions were observed by plotting the population of the size 79 class on the x axis, and the population of the other size class on the y axis. Sizes 79 and 80 were found to be competitively matched such that neither was eliminated from the soup. They quickly entered a stable cycle, which exactly repeated a small orbit. The same general pattern was found in the interaction between sizes 79 and 81.

When size 79 was tested against size 82, they initially entered a stable cycle, but after about 4 million instructions, they shook out of stability and the trajectory became chaotic with an attractor that was symmetric about the diagonal (neither size showed any advantage). This pattern was repeated for the next several size classes, until size 90, where a marked asymmetry of the chaotic attractor was evident, favouring size 79. The run of size 79 against size 93 showed a brief stable period of about a million instructions, which then moved to a chaotic phase without an attractor, which spiralled slowly down until size 93 became extinct, after an elapsed time of about 6 million instructions.

An interesting exception to this pattern was the interaction between size 79 and size 89. Size 89 is considered to be a 'metabolic cripple', because although it is capable of self-replicating, it executes about 40 per cent more instructions to replicate than normal. It was eliminated in competition with size 79, with no loops in the trajectory, after an elapsed time of under 1 million instructions.

In an experiment to determine the effects of the presence of parasites on community diversity, a community consisting of 20 size classes of hosts was created and allowed to run for 30 million instructions, at which time only the eight smallest size classes remained. The same community was then regenerated, but a single genotype (0045aaa) of parasite was also introduced. After 30 million instructions, 16 size classes remained, including the parasite. This seems to be an example of a 'keystone' parasite effect (Paine 1966).

Symbiotic relationships are also possible. The ancestor was manually dissected into two creatures, one of size 46 which contained only the code for self-examination and the copy loop, and one of size 64 which contained only the code for self-examination and the copy procedure (Fig. 3.3). Neither could replicate when cultured alone, but when cultured together, they both replicated, forming a stable mutualistic relationship. It is not known if such relationships have evolved spontaneously.

DISCUSSION

The 'physical' environment presented by the simulator is quite simple, consisting of the energy resource (CPU time) doled out rather uniformly by the time-slicer, and memory space which is completely uniform and always available. In light of the nature of the physical environment, the implicit fitness function would presumably favour the evolution of creatures which are able to replicate with less CPU time, and this does, in fact, occur. However, much of the evolution in the system consists of the creatures discovering ways to exploit one another. The creatures invent their own fitness functions through adaptation to their biotic environment.

Parasites do not contain the complete code for self-replication; thus, they utilize other creatures for the information contained in their genomes. Hyper-parasites exploit parasites in order to increase the amount of CPU time devoted to the replication of their own genomes; thus hyper-parasites utilize other creatures for the energy resources that they possess. These ecological interactions are not programmed into the system, but emerge spontaneously as the creatures discover each other and invent their own games.

Evolutionary theory suggests that adaptation to the biotic environment (other organisms) rather than to the physical environment is the primary force driving

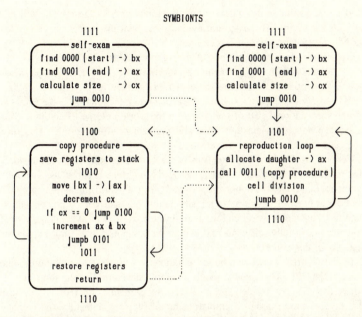

FIG. 3.3. Metabolic flow chart for obligate symbionts and their interactions. Symbols are as described for Fig. 3.1. Neither creature is able to self-replicate in isolation. However, when cultured together, each is able to replicate by using information provided by the other

the auto-catalytic diversification of organisms (Stanley 1973). It is encouraging to discover that the process has already begun in the Tierran world. It is worth noting that the results presented here are based on evolution of the first creature that I designed, written in the first instruction set that I designed. Comparison with the creatures that have evolved shows that the one I designed is not a particularly clever one. Also, the instruction set that the creatures are based on is certainly not very powerful (apart from those special features incorporated to enhance its evolvability). It would appear then that it is rather easy to create life. Evidently, virtual life is out there, waiting for us to provide environments in which it may evolve.

Emergence

Cariani (1991) has suggested a methodology by which emergence can be detected. His analysis is described as 'emergence-relative-to-a-model', where 'the

model . . . constitutes the observer's expectations of how the system will behave in the future'. If the system evolves such that the model no longer describes the system, we have emergence.

Cariani recognizes three types of emergence, in semiotic terms: syntactic,
semantic, and pragmatic. Syntactic operations are those of computation (symbolic). Semantic operations are those of measurement (e.g. sense perception)
and control (e.g. effectors), because they 'determine the relation of the symbols
in the computational part of the device to the world at large'. Pragmatic ('intentional') operations are those that are 'performance-measuring', and, hence
'the criteria which control the selection'.

Cariani has developed this analysis in the context of robotics, and considers
that the semantic operations should act at the interface between the symbolic
(computational) and the non-symbolic (real physical world). I can not apply his
analysis in precisely this way to my simulation, because there is no connection
between the Tierran world and the real physical world. I have created a virtual
universe that is fully self-contained, within the computer; thus, I must apply his
analysis in this context.

In the Tierran world, symbolic operations (syntactic), computations, take
place in the CPU. The 'non-symbolic', 'real physical world' is the soup (RAM)
where the creatures reside. The measurement (semantic) operations are those
that involve the location of templates; the effector operations are the copying
of instructions within the soup, and the allocation of memory (cells). Fitness
functions (pragmatic) are implicit, and are determined by the creatures themselves because they must effect their own replication.

Any program which is self-modifying can show syntactic emergence. As
long as the organization of the executable code changes, we have syntactic
emergence. This occurs in the Tierran world, as the executable genetic code of
the creatures evolves.

Semantic emergence is more difficult to achieve, as it requires the appearance of some new meaning in the system. This is found in the Tierran world
in the evolution of templates and their meanings. When a creature locates a
template, which has a physical manifestation in the 'real world' of the soup, the
location of the template appears in the CPU in the form of a symbol representing its address in the soup. For example, the beginning and end of the ancestor
are each marked by templates. That one 'means' beginning and the other 'means'
end is apparent from the computation made on the symbols for them in the
CPU: the two are subtracted to calculate the size of the creature, and copying
of the genome starts at the beginning address. Through evolution, a class of
creatures appeared which did not locate a template at their end, but rather one
in their centre. That the new template 'means' centre to these creatures is again
apparent from the computations made on its associated symbol in the CPU: the

beginning address is subtracted from the centre address, and the difference is then multiplied by two to calculate the size.

Pragmatic emergence is considered 'higher' by Cariani, and certainly it is the most difficult to achieve, because it requires that the system evolve new fitness functions. In living systems, fitness functions always reduce to: genotypes which leave a greater number of their genes in future generations will increase in frequency relative to other genotypes and thus have a higher fitness. This is a nearly tautological observation, but tautology is avoided in that the fitness landscape is shaped by specific adaptations that facilitate passing genes on.

For a pre-Cambrian marine algae living before the appearance of herbivores, the fitness landscape consists, in part, of a multi-dimensional space of metabolic parameter affecting the efficiency of the conversion of sunlight into usable energy, and the use of that energy in obtaining nutrients and converting them into new cells. Regions of this metabolic phase space that yield a greater efficiency at these operations also have higher associated fitnesses.

In order for pragmatic emergence to occur, the fitness landscape must be expanded to include new realms. For example, if a variant genotype of algae engulfs other algae, and thereby achieves a new mechanism of obtaining energy, the fitness landscape expands to include the parameters of structure and metabolism that facilitate the location, capture, and digestion of other cells. The fitness landscapes of algae lacking these adaptations also become altered, as they now include the parameters of mechanisms to avoid being eaten. Pragmatic emergence occurs through the acquisition of a new class of adaptation for enhancing passing genes on.

Pragmatic emergence occurs in the Tierran world as creatures which initially do not interact, discover means to exploit one another, and in response, means to avoid exploitation. The original fitness landscape of the ancestor consists only of the efficiency parameters of the replication algorithm, in the context of the properties of the reaper and slicer queues. When by chance, genotypes appear that exploit other creatures, selection acts to perfect the mechanisms of exploitation, and mechanisms of defence to that exploitation. The original fitness landscape was based only on adaptations of the organism to its physical environment (the slicer and reaper). The new fitness landscape retains those features, but adds to it adaptations to the biotic environment, the other creatures. Because the fitness landscape includes an ever-increasing realm of adaptations to other creatures which are themselves evolving, it can facilitate an autocatalytic increase in complexity and diversity of organisms.

In any computer model of evolution, the fitness functions are determined by the entity responsible for the replication of individuals. In genetic algorithms and most simulations, that entity is the simulator program; thus, the fitness function is defined globally. In the Tierran world, that entity is the creatures themselves; thus, the fitness function is defined locally by each creature in relation to its environment (which includes the other creatures). It is for this reason that pragmatic emergence occurs in the Tierran world.

In Tierra, the fitness functions are determined by the creatures themselves, and evolve with the creatures. As Cariani states, 'Such devices would not be useful for accomplishing *our* purposes as their evaluatory criteria might well diverge from our own over time.' This was the case from the outset in the Tierran world, because the simulator never imposed any explicit selection on the creatures. They were not expected to solve my problems, other than satisfying my passion to create life.

After describing how to recognize the various types of emergence, Cariani concludes that Artificial Life cannot demonstrate emergence because of the fully deterministic and replicable nature of computer simulations. This conclusion does not follow in any obvious way from the preceding discussions and does not seem to be supported. Furthermore, I have never known 'indeterminate' and 'unreplicable' to be considered as necessary qualities of life.

As a thought-experiment, suppose that we connect a Geiger counter near a radioactive source to our computer, and use the interval between clicks to determine the values in our random-number generator. The resulting behaviour of the simulation would no longer be deterministic or repeatable. However, the results would be the same, in any significant respect, as those obtained by using an algorithm to select the random numbers. Determinism and repeatability are irrelevant to emergence and to life. In fact, repeatability is a highly desirable quality of synthetic life because it facilitates study of life's properties.

Synthetic Biology

One of the most uncanny of evolutionary phenomena is the ecological convergence of biota living on different continents or in different epochs. When a lineage of organisms undergoes an adaptive radiation (diversification), it leads to an array of relatively stable ecological forms. The specific ecological forms are often recognizable from lineage to lineage. For example, among dinosaurs, the *Pterosaur, Triceratops, Tyrannosaurus*, and *Ichthyosaur* are ecological parallels, respectively, to the bat, rhinoceros, lion, and porpoise of modern mammals. Similarly, among modern placental mammals, the grey wolf, flying squirrel, great anteater, and common mole are ecological parallels, respectively, to the Tasmanian wolf, honey glider, banded anteater, and marsupial mole of the marsupial mammals of Australia.

Given these evidently powerful convergent forces, it should perhaps not be surprising that as adaptive radiations proceed among digital organisms, we encounter recognizable ecological forms, in spite of the fundamentally distinct physics and chemistry on which they are based. Ideally, comparisons should be made among organisms of comparable complexity. It may not be appropriate to compare viruses to mammals. Unfortunately, the organic creatures most comparable to digital organisms, the RNA creatures, are no longer with us. Since digital organisms are being compared to modern organic creatures of much greater complexity, ecological comparisons must be made in the broadest of terms.

In describing the results, I have characterized classes of organisms such as hosts, parasites, hyper-parasites, social, and cheaters. While these terms apply nicely to digital organisms, it can be tricky to examine the parallels between digital and organic organisms in detail. The parasites of this study cause no direct harm to their host; however, they do compete with them for space. This is rather like a vine which depends on a tree for support, but which does not directly harm the tree, except that the two must compete for light. The hyper-parasites of this study are facultative and subvert the energy metabolism of their parasite victims without killing them. I cannot think of an organic example that has all of these properties. The carnivorous plant comes close in that it does not need the prey to survive, and in that its prey may have approached the plant expecting to feed on it. However, the prey of carnivorous plants are killed outright.

We are not in a position to make the most appropriate comparison, between digital creatures and RNA creatures. However, we can apply what we have learned from digital organisms, about the evolutionary properties of creatures at that level of complexity, to our speculations about what the RNA world may have been like. For example, once an RNA molecule fully capable of self-replication evolved, might other RNA molecules lacking that capability have parasitized its replicatory function?

In studying the natural history of synthetic organisms, it is important to recognize that they have a distinct biology due to their non-organic nature. In order fully to appreciate their biology, one must understand the stuff of which they are made. To study the biology of creatures of the RNA world would require an understanding of organic chemistry and the properties of macro-molecules. To understand the biology of digital organisms requires a knowledge of the properties of machine instructions and machine language algorithms. However, fully to understand digital organisms, one must also have a knowledge of biological evolution and ecology. Evolution and ecology are the domain of biologists and machine languages are the domain of computer scientists. The knowledge chasm between biology and computer science is likely to hinder progress in the field of Artificial Life for some time. We need more individuals with a depth of knowledge in both areas in order to carry out the work.

Trained biologists will tend to view synthetic life in the same terms that they have come to know organic life. Having been trained as an ecologist and evolutionist, I have seen in my synthetic communities many of the ecological and evolutionary properties that are well known from natural communities. Biologists trained in other specialties will likely observe other familiar properties. It seems that what we see is what we know. It is likely to take longer before we appreciate the unique properties of these new life forms.

Artificial Life and Biological Theory

The relationship between Artificial Life and biological theory is twofold: (1) Given that one of the main objectives of AL is to produce evolution leading to spontaneously increasing diversity and complexity, there exists a rich body of biological theory that suggests factors that may contribute to that process; and (2) to the extent that the underlying life processes are the same in AL and organic life, AL models provide a new tool for experimental study of those processes, which can be used to test biological theory that cannot be tested by traditional experimental and analytic techniques (Ray 1991).

Furthermore, there exists a complementary relationship between biological theory and the synthesis of life. Theory suggests how the synthesis can be achieved, while application of the theory in the synthesis is a test of the theory. If theory suggests that a certain factor will contribute to increasing diversity, then synthetic systems can be run with and without that factor. The process of synthesis becomes a test of the theory.

At the molecular level, there has been much discussion of the role of transposable elements in evolution. It has been observed that most of the genome in eukaryotes (perhaps 90%) originated from transposable elements, while in prokaryotes, only a very small percentage of the genome originated through transposons (Doolittle and Sapienza 1980; Orgel and Crick 1980; Thomas 1971). It can also be noted that the eukaryotes, not the prokaryotes, were involved in the Cambrian explosion of diversity (Barbieri 1985). It has been suggested that transposable elements play a significant role in facilitating evolution (Green 1988; Jelinek and Schmid 1982; Syvanen 1984). These observations suggest that it would be an interesting experiment to introduce transposable elements into digital organisms.

The Cambrian explosion consisted of the origin, proliferation, and diversification of macroscopic multi-cellular organisms. The origin and elaboration of multi-cellularity was an integral component of the process. Buss (1987) provides a provocative discussion of the evolution of multi-cellularity, and explores the consequences of selection at the level of cell lines. From his discussion the following idea emerges (although he does not explicitly state this idea, in fact, he proposes a sort of inverse of this idea, p. 65): the transition from single to multi-celled existence involves the extension of the control of gene regulation by the mother cell to successively more generations of daughter cells. This is a concept which transcends the physical basis of life, and could be profitably applied to synthetic life in order to generate an analogue of multi-cellularity.

The Red Queen hypothesis (Van Valen 1973) suggests that in the face of a changing environment, organisms must evolve as fast as they can in order to simply maintain their current state of adaptation. 'In order to get anywhere you must run twice as fast as that' (Carroll 1865). A critical component of the environment for any organism is the other living organisms with which it must interact. Given that the species that comprise the environment are themselves evolving, the pace is set by the maximal rate that any species may change through evolution, and it becomes very difficult to actually get ahead. A maximal rate of evolution is required just to keep from falling behind. This suggests that interactions with other evolving species provide the primary driving force in evolution.

Much evolutionary theory deals with the role of biotic interactions in driving evolution. For example, it is thought that these are of primary importance in the maintenance of sex (Bell 1982; Charlesworth 1976; Maynard Smith 1971; Michod and Levin 1988). Stanley (1978) has suggested that the Cambrian explosion was sparked by the appearance of the first organisms that ate other organisms. These new herbivores enhanced diversity by preventing any single species of algae from dominating and competitively excluding others. These kinds of biotic interactions must be incorporated into synthetic life in order to move evolution.

Similarly, many abiotic factors are known to contribute to determining the diversity of ecological communities. Island biogeography theory considers how the size, shape, distribution, fragmentation, and heterogeneity of habitats contribute to community diversity (MacArthur and Wilson 1967). Various types of disturbance are also believed to significantly affect diversity (Huston 1979; Petraitis *et al.* 1989). All of these factors may be introduced into synthetic life in an effort to enhance the diversification of the evolving systems.

The examples just listed are a few of the many theories that suggest factors that influence biological diversity. In the process of synthesizing increasingly complex instances of life, we can incorporate and manipulate the states of these factors. These manipulations, conducted for the purposes of advancing the synthesis, will also constitute powerful tests of the theories.

Extending the Model

The approach to AL advocated in this work involves engineering over the first 3 billion years of life's history to design complex evolvable artificial organisms, and attempting to create the biological conditions that will set off a spontaneous evolutionary process of increasing diversity and complexity of organisms. This is a very difficult undertaking, because in the midst of the Cambrian explosion, life had evolved to a level of complexity in which emergent properties existed at many hierarchical levels: molecular, cellular, organismal, populational, and community.

In order to define an approach to the synthesis of life paralleling this historical stage of organic life, we must examine each of the fundamental hierarchical levels, abstract the principal biological properties from their physical representation, and determine how they can be represented in our artificial media. The simulator program determines not only the physics and chemistry of the virtual universe that it creates, but the community ecology as well. We must tinker with the structure of the simulator program in order to facilitate the existence of the appropriate 'molecular', 'cellular', and 'ecological' interactions to generate a spontaneously increasing diversity and complexity.

The evolutionary potential of the present model can be greatly extended by some modifications. In its present implementation, parasitic relationships evolve rapidly, but predation involving the direct usurpation of space occupied by cells is not possible. This could be facilitated by the introduction of a FREE (memory deallocation) instruction. However, it is unlikely that such predatory behaviour would be selected for because in the current system there is always free memory space available; thus, there would be little to be gained through seizing space from another creature. However, predation could be selected for by removing the reaper from the system.

Perhaps a more interesting way to favour predatory-type interactions would be to make instructions expensive. In the present implementation, there is no 'conservation of instructions', because the MOV_IAB instruction creates a new copy of the instruction being moved during self-replication. If the MOV_IAB instruction were modified such that it obeyed a law of conservation, and left behind all zeros when it moved an instruction, then instructions would not be so cheap. Creatures could be allowed to synthesize instructions through a series of bit-flipping and shifting operations, which would make instructions 'metabolically' costly. Under such circumstance, a soup of 'autotrophs' which synthesize all of their instructions could be invaded by a predatory creature which kills other creatures to obtain instructions.

Additional richness could be introduced to the model by modifying the way that CPU time is allocated. Rather than using a circular queue, creatures could deploy special arrays of instructions or bit patterns (analogous to chlorophyll) which capture potential CPU time packets raining like photons on to the soup. In addition, with instructions being synthesized through bit-flipping and shifting operations, each instruction could be considered to have a 'potential time' (i.e. potential energy) value which is proportional to its content of one bits. Instructions rich in ones could be used as time (energy) storage 'molecules' which could be metabolized when needed by converting the one bits to zeros to release the stored CPU time. The introduction of such an 'informational metabolism' would open the way for all sorts of evolution involving the exploitation of one organism by another.

Separation of the genotype from the phenotype would allow the model to move beyond the parallel to the RNA world into a parallel of the DNA-RNA-protein stage of evolution. Storage of the genetic information in relatively passive informational structures, which are then translated into the 'metabolically active' machine instructions would facilitate evolution of development, sexuality, and transposons. These features would contribute greatly to the evolutionary potential of the model.

These enhancements of the model represent the current directions of my continuing efforts in this area, in addition to using the existing model to further test ecological and evolutionary theory.[1]

REFERENCES

Ackley, D. H., and Littman, M. S. (1990), 'Learning from Natural Selection in an Artificial Environment', in *Proceedings of the International Joint Conference on Neural Networks*, i: *Theory Track, Neural and Cognitive Sciences Track* (Washington, DC, Winter 1990) (Hillsdale, NJ: Erlbaum).

Aho, A. V., Hopcroft, J. E., and Ullman, J. D. (1974), *The Design and Analysis of Computer Algorithms* (Reading, Mass.: Addison-Wesley).

Bagley, R. J., Farmer, J. D., Kauffman, S. A., Packard, N. H., Perelson, A. S., and Stadnyk, I. M. (1989), 'Modeling Adaptive Biological Systems', *Biosystems*, 23: 113–38.

Barbieri, M. (1985), *The Semantic Theory of Evolution* (London: Harwood).

Bell, G. (1982), *The Masterpiece of Nature: The Evolution and Genetics of Sexuality* (Berkeley: University of California Press).

—— (1989), *Sex and Death in Protozoa: The History of an Obsession* (Cambridge: Cambridge University Press).

Buss, L. W. (1987), *The Evolution of Individuality* (Princeton: Princeton University Press).

Cariani, P. (1991), 'Emergence and Artificial Life', in Langton *et al.* (1991), 775–97.

Carroll, L. (1865). *Through the Looking-Glass* (London: Macmillan).

Charlesworth, B. (1976), 'Recombination Modification in a Fluctuating Environment', *Genetics*, 83: 181–95.

[1] I thank Dan Chester, Robert Eisenberg, Doyne Farmer, Walter Fontana, Stephanie Forrest, Chris Langton, Stephen Pope, and Steen Rasmussen for their discussions or readings of the manuscripts. Contribution No. 142 from the Ecology Program, School of Life and Health Sciences, University of Delaware.

Cohen, F. (1984), 'Computer Viruses: Theory and Experiments' (Ph.D. diss., University of Southern California).

Dawkins, R. (1987), *The Blind Watchmaker* (New York: Norton).

—— (1989), 'The Evolution of Evolvability', in Langton (1989*b*), 201–20.

Denning, P. J. (1988), 'Computer Viruses', *American Scientist*, 76: 236–8.

Dewdney, A. K. (1984), 'Computer Recreations: In the Game Called Core War Hostile Programs Engage in a Battle of Bits', *Scientific American*, 250: 14–22.

—— (1985*a*), 'Computer Recreations: A Core War Bestiary of Viruses, Worms and Other Threats to Computer Memories', *Scientific American*, 252: 14–23.

—— (1985*b*), 'Computer Recreations: Exploring the Field of Genetic Algorithms in a Primordial Computer Sea Full of Flibs', *Scientific American*, 253: 21–32.

—— (1987), 'Computer Recreations: A Program Called MICE Nibbles its Way to Victory at the First Core War Tournament', *Scientific American*, 256: 14–20.

—— (1989), 'Of Worms, Viruses and Core War', *Scientific American*, 260: 110–13.

Doolittle, W. F., and Sapienza, C. (1980), 'Selfish Genes, the Phenotype Paradigm and Genome Evolution', *Nature*, 284: 601–3.

Eldredge, N., and Gould, S. J. (1972), 'Punctuated Equilibria: An Alternative to Phyletic Gradualism', in J. M. Schopf (ed.), *Models in Paleobiology* (San Francisco: Greeman, Cooper), 82–115.

Farmer, J. D., and Belin, A. (1991), 'Artificial Life: The Coming Evolution', in Langton *et al.* (1991), 815–40.

—— Kauffman, S. A., and Packard, N. H. (1986), 'Autocatalytic Replication of Polymers', *Physica D*, 22: 50–67.

Gould, S. J. (1989), *Wonderful Life: The Burgess Shale and the Nature of History* (New York: Norton).

—— and Eldredge, N. (1977), 'Punctuated Equilibria: The Tempo and Mode of Evolution Reconsidered', *Paleobiology*, 3: 115–51.

Green, M. M. (1988), 'Mobile DNA Elements and Spontaneous Gene Mutation', in M. E. Lambert, J. F. McDonald, and I. B. Weinstein (eds.), *Eukaryotic Transposable Elements as Mutagenic Agents* (Banbury Report 30; Cold Spring Harbor Laboratory), 41–50.

Holland, J. H. (1975), *Adaptation in Natural and Artificial Systems: An Introductory Analysis with Applications to Biology, Control, and Artificial Intelligence* (Ann Arbor: University of Michigan Press).

—— (1976), 'Studies of the Spontaneous Emergence of Self-Replicating Systems using Cellular Automata and Formal Grammars', in A. Lindenmayer and G. Rozenberg (eds.) *Automata, Languages, Development* (New York: North-Holland), 385–404.

Huston, M. (1979), 'A General Hypothesis of Species Diversity', *American Naturalist*, 113: 81–101.

Jelinek, W. R., and Schmid, C. W. (1982), 'Repetitive Sequences in Eukaryotic DNA and their Expression', *Annual Review of Biochemistry*, 51: 813–44.

Langton, C. G. (1986), 'Studying Artificial Life with Cellular Automata', *Physica D*, 22: 120–49.

—— (1987), 'Virtual State Machines in Cellular Automata', *Complex Systems*, 1: 257–71.

—— (1989*a*), 'Artificial Life', in Langton (1989*b*), 1–47.

—— (1989*b*), *Artificial Life: Proceedings of an Interdisciplinary Workshop on the Synthesis and Simulation of Living Systems* (Santa Fe Institute Studies in the Sciences of Complexity, Proceedings, 6; Redwood City, Calif.: Addison-Wesley).

—— Taylor, C., Farmer, J. D., and Rasmussen, S. (1991) (eds.), *Artificial Life II* (Santa

Fe Institute Studies in the Sciences of Complexity, Proceedings, 10; Redwood City, Calif.: Addison-Wesley).

Lotka, A. J. (1925), *Elements of Physical Biology* (Baltimore: Williams and Wilkins); repr. as *Elements of Mathematical Biology* (New York: Dover Press).

MacArthur, R. H., and Wilson, E. O. (1976), *The Theory of Island Biogeography* (Princeton: Princeton University 1967).

Maynard Smith, J. (1971), 'What Use is Sex?', *Journal of Theoretical Biology*, 30: 319–35.

Michod, R. E., and Levin, B. R. (1988) (eds.), *The Evolution of Sex* (Sutherland, Mass.: Sinauer).

Minsky, M. L. (1976), *Computation: Finite and Infinite Machines* (Englewood Cliffs, NJ: Prentice-Hall).

Morris, S. C. (1989), 'Burgess Shale Faunas and the Cambrian Explosion', *Science*, 246: 339–46.

Orgel, L. E., and Crick, F. H. C. (1980), 'Selfish DNA: The Ultimate Parasite', *Nature*, 284: 604–7.

Packard, N. H. (1989), 'Intrinsic Adaptation in a Simple Model for Evolution', in Langton (1989*b*), 141–55.

Paine, R. T. (1966), 'Food Web Complexity and Species Diversity', *American Naturalist*, 100: 65–75.

Pattee, H. H. (1989), 'Simulations, Realizations, and Theories of Life', in Langton (1989*b*), 64–77. Reprinted below as Chapter 15.

Petraitis, P. S., Latham, R. E., and Niesenbaum, R. A. (1989), 'The Maintenance of Species Diversity by Disturbance', *Quarterly Review of Biology*, 64: 393–418.

Rasmussen, S., Knudsen, C., Feldberg, R., and Hindsholm, M. (1990), 'The Coreworld: Emergence and Evolution of Cooperative Structures in a Computational Chemistry', *Physica D*, 42: 111–34.

Ray, T. S. (1991), 'Evolution and Optimization of Digital Organisms', in K. R. Billingsley, E. Derohanes, and H. Brown III (eds.), *Scientific Excellence in Supercomputing: The IBM 1990 Contest Prize Papers* (Athens, Ga.: Baldwin Press), 489–531.

Rheingold, H. (1988), 'Computer Viruses', *Whole Earth Review* (Fall), 106.

Spafford, E. H., Heaphy, K. A., and Ferbrache, D. J. (1989), *Computer Viruses: Dealing with Electronic Vandalism and Programmed Threats* (Arlington, Va.: ADAPSO).

Stanley, S. M. (1973), 'An Ecological Theory for the Sudden Origin of Multicellular Life in the Late Precambrian', *Proceedings of the National Academy of Sciences*, 70: 1486–9.

Syvanen, M. (1984), 'The Evolutionary Implications of Mobile Genetic Elements', *Annual Review of Genetics*, 18: 271–93.

Thomas, C. A. (1971), 'The Genetic Organization of Chromosomes', *Annual Review of Genetics*, 5: 237–56.

Van Valen, L. (1973), 'A New Evolutionary Law', *Evolutionary Theory*, 1: 1–30.

Volterra, V. (1926), 'Variations and Fluctuations of the Number of Individuals in Animal Species Living Together', in R. N. Chapman (ed.), *Animal Ecology* (New York: McGraw-Hill), 409–48.

Wilson, E. O., and Bossert, W. H. (1971), *A Primer of Population Biology* (Stamford, Conn.: Sinauers).

4

FORM AND ORDER IN EVOLUTIONARY BIOLOGY

RICHARD M. BURIAN AND
ROBERT C. RICHARDSON

1. INTRODUCTION

Stuart Kauffman's *The Origins of Order: Self-Organization and Selection in Evolution* (1993) is a large and ambitious attempt to bring about a major reorientation in theoretical biology and to provide a fundamental reinterpretation of the place of selection in evolutionary theory. Kauffman offers a formal framework which allows one to pose precise and well-defined questions about the constraints that self-organization imposes on the evolution of complex systems, and the relation of self-organization and selection. He says at the outset that he wants to 'delineate the spontaneous sources of order, the self-organized properties of simple and complex systems' and to understand how they 'permit, enable and limit the efficacy of natural selection' (1993, p. xiv).[1] As he says somewhat later, the central theme running through his book is that the order in organisms may largely reflect spontaneous order in complex systems (1993: 30). These evolutionary constraints are general and universal constraints intended to apply across the spectrum defined by biological specializations (see Maynard Smith *et al.* 1985 for a description of the range of developmental constraints). If Kauffman is right, he offers a vindication of D'Arcy Thomson's 'principle of discontinuity', emphasizing that 'nature proceeds "from one type to another" among organic as well as inorganic forms; and these types vary according to their own parameters, and are defined by physico-mathematical conditions of possibility' (1952: 1094). The reorientation required has strong philosophical overtones. Kauffman often speaks of

Reprinted (with minor revisions) from A. Fine, M. Forbes, and L. Wessels (eds.), *PSA 1990: Proceedings of the 1990 Biennial Meeting of the Philosophy of Science Association*, ii (East Lansing, Mich.: Philosophy of Science Association, 1991), 267–87. (Part of a Symposium with S. D. Mitchell, R. E. Page, and S. A. Kauffman, on 'Self-Organization, Selection, and Evolution'.)

[1] References are to Kauffman (1993). For an overview, we recommend Kauffman (1992).

complex, integrated systems as 'emergent', and is committed to a novel form of holism together with a revised view of the interrelationship between the biological and the physical sciences. The scope of his analysis is remarkable. He treats at some length the origin of life, neural and genetic networks, the interplay of proteins in metabolism, evolutionary theory, developmental biology and ontogeny, genetics, immunology, and a number of other disciplines. In each case, he looks to generic sources of order. In each case, it is surprising how much he finds.

We intend to focus particularly on the ways in which Kauffman aims to restructure a number of biological disciplines, including his treatment of the sources of order (sect. 2) and the relation between adaptation and organization (sect. 3). With this general groundwork in place, we shall raise a few of the issues that must be faced in understanding his enterprise. These include more specific questions about the role of adaptation in explaining order (sect. 4), and about the limitations of Kauffman's formal approach in explaining the distinctively biological (sect. 5). These are exploratory inquiries rather than objections to Kauffman's enterprise or approach. We hope to stimulate further discussion into the scope and limitations of self-organization in determining the course of evolution. Similarly, it is important to examine the relation of Kauffman's universal, or 'generic', constraints on evolution to more specific local constraints, such as those imposed by the characteristic materials out of which organisms are constructed, the manifestly accidental features characteristic of the *Bauplan* of a lineage, or the even more local vicissitudes of adaptation. We offer, as one would expect, no answers to these large questions. We hope only to focus the questions, and to bring out their importance for Kauffman's enterprise and for theoretical biology generally.

2. GENERIC PROPERTIES AS A SOURCE OF ORDER

The central novelty in Kauffman's approach to theoretical biology is his use of 'self-organized collective properties' or 'self-organizing systems'. These are formally characterized properties of complex systems, determined by the mode of aggregation of their constituent entities. Kauffman argues that these self-organized collective properties are sufficient to determine 'generic properties of complex systems'. *Generic properties*, in turn, are those that are statistically common within an array of systems for whatever reason, whether the consequence of some uniform selective pressure or because of the regularities governing the behaviour of the constituent entities and their organization. If they are due to self-organization, then these generic properties must be largely independent of selection or of the limitations imposed by phylogeny. They are the natural and expected consequences of simple components interacting in simple ways. These generic properties both create and limit the possibilities available to development, evolution, and metabolism. They are, to employ a useful expression from Donna Haraway, 'enabling constraints'.

The first thing to note is that there is nothing *distinctively biological* about the properties of complex systems, or the properties of their components, on which Kauffman draws in delineating these enabling constraints. Kauffman examines the higher level, abstract regularities of complex systems. His focus is on what is typical of classes, or ensembles, of systems specified in terms of their components and organization. The components are relatively simple, and their modes of combination are formally characterized. In contrast, the raw material of closed metabolisms is complex and interaction is highly specific; so is that of organismic development and of evolution. If it is possible to give a minimal—and perhaps minimalist—but correct, mathematical characterization of the features of these complex raw materials and their rules of combination, one then can hope to provide useful information about the ways in which they *can be combined*, the relative ease of combining them in certain ways, the possibilities which their combinations open up, and the behaviour of large ensembles of such entities. One might hope to derive properties of the behaviour of a 'typical' system of such entities from an adequate description of the components of the system and their rules of combination. One might even hope to predict some features of the resulting processes, or some patterns in the resulting taxonomic array. The features to be predicted will be, of course, generic rather than specific. The predictions would govern what would be common, rather than what would be universal; none the less, such predictions would be ambitious and testable. They would reveal, for example, something about what is likely to happen in the course of evolution even in the absence of selection. Just as appeals to genetic drift (Lande 1976; Lande and Arnold 1983) and the neutral theory (Kimura 1968, 1980, 1983) provide useful and important tools for evaluating the significance of selection by providing benchmarks from which to measure adaptive change, so likewise a serious understanding of the generic sources of order would provide an analysis of what is likely to happen in the absence of selection. The establishment of null hypotheses of this sort is a major accomplishment. If well established and relatively precise, they provide expectations against which to test the workings of selection. Deviations of observed genomic architectures or actual distributions of evolutionary trees, compared with Kauffman's null hypotheses, could be used to detect perturbing effects of selection or other 'agents' of evolutionary change. Such null hypotheses would also allow us to evaluate the importance of more local phylogenetic constraints by seeing what aspects of form might be expected even in their absence. Local effects can be seen only against a backdrop that defines what is generally to be expected.

Among the 'predictions' which Kauffman derives from his formal models are the following: typically, evolutionary radiations, even in the absence of selection, will behave like that in the Cambrian explosion, with most of the radiation coming early, followed by pruning and refining among a reduced number of basic body plans. More recently, there has been an explosion of such work, partly following Kauffman's lead. Again, he offers this: evolutionary modifications in early ontogeny will exhibit a 'locking in' of processes in early development; consequently, a similarity in early ontogeny would be expected across a wide array of taxonomic groups. Yet again, we have this: in the development of multicellular organisms with a large number of cell-types, the cells of any particular lineage (if they can switch type at all) will normally be competent to switch to only one, two, or (rarely) three of the cell-types in the body. Finally, we have this: the number of cell-types across lineages will increase roughly as the square root of the number of structural genes.

The predictions just listed may sound cheap, because they represent claims already accepted by many biologists. The crucial point is that they are derived, *without* parameter-fixing or other formal trickery, from elementary mathematical models basic to Kauffman's work—models that *do not incorporate selection or drift*. Kauffman uses such models to make many more predictions, some of which are controversial. For now, let these stand as illustrations of the sorts of results he can be expected to achieve.

Complexity of certain sorts can be mathematically characterized. For example, a soup of prebiotic molecules that interact with one another will have certain probabilities of forming substances which enter into mutually catalytic interactions and of forming a collection of molecules that can produce yet more catalytically interacting molecules of increasing complexity and stability. Such a system, once established, will evolve. This does not require that any single molecule be auto-catalytic or that there be any genetic information or template; it simply requires that the density of molecules that interact—in part by catalysing reactions involving other molecules—be sufficiently great that the molecules act collectively as an auto-catalytic set. Such a scenario—which is, indeed, a moderately plausible one with the additional feature that it includes a path by which template functions and auto-catalysis might enter the picture—is developed at some length in Kauffman's chapter 7 and amplified in chapters 8 and 9. That work has been elaborated in extensive simulation studies, now leading to experimental work. For present purposes, the conceptual basis for these studies yields a take-home moral even without paying serious attention to the details: the likelihood of forming auto-catalytic sets and the likelihood that any that *are* formed will have certain properties is determined by the statistics of the interactions among high numbers of organic molecules within certain ranges of dilutions and boundary conditions.

Molecules may be specified abstractly by their relationships to one another—including, for example, the effects they have on other molecules and their reactions. If one can get a fix on the right boundary conditions, the rules of organic chemistry determine the transition probabilities between chemical species and the changes in those probabilities caused by the addition of particular molecules at particular densities. These probabilities, in turn, determine the likelihood of forming auto-catalytic sets and of those sets having certain properties; for example, they determine the likelihood of properties that do or do not favour formation of RNA or RNA-mediated catalytic reactions. Once auto-catalytic sets of the sorts here hinted at are formed, some of their behaviours (for example, their interactions as wholes) are not readily derivable from the rules of organic chemistry. Such sets are thus 'emergent' entities of a new sort, distinct from that of any simple collection of organic molecules. They could, in short, be the stuff of life.

The treatment of these matters in Kauffman's book is far more serious than in our simple fable. But the *strategy* of argumentation is characteristic of the actual cases Kauffman discusses. For there to be a metabolism, an immune system, evolution of adaptations among competing organisms, or orderly modes of development, there must be a substrate of complexly organized entities. Kauffman's theoretical strategy, typical of that of physicists working on spin glasses and like matters, is to analyse this substrate as an ensemble of relatively simple and uninteresting entities sharing some intrinsic characteristics and modes of interaction. This procedure allows one to abstract from the particularities that distinguish one member of the ensemble from another. The focus is then shifted to what is common among elements of the ensemble: the interaction between these constituents, and the effects of their organization on the evolution of the systems they constitute. This is the stuff of emergence (cf. Bechtel and Richardson 1992, 1993).

Other things being equal, the characteristics of specialized components and their modes of interaction determine what sorts of metabolism, immune system, developmental program, or patterns of evolution are likely and what sorts unlikely; systems consisting of such specialized components will be prone to form complexes of some kinds and not of others, to form networks of some kinds, but not of others, to have histories of some kinds, but not of others. Kauffman systematically abstracts from differences between and among constituents of the systems he is considering. For example, in modelling metabolism, Kauffman ignores differences among polypeptides, instead analysing 'typical' interactions and relationships between them. Similarly, he applies formally identical models in different and disparate domains; for example, a model appropriate to the interaction of polypeptides could also apply to genomes or cell-types, or even to the evolution of species within an ecosystem. Thus, the differences among constituents typically do not enter into Kauffman's characterization of higher-level entities or their evolution. Much of his work involves the extraction of 'generic properties' of higher-level systems through the use of mathematical modelling and computer simulations—but always also with an eye to what is biologically reasonable and realistic. In brief, Kauffman holds that there is a sort of statistical mechanics governing ensembles of complex systems, depending only on formally characterizable properties of underlying entities. These statistical features describe many interesting and important features of major biological systems and their evolution.

3. ADAPTIVE EVOLUTION AND ORGANIZATION

The method of reasoning that Kauffman employs to determine which collective properties are generic, and the consequences of the organizational properties of complex systems, is of quite general interest. We shall illustrate them in this section with two central examples that play a crucial role in his book: fitness landscapes and genomic networks. These examples illustrate, respectively, the relative autonomy of self-organizing properties of complex systems from the limitations of selection and the sources of spontaneous order. We shall see that both embody similar abstract and formal characterizations which, in the terms we have used, contain nothing distinctively biological. None the less, their biological interpretations are of sweeping importance.

3.1. Adaptive Landscapes

The general problem Kauffman poses in examining adaptive landscapes can be understood this way. We can suppose there is an intrinsically favoured generic order for some class, or ensemble, of systems. Suppose they are naturally blue. We can also suppose that there is selection favouring some member or subset of that ensemble, which deviates from the favoured generic order. Selection favours red. Is it likely or even possible that the generic order will be discernible within the population even when it is selected against? Is it, conversely, likely or even possible that the selected subset will constitute a significant, or a dominant, part of the observed order? Will we see blue or red? If the generic order will be discernible even when it is selected against, then its presence when it is not selected against is unremarkable. As Kauffman says, 'if selection can only slightly displace evolutionary systems from the generic properties of the underlying ensembles, those properties will be widespread in organisms,

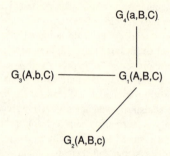

FIG. 4.1. One-step transformations in a haploid model with two alleles at each locus. G_1 can be transformed into any one of three different genotypes (G_2, G_3, or G_4,) by altering a single locus (A, B, or C) to an alternative form (a, b, or c)

not *because* of selection, but *despite* it' (1993: 24). Kauffman demonstrates that the generic order will be discernible across a wide variety of differences in parameter values—blue will shine through—by exploring the statistical structure of fitness landscapes as population size (N) and integration (K) vary. This is what he calls the NK model. Generic order is the result of organization, which dominates selection. We can see the general point fairly easily by looking at the two limiting cases.

For the sake of concreteness and simplicity, consider a simple haploid system with three genes and two alleles at each locus. Any one genotype can be transformed into three others by single mutations. In Fig. 4.1 the genotype G_1 (A,B,C) can be transformed into any of three others, G_2 (A,B,c), G_3 (A,b,C), or G_4 (a,B,C) by modifying exactly one allele to its alternative form. There will be eight possible genotypes, in all, in an ordered space illustrated in Fig. 4.2.

The structure of the space determines the number of mutational steps needed to transform any one genotype into any other. To find an adaptive landscape, we need only calculate the fitness to be assigned to each genotype. The contribution of each gene to the fitness of a genotype will, in general, depend on other genes present at other loci. The fitness contribution of A to the genotype G_1 will not, in general, be the same as the fitness contribution of A to the genotype G_2. Kauffman tells us the fitness w_i of an allele i is a vector composed of the K contributions to w_i, plus i's own contribution. If genes at the second and third loci in our simple model affect the fitness of A in G_1, then w_A can be treated as composed of the independent contribution of A to its own fitness, and the modifications induced by B and C. The fitness of the genotype is then the total of the fitnesses of the N genes in the system. Normalizing to take account for the number of genes, the result Kauffman gives us is this:

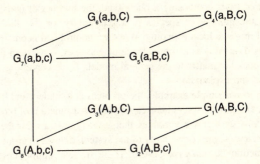

FIG. 4.2. Structure of a space with three dimensions. Once again, each of the genotypes can be modified by single steps into exactly three other forms (D = 3). There are three loci (N = 3), and two alleles at each locus (A = 2)

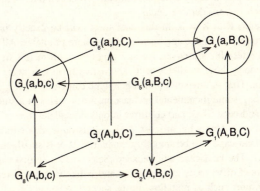

FIG. 4.3. An adaptive landscape in a three-dimensional space (D = 3) with three loci (N = 3) and two alleles at each locus (A = 2). Arrows indicate the direction of higher fitness. So, for example, $W_{G4} > W_{G1} > W_{G2}$. Optima are indicated by circles

$$W_G = (\Sigma w_i)/N$$

What appears initially complex turns out to have a simple form. Having determined the fitness for each genotype—that is, each node—we end up with a directed graph. The simple structure in Fig. 4.2 becomes a three-dimensional fitness landscape in Fig. 4.3. We have an adaptive landscape with two local optima (G_4 and G_7) and two minima (G_3 and G_5).

Notice that, though we have described this as if it were a simple haploid system, nothing depends on that interpretation. N might be the number of genes in the genotype, but it might equally be the number of amino acids in a protein, the number of traits composing a phenotype, the number of conspecifics in a population, the number of species in a community, or, for that matter, the number of firms in a local economy. Whether the problem is one of explaining evolutionary dynamics as a consequence of genomes, ecosystem dynamics, or economics does not matter to the general model. There is nothing distinctively biological in the explanation.

To return to our simple example, the problem is to understand how adaptive walks vary, and how adaptive landscapes vary, as a function of other variables. Kauffman tells us that the variables that matter most are N, the number of components, and K, the connectivity of the system, defined in terms of the number of interactions *for each component*. There are two limiting cases. If K = 0, then there is no interaction among components and fitness is simply additive. The total fitness of a genotype is simply the sum of the intrinsically determined fitnesses of the N genes which constitute it. If K = (N − 1), then every component interacts with every other, and interaction is at a maximum. Kauffman explores each in considerable detail.

Let us begin with K = 0. In this case there will be exactly one optimum genotype, composed of the aggregate of the N more fit alleles. All other genotypes will be less fit. Moreover, for any genotype with m less fit alleles, any alteration among those m alleles to its alternative form will bring us closer to the optimum. That is, any sub-optimal genotype can climb to W_{max} by m steps, each providing some incremental increase in fitness. This is a smooth, highly correlated landscape. If G_1 and G_2 differ in only one allele, then with N alleles, they can differ in fitness by, at most, 1/N. If N is large, this will be relatively small. The landscape will be smoothly graduated. If N is small, any increment will be large. The landscape will be steep. Selection in the first case will have relatively small differences to work with, and is likely to be overcome by disruptive pressures such as mutation. In the second, relatively small differences will yield large effects under disruption. In either case, we should expect shifts away from the optimum. If red occurs only at the peaks, we will see lots of blue.

It is possible to quarrel with the details. As Kauffman notices, normalization is largely responsible for the resulting correlated landscape. It is true that the K = 0 case yields a correlated landscape when N is large: the fitness of any genotype will be a relatively good—that is, a better than chance—predictor of the fitness of any of its one mutant neighbours. But this does not mean that all changes are equally good. If G_1 differs from both G_2 and G_3 by only one step, then either change can result in a maximum improvement of 1/N, but the magnitude of the changes could also differ by several orders of magnitude. A change from G_1 to G_2 might result in a change in fitness of 1/N, while a change from G_1 to G_3 might result in a change in fitness of 1/1000N. At a smaller scale, the fitness landscape might look very rugged indeed.

Now consider the other extreme, when $K = (N - 1)$. These are fully integrated networks, where each component interacts with every other. Any change in any unit changes everything everywhere else too. These are Cuvier's organisms, and Leibniz's world. The differences between this and the $K = 0$ case are striking. Even if there is only one *global* optimum, there will be a plethora of local optima, and it will be hard to find the global optimum in the space of possibilities. Kauffman shows that the expected number of local optima is, in fact, $2^N/(N + 1)$. As N increases the number of local optima increases drastically. Moreover, fitness values—even for neighbours removed by one step— are entirely uncorrelated; that is, a mutant differing by only one locus differs randomly from its parent. This 'rugged fitness landscape' has two important dynamic consequences. First, adaptive walks will reach only a small fraction of the local optima, and, therefore, they are unlikely to reach the global optimum. Once again, we should be able to see any generic order in the ensemble. Blue will show through. Second, since there is massive interaction, there will be conflicting constraints on every gene; satisfying conflicting constraints will cause adaptive peaks to fall towards the mean fitness of the ensemble. It is harder to satisfy two people than one, and impossible to satisfy everyone. 'Accessible optima', Kauffman tells us, 'become ever poorer. Fitness peaks dwindle' (1993: 52). As a consequence 'Optima become hardly better than chance genotypes in the space of possibilities' (1993: 53). Correlation between the fitness of alternative genotypes therefore increases. Heritability of fitness decreases, and the response to selection slows. As the fitness peaks dwindle, approaching the mean fitness, alternative local optima will become more readily accessible, and disruptive forces should spread the population across the landscape. We see more blue.

Kauffman says this reveals a 'fundamental restraint facing adaptive evolution' (1993: 53). Everything depends on N and K. If K is much smaller than N, then there will be high optima, but any genotype will be only marginally better than its neighbours in the space of genotypes. If N is approximately the same order as K, then there will be a host of local optima, but any one genotype will be only marginally better than the average. In both cases, sub-optimal forms will be common: '. . . powerful spontaneously ordered properties typical of most ensemble members will almost certainly still be found [even] in the presence of strong selection' (1993: 29).

Kauffman goes on to consider various wrinkles in this basic model and their implications for adaptive evolution and organization. He considers the effects of accumulated mutations, longer jumps in the adaptive space, recombination, variable environments, sex, and much more. In every case, the implications are explored with a careful eye to realistic development, and rigour.

The power of the resulting vision is considerable. Let us briefly point towards two implications. First, consider what is often called 'Von Baer's law'

(Gould 1977; Wimsatt 1986; Wimsatt and Schank 1988): there is generally greater resemblance among embryonic forms than adult forms, and greater resemblance among early embryos than later ones.[2] Differentiation occurs only later in ontogeny. Why would modifications of earlier stages be less common?[3] Kauffman observes that if early modifications affect many traits, then mutations affecting (early) embryonic stages will be adapting on highly uncorrelated fitness landscapes. It will be harder to find viable mutants. Correspondingly, mutations affecting later stages will be adapting on relatively correlated fitness landscapes. Finding viable alternatives will be relatively easy. Second, Kauffman offers an explanation of the pattern of rapid proliferation and subsequent constriction found in the Cambrian explosion. The initial explosion at higher taxonomic levels occurs because even jumps of a broad scale will find locally adapted peaks (or comparable peaks); but after this initial success, the landscape will become more differentiated. Finding improvements will get harder and harder.

3.2. Genomic Regulatory Networks

If the story we have just recounted from Kauffman is correct, the origins of generic order do not lie in adaptive evolution. One source of such order, Kauffman claims, lies in intrinsically organized mechanisms, or in self-organization. The general strategy Kauffman employs in exploring the importance of self-organization can be illustrated by turning to genomic regulation (which occupies Kauffman's attention in chapters 11–13). The problem Kauffman poses is *how* genetic regulatory systems can be maintained in the face of genetic mutation and recombination, both of which should tend to disrupt and disaggregate them. Kauffman describes his project this way:

The genome is a system in which a large number of genes and their products directly and indirectly regulate one another's activities. The proper aim of molecular and evolutionary biology is not merely to analyse their structure and dynamical behaviour, but also to comprehend why they have more or less the architecture and behaviour observed and how they may evolve in the face of continuing mutations. I shall suggest that we must build statistical theories of the expected structure and behaviour of such networks. Those expected properties then become testable predictions of the body of theory. If discovered in organisms, those properties then find their explanation as the typical or

---

[2] Historically, this is only a rough and misleading approximation. Von Baer did hold that there was greater resemblance among embryonic forms than adult forms, and greater resemblance among early embryos than later ones; but this was because he thought earlier forms were relatively *unformed and undifferentiated*. Evolution, like development, he thought of as a process of differentiation, and thus not a matter of divergence so much as specialization.

[3] But see Raff (1987), Raff and Wray (1989), and Raff *et al.* (1990) for a discussion of ontogenetic processes in sea urchins which suggests this is simply false.

generic properties of the ensemble of genomic regulatory systems which evolution is exploring. (1993: 412)

The problem is one of understanding how to maintain an optimal or nearly optimal network in the face of mutational pressure, which will tend to create sub-optimal genotypes. Mutation pressure can be thought of, as we have said, as tending to distribute genotypes more broadly over a fitness landscape, whereas selection would tend to concentrate the distribution of genotypes within a population over a narrower and more optimal region of the space. In genomic regulatory systems, mutations alter the structure of connections within the system. However, an additional problem derives from research on the mechanisms of gene expression. There are, as is well known, complex sets of genes which regulate the expression of other genes. The more complex the regulatory system, the more unstable and delicate it would seem to be; for the more complex it is, the more targets there are which can be disrupted by mutation. Moreover, mutations or transpositions in regulatory genes would alter the expression of genes as much—and in fact more—than would mutations in non-regulatory genes. High selection pressures would be required to counter the mutation rate and maintain the regulatory system. Given the actual complexity of the genome, Kauffman concludes it is implausible that selection could maintain order.

Kauffman suggests, alternatively, that the stability of the regulatory system is not something that requires a special explanation in terms of selection. If the genome consists of large ensembles of genes, mutually influencing and regulating one another, then, he argues, there will be a natural, generic, order to the system which is maintained independently of the influence of selection. The genome is a *spontaneously self-organizing system*. To support this suggestion, he turns to the statistical features of systems with multiple interconnections. Kauffman looks at the patterns of interactions between genes instead of the specific effects of any single gene or set of genes. In many cases, he claims, the critical determinant of the genome's behaviour is the self-organizing pattern of connections; no particular gene or set of genes must be maintained by selection.

Kauffman models genetic networks abstractly, just as he models adaptive change abstractly. He assumes as a first approximation that genomic networks can be modelled as Boolean switching networks (1993: 441 ff.). Each gene will 'regulate' other genes, either directly or indirectly, and either alone or in conjunction with other genes. When a gene directly or indirectly regulates its own behaviour, we have a feedback loop. Since we are limited to Boolean operations and a finite number of nodes, a finite number of states (defined in terms of configurations of nodes) will be possible. It follows that such a network must eventually return to a previous state. Since a Boolean system is deterministic, these are cycles in the state space. The cycles constitute stable *dynamical*

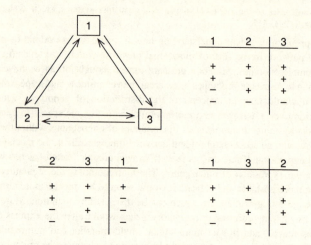

1	2	3
+	+	+
+	−	+
−	+	+
−	−	−

2	3	1
+	+	+
+	−	−
−	+	−
−	−	−

1	3	2
+	+	+
+	−	+
−	+	+
−	−	−

FIG. 4.4. A Simple Boolean Network with Three Nodes and Eight Possible States. Unit 1 is an AND gate, assuming a + value iff both units 2 and 3 assumed a + value on the previous cycle. That is, we have a function from <...+ +> to <+......>. Units 2 and 3 are OR gates, assuming a + value if any other unit assumed a + value on the previous cycles, and otherwise assuming a − value. That is, we have a function from either <+......> or <......+> to <...+...> and from either <+......> or <...+...> to <......+>

attractors for the network: once a system enters a cycle, it will repeat that cycle indefinitely.

As a simple illustration, we can consider a system consisting of three units, each sending activation signals to the other two, in which the response of each unit to the incoming signals is a Boolean AND or OR operation. A system with three 'genes' has eight possible patterns of activation (arrayed in a space isomorphic to the genotype space of Fig. 4.2). In the specific network shown in Fig. 4.4, the value of unit 1 is + if the values of both units 2 and 3 were + on the previous cycle. It is governed by an AND function. Units 2 and 3 will record a + value if any other unit assumed a + value in the previous cycle, and otherwise will assume a − value. They are OR Gates. We assume the network is synchronously updated: a pattern at time t completely determines the new pattern to be found at t + 1. Since there are a finite number of states, and deterministic transitions, the system will inevitably encounter cycles, which it will repeat indefinitely. These are dynamical attractors, or attractor state cycles. For example, the alternation between <--+> and <-+-> is a stable cycle. Which cycle a given network will settle into depends totally upon the starting-point.

Kauffman assumes that the genes within a genomic regulatory network can be treated as nodes in the model. The connections between nodes provide the vehicle for one 'gene' to regulate the behaviour of another. He then analyses the statistical properties of such networks, by looking at the effects of different connectivity, different rules, different numbers of genes, and the effects of mutation on the resulting networks. As with adaptive landscapes, the ratio of connections to nodes turns out to be highly important: the ratio of the number of connections within the system (M) to the number of genes (N) affects the expected number of genes any gene influences directly and the connectivity of the network.[4] This in turn affects how many steps are required for a gene to communicate to all the genes it regulates. It likewise affects the size of feedback loops, and the chances of a given gene receiving feedback, via a loop, from itself. If M is significantly less than N, then there will be a number of relatively independent sets of nodes connected with one another in a tree structure. As M increases, the average size of these trees grows and they tend to overlap and merge; moreover, feedback loops form. Once M exceeds N, we have a richly interconnected tree with multiple feedback loops (ch. 11, *passim*.).

Kauffman also assumes that genetic regulatory networks exhibit a relatively low average connectivity. Given a physical interpretation, this means that the regulatory functions of genes are highly specific: any given gene will regulate, and be regulated by, relatively few genes. Kauffman develops models that specify some of the details of interactions within such networks. He considers Boolean networks where each unit (gene) can have one of two values (on, off) and sends out signals to other units. The inputs to other units determine the next value of these units, again using Boolean operations. He focuses especially on systems in which the value of one regulating unit can suffice to guarantee that the regulated unit assumes one of its two values. He calls these *canalyzing functions*, and says that the majority of known genes in bacteria and viruses are governed by such Boolean functions. (The AND function governing unit 1 above is a canalyzing function, since a negative value for either unit 2 or unit 3 is sufficient to ensure that 1 will be negative on the next cycle. Likewise OR is a canalyzing function, since a positive value for either input unit is sufficient to ensure a positive value in the target unit on the next cycle.) Kauffman's procedure is then to look at the total set, or ensemble, of large regulatory systems (10,000 < N < 250,000) under the constraints of a low K and a limitation on the allowable Boolean operations. This tells us what to expect, statistically, given just these local constraints. It is a Kauffmanian null hypothesis governing the expected features of genomic systems (1993: 470 ff.).

---

[4] It is worth emphasizing that M is the number of connections within a network, whereas K is the number of connections per component. That is, K is just M/N where N is the number of components. When faced with systems that exhibit relatively low connectivity (K), Kauffman tends to look at the consequences of variations in M.

Once again we have a general and simple formal model, depending on no assumptions that are distinctively biological. Kauffman suggests that each distinct attractor-state cycle can be interpreted as a distinct cell-type in the repertoire of the genomic system. When the system settles into one cycle, it produces one cell-type. When it settles into another cycle, it produces another cell-type. These are the cell-types into which the system settles naturally. To support the claim that his network provides a model of such cell-types, Kauffman identifies a number of similarities between the properties of the attractor-state cycles and the cell-types found in eukaryotes: (1) The number of cell-types in an organism and the number of attractor-state cycles in a network both roughly equal the square root of the number of constituent genes; (2) a large core of units in networks, as well as genes in organisms, are ubiquitously active in all attractor states or cell-types in an organism; (3) the patterns of activation in attractor states as well as the patterns of gene expression in different cell-types are highly similar; (4) a network attractor state or a cell-type can be induced to differentiate directly only to a few neighbouring attractor states or cell-types; and (5) both networks and cell-types are highly stable and resistant to change in the face of alteration in the network.

Kauffman is able to explore the conditions under which such networks maintain their stability and the role selection might play in maintaining such stability. He begins by examining the behaviour of highly interconnected systems undergoing random mutations, investigating the effects of these mutations on fitness and the selection strength necessary to maintain the network in a high fitness state. He stipulates, arbitrarily, that some specific set of connections is to count as optimal, and specifies a measure of fitness, in terms of the percentage of connections which are 'correct' by comparison with the standard. The fitness for a given network, W_x, is defined thus (1993: 429):

$$W_x = b + (1 - b)(G_x/T)^a$$

where T is the total number of regulatory connections in the network, G_x is the number of 'good' connections in x, and b is a residual basal fitness in the absence of any 'good' connections. The value of a corresponds to the three broad ways fitness might correlate with the fraction of good connections; that is, it determines the shape of the fitness curve. If $a = 1$, fitness falls off linearly in proportion to the percentage of bad connections; if $a > 1$, fitness falls off sharply as G falls below T and then levels off; if $a < 1$, fitness initially drops off slowly, and then more rapidly.

The general qualitative results are straightforward. If we assume a fixed mutation rate μ, and a basal fitness of zero ($b = 0$), then the equation above reduces to this:

$$W_x = (G_x/T)^a$$

There are three cases, depending on the value of a. When a = 1, the fitness of a network is a linear function, proportional to the number of good connections and inversely proportional to the number of bad connections. A mutation in the network can increase or decrease the fitness of the network only incrementally. Fitness, in short, is additive. When a < 1, the fitness curve is convex. W_x falls off slowly at first, then more quickly. A limited number of bad connections is tolerated, but there will be a threshold (depending on μ) beyond which W_x declines precipitously. When a > 1, the fitness curve is concave. W_x falls off steeply at first, and then levels off with 0 as the limit. In this case, networks are relatively intolerant to error, but networks with errors are not significantly different from one another.

These results generally replicate the NK model discussed in section 3.1. The case in which a > 1 corresponds to high K, and a < 1 to relatively low K. Just as in the previous case, the complexity of the network matters greatly. Complexity here is essentially a function of T, the number of regulatory connections in the network. As T increases, mutation is more able to drive networks off the adaptive peaks. Once again, we assume μ is constant. Since the power of selection is inversely proportional to the number of connections, as the number of connections increases the impact of selection on any given node decreases. Increasing T thus decreases the relative strength of selection. Depending on the specific value of a, as T increases, the population will move away from the optimum more or less quickly. This is the error catastrophe revisited.

A high basal fitness value for b means that even a randomly ordered network can approach the optimum. In the limiting case in which b = 1, there is no difference at all between networks. With intermediate values of b (1 > b > 0) and given that a $\gg$ 1, two alternative stable states emerge—one with low, and one with high, mean numbers of good connections. Which state a network ends up in depends on its history, just as with state cycles in Boolean networks. If one starts an evolving population of genetic networks as a small network with high fitness and gradually increases the number of connections, the population will remain near optimal fitness even as it becomes more complex. It resists mutation pressure. If one starts with low fitness values, it will tend to stabilize at the lower value, and is unlikely to achieve the higher fitness value. Moreover, there is a threshold for the number of connections in such a network above which the system, even if started in an optimal condition, will lose fitness. There will be values of T and a at which μ will overwhelm selection. Once again, we have a complexity catastrophe.

Kauffman offers his models as useful characterizations of the null state against which selection must be assessed. He contends that without a characterization of the null state, evolutionists are prone to attribute too much power to natural selection, viewing it as capable of generating almost any possible genetic state that is highly adaptive. Kauffman contends that the null state has quite power-ful properties and that selection is generally powerless to overcome them. In particular, he contends that the usual treatments of the means by which selec-tion maintains complex regulatory systems rest on mistaken presuppositions. Selection is not able by itself to produce (rather than merely maintain) patterns of connectivity radically different from the base line—and this base-line con-nectivity turns out to be relatively stable. Once a system settles into this kind of pattern, even massive selection pressure is powerless to alter it. Again, we have what appears to be a fundamental limitation on adaptive evolution.

4. CO-EVOLUTION AND COMPLEX ADAPTATION

We now turn to two questions concerning Kauffman's treatment of adaptation and complexity. One concerns the impact of co-evolution on models of evolu-tionary dynamics. The other focuses on the generic character of Kauffman's constraints on evolution.

4.1. Co-evolution

As we explained in section 3.1, Kauffman's appeal to the NK model motivates his scepticism about the power of selection. Recall that by increasing the con-nectivity, K, one increases the ruggedness of the adaptive landscape. When K = 0, we have a highly correlated landscape with a single adaptive peak, and fitness is additive. When K = (N − 1), we have an uncorrelated landscape with multiple adaptive peaks, and fitness is non-additive. Since, in the K = 0 case, the landscape is highly correlated and the selective effect of a single allelic change is correspondingly low, disruptive pressures will be able to counteract selection. Since, in the K = (N − 1) case, there are multiple constraints, local optima will tend to be depressed, and, once again, disruptive pressures will be able to counteract selection. At one point, Kauffman makes the point this way:

... as K increases, landscapes must change from smooth through a family of increasingly rugged landscapes to fully uncorrelated landscapes. *Increasing the richness of epistatic interactions K increases the ruggedness of fitness landscapes.* Since increasing epistatic interactions simultaneously increases the number of conflicting constraints, increased multipeaked ruggedness of the fitness landscape as K increases reflects those increasingly complex mutual constraints. (1993: 47)

The conclusion appears to be robust. As we move from cases with additive fitness through to highly integrated systems by increasing K, we simultaneously increase the number of adaptive constraints and reduce the relative advantage. The trade-off bodes ill for the power of selection.

But we should be reluctant to embrace this conclusion without further consideration. One possibility which must be taken seriously is the prospect of increasing K without increasing conflicting adaptive constraints. Flightless birds, for example, are often neotenic relative to their nearest relatives. They retain a longer leg length, reduced breast muscles, and a less developed sternum. Or to take a slightly different example, regressive evolution among cave fauna affects a complex group of traits. Among other things, adaptation to the cave environment means reducing optic sensory organs and increasing non-optic sensory organs. There is reason to think that there is selection acting on both traits, but probably not independently (cf. Culver *et al*. 1990; Kane *et al*. 1990; and Jones *et al*. 1992). These are not, from a functional perspective, independent traits; rather they form an adaptive complex. Clearly, there is interaction, but no constraints that conflict. The same is true in general for mosaic evolution. Evolution operates at different rates on different characters, but often affects character-complexes rather than simple characters. Correlation in character sets provides the compromise between landscapes that are too smooth and those that are too rugged, thus allowing adaptive evolution. Kauffman says, '. . . there are general principles characterizing complex systems able to adapt: They achieve a "poised" state near the boundary between order and chaos, a state which optimizes the complexity of tasks the systems can perform and simultaneously optimizes evolvability' (1993: 173).

The same general concern can be raised at a higher level. Consider the analogous case a level or two up. Van Valen (1973) found that there was a roughly constant rate of extinction among taxa. Ammonoids, Echinoids, and Foraminifera have similar survivorship curves, indicating that survivorship is independent of age (contrary to the expectation of, among others, Hyatt). To explain this observation, Van Valen proposed what he called the 'Red Queen Hypothesis'. The environment constantly degrades because of interactions with other species, whether they are predators or competitors. As a consequence, extinction rates are essentially stochastic. The more general point, already emphasized by Darwin (1859), is that the relevant selective environment of an organism, or a species, is largely biotic. Correspondingly, evolution is largely co-evolution. This may lead to a kind of 'arms race' with a constantly deforming adaptive landscape (Dawkins 1982) or to an equilibrium state (Stenseth and Maynard Smith 1984). In either case, fitness landscapes are largely formed and informed by other species. The connectivity here will be limited, but, more importantly, it will be localized.

At whatever level we may address the problem, the question is relatively simple. Granted that the extreme cases of no connectivity, ($K = 0$), and maximal connectivity, $K = (N - 1)$, leave adaptive evolution only a secondary role, will the intermediate cases suffer from the same dilemma? Or, put positively, under what conditions of connectivity will the dilemma be escaped? The general outline of Kauffman's answer is clear. Co-evolution will be understood in terms of the interaction of fitness landscapes in a hyperspace. Kauffman says that '... in a *coevolutionary process*, the very adaptive landscape of one actor itself heaves and deforms as other agents make their own adaptive moves' (1993: 238). What is needed is to find parameter values which allow improvement without falling into chaotic fluctuations. The solution is to couple the fitness landscapes in modelling co-evolution (1993: 243 ff.). In a multiple-species system, this means introducing a parameter C for the interaction effect. Fitness depends not only on the K interactions within the system but on the C interactions between systems. The NK model becomes an NKC model. Again, everything depends on the details. The relative values of K and C matter; so does the number of co-evolving species. Kauffman argues that co-evolution requires that the interaction between co-evolving species be weaker than the interaction within either population. In Herbert Simon's (1981) sense, the systems must exhibit *near decomposability*. In consequence, evolution will occur on *correlated* rather than *uncorrelated* fitness landscapes—close to, but not within, the chaotic regime. Adaptation, in Kauffman's delightful phrase, occurs 'at the edge of chaos' (1993: 255). This allows us to pose a difficult question, one with considerable mathematical and biological depth: Can one avoid the 'complexity catastrophe' with the right pattern of connectivity? Can selective interconnections structure fitness spaces and their interactions so that an increase in K need not depress the fitness peaks? The answer, to us at any rate, is not clear.

4.2. Development and Evolution

It is worth at least remarking on how radical Kauffman's vision is. Kauffman proposes that intrinsic organizational constraints are critical in the evolutionary process, and that at least the 'generic' properties will be unaltered by selection. Others, such as Alberch (1982), hold similar views. For many of us, this requires a kind of gestalt shift. One way to think of developmental mechanisms such as heterochrony or allometry is to think of these as the *targets* of selection. So, for example, there may be selection for genes that attenuate development. Selection may favour genes that affect antennal length and which only incidentally affect limb length; or there may be selection for larger body size, only incidentally affecting length (cf. Kane *et al.* 1990). Evolution in which developmental stages are dissociated is apparently quite common. This provides for at least two important ontogenetic changes (cf. Raff and Kaufman 1983): one of these is mosaic evolution; the other is a dissociation of larval from adult development. Approached another way, developmental mechanisms are additional constraints on evolution. Thus, Alberch says that evolution is 'the product of two independent processes, where diversification . . . precedes adaptation' (1982: 19). Phenotypic evolution is controlled by processes regulating variation in body plan and by adaptive processes. Kauffman carefully argues that generic constraints typically dominate selection. Form rules, function follows.

5. THE DISTINCTIVELY BIOLOGICAL

We have repeatedly emphasized that Kauffman's models focus on more formal constraints, and pay limited attention to biological contingencies. This does not mean that he pays no attention to biological details. He often does, as we illustrated above in discussing genomic regulatory networks. In emphasizing the 'distinctively biological', we mean to emphasize the difference between local and global constraints, including both what is characteristic of biological as opposed to abiotic systems and what is characteristic of some biological systems but not others. To what extent is Kauffman's approach capable of capturing what is distinctively biological? Is it, like many other attempts to develop physics-based analyses of biological subject-matter, fated to yield serious misrepresentations of the systems to which it is applied, or does it provide a central core from which more specifically biological analyses can comfortably proceed? What does it do well and what does it leave for others to do better? In the end, these questions must be answered by detailed examination of attempts to apply the new apparatus to biological problems, but, as we shall now argue, some general considerations let us localize issues that are particularly sensitive to these questions.

5.1. Historical Contingency

Kauffman's approach, by and large, does not pretend to answer questions about historical contingencies and is ill equipped to do so. Thus his work speaks to the statistical distribution of patterns of evolutionary radiation, but says virtually nothing about which organisms or which lineages will play a role, if any, in a radiation. Kauffman's results are based more on abstract rules of combination than on the details of chemistry or biology. As such, they might yield, for example, the expected architecture of genetic networks, the likely patterns of differentiation in cell lineages, or the likely branching patterns in evolutionary trees, but not the particular functions of, or connections among, particular genes, the sorts of cells that will appear in particular lineages, or the likely tree for a particular monophyletic group. Similarly, Kauffman argues that evolutionary change and adaptation are most likely to occur when ecological systems are 'poised on the edge of chaos', but his apparatus can say little or nothing about the concrete details of the changes that move an ecology closer to or further from the edge of chaos.

To put the point generally, Kauffman's theoretical apparatus is not intended to handle the contingent details of the structure or function of particular genes, proteins, cells, stages of ontogeny, and so on, or to resolve questions about the particular ecological or evolutionary interactions of particular populations or species. There may be important interactions between his results and the investigations of biologists interested in such issues, but, in general, they will turn up only after independent investigations of the contingencies of structure, function, and history.[5] In this sense, there is a very large set of issues of central concern to many biologists to which Kauffman's work speaks only indirectly or not at all.

There is a sense of contingency which Kauffman's approach can accommodate, as he shows using another formal model—this time based on random grammars—in chapter 10. The point he makes is actually quite general: history is sensitive to small perturbations. What might appear to be minor details can have effects which are amplified with time. When history is treated as a walk in an adaptive space, it is clear that small differences in initial conditions or minor perturbations of parameter values can significantly affect the result. Thus Kauffman can explain how it is that there is contingency to history. However, the particular contingencies which govern our world remain beyond the reach of his formal apparatus. For example, it appears to be simply accidental that terrestrial life relies on L-amino acid isomers and D-ribose rather than D-amino acids and L-ribose. We would expect it to rely on one or the other even if this reliance is a consequence of a random walk, but we know, at least as yet, of no general reason to expect one rather than the other or to explain why terrestrial life actually relies on L-amino acids and D-ribose. It is contingencies such as this that appear beyond the reach of Kauffman's formal apparatus, even though the general fact of contingency is not.

On the other hand, there are many traditional biological questions on which his work, if sound, has immense impact. Take two seemingly simple questions: To what extent does selection affect the general patterns of evolution? To what extent are the patterns of ontogeny the result of selection? These questions have

---

[5] A possible exception concerns Kauffman's suggestions for experimental design of novel peptides. At the end of chapter 8, he argues on general grounds that the best path to follow in such work may well be to establish sets of interacting novel enzymes under appropriate constraints; the efficiency of the search for an enzyme that can perform a novel catalytic task may be easier from such starting-points than from the positions currently occupied in 'catalytic task space'.

typically been posed in ways that make attempts to answer them misleading and confused. To ask after causal responsibility is to ask what difference the presence of the putative causal factor makes in the relevant context. To resolve such a question, one must know the way the world *would have been* in the absence of the factor in question in order to compare it with the way it *is* in the presence of that factor. It is obvious that the relevant comparisons required to answer our questions about selection are inaccessible to biologists. We do not have access to systems in which there has been no selection and we are rarely if ever in a position to compare systems virtually free of selection with others, otherwise similar, in which selection plays a major role. Correlation and causation are confounded. Kauffman's work at least allows an intelligible formulation of such comparisons by providing a theoretical (re)construction of what would happen to systems that meet the combinatorial conditions with which he works in the absence of selection. To the extent that such theoretical reconstructions are sound, his work allows us to pose clearly some crucial questions about evolutionary patterns that were already raised obscurely by Darwin but which, frustratingly, have remained unclearly formulated and unresolvable to this day.

5.2. Biological Laws

In our pursuit of the distinctively biological, let us turn from historical contingencies to the place of laws and regularities in the biological sciences. We have in mind, for example, the regularities of biochemistry as they pertain to organisms, and not the chimerical, logically universal, laws of philosophers. For lack of space, we shall simply embrace an admittedly controversial claim, namely that *there are no universal and distinctively biological laws of nature.* Such biological laws as there are are, in a strong sense, contingent.[6]

To provide some content for this claim, note that the principle of natural selection is not a law, but is a schema requiring specification by means of an account of the physico-chemical and ecological factors affecting survival and reproduction (cf. Brandon 1978 and 1990). Note also that such evolutionary 'laws' or rules as Allen's and Bergmann's rules and such 'laws of development' as those that specify the consequences of spiral cleavage are nothing like universal generalizations under any plausible interpretation. Note, finally, that all biochemical rules that are not narrowly chemical—perhaps, the rules connecting nucleotide triplets with amino acids via the genetic code or connecting certain sequences of amino acids with protein conformation (or with catalytic roles)—

---

[6] See Beatty (1995). We owe the initial suggestions that led us to undertake this treatment of laws here to John Beatty.

are contingent on the physiological contexts secured in the course of evolution. This fact provides strong grounds for denying that such rules have the generality over evolutionary time that would be required of laws as these are often understood.

To the extent that the contingencies of evolution underlie biochemical, ontogenetic, and ecological regularities, Kauffman's devices for capturing generic properties and regularities cannot be expected to produce the specific regularities with which biologists have typically been concerned. First-order biological regularities are, in the end, historical contingencies of just the sort from which Kauffman abstracts in defining his generic regularities. If historical contingencies—whether they have their source in adaptation or in phylogeny—underlie the regularities of biology, a statistical mechanics based on abstract combinatorial rules will not be able to (re)produce those regularities. To the extent that biological 'laws' are the products of evolution, then, Kauffman's abstract mechanics will produce patterns of a higher order, but not biological laws; in full abstraction, the underlying combinatorics employed in his mechanics must be independent of biological evolution. In the case of biochemistry, for example, the underlying combinatorial rules are those of organic chemistry, and they do not change in the course of biological evolution.[7]

5.3. Functional Claims

The most obvious remaining bastion of distinctively biological claims concerns the functions of various entities and processes—the various functions of DNA and RNA molecules (and of specific segments of such molecules), of particular enzymes, proteins, lipids, organelles, organs, etc., and also of behaviours, of circadian and seasonal cycles that affect the physiological states of organisms, and so on. Briefly put, the point is that the functions of a molecule—say an arbitrary hormone or an arbitrary gene product—depend on its physiological context. They depend on whether there are receptors for that molecule, and if so where, on whether there are enzymes that process it as part of a reaction chain, and if so on whether the substrates for that activity are available. No intrinsic analysis of the molecule can reveal its actual functions. Parallel claims are true, though perhaps to a lesser degree, for organs—where, as John Beatty (1980) shows, engineering analyses are sometimes possible which, arguably, are somewhat less context-dependent—and for behaviours. Here, too, *the specific*

---

[7] As Marjorie Grene and Norman Gilinsky have pointed out to R. B. in discussion, the combinatorial rules of organic chemistry may well depend on cosmological evolution. Our claim is relative: given the laws of organic chemistry, the distinctively biological laws of biochemistry (which deal, for example, with the products and functions of particular molecules in physiological settings) are contingent on the pathways of biological evolution.

functions of specific entities or processes are not amenable to the sort of statistical mechanics that typifies Kauffman's approach to biological regularities.

It will help to anchor these claims if we return to one example for a very brief discussion. There is a generic genomic architecture that, according to Kauffman's analysis, is to be expected in typical cells of typical organisms merely on grounds that genes produce products and, directly or indirectly, influence other genes while retaining stable and heritable interrelationships. In this architecture, some genes are turned on in most cell-types, the activity of most genes is affected by a small number of other genes, and whole batteries of genes are switched on in a cascade if one—or, more likely, a few—critical genes are turned on. Kauffman's results, as we have said, are rather more complicated than this, but this captures the spirit of the enterprise. His account of the architecture follows from minimal assumptions that say nothing (and allow no conclusions) about the functions of particular genes. This is not a shortcoming in Kauffman's approach, nor do we mean to suggest that it is. It simply characterizes his enterprise. To the extent that the characterization is fair, it makes it clear that there is no easy way for him to provide a functional analysis of particular genes.

Strongly analogous claims apply to Kauffman's treatment of metabolic networks, of ontogenies, and of fitness landscapes. The power of his constructional principles rests on the fact that they are built by reference to the statistics of *typical* genes (or proteins, cells, organisms, or species), taken as indifferently alike for the analysis of the systems of which they are components. The weakness of his constructional principles is that they abstract from the particular case. This makes it an open question to what extent such constructional principles can capture the distinctive features of metabolisms, genomes, ontogenies, and evolutionary patterns that have been of central interest to biologists. It also leaves open the question whether Kauffman's transformative vision will prove so powerful that the centre of biological interest shifts to the novel questions placed at the centre of investigation by his formal apparatus.

6. CONCLUSION

Kauffman's approach to a large suite of major biological issues is that of a physicist studying complex materials and complex systems. His approach opens up new vistas. It suggests that the behaviours of metabolisms, immune systems, genetic networks, and ecological communities are driven by dynamics different from those that most orthodox biologists recognize or accept. He puts forward important hypotheses about the origin of life, the power of selection, the conditions under which evolution will be rapid, the structure of the genome and immune systems, and much more.

One consequence of thinking like a physicist here is that one is primarily, and perhaps solely, concerned with higher-level regularities. That implies that one no longer focuses on the details of the systems of concern; those details are mere contingencies, buried and inaccessible to analysis. Kauffman is of two minds here. In his conciliatory moments, he sides with Darwin, treating the higher-level results as providing null hypotheses against which we might judge the importance of more local constraints, including those of selection. Thus, he says in his Epilogue: 'I have tried to take modest steps toward character-izing the interaction of selection and self-organization.' In this mood, self-organizational properties are simply formal constraints on evolution (1993: 644).

When he is in a more radical mood, the generic characteristics overwhelm the particularities. Here he sides with D'Arcy Thompson—as he himself ac-knowledges just prior to the last remark quoted. There he says that his book 'is an effort to continue in D'Arcy Thompson's tradition, with the spirit now animating parts of physics. It seeks the origins of order in the generic properties of complex systems' (1993: 644). On one standard view, biology studies fea-tures of physical systems that contribute to the functioning of living systems (Bechtel 1993). Biology is a science of function rather than form. When Kauffman sides with D'Arcy Thompson's program, his denies this character-ization of biology. Form dominates, and, to that extent, Kauffman's *The Ori-gins of Order* seeks to bring about a transformation of biology into a science of form, a transformation which, we believe, will be a focus of debate for some time to come.[8]

REFERENCES

Alberch, P. (1982), 'The Generative and Regulatory Roles of Development in Evolution', in D. Mossakowski and G. Roth (eds.), *Environmental Adaptation and Evolution* (Stuttgart: Gustav Fischer), 19–36.

Beatty, J. (1980), 'Optimal-Design Models and the Strategy of Model Building in Evolutionary Biology', *Philosophy of Science*, 47: 532–61.

—— (1995), 'The Evolutionary Contingency Thesis', in G. Wolters and J. Lennox, in collaboration with P. McLaughlin (eds.), *Concepts, Theories, and Rationality in the*

[8] This began as two papers, and evolved into a joint enterprise. The order of authors is only alphabetical. We are grateful to Marjorie Grene for arranging the symposium in which this work was presented, and for her encouragement in this project as well as everywhere else. We also thank Stu Kauffman for his patient help and discussion as we struggled to understand his views. We both benefited greatly from a workshop at the Santa Fe Institute, and from the participants there. R.C.R is indebted to the National Science Foundation (DIR-8921837) for supporting this work.

Biological Sciences (Konstanz: Universitätsverlag Konstanz, and Pittsburgh: University of Pittsburgh Press, 1995), 45–81.

Bechtel, W. (1993), 'Integrating Sciences by Creating New Disciplines: The Case of Cell Biology', *Biology and Philosophy*, 8 (1993), 277–300.

—— and Richardson, R. C. (1992), 'Emergent Phenomena and Complex Systems', in A. Beckerman, H. Flohr and J. Kim (eds.), *Emergence or Reduction?* (Berlin and New York: Walter de Gruyter), 257–88.

—— —— (1993), *Discovering Complexity* (Princeton: Princeton University Press).

Brandon, R. (1978), 'Adaptation and Evolutionary Theory', *Studies in History and Philosophy of Biology*, 9: 181–206.

—— (1990), *Adaptation and Environment* (Princeton: Princeton University Press).

Culver, D., Kane, T. C., Fong, D. W., Jones, R., Taylor, M. A., and Sauereisen, S. C. (1990), 'Morphology of Cave Organisms—Is It Adaptive?', *Mémoires de Biospéologie*, 17: 13–26.

Darwin, C. (1859), *On the Origin of Species*, 1st edn. (London: John Murray).

Dawkins, R. (1982), *The Extended Phenotype: The Gene as the Unit of Selection* (Oxford and San Francisco: W. H. Freeman).

Gould, S. J. (1977), *Ontogeny and Phylogeny* (Cambridge, Mass.: Harvard University Press).

Jones, R., Culver, D. C., and Kane, T. C. (1992), 'Are Parallel Morphologies of Cave Organisms the Result of Similar Selection Pressures?' *Evolution*, 46: 353–65.

Kane, T. C., Richardson, R. C., and Fong, D. (1990), 'The Phenotype as the Level of Selection: Cave Organisms as Model Systems', in *PSA 1990*, Volume 1, A. Fine, M. Forbes and L. Wessels (eds.), East Lansing: Philosophy of Science Association, 151–164.

Kauffman, S. (1992), 'The Sciences of Complexity and "Origins of Order"', in J. Mittenthal and A. Baskin (eds.), *Principles of Organization in Organisms* (Reading, Mass.: Addison-Wesley), 303–19.

—— (1993), *The Origins of Order: Self-Organization and Selection in Evolution* (Oxford: Oxford University Press).

Kimura, M. (1968), 'Evolutionary Rate at the Molecular Level', *Nature*, 217: 264–6.

—— (1980), 'A Simple Method for Estimating Evolutionary Rate of Base Substitutions through Comparative Studies of Nucleotide Sequences', *Journal of Molecular Evolution*, 16: 111–20.

—— (1983), *The Neutral Theory of Molecular Evolution* (Cambridge: Cambridge University Press).

Lande, R. (1976), 'Natural Selection and Random Genetic Drift in Phenotypic Evolution', *Evolution*, 30: 314–34.

—— and Arnold, S. (1983), 'The Measurement of Selection on Correlated Characters', *Evolution*, 37: 1210–26.

Maynard Smith, J., Burian, R., Kauffman, S., Alberch, P., Campbell, J., Goodwin, B., Lande, R., Raup, D., and Wolpert, L. (1985), 'Developmental Constraints and Evolution', *Quarterly Review of Biology*, 60: 265–87.

Raff, R. (1987), 'Constraint, Flexibility, and Phylogenetic History in the Evolution of Direct Development in Sea Urchins', *Developmental Biology*, 119: 6–19.

—— and Kaufman, T. C. (1983), *Embryos, Genes, and Evolution* (New York: Macmillan).

—— and Wray, G. A. (1989), 'Heterochrony: Developmental Mechanisms and Evolutionary Results', *Journal of Evolutionary Biology*, 2: 409–34.

—— Parr, B. A., Parks, A. L., and Wray, G. A. (1990), 'Heterochrony and Other Mechanisms of Radical Evolutionary Change in Early Development', in M. Nitecki (ed.), *Evolutionary Mechanisms* (Chicago: University of Chicago Press), 71–98.

Simon, H. (1981), *The Sciences of the Artificial*, 2nd edn. (Cambridge, Mass.: MIT Press).

Stenseth N. C., and Maynard Smith, J. (1984), 'Coevolution in Ecosystems: Red Queen Evolution or Stasis', *Evolution*, 38: 870–80.

Thompson, D. W. (1952), *On Growth and Form*, 2nd edn. (Cambridge: Cambridge University Press).

Van Valen, L. (1973), 'A New Evolutionary Law', *Evolutionary Theory*, 1: 1–30.

Wimsatt, W. (1986), 'Developmental Constraints, Generative Entrenchment, and the Innate-Acquired Distinction', in W. Bechtel (ed.), *Integrating Scientific Disciplines* (Dordrecht: Martinus-Nijhoff), 185–208.

—— and Schank, J. C. (1988), 'Two Constraints on the Evolution of Complex Adaptations and the Means for their Avoidance', in M. Nitecki (ed.), *Evolutionary Progress* (Chicago: University of Chicago Press), 231–73.

5

EVOLUTION—NATURAL AND ARTIFICIAL

JOHN MAYNARD SMITH

There are two kinds of question one can ask about the simulation of evolution on a computer. The first is whether it is an efficient way of answering practical questions—the design of railway timetables, aeroplane wings, or what have you. I am interested in this question, but have nothing to contribute to an answer. The second is whether it can contribute to our understanding of evolution. It is this question that I shall discuss. I shall do so mainly by saying where I think we stand in evolutionary biology, rather than by discussing particular examples of artificial life. My hope is that this will help philosophers and computer scientists to see where the real questions are.

First, there is a confusion that sometimes arises in discussions about evolution, both within biology and among students of genetic algorithms. This is the belief that the genetic system of real organisms is optimal for the evolution of adaptation. This would be true if natural selection worked only by favouring the survival of some species at the expense of others. Between-species selection does of course happen, but it is a weak force compared with selection favouring some individuals, or some genes, at the expense of others, within populations. The point is obvious if we think about the evolution of the mutation rate. Most mutations reduce the fitness of their carriers. There is therefore strong selection tending to reduce the mutation rate. Its actual value (approximately 10^{-10} per base, per replication) is probably as low as it can be, without paying an excessive cost in slower replication. To optimize the evolution rate of the species, it might well pay to have a higher mutation rate.

There is an extensive literature on the evolution of genetic systems, concentrating in particular on the evolution of sex and recombination. Some of this work has depended on computer simulation, but the simulations have been of precisely defined genetic systems, resembling those found in nature. The problems are by no means all solved. There remains the question whether selection for genes causing recombination arises mainly from their role in generating new selectively advantageous combinations, or from their role in facilitating the elimination of harmful mutations. I think, however, that we probably now have the necessary theoretical models, and what we need are the data that will enable us to choose between them. What is the deleterious mutation rate per genome per generation? Do deleterious mutations have multiplicative or synergistic effects on fitness? How important are parasites as selective agents favouring sex? How ancient are the oldest asexual populations?

The theoretical study of the evolution of genetic systems has been a branch of population genetics, based on realistic genetic assumptions. Are there more general questions that studies of artificial life can illuminate? Biologists are in the embarassing position of having only one case to study: in all likelihood, all the living organisms we have access to have a single origin. It is therefore hard for us to decide whether features common to all organisms (for example, the genetic code) are mere historical contingencies—what Crick has called 'frozen accidents'—or are necessary features of any evolving system. I shall discuss briefly three rather general questions. Has there been time for natural selection to produce the complex creatures we see around us? What is the nature of the adaptive landscape? What features of the genetic system are necessary and what contingent?

From time to time some physicist or mathematician—usually not a computer scientist—announces that there has not been time for natural selection to produce the results biologists claim. An odd feature of these objections is that the objector never attempts to calculate how much time *would* be needed. Twice as long? A million times as long? It is not easy to calculate how long would be needed, but one can at least have a rough shot. The starting-point has to be, I think, that the genome of higher animals and plants contains 10^8 to 10^9 base pairs of informative DNA: the total DNA in the nucleus is substantially greater, but much of it is thought to be 'junk'. If we take the conservative figure of 10^9 base pairs, this implies 2×10^9 bits of information (there are four alternative bases, with roughly equal frequencies). Presumably, this is enough, together with the environment and the laws of physics and chemistry, to specify the structure of the adult organism: after all, what else could specify it? To be fair, although the field is exploding right now, we still know too little about the role of genes in development to know whether 10^9 bits are really necessary. Perhaps, with a more efficient coding system, 10^6 would be enough. But we do know that 10^9 bits are sufficient, and the objection we are usually faced with is, not that there is insufficient information in the genome to program development, but that there has not been time for selection to generate that much information.

To get a handle on the question, suppose that we start with a set of random DNA sequences, and try, by selection, to produce a unique optimal sequence. Obviously, if in each generation we are allowed to weed out half the sequences—a not unreasonable intensity of selection—we can specify one base in two generations, or 10^9 bases in 2×10^9 generations. The time available since the origin of life is approximately 4×10^9 years, and during most of that time most organisms got through many generations a year, so it would seem that there has been plenty of time.

There are two modifications that should be made to this overly crude model. First, new genetic information does not usually arise by generating a set of random sequences, and then evolving an optimal one by selection. Typically, a gene is duplicated, and one copy is then modified. To have two copies of the same gene does not add to the information available. But to start with two identical copies, and then modify a few bases in one of them so as to produce a gene with a new function, does add to the coding DNA, and so has been counted in the estimate of total informative DNA assumed above. This suggests that the excess of the time available over the time needed is even greater than the calculation suggests. There is, however, a second modification which leads us to adjust the calculation in the opposite direction. If new information arises by modification of a duplicated sequence, novelty arises as a single mutation in a single member of the population. To fix such a mutation in the population requires more than one generation of selection, with a 50 per cent culling rate. For example, if the population consists of a million individuals, it would take about twenty generations, increasing the time required by a factor of 20. Probably these two modifications roughly cancel out, leaving us with time to spare.

There are other processes one should perhaps allow for, notably recombination and symbiosis (in this context, uniting two genomes into one). But it is interesting that one can quantify both changes in the genome, and selection, in the same units—bits of information. Unfortunately, we have at present no way of quantifying the information needed to generate a particular phenotype in the same units.

Students of artificial evolution have been much concerned with the nature of the adaptive landscape, and with evolution on a rugged landscape. This is a topic on which biologists are divided, in part because Sewall Wright was an American and R. A. Fisher an Englishman, separated by an ocean and a common language. As a student of Haldane's, I can of course take an impartial stand. In essence, Fisher's view was that evolution by natural selection is a hill-climbing process that can happen only on a smooth landscape. If mutational steps are small, and populations large and random-mating, it is hard to escape this conclusion. However, it may not be quite as limiting as it seems at first sight. We may be hill-climbing on an undulating landscape, but that landscape does not remain still. For each species, the fitness landscape is determined not only by the physical environment but also by other species, its competitors, predators, parasites, and prey, which can also evolve. The appropriate image is of hill-climbing on a surface resembling that of the open ocean. We do not get trapped on local wave-tops, because the surface changes all the time.

Wright tried to escape the dilemma of a rugged landscape by abandoning the assumption of a large random-mating population. If a species is divided into a large number of small and partially isolated populations, a small population may occasionally jump across a local valley, purely by chance. Once a new adaptive peak has been reached, the new type can selectively replace the old. I have always been doubtful about the relevance of Wright's idea: perhaps I am not as free of chauvinism as I like to think. There are two difficulties. First, the valleys must be small: for example, the change from *ab* to the fitter *AB*, when the intermediates *aB* and *Ab* are of lower fitness. The mechanism will not help us to cross large valleys. A second difficulty concerns the role of sex. The crossing of a small valley, *ab* → *AB*, requiring two mutations, is quite possible for an asexual population: one has only to wait for the (rare) double mutant to arise by chance. But it is impossible if recombination is common, because the new genotype, *AB*, even if it arises, is immediately destroyed by recombination. It was for this reason that Wright introduced population subdivision. So, if the ability to make such transitions has been important in evolution, it is hard to understand why sex is so widespread. The prevalence of sex is a reason for thinking that adaptive landscapes are usually smooth.

A more sophisticated approach to evolution on a rugged landscape is Eigen's idea of a 'quasispecies'. He imagines that, in early evolution, a particular optimal sequence was surrounded by a cloud of similar sequences, separated by 1, 2, 3 . . . mutations, the whole population constituting a quasispecies able to explore a rugged landscape, provided the valleys were not too wide. For small genomes, the model works well. For example, if the only mutations allowed are single base substitutions, an RNA molecule 100 bases long has 300 neighbours that can be reached by one mutation, and about 3×10^7 that can be reached by three mutations. A quasispecies of such molecules could successfully explore a landscape with many small fissures, provided, of course, that recombination was rare or absent. Eigen is probably right in thinking that the early exploration of 'gene space' by simple replicators depended on the variability of quasispecies. But the arithmetic is quite different for organisms with 10^9 base pairs.

My suspicion, then, is that evolution has depended on local hill-climbing, and that long-term entrapment on local peaks has been avoided because the landscape is always changing. Of course, this does not mean that there are not peaks that cannot be reached. For example, animals have never evolved the wheel and axle, although, on a molecular scale, bacteria have flagella that rotate. One could argue that there is not much point in having wheels if there are no roads, but this overlooks the value of rotors in flying. Aerodynamically, hoverflies are helicopters, but they achieve this with a reciprocating wing of fiendish ingenuity, and have even evolved a reciprocating gyroscope as a sense organ. The wheel, then, may be an unreachable peak, but animals have evolved effective alternatives.

One can get an idea of how attainable various adaptive features are by asking how often they have evolved independently. For example, powered flight has evolved four times. Multicellular organisms with many different kinds of cells have evolved three times (animals, plants, fungi). Advanced image-forming eyes, of varying design, have evolved several times, although recent genetic evidence suggests that they may all be derived from simple light-sensitive organs in a common ancestor. In contrast, some fundamental features have evolved just once. Examples include the genetic code, sex involving the fusion of gametes, and language with grammar.

Turning now to the nature of the genetic system, I have already argued that we need models of systems closely resembling those actually found. There is, however, the deeper problem of explaining features that are common to all real genetic systems. There are two features which, I think, are necessary for any genetic system that is to support adaptive evolution. The system should be digital, and should not permit the 'inheritance of acquired characters'. The need for a digital system arises from the familiar difficulty of maintaining information in a system able to vary continuously. The reason for avoiding 'Lamarckian' inheritance is equally obvious. Most changes induced in organisms by the impact of the environment are non-adaptive: they are the effects of injury, disease, and ageing. A genetic system equipped with a mechanism of reverse translation, able to incorporate information about the adult phenotype into the genetic message transmitted to the next generation, would lead to deterioration, not to adaptation. Of course, if there was some way of selecting for transmission only those phenotypic changes that were adaptive, this would speed up adaptive change. There is a sense in which cultural evolution achieves this end, or would do if we were sensible enough to teach our children only those things which we have learnt to be useful.

The claim that digital coding and non-Lamarckian inheritance are necessary features of a genetic system able to support evolution is based on a sample of one. The study of artificial evolving systems may confirm or refute this claim, and may throw up other necessary characteristics.

A related set of questions concerns the conversion of genetic information into phenotypic structure. Selection acts on the phenotype. Whether the fitness landscape will be smooth, therefore, depends on the mapping of genotypes on to phenotypes. A smooth landscape requires that unit steps in genotypic space (mutations) should cause small changes in phenotypic space, or, at least, that a substantial proportion of mutations should do so. In the natural system, the simplest type of mutation is the replacement of one base by another: the typical effect is a protein differing by one amino acid. There is no guarantee that the new protein will do anything useful, but it may. I am ignorant of how students of artificial evolution ensure that a reasonable proportion of their mutations produce results that are at least candidates for selection. A random change in the kind of program I write would, almost always, result in an error message. It is clear to me that this is a topic I ought to learn something about.

The process of recombination raises similar difficulties. It would seem sensible to have a recombinational process whereby whole sub-routines could be exchanged. In bacteria, such processes do exist. There are various kinds of accessory genetic elements (plasmids, transposons) that can be acquired as a unit by a bacterial cell, and that confer upon it new abilities—for example, to resist one or more antibiotics, to utilize new substrates, or to survive toxins or heavy metals. Much short-term adaptive evolution in bacteria depends on the acquisition of such elements.

This ability to acquire whole sub-routines is less widespread in animals and plants, although still important. For example, some fish are luminous because, when young, they swallowed luminous bacteria and passed them to special luminous organs; leguminous plants can fix nitrogen because they form a symbiotic union with nitrogen-fixing bacteria. But most recombinational events in higher organisms are the result of the sexual union of two gametes carrying very similar genetic messages. Hybridization between substantially different individuals, from different genera and often from different species, leads to inviable or infertile offspring. Hence recombination is between very similar messages. Provided that, before exchange, both parental messages are cut at precisely the same point, most recombinational events give rise to functional products, very similar to the parental ones. Again, I am ignorant of how far the 'recombination' introduced into artificially evolving systems involves the acquisition of sub-routines or functional units, analogous to the acquisition of plasmids and transposons by bacteria, and how far it resembles the 'homologous recombination' that occurs in the sexual process of higher organisms.

In this chapter, I have discussed some of the fundamental features of naturally evolving populations. I hope this will help workers in artificial evolution to see more clearly the relation between these natural systems and the artificial ones that they study.

6

ANIMALS AS COST-BASED ROBOTS

DAVID J. MCFARLAND

From the behavioural point of view, what are the fundamental differences between animals and robots? Apart from the obvious, though behaviourally trivial, differences—such as that they are made from different hardware—we can say that animals are more sophisticated, have better sensors, etc. As scientists, we are not inclined to say that robots are machines whereas animals are not, or that the behaviour of robots is predetermined whereas that of animals is not. As scientists we believe that a deterministic philosophy applies to both animals and robots, and this attitude enables us to entertain the notion robots may, one day, be analogues of animals.

What we are interested in, when asking this question, is what are the basic differences in architecture between animals and robots. We want to know what architecture we should give robots to make them more like animals. This is the hidden agenda of this paper.

THE ROBOT'S DILEMMA

Pylyshyn (1987) has edited an interesting book, called *The Robot's Dilemma*, which has to do with the frame problem in artificial intelligence. For those not familiar with this problem, the book contains an excellent overview by Janlert. The book is interesting, because it seems to point to an ailment that afflicts the application of classical artificial intelligence in robotics.

There are many versions of the frame problem, but it is convenient to start with Dennett's (1987) description, because it is not far removed from a description of the type of problem that might confront an animal.

Once upon a time there was a robot, named R1 by its creators. Its only task was to fend for itself. One day its designers arranged for it to learn that its spare battery, its precious energy supply, was locked in a room with a time bomb set to go off soon. R1 located

Reprinted from *International Studies in the Philosophy of Science*, 6 (1992), 133–53. Reprinted by permission of Carfax Publishing Company, PO Box 25, Abingdon OX14 3UE, UK.

DAVID J. MCFARLAND

the room, and the key to the door, and formulated a plan to rescue its battery. There was a wagon in the room, and the battery was on the wagon, and R1 hypothesized that a certain action which it called PULLOUT (WAGON, ROOM) would result in the battery being removed from the room. Straightaway it acted, and did succeed in getting the battery out of the room before the bomb went off. Unfortunately, however, the bomb was also on the wagon. R1 *knew* that the bomb was on the wagon in the room, but didn't realize that pulling the wagon would bring the bomb along with the battery. Poor R1 had missed that obvious implication of its planned act.

Back to the drawing board. 'The solution is obvious', said the designers. 'Our next robot must be made to recognize not just the intended implications of its acts, but also the implications about their side effects, by deducing these implications from the descriptions it uses in formulating its plans.' They called their next model, the robot-deducer, R1D1. They placed R1D1 in much the same predicament that R1 had succumbed to, and as it too hit upon the idea of PULLOUT (WAGON, ROOM) it began, as designed, to consider the implications of such a course of action. It had just finished deducing that pulling the wagon out of the room would not change the colour of the room's walls, and was embarking on a proof of the further implication that pulling the wagon out would cause its wheels to turn more revolutions than there were wheels on the wagon—when the bomb exploded.

Back to the drawing board. 'We must teach it the difference between relevant implications and irrelevant implications', said the designers, 'and teach it to ignore the irrelevant ones.' So they developed a method of tagging the implications as either relevant or irrelevant to the project in hand, and installed the method in their next model, the robot-relevant-deducer, or R2D1 for short. When they subjected R2D1 to the test that had so unequivocally selected its ancestors for extinction, they were surprised to see it sitting, Hamlet-like, outside the room containing the ticking bomb, . . . 'Do something!' they yelled at it. 'I am', it retorted. 'I'm busily ignoring some thousands of implications I have determined to be irrelevant. Just as soon as I find an irrelevant implication, I put it on the list of those I must ignore, and . . .' the bomb went off. (Dennett 1987: 41–2)

According to Dennett (1987), all these robots suffer from the frame problem, first formulated by McCarthy (1959) and first promulgated by McCarthy and Hayes (1969). (An excellent introduction is to be found in Pylyshyn (1987), especially in the contribution by Janlert (1987).) For Hayes (1987) the frame problem is strictly one of reasoning about a changing world, but for others it is a broader problem. Thus for Fodor (1983) it is a holistic problem for cognitive science, while for Janlert the general frame problem is the problem of 'finding a representational form permitting a changing and complex world to be efficiently and adequately represented' (Janlert 1987: 7–8).

For our present purposes the frame problem is a problem that arises when an agent attempts to assess the consequences of future behaviour. Strictly, it is a problem of modelling that arises during planning. The problem arises because many of the possible consequences of a planned action are not really relevant to the decision whether to perform the action.

What would have happened if R1 had been an animal? Let us assume that we are thinking of an animal designed to occupy the bomb-disposal niche. Our story would be the same as Dennett's up to the point that R1 enters the room. Upon entering the room R1 immediately sets about removing the wagon from the room, in accordance with its plan. Upon entering the room, our animal would immediately undergo a large change in motivational state. It would see the bomb and this perception would lead to an increase in fear, or some other relevant aspect of motivation. The change in motivational state might cause the animal to embark upon a number of alternative activities: to defuse the bomb quickly, to run away, or to take the bomb off the trolley and pull out the trolley. What it would not do is wait until the bomb went off, because if its ancestors had employed that strategy, it would not be here for us to study.

THE ECOLOGICAL NICHE

If we are to take ethological design of robots seriously, then we should first consider the *ecological niche* that the proposed robot is to occupy. In animal ecology, the niche is the role that the animal plays in the community in terms of its relationship both to other organisms and to the physical environment. Thus a herbivore eats plant material and is usually preyed upon by carnivores. The species occupying a given niche varies from one part of the world to another. For example, a small-herbivore niche is occupied by rabbits and hares in northern temperate regions, by the agouti and viscacha in South America, by the hyrax and mouse deer in Africa, and by wallabies in Australia.

Niche occupancy usually implies ecological competition. When animals of different species use the same resources or have certain habitat preferences or tolerance ranges in common, niche overlap occurs. This leads to competition between species, especially when resources are in short supply. There is a competitive exclusion principle which states that two species with identical niches cannot live together in the same place at the same time when resources are limited. The corollary is that, if two species coexist, there must be ecological differences between them.

If our robot is to be employed as a bomb-disposer, then it must be able to compete in the market-place with human bomb-disposers. Of course, the two species of bomb-disposer will not be alike in every (bomb-disposing) respect. Employers will value one for certain qualities, and the other for other qualities. In other words there will be only partial niche overlap. Nevertheless, employers will apply roughly the same cost-efficiency criteria to each species, and these criteria will supply the selective pressures characteristic of the bomb-disposer niche. These selective pressures provide the main ingredients of the *cost function* that is characteristic of the environment in which the robot is to operate.

An animal in a particular state runs a (specifiable) risk of incurring real costs.

DAVID J. MCFARLAND

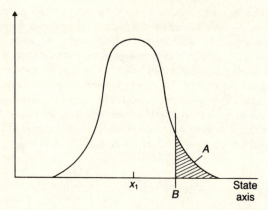

FIG. 6.1. The probability of the state x moving to a new position along the state axis. Area A is the probability of crossing boundary B. From McFarland and Houston (1981)

It is obvious that it is more risky to be in some states than others, and it seems reasonable to suppose that the risk of death must increase steeply the nearer a variable is to its lethal boundary. Thus it is obviously dangerous to allow hunger to approach lethal levels if the food supply is not guaranteed. In animal behaviour studies, the term *cost* is generally used to signify the risk of death plus other factors that may lead to a decrement in Darwinian fitness. This is a useful term for general discussion, although we have to remember to distinguish between the actual cost and the animal's notional cost (see below).

Cost considerations apply to robots as well as animals. The bomb-disposing robot that runs out of fuel may as well be dead as far as its usefulness is concerned. Such a robot would have low fitness in the sense that it would not fare well in the market-place. In considering the question of the fuel supply of our bomb-disposing robot, we assume that the robot has some sort of on-board energy store, and that robot activity is an energy-consuming business. The robot is equipped with a sensor for monitoring the fuel level, but this is not perfectly accurate. In Fig. 6.1 we assume that x is the state of the fuel reserves at a particular time and that the probability P of the state x moving to a new position along the state axis is given by a normal distribution. As the robot goes about its business, the state x moves towards the boundary B at which the fuel reserves are zero. The area A represents the probability of crossing the boundary B. The area A increases as the square of the distance ox, as shown in Fig. 6.2. In other words, the risk of crossing the boundary B increases as the square of the fuel deficit.

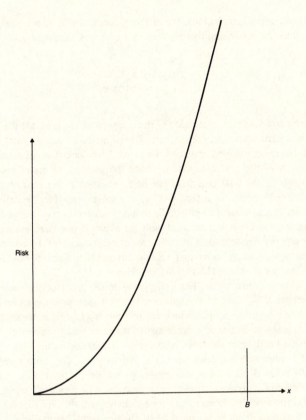

FIG. 6.2. The risk of crossing the boundary B, based on Fig. 6.1

The exact parameters of this function will depend upon the ecology of the refuelling situation. The frequency and reliability of refuelling opportunities will obviously be important factors in influencing the risk of running out of fuel. The cost of the refuelling behaviour must also be taken into account. In the present case, we assume that the robot refuels by replacing its old run-down battery with a new recharged one. So it is the availability and location of the new batteries that matters.

In animal behaviour, real costs can be studied experimentally in the field. To obtain equivalent information about the costs and benefits of robot behaviour, it would be necessary to do similar studies. Reliability studies of motor cars provide an example of this sort of approach. To evaluate the risks, costs, and benefits of a robot launched into the market-place, it would be necessary to do some ecological modelling that resulted in a cost function.

COST FUNCTIONS

In general cost functions must specify three aspects of the cost: (1) the cost of being in a particular state, (2) the cost of performing an activity, and (3) the cost of changing between activities. Once we have looked at all the various components of the cost function, we have the problem of combining these components. If the total cost $C(x)$ can be represented as the sum of the cost associated with each x in x then $C(x)$ is said to be separable. Separability is approximately equivalent to probabilistic independence of the various factors. This means that the risk associated with the value of one state variable (e.g. energy supply) is independent of the values of other variables. In assessing the cost functions of animal behaviour, separability has been found to hold in some studies but not in others (McFarland and Houston 1981).

Let us now return to our bomb-disposing robot, and (for the sake of the exercise) see if we can find a simple cost function appropriate to its ecological niche. Apart from fuel supply, which we have already looked at, the other main selective pressure influencing the design of the robot will be related to bombs. On the one hand, since the robot is to occupy a bomb-disposing niche, it must be able to approach and detect bombs to defuse them. The more bombs successfully defused by a robot, the greater its success in the market-place. So bomb-defusing is somewhat akin to the production of viable offspring in animals. On the other hand, the robots are expensive, and the type that frequently blows itself up will not be favoured by purchasers, so the bomb-disposing robot must give high priority to avoiding exploding bombs.

Let us assume that the robots are designed to deal with time-bombs, set to go off at a particular time. We will also assume (for the sake of the exercise) that the robots have some information as to when a particular bomb is likely to explode. So estimated time to explosion, T, will be an important variable in our cost function.

If a bomb does explode, then the distance D, from the robot to the bomb, will be a factor determining the likelihood of the explosion killing the robot (for simplicity we shall ignore the possibility of injury). In fact, we can regard $D = 1$ as lethal and, using an argument similar to that used for the probability of running out of fuel (above), we can suppose that the cost in relation to an explosion is the square of the proximity P of the robot to the bomb (where $P = 15 - D$) as shown in Fig. 6.3.

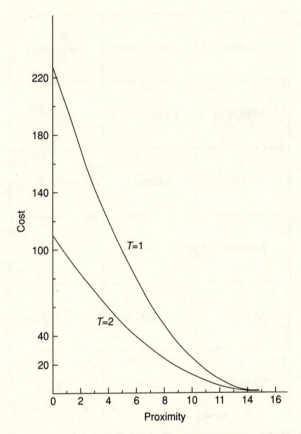

FIG. 6.3. Cost as a function of proximity to the bomb. Proximity = 15-D, where D is the distance from the bomb. The cost function is parametized by the time T to the explosion

Because this cost is also influenced by the time to explosion, we divide this quantity by T, as shown in equation (1).

$$C = Ax_f^2 + Bx_b \qquad (1)$$

where C = the (instantaneous) cost, x_f is the state of the fuel reserves, $x_b (= P^2/T)$ is the (risk) state of the robot in relation to the bomb, and A and B are scaling parameters.

So far we have considered the cost (C) in relation to the state variables (fuel)

Activity	Time usage	Energy usage
APPROACH	3 steps / T	1.0 E/T
AVOID	3 steps / T	1.0 E/T
DISPOSE	$T=1$	$E=0.5$
DEFUSE	$T=3$	$E=0.5$
PULLAWAY	$2D/T$	1 E/T

FIG. 6.4. The behavioural repertoire of the bomb-disposing robot, and the consequences of each activity in terms of time and energy. T = time to explosion, E = energy debt in arbitrary units

and (bomb), and we are assuming (for the sake of the exercise) that these are the only essential state variables. However, we should also consider the costs associated with activity. To do this we have to look at the robot's behaviour repertoire.

Let us assume that our robot is capable of the five activities listed in Fig. 6.4. These activities will have consequences in terms of time and energy usage, and of some other changes in the state of the robot. Strictly, the rate of an activity u would be variable, but for simplicity I have assumed that all activities take place at a constant rate. This means that costs of performing an activity will be proportional to the time spent performing the activity, and the cost function will look something like equation 2.

$$C = Ax_f^2 + Bx_b + Ku_c \qquad (2)$$

where K and u_c relate to the current activity.

We are now in a position to determine what costs are incurred by the robot being in a particular state and engaging in a particular activity. As mentioned above, these can be considered under three headings: (1) the cost associated with the state, (2) the cost associated with the current activity, and (3) the cost of changing from one activity to another. For simplicity, we shall ignore the last of these (but see McFarland 1989, ch. 1, for a review) in considering the behaviour of our bomb-disposing robot (i.e. we assume that all costs of changing are zero). The next step is to look at the consequence of behaviour in terms of their effects upon the state of the agent.

CONSEQUENCES OF BEHAVIOUR

Let us suppose that our bomb-disposing robot has been informed about the bomb on the trolley in the room mentioned in Dennett's original (1987) example. The first thing the robot will do is approach the bomb from a distance (say) of 15 m. In each unit of time the robot will cover 3 m.

We can plot the consequences of approach behaviour in terms of the robot's motivational state. Two aspects of the robot's state are relevant here. The first is the state of the fuel reserves, which we may conveniently refer to (in motivational terms) as hunger H. The second is the motivational state in relation to the bomb, which we may conveniently term fear F. Let us assume that this is directly related to the cost associated with the bomb, indicated in equation (2), so that $F = \sqrt{risk}/T$.

In plotting the consequences of approach behaviour in terms of these motivational variables, as is illustrated in Fig. 6.5, we are defining a trajectory that describes the changes in motivational state that occur as the robot approaches the bomb.

When the robot makes contact with the bomb, there are a number of options open to it. Like Dennett's R1, it could pull away the trolley with the bomb on board. It could dispose of the bomb, throwing it off the trolley, and then pull away the trolley with the battery on board. Since the robot is supposed to be a bomb-disposer, the best option would seem to be to defuse the bomb, and we shall explore this option first.

It takes $3\ T$ units to defuse the bomb, and during this time the risk of

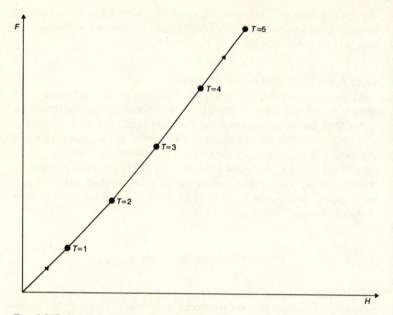

FIG. 6.5. Trajectory in the state plane, representing the consequences of approach behaviour in terms of motivational variables *F* and *H*

explosion is increasing. However, assuming this time is fixed (i.e. the robot is skilled at defusing) then it will be safe to start to defuse the bomb, provided the task is started sufficiently early, and provided the robot has accurate information about the time that the explosion is due. Uncertainty about this factor is incorporated into our formulation of the cost function, so we can look at the costs involved to see what risks are being run by the robot.

Figure 6.6 shows instantaneous cost as a function of time for a robot that decides to defuse the bomb. If the robot succeeds in defusing the bomb the risk of explosion drops to zero, but there is still an energy debt to be repaid.

The risk of explosion depends upon both time and distance from the bomb, variables which the fear variable is designed to reflect. (*Note:* motivational variables are designed to reflect the situation as determined by the ecological niche.) Therefore, the robot can base its decisions upon its motivational state, as shown in Fig. 6.7. Such a robot would be an *automaton*, meaning that its behaviour will be entirely determined by its state. Almost certainly some animals

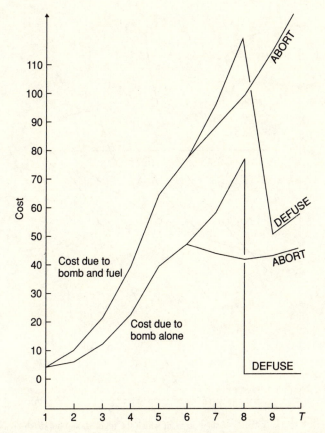

Fig. 6.6. Instantaneous cost as a function of time for a robot that decides to defuse the bomb at time $T = 6$, or decides to abort (i.e. the rest of the time is spent in avoid activity) at this time. If the robot succeeds in defusing the bomb the risk of explosion drops to zero, but there is still an energy debt to be repaid

are automata of this type (probably most insects). The advantage of the well-designed automaton is that it can achieve a lot with a small brain. The capital costs are therefore small (McFarland 1991a). The main disadvantage is that they lack flexibility. Bomb-disposing automata would not be expensive, but many would be lost in the course of duty. It may be better to design an *autonomous* bomb-disposer.

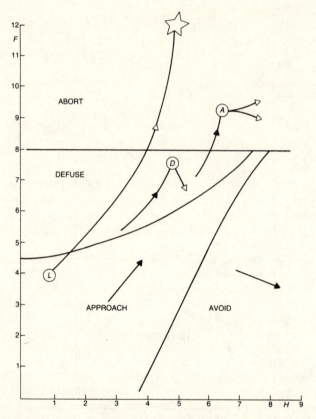

FIG. 6.7. Regions of the *F–H* state plane in which the robot should approach, avoid, or defuse the bomb, or abort the mission. *L* is the lethal trajectory that would result if the robot simply persisted in approaching the bomb. *D* is the trajectory resulting from approach followed by defuse, *A* is the trajectory resulting from approach followed by avoid

AUTONOMY

The first point to make here is that autonomy is a separate issue from self-sufficiency. In nature there are many types of autonomy that are self-sufficient. The basic principles of self-sufficiency apply to both animals and robots, but these principles are different from those of autonomy. McFarland (1992*a*) has highlighted this distinction.

Autonomy implies freedom from control. In ordinary terms, A controls B if and only if the relation between A and B is such that A can drive B into whichever of B's normal range of states A *wants* B to be in.

Certain types of machines are controllable. That is, provided the controller knows enough about the state of the machine, the machine can be made to behave as the controller wishes. To control a machine completely, the controller would have to know the state of the machine, the environmental forces acting upon it, and the rules for translating state into behaviour. For example, a boy could control a model aeroplane by radio if he knew enough about the forces acting on the plane, such as gravity, wind, etc., and the rules for translating this information into behaviour. These rules must include not only how the controls work in general, but the detailed effects of manipulation of the controls on the behaviour of the aeroplane. In addition, to control a machine, the controller must *want* to make the machine behave in a particular way. In other words, the controller must have some relevant motivation.

An autonomous robot would not be completely controllable and observable by an outside agent (this is what we usually mean by autonomy). We normally think of a dog as being autonomous in the sense that its behaviour is not readily controllable. Humans can control the behaviour of dogs to some extent, but the extent of this control depends partly upon the animal's internal state and partly upon its internal organization, or architecture. Thus a human is usually more successful in influencing the behaviour of a dog than a cat, because the one is more amenable than the other. Dogs like to be cooperative, while cats do not. Autonomous robots, like dogs and cats, would be self-controlling and not completely controllable by outside agents.

Autonomous systems are capable of (at least) elementary cognition, and this makes a difference to their motivation. Motivation in an automaton is simply that aspect of the total state that determines the behaviour. In an autonomous agent, the motivational state includes a cognitive evaluation of the likely consequences of possible future behaviour. Cognition in animals can be considered as the manipulation of declarative knowledge, in the sense that the agent knows that something is the case (see McFarland 1991*b*). This knowledge can influence various aspects of behaviour, and is not tied to any one procedure. Cognitive evaluation requires judgement about the likely consequences of future behaviour. Such evaluation implies optimization with respect to some motivational criterion. So the process of decision-making in an autonomous agent is different from that of an automaton.

Whatever the decision-making mechanism employed by an agent, it must cope with the following tasks: (1) the numerous behavioural alternatives are somehow reduced to a manageable number of candidates for behavioural expression (the breadth-of-search task); (2) to evaluate the alternatives, the animal must have some knowledge of the probable consequences of the alternative activities (the depth-of-search problem). If the agent is an automaton, then these two tasks are accomplished by means of built-in procedures. The breadth-of-search task is circumvented because the animal simply performs that activity dictated by its current state. The depth-of-search task does not arise because the possible consequences of an activity are not evaluated, but simply assumed as part of the design process. In other words the required knowledge is implicit in the design.

If the animal is autonomous, then these two tasks become problems for the individual. In artificial intelligence terminology, they are both aspects of planning. As we saw with R1D1, the major problem with behaviour-planning based on search procedures is the amount of computation required for a thorough search. The amount of search can be reduced by the application of appropriate heuristics in the form of rules of thumb, indicating solutions which may work but are not optimal.

Planning must ultimately be based upon some internal representation of the cost function, which in ethology is called the *goal function* (McFarland and Houston 1981), but for which the term *value system* (after Vershcure *et al.* 1992) may be more appropriate in robotics. Note that the value system (or goal function) may be a good or a bad representation of the cost function, and the degree to which an agent is well adapted behaviourally will depend upon the accuracy of this representation (see McFarland and Houston 1981). In the case of our bomb-disposal robot, the architecture would be something like Fig. 6.8.

Planning does not allow the agent to escape from the realities of its ecological niche. It is still subject to the discipline summarized by the cost function. So what advantage can be gained by planning? The extra flexibility that could be obtained in our bomb-disposal example is summarized in Fig. 6.9.

IMPLEMENTING THE COST-BASE

In suggesting that animals are cost-based robots, I am claiming (1) that animal behaviour is governed by mechanisms no different in principle from those that could be put into a robot; (2) that these mechanisms are optimized (through evolution) with respect to the real costs that are characteristic of the animal's ecological niche; and (3) similar design principles could be used in robotics. To demonstrate the last of these claims it would be necessary to implement the cost-base for a robot. That is, once the ecological niche of the robot has been specified, and once an appropriate cost function has been formulated, some way of translating these functional descriptions into mechanisms has to be found.

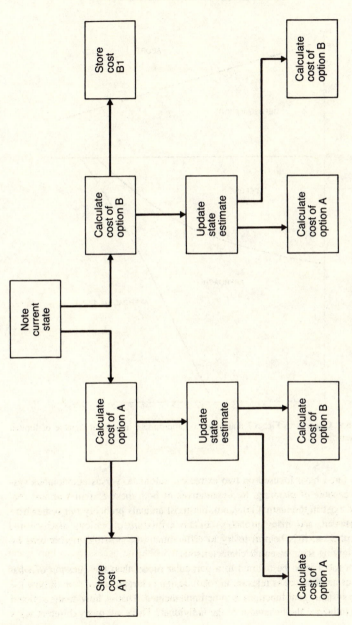

FIG. 6.8. Architecture of a simple planning system

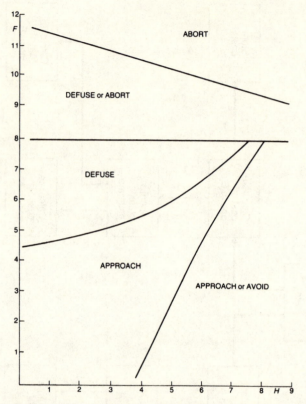

FIG. 6.9. Changes to Fig. 6.7 that might be appropriate in a robot capable of limited autonomy

So far, I have focused on two extremes: automata, versus autonomous systems capable of planning. Representatives of both these extremes almost certainly exist in the animal kingdom, but most animals probably fall somewhere in between, and many probably contain a mixture of various mechanisms. Nevertheless, it is helpful to try to differentiate the possible mechanisms by highlighting their essential characteristics.

If a robot is to be tailored to a particular niche, then the question of what kind of architecture is relevant in robot design is largely a question of how the value system (goal function) is to be implemented. That is, how do the notional costs influence the behaviour of the individual? There are many different ways in which the information inherent in the value system may, or may not, be made use of by the decision-making mechanisms of the individual agent. It may be that the notional costs are estimated by the individual in a cognitive manner; it may be that they are simply monitored by the individual; it may be that the individual receives no information about the notional costs, but merely behaves (through the use of decision-rules) as if the costs were relevant. These are all alternative ways of implementing the design that is specified by formulating a particular value system. Let us return to our example.

First we must look at the fundamental design of our bomb-disposing robot. The robot is designed to perform various activities. To perform these, the robot must receive information about various environmental variables. Let us assume that the robot has sensors specially designed to detect the values of these variables. The outputs of the sensors cannot drive behaviour directly. They must first be calibrated in terms of their relative importance to the robot. The calibration transforms each sensor-output into a motivational variable, on the basis of which decisions can be made. When we come to the question of how the sensor-outputs are to be calibrated, there are two basic design strategies that we should think about. We can call these the 'procedural' strategy and the 'cognitive' strategy.

1. The *procedural strategy* is that normally assumed to apply to primitive (non-cognitive) animals, and to automata. According to this strategy, the calibrations should be designed to reflect the animal's ecological circumstances, as outlined by Houston and McFarland (1976). The calibrated motivational variables then directly reflect the 'importance' of the various sensory inputs, in terms of survival value or fitness. The animal, or robot, can then act on this information in accordance with fairly simple procedures.

2. The *cognitive strategy* is more anthropocentric in inspiration. According to this strategy, the calibrations should be designed to reflect the 'facts' as represented by the sensory outputs. Some sensors will, by their very nature, distort the incoming information. Such distortions can sometimes be compensated by suitable calibration. The aim of the design is to present an accurate picture of the world that is monitored by the sensors. The calibrated variables then provide a body of knowledge that is 'declarative' in the sense that it can be used for a number of purposes, and is not tied to any particular procedure. The manipulation of such declarative knowledge is essentially a cognitive exercise.

The two strategies, as outlined here, represent extremes, and it is perfectly possible to imagine a design that combines them. For our present purposes, however, we proceed beyond the calibration stage to enquire how the value system might be incorporated into such designs.

There is a spectrum of possibilities. At the extreme 'procedural' end of the spectrum is the possibility that the design incorporates no information about the value system, but the behaviour-control system is put together in such a way that the animal or robot behaves as if it were guided by the relevant notional costs. Such a system would be analogous to a physical system in which the behaviour conforms with some extremal principle. This possibility is discussed below.

Another possibility is that the sensor-outputs are weighted by elements of the value system. The resulting motivational variables would then represent the relative importance of the sensory inputs, and could be used directly in rules of procedure leading to a behavioural outcome. The most obvious rule of procedure is that the strongest motivational tendency wins in a competition for behavioural expression. The behavioural outcome would then reflect the most important (in terms of the value system) of the alternatives. This design has the merit of being simple and straightforward, but it has a number of disadvantages, which have been aired in the animal behaviour literature (e.g. McFarland 1989, ch. 1).

At the 'cognitive' end of the spectrum is the possibility that the sensor-outputs are calibrated purely in terms of the stimulus properties, thus providing a representation of the state of affairs monitored by the sensors. An advantage of this design is that the state-representation so achieved could be used for a number of purposes. It is a form of declarative knowledge. To achieve a behavioural outcome that also took the value system into account, it would be necessary to evaluate the state in relation to the value system. This would require a separate representation of the value system. A disadvantage of this approach is that it is more complicated than the procedural device, and would require a larger brain (McFarland 1991*a* and *b*).

The essential differences between these possibilities relate to the nature of the representation of the value system. In the procedural design, there is no explicit representation of the value system, but it may be functionally represented in the calibration of the sensor-outputs. This type of representation is sometimes called a tacit representation. In the cognitive design, on the other hand, the value system is explicitly represented, like a table of values that can be consulted from time to time. In the procedural design, there is no evaluation process apart from that embodied in the rules of procedure. In the cognitive design on the other hand, there is an explicit evaluation process which works out the best (in terms of the value system) behavioural outcome in relation to the prevailing state. This process will generally be a cognitive process, because the information that it utilizes is represented in a declarative form, capable of being used for a number of purposes.

1. Implicit Value System

The use of optimality principles in accounting for animal behaviour can be seen as analogous to the use of extremal principles in physics (see McFarland 1992b). A stone thrown through the air obeys a 'least action' law, minimizing a particular function of kinetic and potential energy. The stone behaves as if seeking an optimal trajectory, although its behaviour is in fact determined by forces acting in accordance with Newton's laws of motion. Similarly, an animal may behave as if seeking an optimal trajectory through the state space (Sibly and McFarland 1976; McFarland and Houston 1981) but such an account says little about the mechanisms involved. Optimality principles are, in effect, functional explanations which describe how the animal ought to behave in order to attain some objective. For a causal explanation, the equivalent of physical forces must be established. These will presumably take the form of a set of rules of thumb governing behaviour, or of some equivalent cognitive mechanism.

It is possible for the rules governing behaviour to conform to some extremal or optimality principle, without there being any obvious sign of this in our formulation of the control system. For example, McFarland (1991a) discusses, as a simple example, a cost function of the form

$$C(x) = Kx_1^2 + Lx_2^2 + Mu_1^2 + Nu_2^2 \tag{3}$$

and points out that this function can be optimized by an agent that follows the simple behavioural rule

if $x_1u_1 > x_2u_2$ perform activity u_1, else perform activity u_2

Animal examples are provided by Sibly and McFarland (1976), McFarland and Houston (1981), and Stephens and Krebs (1986).

The point is that rules of thumb can be incorporated into a simple model, or mechanism, which makes no explicit reference to the cost function, but nevertheless produces behaviour that conforms with the cost function.

2. Embedded Value System

In animals, stimuli are monitored by sensors and calibrated to produce cues. If we could measure them, we would expect to find that these cues were related to the survival values associated with the relevant states and stimuli. For example, Houston and McFarland (1976) consider the plight of the desert lizard *Aporosaura anchietae*, foraging on the surface of sand dunes. The probability of death due to thermal stress can be represented as a function of temperature, as shown in Fig. 6.10(a). The probability of death from predation is also likely

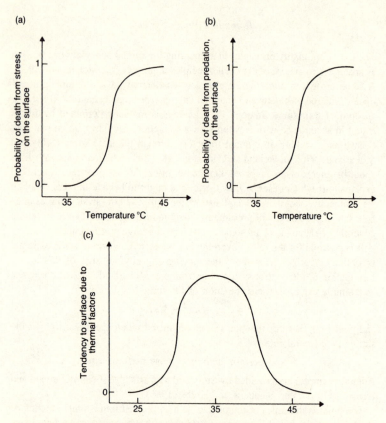

Fig. 6.10. Hypothetical functions relating temperature and survival for the lizard *Aporosaura*. (*a*) and (*b*) are cumulative probability functions. (*c*) is a calibration function derived from (*a*) and (*b*). After Houston and McFarland (1976)

to be a function of temperature (Fig. 6.10(*b*)), because the lizards are less mobile at lower temperatures. Taking these two aspects of survival into account, we might expect the calibration of thermosensitivity to be somewhat like that illustrated in Fig. 6.10(*c*). In other words, the motivational variable that results from the calibration can be thought of as that part of the tendency to be active on the dune surface which is due to thermal factors. This variable is calibrated in such a way that it reflects the risk (due to thermal factors) of being on the dune surface. Other factors which also affect the tendency to forage on

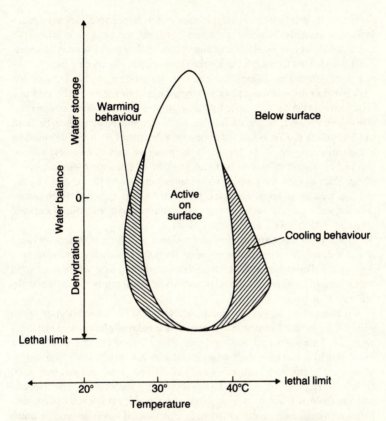

FIG. 6.11. Two-dimensional representation of the physiological states at which *Aporosaura* might be expected to be below the surface of the sand, or above the surface and involved in warming or cooling behaviour, or actively foraging. Boundary lines indicate transitions between one type of behaviour and another. After Houston and McFarland (1976)

the surface, notably hunger and thirst, are discussed by Houston and McFarland (1976).

If we restrict ourselves to consideration of the thermal and hydration factors affecting the lizard, then we can construct a 'survival space' within which the animal can be safely active on the surface of the dunes. An example is illustrated in Fig. 6.11.

On the basis of the calibrations illustrated in Fig. 6.10, and of a similar calibration for hydration factors, Houston and McFarland (1976) constructed alternative models which would produce different possible survival spaces depending upon the assumptions incorporated into the models. In particular, they pointed out that in addition to appropriate calibration of sensory information, there also has to be some appropriate combination rule relating the information from different modalities. For example, the tendency to be active on the surface due to thermal factors has somehow to be combined with the tendency to be active on the surface due to hydration factors. Different combination rules give different results, as illustrated in Fig. 6.12. The main point made by Houston and McFarland (1976) is that the optimal combination rule is not independent of the calibration functions. So that in designing an animal (or robot) calibration and combination have to be taken together in a holistic optimization exercise. They suggest the conjoint measurement approach (Krantz and Tversky 1971) as a means of approaching this problem. Another approach which tackles both the scaling of the variables and their combination rules is the 'functional measurement' approach of Anderson (1978).

In relation to robot architecture, the problem with the calibration approach is that it cannot be conducted in isolation from the combination rules, or their equivalents. The performance of the robot (or animal) as a whole must fulfil certain criteria, and not all the responsibility for this can be placed upon the calibration of sensory input.

In relation to our lizard example, the problem is to find an architecture which will ensure that the lizard will not incur undue risks of predation in venturing on to the dune surface to find food and water. Effectively this means that a lizard should not expose itself when its muscles are insufficiently warmed up to enable it to run with sufficient speed to dive into loose sand and bury itself (Louw and Holm 1972). An architecture involving a simple permissive temperature threshold will not be adequate, because the risk of predation is counterbalanced by risks of starvation. Normally, the animal has little time in which to forage for food, because the temperatures are too high in the middle of the day and too cold at night (Fig. 6.13). As usual, the architecture must permit compromise and trade-off among conflicting requirements.

3. The Explicit Value System

A basic problem in robotics is planning movements to solve some prespecified task, and then controlling the robot as it executes the commands necessary to achieve those movements. In this context, planning involves deciding on a course of action before acting. The robot is designed with some problem-solving system that can formulate a plan to achieve some stated goal, given some initial situation. The plan is a representation of a course of action for achieving the goal.

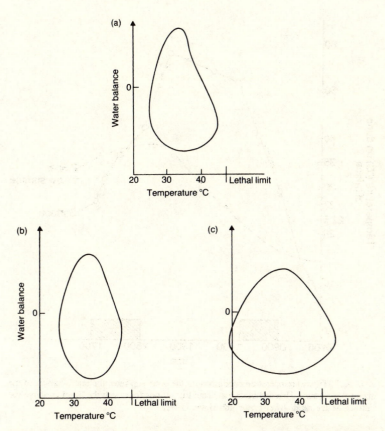

FIG. 6.12. Two-dimensional representation of the physiological states at which *Aporosaura* might be expected to be above or below the sand. (*a*) Boundary line transposed directly from Fig. 6.11. (*b*) Boundary line based on an additive combination rule. (*c*) Boundary line based on a multiplicative combination rule. After Houston and McFarland (1976)

The formulation of plans, or representations of possible courses of action, is not without its computational difficulties. These have been admirably reviewed by Janlert (1987). Ethologists have no argument with the definition of a plan, but we might disagree with the traditional views of how plans should be transformed into behaviour. One problem is that goal-directed (or means-end) formulations are deficient because they violate the trade-off principle (McFarland

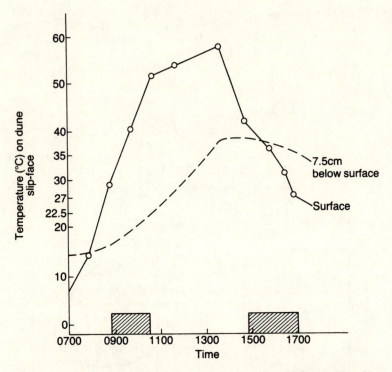

FIG. 6.13. Typical temperature conditions on the dune slip-face, the micro-habitat of the lizard *Aporosaura*. Hatched blocks indicate the periods for which the lizard is above the surface of the sand. After Louw and Holm (1972)

1989, ch. 5). While means-end analysis may be acceptable as a way of formulating a plan, as a recipe for behaviour it is primitive and restricted in its applicability. In a rational system, good design should be based upon evaluation of options in terms of broad relevant criteria, such as those provided by a value system.

This means that, in deciding among alternative possible courses of action (once their implications have been evaluated) the agent should compare them in terms of their ultimate value or utility. To do this it is necessary to have an explicit representation of the value system. Moreover, as we see if we think about the frame problem, the evaluation of implications of possible courses of action is not without computational problems.

Returning to our bomb-disposing robot, we might think that its performance

(Fig. 6.9) could be further improved by learning. We must realize, however, that learning requires feedback about success and failure, and this feedback must be based upon an immutable set of values (see below). In other words, learning has to operate in relation to the value system, so the improvement in performance that results from learning is an improvement in relation to the value system. Now the value system may or may not be a good representation of the cost function that is characteristic of the robot's ecological niche. In animals it can never be a perfect representation, because of evolutionary lag, genetic diversity, and ecological competition (McFarland and Houston 1981). In robots the same logic holds. This means that learning is not always adaptive. Learning in robots is adaptive only in so far as the value system resembles the cost function (McFarland 1991a).

COST-BASED LEARNING

For learning to be adaptive (i.e. of advantage) the (predefined) value system must reflect the cost function that is characteristic of the ecological niche. The more the set of values, or goal function, resembles the cost function, the better adapted will be the agent. Note that it is *not possible* for the agent to learn to modify the value system to make it more like the cost function. Since learning is itself dependent upon the goal function to provide reinforcement value, it cannot itself modify the value system (McFarland and Houston 1981; McFarland 1991a). This is why the value system must be a predefined value system.

At this point we may wonder whether there is anything to be gained by learning. In animals learning is not always worth while (McFarland and Houston 1981; Tovish 1982). Sometimes, the animal has a choice between a mastered situation with relatively low pay-offs, and a to-be-learned situation with higher pay-offs. If the cost of learning is high, then the mastered situation may be the better option.

Learning may alter either the availability or the accessibility of resources. In general, the availability of a resource determines the extent to which changes in the rate of behaviour affect the consequent changes in state, while the accessibility of a resource is a constraint upon the rate at which the resource can be handled. In a foraging animal, for example, the availability of prey is an environmental parameter which influences how quickly the animal can find prey. The accessibility of prey has to do with the predator's ability to handle the prey. If it takes a squirrel a long time to open a nut, then the nut-handling time acts as a constraint upon the rate at which the squirrel can take in nuts. The squirrel could alter the constraint by improving its skill in handling nuts, so the accessibility of the resource is really a property of the animal rather than of the environment.

In terms of cost-based learning, the animal/robot may learn to improve the availability of resources, or the accessibility of resources. For example, if the bomb-disposing robot could learn to reach the bomb more quickly, it would be learning to improve the accessibility of resources, because it would be improving the consequences of its chosen behaviour. If it could learn to defuse the bomb more quickly, it would be learning to increase the accessibility of resources, because it would be altering a constraint on its behaviour (see McFarland and Houston 1981; Tovish 1982). The learning process itself may involve costs, often because the resulting trajectory (in the state space) is more costly in the early stages of learning than the trajectory that would result if the robot stuck to its old ways.

Finally, what about the frame problem? A well-designed bomb-disposing robot will be tailored for its niche. This means that its decision-rules, (autonomous) choice mechanisms, and learning processes will be optimized (as far as possible in the face of the constraints) with respect to the cost function that is characteristic of the niche. In these respects, the robot will be similar to an animal, and the frame problem will have been circumvented at the design stage. Indeed, if we believe animals to be deterministic agents, in the sense that their behaviour is fully determined in the cause–effect terms, then we should regard animals as cost-based robots.

REFERENCES

Anderson, N. H. (1978), 'Methods and Designs: Measurement of Motivation and Incentive', *Behavior Research Methods and Instrumentation*, 10: 360–75.

Dennett, D. C. (1987), 'Cognitive Wheels: The Frame Problem of AI', in Pylyshin (1987).

Fodor, J. (1983), *The Modularity of Mind* (Cambridge, Mass.: MIT Press).

Hayes, P. J. (1987), 'What the Frame Problem is and isn't', in Pylyshin (1987).

Houston, A., and McFarland, D. (1976), 'On the Measurement of Motivational Variables', *Animal Behaviour*, 24: 459–75.

Janlert, L. (1987), 'Modeling Change—The Frame Problem', in Pylyshyn (1987).

Krantz, D. H., and Tversky, A. (1971), 'Conjoint-measurement Analysis of Composition Rules in Psychology', *Psychological Review*, 78: 151–69.

Louw, G. N., and Holm, E. (1972), 'Physiological, Morphological and Behavioural Adaptations of the Ultrasammophilous Namid Desert Lizard *Aporosaura anchietae* (Bocage)', *Madogua*, 1: 67–85.

McCarthy, J. (1959), *Programs with Common Sense* (Proceedings of the Teddington Conference on the Mechanisation of Thought Processes; London: Her Majesty's Stationery Office).

—— and Hayes, P. J. (1969), 'Some Philosophical Problems from the Standpoint of Artificial Intelligence', in B. Meltzer and D. Michie (eds.), *Machine Intelligence 4* (Edinburgh: Edinburgh University Press).

McFarland, D. (1989), *Problems of Animal Behaviour* (London: Longman).

—— (1991*a*), 'What it Means for Robot Behaviour to be Adaptive', in: J. Meyer and S. W. Wilson (eds.) *From Animals to Animats* (Cambridge, Mass.: MIT Press).

—— (1991*b*), 'Defining Motivation and Cognition in Animals', *International Studies in the Philosophy of Science*, 5: 153–70.

—— (1992*a*), *Autonomy and Self-sufficiency in Robots* (VUB, A1 memo).

—— (1992*b*), *Rational Behaviour of Animals and Machines* (in press).

—— and Houston, A. (1981), *Quantitative Ethology: The State-Space Approach* (London: Pitman Books).

Pylyshyn, Z. W. (1987) (ed.), *The Robot's Dilemma: The Frame Problem in Artificial Intelligence* (Norwood, NJ: Ablex Publishing Corporation).

Sibly, R. M., and McFarland, D. J. (1976), 'On the Fitness of Behaviour Sequences', *American Naturalist*, 110: 601–17.

Stephens, D. W., and Krebs, J. R. (1986), *Foraging Theory* (Princeton, NJ: Princeton University Press).

Tovish, A. (1982), 'Learning to Improve the Availability and Accessibility of Resources', in: D. McFarland (ed.), *Functional Ontogeny* (London: Pitman Books).

Vershcure, P., Krose, B., and Pfeifer, R. (1992), 'Distributed Adaptive Control: the Self Organisation of Structured Behaviour', *Robotics and Autonomous Systems* (in press).

PART III

PART II

7

FROM ROBOTS TO ROTHKO: THE BRINGING FORTH OF WORLDS

MICHAEL WHEELER

1. INTRODUCTION

It would be a gross understatement to say that the murals from Mark Rothko's Seagram Project have presence. They *ooze* it. The viewer is humbled by the huge canvases with their enormous, bursting rectangles, painted in sombre blacks, maroons, and reds.[1] My use of the word 'humble' here might be taken as evidence that I subscribe to the widely held view of Rothko's paintings as suggestive of spiritual or religious realms. And a mystical interpretation of Rothko's work might seem to be justified, given that Rothko described his own personal experience of painting as a 'religious experience' (Rosenblum 1975), and taking into account the fact that one of his most famous works is 'The Rothko Chapel' in Houston. But Rothko maintained that he was a materialist. Hence he consistently resisted 'otherworldliness' (Ashton 1983). How can we reconcile these apparently conflicting positions?

Answering that question will take us on a long journey. If I were a cognitive scientist, one might expect this to be the signal for a computational analysis of our experience of art, in terms of either symbolic data structures and heuristically guided search algorithms, or distributed representations realized as patterns of activation spreading through networks of interconnected processing units. Well, as it happens, I am a cognitive scientist. I count myself an enthusiastic supporter of the idea that cognition is a phenomenon which is wholly amenable to scientific investigation. But I urge scepticism about the potential for *orthodox* cognitive science to shed light on the constitutive nature of, or the causal processes underlying, our cognitive encounters with works of art. To achieve

Partly based on a paper to be published in C. Murath and S. Price (eds.), *The World, the Image, and Aesthetic Experience* (Bradford: Interface, 1995).

[1] London's Tate Gallery owns selections from the third series of canvases which Rothko produced for this project. It is these murals to which I refer here. The works were commissioned for the Four Seasons Restaurant in the Seagram Building in New York, but were never delivered.

these explanatory goals, we need a radically different way of conceptualizing matters, and a rather different set of explanatory tools. Both the conceptual framework and the set of explanatory tools to which I refer have been playing distinctive and significant roles in the developing discipline of Artificial Life.[2]

Techniques such as genetic algorithms (see sect. 5), which are often associated with A-Life, can be used to produce works of art (e.g. Todd and Latham 1992). Moreover, it has been suggested that the process of 'doing' A-Life is itself analogous to artistic creation (Bonabeau and Theraulaz 1994). Fascinating as these issues are, neither is directly relevant to the subject-matter of this paper. What I aim to make plausible is the claim that A-Life-oriented accounts of cognition have the potential to help us explain our experience and understanding of art. In spite of this eventual goal, most of what follows will not be an exercise in aesthetics, because my point of departure is the (surely uncontroversial) assumption that our encounters with art do not take place in a cognitive vacuum. Rather we can make headway on the problem of explaining our understanding and experience of art only in the context of an account of cognition as a whole. Therefore, in this paper, considerable time will be spent on justifying and on explicating an A-Life-based approach to cognition as a phenomenon. Then we shall be in a position to identify the ways in which A-Life can help with the more specific case.

2. FROM ANIMATS TO HERMENEUTICISTS

'A-Life' is an umbrella-term, covering a diverse range of research projects, from models of RNA replication and sensory-motor activity to studies of collective intelligence and population dynamics. For the purposes of this chapter, I shall concentrate on a particular strand of A-Life research—a strand sometimes known as 'the animat approach'.[3]

Animats are *artificial animals*, or, to give an alternative definition, *artificial autonomous agents*. The class of such systems includes autonomous robots with actual sensory-motor mechanisms, and simulated autonomous agents embedded in simulated environments. In this context, an autonomous agent can be defined as any adaptive system which, while in continuous long-term interaction with its environment, actively behaves so as to achieve certain goals. From this definition it follows that, for a system to be an autonomous agent, it must exhibit *adaptive behaviour*, behaviour which increases the chances that

---

[2] Henceforth I shall abbreviate 'Artificial Life' to 'A-Life', and 'Artificial Intelligence' to 'AI'.

[3] The term 'animat' is due to Wilson (1985). Meyer and Guillot (1994) provide a recent review of work within the paradigm. In characterizing the animat approach, I merely make explicit views which, I take it, are held by most (if not all) of the field's practitioners.

that system can survive in a noisy, dynamic, uncertain environment. We should identify a system as an adaptive system only in those cases where it is useful to attribute survival-based purpose and purposes to that system. So rivers do not count as adaptive systems, but moths do. Naturally occurring adaptive behaviour is the result of evolutionarily determined pressures on the survival and reproduction prospects of embodied systems. However, once we are in the animat domain, the notion of 'adaptiveness' no longer applies only to evolved systems. Adaptiveness is a matter of surviving long enough in an environment to achieve certain goals. These goals may not necessarily include reproduction. But having said that, design methodologies based on *artificial* evolution may well be powerful ways to produce robust control systems for animats (see sect. 5).

As with most definitions of concepts, there are potential problem cases. By the definitions on offer here, amoebas and some plants, for example, might count not only as adaptive systems, but also as autonomous agents. It seems to me a matter for dispute whether this is a sign that the proposed definition of 'autonomous agency' is too liberal, or a sign that our intuitions in this area are prone to being too restrictive. In any case, with respect to the natural world, this chapter is concerned only with insects, fish, reptiles, birds, non-human mammals, and humans.

The guiding idea behind the animat approach is that we can increase our understanding of adaptive behaviour—the nature of the phenomenon, and of the mechanisms underlying it—through the synthesis and analysis of artefacts. On evolutionary grounds, it seems reasonable to suppose that human linguistic competence and deliberative thought are overlays on a prior (and, in terms of survival, more fundamental) capacity for adaptive behaviour. Thus the field starts not with the aim of understanding the reasoning capacities possessed by humans, but with the goal of explaining the adaptive behaviours performed by simpler (although whole) natural or artificial creatures, who perceive and act in their environments.

Some texts of a philosophical nature which are consonant with, and have influenced work within, animat research (and A-Life in general) draw on hermeneutical accounts of understanding.[4] In developing the explanatory framework on offer here, I too shall draw on such accounts. So let us focus on a specific statement of the hermeneutical situation, as identified by Gadamer (1976). The phenomenon of understanding is an ongoing series of historically embedded events. In characterizing such events, we cannot make fully explicit,

---

[4] Palmer (1979) provides a comprehensive introduction to the different strands of thought that come under the banner of hermeneutics. Varela *et al.* (1991) argue for a philosophical position which is hermeneutical, and in harmony with A-Life.

ignore, or eliminate the role played by the understander's specific socio-cultural biases, precisely because those biases are constitutive elements in the very process through which the understander makes sense of things. They are the 'prestructures' of understanding, a product and expression of the understander's specific place in socio-cultural history, and they must be taken as 'the given' in any understanding-event (such as, for example, an encounter with a work of visual art).

This should immediately suggest a prima facie tension in the project I have set myself. The claim that understanding is hermeneutical would seem to be in conflict with the naturalistic approach to mind to which any cognitive science must, presumably, be committed. Naturalism in the philosophy of mind is the view according to which (i) all there is is physical stuff, and (ii) the study of mind is continuous with work in the natural sciences. Thus to naturalize under-standing, one would have to show *how* it is that the capacity to make sense of things is the sort of property that a physical system could possess. From the hermeneutical perspective, naturalism seems to demand that it be possible to objectify—in the tradition of science—whatever those prestructures are that determine the knower's process of understanding. And that is precisely what the hermeneuticist denies is possible. The cognitive scientist, attempting to explain understanding, is embedded in a particularly acute hermeneutical situ-ation, because whilst she cannot make explicit the prestructures of her own understanding, it is that very 'making explicit' that would be required, in order for her to reach the required position of scientific objectivity with respect to her subject-matter.[5]

A second worry stems from the fact that, for many hermeneuticists (e.g. Gadamer 1976), the prestructures of understanding are linguistic phenomena, in the sense that the traditions and heritage which shape understanding are thought to be embedded in language. Skills, crafts, and *works of visual art*—things which are not in themselves linguistic—are held to be intelligible only in so far as they can be brought to articulation in language. By contrast, as we have seen, the animat approach in A-Life concentrates on the synthetic counterparts of non-linguistic animals. Most A-Lifers wish to claim—as I do—that concepts such as understanding and knowledge can be used non-metaphorically to ac-count for the behaviour of non-linguistic agents. It would seem that the best advice anyone could give to such people is 'steer well clear of hermeneutics'.

Since I intend to ignore my own advice, it seems that we are about to go deep into a dangerous philosophical territory. So, in order to avoid getting lost, let us take one step back, and find our conceptual bearings.

---

[5] The relationship between hermeneutics and cognitive science is discussed elsewhere by, for example, Varela *et al.* (1991) and Drury (1994).

3. DESCARTES'S LAST STAND

Thus Murphy felt himself split in two, a body and a mind. They had intercourse apparently, otherwise he could not have known that they had anything in common. But he felt
his mind to be bodytight and did not understand through what channel the intercourse
was effected nor how the two experiences came to overlap. (From 'Murphy' by Samuel
Beckett)

Murphy is trapped in the aftermath of the Cartesian divorce in which the
cognizer's mind was severed from her body and her environment. The prime
source of his anxiety might seem to be Descartes's most famous conclusion—
that the mind is an essentially independent realm of operations which causally
interacts with the material world on an intermittent basis (Descartes 1641).
And, of course, Cartesian substance-dualism does suffer from all sorts of seemingly insurmountable difficulties (well documented elsewhere) to do with the
supposed causal interactions between the two kinds of stuff (the mental and the
material). But the problems of substance-interaction are not the focus of this
investigation. Descartes's legacy was not merely to give a whole new (although
now largely discredited) respectability to the thesis of mind–matter substance-
dualism. In effect, he helped to open up an *explanatory* divide between mind
and world, according to which a fundamentally 'internal' subject relates to an
'external' world of objects via some interface. Whether that interface is the
pineal gland or the boundary of the brain or central nervous system does not
much matter (cf. Hornsby 1986). So, even if Beckett's anti-hero were a committed physicalist, without the burden of substance-dualism, he could still adopt
a recognizably Cartesian attitude towards the phenomena in question. And
where the anti-hero goes, so goes many a cognitive theorist.[6]

Cognitive science has been dominated by the complementary dogmas of
representationalism and computationalism. Despite the fact that the concept of
'representation' has been a key theoretical term in cognitive science, the question of how we might go about recognizing a representation when we come
across one is far from decided. Every available characterization (including the
one I am about to offer) is almost certainly incomplete, or falls prey to counter-
examples. Nevertheless, it seems as if something like the following must be
going on. Consider an agent, A, one of A's internal states, S, and some feature,
F, of A's environment (where F may be an aspect of A's surroundings, or of
A's own activity). A, S, and F are all picked out by some external observer, O.
O correctly identifies S to be a representation of F if, on those occasions when

---

[6] The conclusion that orthodox cognitive science is fundamentally Cartesian in one respect or
another has also been reached, although via routes other than the one followed here, by (at least)
Dreyfus (1991), Dreyfus and Dreyfus (1988), Harvey (1992), Haugeland (1993), van Gelder (1992),
and Varela *et al.* (1991).

O's best explanation of A's behaviour is that A is coordinating its behaviour reliably with respect to F,

1. S is a cause of A's behaviour, and
2. S has been previously (or is now) a cause of A's behaviour on an occasion when F was (is) not actually present to A, but—according to O's best theory—A was (is) still coordinating its behaviours with respect to F.

If this second condition is not met, S is not a representation of F, but merely part of a recurring causal correlation between F, S, and some aspect of A's behaviour.

In order for O to judge whether or not condition 2 is met, she would need to have a theory of the role that S plays in A's overall cognitive organization. So now consider the hypothetical organization of the cognitive system, as proposed in orthodox cognitive science. A perception-module constructs a model (a set of representations) of the external world. This world-model is then delivered to a central system made up of sub-modules for specialized sub-problems such as reasoning and planning. These sub-modules manipulate the representations in accordance with certain computational algorithms, and then, usually after a process in which various sub-modules communicate with each other, 'cognition-central' outputs a further set of representations (this time of the desired actions) to which the action-mechanisms then respond. Thus ongoing activity is organized as a sense-plan-act cycle, in which each stage is conceptually distinct (cf. the analysis of classical AI by Brooks (1991)). Given this architecture, the representational content of any particular S is determined by the information about A's environment that, according to O's best theory, the internal modules or sub-modules concerned are communicating to each other. (So we can ask questions such as: 'what does the agent's visual system tell the agent's planning system?') In this way, the content of S is at least partly determined by the role that S plays in O's theory of A's overall cognitive organization.

In one form or another, representationalism has been around for centuries. But cognitive science as we know it was launched when the computational theory of cognition was annexed to the representational theory of mind. Indeed, the putative existence of in-the-head computational mechanisms seems to provide a powerful solution to the problem of how a physical system (such as a brain) could ever realize a representational system (such as—so the story goes—a mind). On this view, representations are ultimately physical states of physical systems, and computations are ultimately physical processes occurring in those same physical systems. Hence we are presented with a promising way to naturalize our capacity to make sense of our world. Surely nothing could be further from Cartesian dualism.

Appearances can be deceptive. First, like Descartes, orthodox cognitive scientists hold that inner states and inner processes are the essence of mind. Indeed, by identifying—in a more or less sophisticated manner—mind with brain, the Cartesian physicalist can buy into a concrete, 'between-the-ears' sense of the 'inner-ness' of mind. Secondly, even if mental representations are ultimately physical states of the brain or central nervous system, the role of those states in causally explaining behaviour remains the same as in Descartes's account. Thirdly, for Descartes, perception, thought, and action must be temporally distinct and theoretically separable. The cognizer's body is essentially a courier system, delivering sensory-input messages to, and collecting motor-output messages from, the thinking thing. And that picture of perception, thought, and action bears an uncanny resemblance to the sense-plan-act cycle adopted in orthodox cognitive science. Brooks (1991) dubbed the architectural assumptions of orthodox cognitive science 'decomposition by function'. He might as well have called them 'decomposition by Descartes'.

Here we should deal with a possible misunderstanding. At root, this is not an issue of classicism versus connectionism in cognitive science. Whilst functional decomposition is part and parcel of the classical approach, the cognitive scientist who discards classicism in favour of connectionism need not—and, typically, does not—also discard the commitment to functional decomposition. Standard connectionist networks are usually trained to execute some functionally well-defined sub-task, abstracted away from cognition as a whole. The sub-task in question is conceptualized as a matter of executing transformations between input representations (which, in theory, arrive from elsewhere in the cognitive architecture) and output representations (which, in theory, are sent on to other functionally identified sub-modules).

The conclusion of this section is that, despite the field's physicalist assumptions, orthodox cognitive science is still in the grip of a recognizably Cartesian picture of ongoing perception and action in an environment. So what is different about A-Life?

4. A-LIFE AND THE PERCEPTION-ACTION CYCLE

[What's] noteworthy about our refrigerator aptitudes is not just, or even mainly, that we can visually identify what's there, but rather that we can, easily and reliably, reach around the milk and over the baked beans to lift out the orange juice—without spilling any of them. (Haugeland 1993: 11)

In animat research, the thesis of *active perception* has come to the fore. This is the view that perception should be conceptualized as an *activity*, performed by an autonomous agent in the context of ongoing adaptive behaviour. From this perspective, it is a mistake to conceptualize, say, visual perception as a process of recognition and identification, in which an organism takes what are, in effect, a series of sophisticated photographic snapshots, intended for use by the central modules in processes of classification and categorization. Indeed, far from thinking that perception and action can be investigated separately, animat researchers tend to think in terms of a unitary phenomenon, the *perception-action cycle*. This idea is not original to A-Life. Variations on the theme of the perception-action cycle can be found in, for example, the philosophy of Merleau-Ponty (1963), the brain theory of Arbib (1989), and in the AI vision research of Ballard (1991). But an approach that concentrates on the situated activity of whole agents is particularly well positioned to investigate the implications of adopting such a view. Thus the concept of active perception finds a particularly clear expression in those research projects in situated robotics concerned with the role of sensory-motor control in achieving adaptive behaviour. These projects are either examples of, or obvious forerunners of, the animat approach in A-Life (see e.g. Horswill and Brooks 1988; Brooks 1991; Cliff 1991; Franceschini *et al.* 1992; Cliff *et al.* 1993; Webb 1994).

To get by in life, animals and animats need to act adaptively, in real time, in a relatively unconstrained environment. As many commentators (from A-Life and AI) have observed, these capacities were painfully absent from the behavioural repertoires of (the few) robots built according to orthodox principles (e.g. *Shakey* (Nilsson 1984)). Hence there is some plausibility to the suggestion that, rather than looking for time-consuming general-purpose perception and planning systems, we should expect at least some of the mechanisms underlying ongoing activity to be somewhat rough-and-ready affairs, dedicated to the just-good-enough real-time completion of certain specific behaviours of high adaptive significance.

In this context, consider the concept of a *subsumption architecture*, as pioneered by Brooks and his colleagues (see e.g. Brooks 1991). In this approach to robot control, individual behaviour-producing systems—'layers'—are designed to be individually capable of (and to be generally responsible for) connecting the robot's sensing and motor activity, in order to achieve some ecologically relevant behaviour. So each layer is coupled to the robot's environment along what might be called a 'channel of ecological significance'. Starting with layers that achieve simpler behaviours (such as 'avoid objects' and 'explore'), layers are added, one at a time, to a debugged, working robot, so that overall behavioural competence increases incrementally. The layers run in parallel, affecting each other only by means of suppression or inhibition mechanisms. No detailed messages can be passed between layers (as they can between procedures in a robot designed according to classical principles).

To appreciate the potential applicability of this specificity claim to naturally occurring control systems, consider Webb's robot-implementation of a hypo-thesized mechanism for cricket phonotaxis (the ability to track an auditory signal produced by another cricket) (Webb 1993, 1994). Female crickets locate potential mates by tracking an auditory advertisement produced by the male. The female cricket's control system is a layered, parallel architecture of behaviour-producing systems. Each of these layers involves specialized links between sensing and motor behaviour, in a way which is clearly analogous to a subsumption architecture. Cricket phonotaxis is achieved through the opera-tion of one of these layers.

It is worth highlighting just how the phonotaxis-enabling mechanism em-bodies the principle of specificity. A tracheal tube of fixed length connects the female cricket's ears and spiracles. When the male's signal is picked up, a phase cancellation occurs, producing a direction-dependent intensity difference at each ear-drum. This intensity difference provides the basis for the female cricket's successful movement towards the sound source (the male), because the side closer to the sound source will have the stronger response. The key point for current purposes is the close coupling between the male's auditory signal and the mechanism underlying phonotaxis in the female. The mating signal has to be at a specific frequency, because the whole process depends on the fixed length of the trachea.[7] As Webb (1993: 1092) puts it, '[There] is no need to process sounds in general, provided this sound has the right motor effects. Indeed, it may be advantageous to have such specificity built in, because it implicitly provides "recognition" of the correct signal through the failure of the system with any other signal'. Moreover, the way that the mechanism operates means that there is no need to hypothesize the existence of two separate pro-cesses—one to recognize the song, and one to determine the direction in which to move.

Dedicated mechanisms that link sensing to motor behaviour may be highly specific to some particular adaptive behaviour of high ecological significance, as in the case of cricket phonotaxis. Alternatively, they may negotiate domains reflecting behavioural patterns which are grouped together—naturally—by the capacities of the system and the way it is embedded in its ecological niche. For example, neurophysiological studies of monkeys have demonstrated the exist-ence of specialized cortical areas for behaviours that use foveal motion and for behaviours that use peripheral motion (Komatsu and Wurtz 1988).

The success of these special-purpose mechanisms should not be judged according to any criterion of optimal performance by that mechanism in its own sub-domain, abstracted away from the overall behavioural success of the

---

[7] I have simplified matters somewhat, for the sake of clarity. The mechanism actually operates such that the signal has to be of the appropriate temporal pattern as well as the appropriate frequency (see Webb 1994: 46–7).

complete agent. For instance, Horswill and Brooks (1988) report on the development of a robot whose overall goal is to approach arbitrary moving objects in real time, using vision as the only sense. This involves the performance of visual segmentation and motion-tracking sub-tasks. As a complete agent, the robot behaves quite well in an unconstrained, dynamic, real-world environment, whilst being rather poor at each of the sub-tasks considered individually. The structure of the interactions between the agent and its environment suffices to secure overall adaptive success. And if this is the case for a robot designed by humans, there seems little doubt that wherever similar mechanisms are found in nature, evolution will have ensured that the overall organization and flow of control will be opportunistic and sub-optimal—but that's life.[8]

The moral of this section is that, in characterizing autonomous agent behaviour, we should be careful to distinguish between the situated agent and the mechanisms which enable that agent to behave adaptively in its environment. An ongoing perception-action cycle is an achievement of a whole agent. It is grounded in—as opposed to being the same process as—a set of adaptive sensory-motor couplings.

5. EVOLUTIONARY ROBOTICS

There is a strategy for designing animats which is directly inspired by the design-history of biological agents. In *Evolutionary Robotics*, genetic algorithms are used to develop control systems for animats. (The work on which I concentrate here is by the Evolutionary Robotics Group at the University of Sussex. For more details, see Cliff *et al.* (1993), Harvey *et al.* (1994), and Husbands *et al.* (1995).)[9] Loosely speaking, the evolutionary methodology is to set up a way of encoding robot control systems as genotypes, and then, starting with a randomly generated population of controllers, and some evaluation task, to implement a selection cycle such that more successful controllers have a proportionally higher opportunity to contribute genetic material to subsequent generations, that is, to be 'parents'. Genetic operators analogous to recombination

---

[8] It does not follow from the sub-optimality of some internal mechanisms that evolutionary biologists cannot use optimality models to provide normative explanations of animal behaviour (see sect. 8). In specific instances where phenotypic behaviour diverges from optimality, such internal sub-optimality may help us to understand why that divergence has occurred. Moreover, it does not seem inconceivable that sets of interactions between strictly sub-optimal internal mechanisms could result in optimal behaviour (or close to it) at the level of the whole agent.

[9] I have benefited enormously from many discussions with Phil Husbands, Inman Harvey, and Dave Cliff on the practical, theoretical, and philosophical issues raised by evolutionary robotics. In the course of what follows, I use various features of their work to illustrate philosophical points. The evolutionary roboticists themselves may not agree with every aspect of my philosophical interpretation.

and mutation in natural reproduction are applied to the parental genotypes to produce 'children', and a number of existing members of the population are discarded so that the population size remains constant. Each robot in the resulting new population is then automatically evaluated, and the process starts all over again. Over successive generations, better-performing controllers are discovered.

In the work at Sussex, the robot control systems are made up of sensors (tactile and visual), motors (which drive wheels), and non-standard artificial neural networks featuring subsets of the following sorts of properties (some of which reflect certain properties of biological neural networks): continuous-time processing, real-valued time delays on the connections between the units, non-uniform activation functions (that is, the activation profiles of different units from within the same network can be described by different mathematical functions), deliberately introduced noise, and connectivity which is not only both directionally unrestricted and highly recurrent, but also not subject to symmetry constraints (that is, any two units in the network can be connected to each other, and any single unit can be connected to itself).

But now how should one of these control systems be 'wired up', in order to achieve a particular task? One general commitment of this work is that as few restrictions as possible are placed on the potential structure of the control system. The evolutionary roboticist decides on the robot's immediate task, but endeavours to stay out of the business of how the robot's 'nervous system' should work in order to achieve the appropriate behaviour. In accordance with this 'hands-off' principle, the number of internal units, the number, directionality, and recurrency of the connections, and certain parameters of the visual system are placed under evolutionary control. The job of artificial evolution is to tune the control-system dynamics to the environment in such a way that the robot can complete the evaluation task.

This approach has resulted in the artificial evolution of sensory-motor controllers which succeed in guiding robots (real and simulated) in the performance of simple homing and target-tracking tasks. These controllers are adaptive in that they exhibit considerable robustness when tested on generalized versions of the specific tasks for which they were actually evolved. So let us consider a specific example. A (simulated) visually guided robot is placed in a (simulated) circular arena with a black wall and a white floor and ceiling. (The simulation incorporates detailed models of the Newtonian physics of the interactions between the agent and its environment, based on observations of a real robot.) From any randomly chosen position in the arena, the robot's task, as encoded in the evolutionary evaluation function, is to reach the centre of the arena as soon as possible and then to stay there. (Notice that there is no sense in which the robot already 'knows', at the outset, what its task is.)

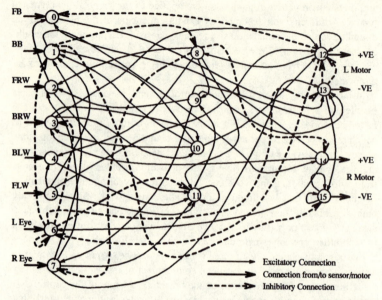

FIG. 7.1 An evolved control network for the room-centring task. The units on the left hand side are originally designated as input units, although artificial evolution has re-wired the connections so that some of these units have, in effect, become inter-neurons. FB = Front Bumper, BB = Back Bumper, FRW = Front Right Whisker, BRW = Back Right Whisker, BLW = Back Left Whisker, FLW = Front Left Whisker. Diagram reproduced with kind permission

The room-centring scenario requires little of the robot in the way of behavioural complexity, and some successful controllers soon evolve. Nevertheless, the control systems present some suggestive interpretive problems; and there seems no reason to assume that control systems evolved for more complex tasks will be any different. The artificially evolved networks bear little resemblance to the human-designed networks, so often employed in mainstream connectionism, in which activation passes from input to output layer in a straightforward, orderly fashion. In fact, the networks evolved for the room-centring task tend to resemble bowls of spaghetti. Figure 7.1 shows the wiring diagram for one successful controller. Even after redundant units and connections (which may be left over from earlier evolutionary stages) have been eliminated, and the significant sensory-motor pathways have been identified, the channels of activation in the network still flow in complex and counter-intuitive ways, due to the nature of the connectivity and the existence of feedback loops (Fig. 7.2).

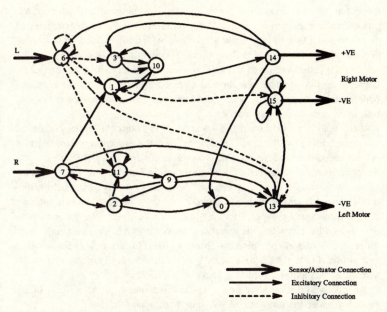

FIG. 7.2 The same evolved control network as shown in Figure 7.1, but with only the salient pathways in the network shown. Notice that the robot has evolved to use only visual guidance in achieving the goal. Diagram reproduced with kind permission

How compelling is a representational/computational explanation of the observed behaviour? In fact, how do we go about answering that question? One way would be to appeal to the 'objective' causal structure of the control system. It is worth pursuing this idea for a moment, to see where it takes us. We are confronted by complex channels of activation in a fully integrated control system. It is no longer *obvious* that we should, or even that we could, decompose the agent's causal structure into functionally well-defined sub-systems that communicate with each other, in such a way that it makes sense to think in terms of a sense-plan-act cycle. That is the 'penalty' for letting evolutionary design mechanisms loose on the problem of structuring non-standard artificial neural networks. Hence, someone might say, there is no orthodox interpretation of the robot's behaviour.

At this point care is required. We need to take account of the (hermeneutical) fact that deciding on the causal profile of a complex system is something which is not neutral with respect to the external theorist, and the set of preconceptions which she brings to the phenomena under investigation. For example, if a theorist approaches an evolved control system *as* a computational information-processing device, then her proposed decomposition of the causal structure of the system will tend to proceed in accordance with the principles of functional decomposition. This appeal to the preconceptions of the theorist does not make the internal causal profile of the system entirely arbitrary. It is the interaction between, on the one hand, the theorist's preconceptions and, on the other, the understanding of the system thereby obtained, that makes one proposed explanation more compelling than another.

If our goal is to understand the workings of orthodox AI-systems (classical or connectionist), or electronic calculators, then the explanatory framework of computationalism (and the style of representationalism that goes with it), plus the organizational principles of decomposition by function, are entirely appropriate. However, for other systems, such as rivers or weather fronts, the orthodox framework seems entirely inappropriate. (Just because we can simulate fluid dynamics on a computer does not mean that the river 'behaves' in the way that it does by computing its moment-to-moment moves. We can build computer models of non-computational theories (Beer, forthcoming).) So on which side of the divide should we place the artificially evolved control system described above, and the control systems of animals?

Anyone who comes down firmly on the 'computers and calculators' side is probably under the influence of the view that, whatever else an animal (or a successful animat) may be, it is most certainly an *information-processing system*; that is, any proposed framework for understanding cognition must explain how an agent's cognitive system consumes, stores, and manipulates information. And computers are particularly good at that sort of thing (with a little help from human programmers). But do we have to conceptualize cognition as information-processing? The way to answer that question is to see if we can find a credible alternative.

6. DYNAMICAL SYSTEMS

A dynamical system is any system for which we have a rigorous analysis of the way it evolves over time. Formally, this is any system for which we can provide (1) a finite number of state variables which, given the interests of the observer, adequately capture the state of the system at a given time, and (2) a set of state space evolution equations describing how the values of those variables change with time. Given (1), we can produce a geometric model of the set of all possible states of the system called the *state space* of that system. A state space has as many dimensions as there are state variables for the system, and each possible state of the system is represented by a single point in that space. Given (2), and some initial conditions—a point in the state space—subsequent changes in the state of the system can be plotted as a curve in the state space. Such a curve is called a *trajectory* of the system, and the set of all such trajectories is the system's *phase portrait*.

An *attractor* is a state of the system to which trajectories passing nearby tend to converge. Now consider some attractor P. The set of states such that, if the system is in one of those states, the system will evolve to the attractor P, is called P's *basin of attraction*. The trajectories which pass through points in the basin of attraction on the way to the attractor, but which do not lie on the attractor itself, are *transients* of the system. There may well be several attractors in a single state space, and these attractors may be of different types. For instance, *point* attractors are single points in the state space which represent constant solutions to the system, whilst *periodic* attractors represent oscillatory solutions.[10]

The ongoing behaviour of a dynamical system is specified by the current state of the system and the evolution equations which govern how the system changes through time. Certain values in a state space evolution equation specify quantities that affect the behaviour of the system without being affected in turn; these are called the parameters of the system. The relation of *coupling* obtains when two theoretically separable dynamical systems are bound together in a mathematically describable way, such that, at any particular moment, the state of either system fixes the dynamics of the other system, in that some of the parameters of each system either become, or become functions of, some of the state variables of the other. Now consider two coupled dynamical systems, X and Y: X is said to *perturb* Y when changes in the state variables of X result in changes in the parameter-values determining the phase portrait of Y, thereby resulting in changes in that phase portrait. At some critical parameter-values a system may become *structurally unstable*, in that tiny changes in certain parameter-values may result in the immediate emergence of a qualitatively different phase portrait. These qualitative changes are called *bifurcation points*.

Husbands *et al.* (1995) demonstrate how techniques based on dynamical systems theory can be used to gain an understanding of the situated activity of the room-centring robot.[11] In essence, the approach is to identify the ways in which the robot's visual world (which is determined by the evolved visual morphology) interacts with the dynamics of the control network to enable the

---

[10] Abraham and Shaw (1992) provide a friendly but thorough introduction to dynamical systems theory (including chaos theory).

[11] For coverage of other ways in which dynamical systems theory can play a role in animat research and cognitive science, see Beer (forthcoming), Smithers (1992), van Gelder (1992), and Wheeler (1994).

robot to achieve its goal. An analysis of the dynamics present in the significant visuomotor pathways in the control system is combined with a two-dimensional state space representing (to the observer) the robot's visual world (that is, the visual signals which would be received at different positions in the world). The result is a phase portrait predicting the way in which—according to the dynamical systems model of the 'physical' system—the robot will tend to move through the state space.

Now consider the specific control system shown in Figs. 7.1 and 7.2. The phase portrait for the behaviour of the robot in an environment of wall-height 15 (the environment in which the control system was evolved) features a single point attractor in the visuomotor space. This attractor corresponds to a very low radius circle about the centre of the world. The whole state space is, in effect, a basin of attraction for this attractor. In short, the model predicts that the robot will *always* succeed at its task, a prediction which was borne out by empirical demonstration. (It is important to stress that certain details of this particular dynamical analysis are contingent upon the nature of the specific scenario. For example, the symmetries of the environment allow the observer to generate the visuomotor state space used. However, for our purposes, it is the general *style* of analysis that matters, not the specific details.)

The next stage was to investigate the adaptiveness of the control system by analysing the behaviour of the robot in an arena with wall-height 5, that is, in an environment for which the control dynamics were not specifically evolved. The change in wall-height means a change in the structure of the robot's visuomotor state space. The same process of analysis now yields a phase portrait featuring two point attractors in visuomotor space, both corresponding to successful behaviours. Once again the model was confirmed by empirical demonstration. So the dynamical systems analysis correctly predicts that the control system is general in that it will achieve its goal by exhibiting different situated dynamics in different environments.

The observed behaviour rewards an interpretation in terms of active perception (Husbands *et al.* 1995). The robot is actually very poorly sighted indeed. (Each eye features only one pixel, and returns a single grey-scale value.) Moreover, this particular evolutionary solution to the problem is such that only one of the two eyes is ever used at any specific moment. Minimal monocular vision is no basis for building models of the world, which could then be used to make decisions about how to proceed. The robot succeeds in its task by exploiting its own movements to create variations in light inputs. Thus the ways in which the sensory-motor mechanisms are coupled to the world enable the robot to complete the task, given its ongoing activity as a whole agent.

Let us now attempt to extract a general principle from this analysis. The scientist using dynamical systems theory as an explanatory tool has to make certain decisions about how to divide up the phenomenon under investigation. In the context of the science of autonomous agents, the framework provides a natural way to cash out the claim, made earlier, that where to draw boundaries (interfaces) between the different internal modules in an evolved control system is, to some extent, up to the observer in her search for an understanding of behaviour. But now we can make a more radical claim. It is also up to the observer to decide when and where to draw boundaries between the 'internal' states of the agent and the 'external' states of the environment. For certain purposes (for example, to gain an understanding of salient aspects of a control system's internal dynamics), it is useful to think of, say, an animal's nervous system and the physical medium in which it operates as separate, but coupled, dynamical systems, such that each system biases the intrinsic possibilities for change already present in the other. But this is only one stage in understanding how the dynamics of a control system interact with the dynamics of an environment to produce well-tuned adaptive behaviour. In a sense, it is the one agent-environment system which is *primary*. An analysis in terms of coupled dynamical systems is an *abstraction* that may not always be the best method of understanding what is going on, and, in some cases, may not even be practically possible.[12]

The visuomotor phase portraits, which were constructed to understand the behaviour of the room-centring robot in different environments, could be thought of as an attempt to capture how the robot moves through its visuomotor world. The dynamical structure of that world (the phase portrait) changes when the robot's 'physical' environment (to which it is coupled) changes, although the structure of the control system itself does not change. Thus amputating the robot's environment from the explanation would leave one with, at best, a radically incomplete understanding of the embedded behaviour.

How we analyse the control systems and the sensory-motor mechanisms that enable agents to achieve adaptive behaviour depends on how we conceptualize the phenomenon at issue. Hence we shall be misled by inappropriate preconceptions about the nature of that phenomenon. One key implication of the general principle just expressed is that any account of cognition starting from the Cartesian perspective of a divided subject and object is bound to founder, because it takes what is an abstraction to be the most fundamental fact about the nature of agents and their worlds. This idea has a heavy-weight philosophical relation.

---

[12] Many thanks to Phil Husbands for discussion of this point.

7. A HEIDEGGERIAN PERSPECTIVE

Many key passages in Heidegger's *Being and Time* are dedicated to rejecting the idea that our everyday dealings involve encounters with value-free objects on which a subject then confers meaning. The subject–object dichotomy is basic to the Cartesian account of mind-world relations, and to the philosophical foundations of orthodox cognitive science. It has its place in the Heideggerian picture; but, far from being in any sense fundamental, it is held to be a derivative mode of encounter which depends on, and comes after, a more direct and revealing relation.[13]

Heidegger uses the term 'Dasein' (literally 'being-there') to characterize human being (the way in which humans are). According to Heidegger, the fundamental character of the entities with which Dasein has dealings in everyday practical activity is that of *equipment*. We encounter entities as being *for*, for instance, throwing, writing, transportation, or working. This is Heidegger's notion of the *ready-to-hand*.

The less we just stare at the hammer-thing, and the more we seize hold of it and use it, the more primordial does our relationship to it become, and the more unveiledly is it encountered as that which it is—as equipment. The hammering itself uncovers the specific 'manipulability' of the hammer. The kind of Being which equipment possesses—in which it manifests itself in its own right—we call 'readiness-to-hand'. (Heidegger 1926: 96)

So our most direct and revealing understanding of equipment comes about not through some detached intellectual or theoretical consideration, but through our manipulative dealings with those entities; that is, it is essentially an *activity-based* account of everyday understanding.

The meaning of a piece of equipment is given by the possibilities of interaction which it presents to Dasein—its normal functioning in Dasein's way of life. Such entities are part of a socially and historically embedded totality of *involvements* which, in the end, refer back to the agents who use those entities. Heidegger's example is of the hammer which is involved in an act of hammering; that hammering is involved in making something fast; the making something fast is involved in achieving protection against the weather; and finally, protection against the weather is to shelter the agent. The totality of such involvements is a relational whole which, in the end, pertains to Dasein. The hammer is intelligible as what it is only with respect to the shelter and indeed

---

[13] It is impossible, in the limited space available here, to do justice to a book such as *Being and Time*. What follows is already heavily oriented towards the specific subject-matter at hand, and many nuances will be passed over. Dreyfus' book-length commentary (Dreyfus 1991) provides a clear and detailed analysis of Heidegger's ideas.

all the other items of equipment to which it meaningfully relates in Dasein's normal practices. For Heidegger, a 'world' *is* the totality of an involvement-whole, inseparable from the skills and practices definitional of that whole. This is a radical holism.

Corresponding to primordial understanding as an activity-based phenomenon is Heidegger's concept of *circumspection*. This is identified as a fundamental feature of our typical everyday activity, for which divisions between subject and object have no purchase. We are *absorbed* in our activities in such a way that we skilfully *cope* with developments and eventualities without being ex-plicitly aware of events or objects. In this mode, flexible common-sense know-how operates without thoughts-that or thoughts-about, and awareness of objects and thematic self-awareness are not present. Hence Heidegger would deny that 'mental content', as traditionally understood in terms of a subject relating to objects, is a feature of our most basic directed activity. The term that Heidegger introduces to express the fundamental form of intentionality is *comportment*, defined as 'being-directed-toward'. This is held to be a feature of human activ-ity in general, and should, in itself, carry no overtones of conscious or delib-erate goal-driven action, or of propositional attitudes or mental content.

But has Heidegger really been concerned with what is our *most fundamental* way of encountering *all* the entities in our world? The notion of the ready-to-hand might be plausible for hammers and shelters (things that we design), but what about rocks and twigs (naturally occurring entities)?[14] Surely our most fundamental way of encountering these entities is precisely as value-free ob-jects? To answer this objection, we need to be clear about the priority relation at issue. First let us consider man-made entities: Heidegger would not wish to deny that there are causally efficacious properties of nature which explain why it is that you can make hammers out of wood and metal, but not out of jelly and ice cream. The physical sciences can explain 'how it is' that the hammer does what it does, but not 'what it is' that the hammer is, what its meaning/function is in our world. As we have just seen, for Heidegger, a 'world' is a totality of involvements, defined with reference to Dasein's skills and practices. Now to the extent that naturally occurring entities show up in such a totality (that is, when Dasein *uses* such entities as tools, missiles, etc.), they too have their way of being for Dasein defined by what they afford Dasein in ongoing everyday activity. This does not mean that naturally occurring entities cannot show up in other ways (that is, as value-free objects) when they are not relevant to Dasein's absorbed coping. But, as we are about to see, this is also true of hammers.

Ongoing coping operates within the equipmental whole. But there can be

---

[14] Many thanks to Maggie Boden for reminding me of the relevance of this point.

disturbances in this referential network which allow another mode of the being-of-entities to come to the fore. The most graphic cases are breakdowns (for example, when the head falls off the hammer). When equipment breaks, the mode of Dasein's encounter with the entity changes. In cases where the equipment malfunctions or impinges on Dasein's activity in such a way that Dasein cannot immediately switch to a new mode of coping, that equipment exhibits a way of being that Heidegger calls *un-ready-to-hand*. Resolving the situation will require deliberate action and/or deliberative reasoning (explicit planning). Now that ongoing coping has ceased, the referential relationships making up the equipmental whole have been disturbed, and there has emerged a separation between Dasein and the piece of equipment. However, in this situation, the entity is still not merely an object with pre-given determinate properties. 'Being too heavy for this job' is not a simple property of the hammer. Moreover, it is not a simple relation between Dasein and the hammer, but a situational feature which is identifiable only given a particular context and a particular set of background practices. Dasein's deliberate problem-solving will take place against this background. However, we sometimes deal with entities either as objects of theoretical investigation by the physical sciences, or as objects of pure contemplation. Under these circumstances, the entities concerned have become completely decontextualized from the equipmental whole of everyday practice, and their way of being has changed to *present-at-hand*. At this stage of our dealings, the subject–object dichotomy is fully applicable.

We are now in a position to clarify Heidegger's notion of understanding, via the introduction of a Heideggerian concept which, in the original German, is 'Rede.' Most commentators translate this as 'talk' but, as Dreyfus observes (Dreyfus 1991), this is misleading, as, for Heidegger, 'Rede' does not have to be linguistic. Dreyfus suggests that a more accurate translation would be *telling*, as in 'telling the time' or in 'telling the difference between different wines'. I shall follow Dreyfus's translation. Telling is the way in which Dasein articulates the structure of the involvement-whole, just by telling things apart in use. So hammering a fence post into the ground articulates one of the hammer's significances. But many such significances do not possess names in our language. I do not have words for all of the subtle actions I performed with a squash racquet in last night's match. Hence, although we can often express significances in language, articulation and telling do not have to be linguistic. But in whichever form telling occurs, it will presuppose the referential whole of the totality of involvements.

But what is the source of the significances that define equipment? The normative aspect of significance is assured by the fact that *being-with* other Daseins is fundamental to Dasein's being-in-the-world; that is, Dasein is socialized. It is essential to get this feature of Dasein's being absolutely clear. Dasein does not start out as 'un-socialized' and then later 'become socialized', Dasein *is* socialized. So, by this criterion, *animals and infants cannot be Dasein*. The nature of the socialization is also crucial. Dasein is 'always already outside', because Dasein exists in that it is socialized into ways of acting. These ways of acting are the background practices that define cultures and societies; and they constitute the norms that allow the involvement-whole to exist. So it is with our socialization into our culture that equipment becomes significant. Hence it is here that we find the prestructures of understanding, and the genesis of the hermeneutical situation.

Given all this, there might seem to be an enormous conceptual gulf between Heidegger's account of Dasein's being-in-the-world, and the dynamical systems-based understanding of the room-centring robot. However, there are intriguing parallels. In fact, I suggest that if the Heideggerian picture is compelling, then there is good reason to think that the dynamical systems perspective, as set out in this chapter, combined with the concept of active perception, provides a compatible framework for the scientific investigation of the mechanisms under-lying world-embeddedness.

Conceptually, we move from the ready-to-hand to the present-at-hand (via the un-ready-to-hand), as a result of the inhibition (or the prevention) of the unreflective activity that constitutes everyday understanding. All these various ways of being presuppose the totality of involvements, the phenomenon of world; but only the present-at-hand is correctly characterized in terms of a full-blown subject–object dichotomy. Now recall that the moral of section 6 was that when the external observer attempts to understand the ongoing activity of an environmentally embedded autonomous agent, she needs a framework for thinking about that agent's ongoing behaviour which does not assume the subject–object dichotomy as primary. One might capture the connection in the following thought: the conceptual hyphens in Heidegger's concept of 'being-in-the-world' are partners of the empirical hyphen in the dynamical systems no-tion of an agent-environment system.[15] The separation of agent and environment into two (or, indeed, any number of) systems is something to be imposed in context, by the external theorist, on those occasions where the nature of the behaviour is most satisfactorily characterized in those terms. Thus both the Heideggerian account of world-embeddedness and the scientific framework for animat research sketched in this chapter stand in opposition to Cartesian ways of thinking about the relationship between agents and their worlds.

---

[15] This way of putting things evolved out of a conversation with Michael Morris.

8. THE BRINGING FORTH OF WORLDS

These speculative, but (to me, at least) suggestive, observations might seem to embody a deep tension, given Heidegger's claim that the significances articulated during ongoing activity are determined by socio-cultural norms. As mentioned earlier, it looks as if Heidegger has to deny that non-human autonomous agents even have worlds of meaning (domains of significance). This would seem to be in conflict with the animat approach. But can we retain a recognizably Heideggerian perspective, and, at the same time, champion the existence of animal (and animat) worlds?

If we continue to maintain, with Heidegger, that 'being embedded in a culture' is the only source of significance, then we might as well throw in the towel. And a Heideggerian notion of significance makes sense only if we can identify normative constraints to do the job of structuring a meaningful world. But where else can we find norms of behaviour, except, that is, in societies and cultures? The answer I shall offer will not go down well with hard-line Heideggerians.

Consider an adaptive behaviour such as catching some prey. In achieving this behaviour, an animal will coordinate its activities with respect to ecologically significant objects, events, or situations which, to borrow a term from Miller and Freyd (1993), I shall call *fitness affordances*. Fitness affordances 'point both ways'. A prey is only a prey with respect to some predator. It may, itself, be a predator to some other creature on which *it* preys. Consequently, fitness affordances are irreducibly cospecificationary, whilst being perceiver-independent in the sense that 'fitness effects are imposed by natural selection whether the organism likes it or not; they cannot be eliminated through subjective denial or wishful thinking' (Miller and Freyd 1993: 16). Fitness affordances are best understood as properties of an agent-environment system.

The good or ill of a fitness affordance is determined by the effects it is likely to have on the positive or negative survival prospects—the Darwinian fitness—of the animal. 'But', the hard-line Heideggerian will respond, 'surely you don't believe that norms can be generated from evolutionary selection pressures? The results of evolution just *are*; there is no sense in which things *should* occur one way or another. Don't confuse causal processes with normative constraints.'[16] Although I do not have the space to give this response the attention it deserves, it seems, to me, to involve a misunderstanding about the normative role that *optimality models* play in the biological sciences.[17] The term 'optimality

---

[16] Of course, it is not only Heideggerians who would level such a criticism (see e.g. Morris 1992).

[17] Parker and Maynard Smith (1990) provide a key discussion of the theoretical and practical issues arising from the deployment of optimality models in evolutionary biology.

models' should be taken to include models of 'simple' scenarios, in which the optimal behaviour for an individual is independent of what other individuals do (e.g. in solitary foraging), and more complex multi-agent scenarios, where what counts as the best strategy for an individual will depend on the strategies adopted by the other agents in the relevant eco-system (e.g. in ritualized combat). In multi-agent scenarios, a strategy is considered optimal when it is *evolutionarily stable*; that is, if that strategy is adopted by most members of a population, that population cannot be invaded by a mutant playing a rare alternative strategy (Maynard Smith 1982). So fitness is maximized in the sense that individuals not adopting the ESS do worse. This is 'competitive optimization' (Parker and Maynard Smith 1990).

The optimality approach assumes that adaptation is common in nature, and that adaptation is to be explained by natural selection. Of course, present-day animals should not be thought of as optimal solutions to some set of adaptive problems posed in the primeval swamp. And the optimality of behaviour may well only ever be approximate, because the process of adaptation may lag behind environmental changes (e.g. in co-evolutionary scenarios). But optimality models do not assume—nor do they attempt to demonstrate—that animal behaviour is always optimal. Rather, optimality models provide a way to make sense of the claim that if we can correctly identify the costs and benefits of ecologically-embedded behaviour patterns, then we will be able to explain why the animal in question *should* behave in certain ways. The failure of such a model to predict at least the qualitative patterns in an animal's behaviour indicates that our theories about that animal's ecological niche are either incomplete or just false, not that the concept of optimal fitness is of no use in understanding the selective pressures at work in animal worlds.

Different animals inhabit different ecological worlds. The significances which characterize those worlds can be identified by appeal to the norms of optimally fit adaptive behaviour. Thus fitness affordances are the evolutionary prestructures of understanding. And, of course, humans are just as embedded in evolutionary history as are non-human animals; so we should expect our domains of significance to be codified not only by cultural norms, but also by evolutionary norms. Indeed, the significances articulated in Dasein's building of a shelter (Heidegger's own example; see sect. 7) are more naturally cashed out by an appeal to evolutionarily determined, survival-based norms. And given that biology is part of natural science, human understanding will be naturalized to the extent that fitness affordances, as opposed to social norms, codify our worlds. To extend the proposed framework to animats, we merely have to add that, in many cases, an animat's fitness will be calculated from how well that agent does in achieving some task decided by the human designer. In these cases the most fundamental fitness affordances will derive from these externally imposed goals.

The relationship between mechanism and meaning here was already implied by the earlier discussion of active perception. Consider the use of specific sensory-motor couplings along channels of ecological significance. The physical stimuli to which sensory mechanisms respond are not, in themselves, meaningful properties of the agent's world. Moreover, the agent's internal mechanisms are not the source of meaning. To focus on the evolutionary case, the way in which the complete agent, embedded in its environment, exploits fitness affordances during ongoing activity brings forth (articulates) significance. But how an agent exploits fitness affordances is, of course, just the cumulative result of the ongoing operations of sets of adaptive sensory-motor couplings. Hence it is on the basis of the way in which the female cricket's control system is tuned to the auditory stimulus produced by the male (and vice versa) that the male's auditory output becomes (at the level of the whole organism) a call-to-mate, a meaningful property (fitness affordance) of the female cricket's ecological world.

9. ART AND LANGUAGE

Finally, it is time to return to the experience and understanding of visual art. First consider Gadamer's hermeneutical account, in which meaningful worlds come to stand through the interaction of interpreter and work (Gadamer 1976). On this view, we do not understand a piece of art by reconstructing some subjective meaning on behalf of the author or artist which is somehow encapsulated in the work. According to Gadamer, the work of art 'lives' in its presentations, what it 'says' to every interpreter in every age. Such events of understanding depend on both what we bring to the work (our history and tradition) and what the work brings to us. As a result of a dialogue between interpreter and work, the horizons of both are fused, and a world is brought forth. Given the theme of this chapter, we might throw caution to the wind, and put a dynamical systems gloss on this event, by saying that the one interpreter-work-of-art system is explanatorily primary. Neither system, considered separately, is adequate to explain the nature of the event.

As we saw earlier, for Gadamer, the medium in which understanding-events take place is language. The norms making up our socio-cultural heritage are thought to be embedded in the language that we use. Thus the prestructures of understanding are linguistic, and language creates the possibility of a domain of significance. But, in our investigation of an A-Life-based approach to cognition, we found reason to reject the primacy of language in the process of understanding, even in a hermeneutical account of that process. Strangely enough, this helps us to understand the sense of mysticism engendered by Rothko's rectangle paintings. If human understanding is not primarily linguistic, yet a distinctly hermeneutical account of understanding still makes sense, then not only the visual, but the musical, and performing arts may be able to affect us in fundamental ways which constitute non-linguistic, but, nevertheless, hermeneutical forms of understanding. Consider our experience of jazz. Surely we do not understand Charlie Parker's saxophone improvisations or Buddy Rich's drum patterns by bringing them to articulation in words (whatever that could possibly mean). Tapping our feet would seem to be a better way of expressing our half of the hermeneutical dialogue.[18]

To my mind, the tendency to experience Rothko's paintings as somehow mystical can be traced to a distinctive ingredient in the whole Rothko experience. The viewer is drawn into—even engulfed by—the spaces occupied by the paintings. These spaces are, of course, not the fixed two-dimensional planes 'actually' occupied by the surface of the paintings, but transient, virtual spaces opened up by the interaction between viewer and work. In an attempt to understand this hermeneutical (and dynamical) phenomenon, we can begin by noticing that the amorphous horizontal borders dividing the rectangles in many of Rothko's paintings often display an uncanny affinity with the horizons depicted in the romantic landscapes of Caspar David Friedrich (cf. Haftmann 1971; Rosenblum 1975). Equally striking, however, is an important difference between Friedrich and Rothko. Friedrich often (although not always) incorporated a figure into his landscapes—a lone figure facing nature in all its vastness. In Rothko's paintings, there are no figures, save the viewer herself, who is no longer a spectator, but becomes part of the very dynamics of the event. This experience of being drawn into, or embedded in, a surreal landscape seems beyond the bounds of articulation in language. No wonder the paintings have such an extreme effect on many of those who encounter them.

Hermeneutics—purged of linguophilia—can certainly provide us with a compelling phenomenological account of our experience of Rothko's paintings (and the rejection of language as the only basis of articulation is already apparent in Heidegger's concept of 'telling'). But can science can add to our understanding of such processes? I have described, in broad terms, a scientific framework which rejects many of the assumptions made in orthodox cognitive science. In developing the alternative approach, I have used evidence from existing A-Life research to shape an account of the phenomenon of cognition, and the mechanisms underlying it. The resulting framework is in harmony with a non-linguistic hermeneutics, and this opens up the possibility that we can understand the Rothko experience not only from the perspective of phenomenology, but also

---

[18] Raffman (1993) develops a more orthodox theory (from the perspective of cognitive science) of why certain features of our experience of music are inexpressible in language. The example of jazz was suggested to me by Maggie Boden.

from the perspective of science. This is something which seems quite beyond orthodox cognitive science, restricted, as it is, to the subject–object dichotomy, and the language of representation and computation.[19]

REFERENCES

Abraham, R. H., and Shaw, C. D. (1992), *Dynamics: The Geometry of Behavior*, 2nd edn. (Redwood City, Calif.: Addison-Wesley).

Arbib, M. A. (1989), *The Metaphorical Brain 2: Neural Networks and Beyond* (New York: John Wiley and Sons).

Ashton, D. (1983), *About Rothko* (New York: Oxford University Press).

Ballard, D. H. (1991), 'Animate vision', *Artificial Intelligence*, 48: 57–86.

Beer, R. D. (forthcoming), 'Computational and Dynamical Languages for Autonomous Agents', in T. van Gelder and R. Port (eds.), *Mind as Motion: Explorations in the Dynamics of Cognition* (Cambridge, Mass.: MIT Press).

Bonabeau, E. W., and Theraulaz, G. (1994), 'Why do we Need Artificial Life?', *Artificial Life*, 1/3: 303–25.

Brooks, R. A. (1991), 'Intelligence without Reason', in *Proceedings of the Twelfth International Joint Conference on Artificial Intelligence* (San Mateo, Cal.: Morgan Kaufman), 569–95.

Cliff, D. (1991), 'The Computational Hoverfly: A Study in Computational Neuroethology', in J.-A. Meyer and S. W. Wilson (eds.), *From Animals to Animats: Proceedings of the First International Conference on Simulation of Adaptive Behavior* (Cambridge, Mass.: MIT Press/Bradford Books), 87–96.

—— Harvey, I., and Husbands, P. (1993), 'Explorations in Evolutionary Robotics', *Adaptive Behavior*, 2: 73–110.

Cliff, D., Husbands, P., Meyer, J.-A., and Wilson, S. W. (1994) (eds.), *From Animals to Animats 3: Proceedings of the Third International Conference on Simulation of Adaptive Behavior* (Cambridge, Mass.: MIT Press/Bradford Books).

Descartes, R. (1641), *Meditations on the First Philosophy in which the Existence of God and the Real Distinction between the Soul and the Body of Man are Demonstrated*, in *Discourse on Method and the Meditations*, trans. F. E. Sutcliffe (1968) (London: Penguin).

Dreyfus, H. L. (1991), *Being-in-the-World: A Commentary on Heidegger's Being and Time, Division 1* (Cambridge, Mass. and London: MIT Press).

—— and Dreyfus, S. E. (1988), 'Making a Mind versus Modelling the Brain: Artificial Intelligence back at a Branch Point', *Artificial Intelligence*, repr. in M. Boden (ed.), *The Philosophy of Artificial Intelligence* (Oxford Readings in Philosophy; Oxford: Oxford University Press).

Drury, J. (1994), 'Cognitive Science and Hermeneutic Explanation: Symbiotic or Incompatible Frameworks?', *Philosophy, Psychiatry and Psychology*, 1/1: 41–50.

Franceschini, N., Pichon, J. M., and Blanes, C. (1992), 'From Insect Vision to Robot Vision', *Philosophical Transactions of the Royal Society, series B*, 337: 283–94.

[19] This work was supported by British Academy award no. 92/1693. Many thanks to Maggie Boden and Matthew Elton for their helpful comments on an earlier version of this paper.

Gadamer, H. G. (1976), *Philosophical Hermeneutics* (Berkeley and Los Angeles: University of California Press). A collection of essays translated and edited by D. E. Lange.

Haftmann, W. (1971), Introduction to the catalogue for an exhibition at the Kunsthaus Zurich Museum of Fine Arts, 21 March to 9 May 1971.

Harvey, I. (1992), 'Untimed and Misrepresented: Connectionism and the Computer Metaphor' (Cognitive science research paper 245, University of Sussex).

—— Husbands, P., and Cliff, D. (1994), 'Seeing the Light: Artificial Evolution, Real Vision', in Cliff *et al.* (1994), 392–401.

Haugeland, J. (1993), 'Mind Embodied and Embedded', Draft of paper to appear in Y.-H. Houng (ed.), *Mind and Cognition: Proceedings of the First International Conference on Mind and Cognition* (Taipei: Academia Sinica).

Heidegger, M. (1926), *Being and Time*, trans. J. Macquarrie and E. Robinson (1962) (Oxford: Blackwell).

Hornsby, J. (1986), 'Physicalist Thinking and Conceptions of Behaviour', in P. Pettit and J. McDowell (eds.), *Subject, Thought and Context* (Oxford: Oxford University Press), ch. 3.

Horswill, I. D., and Brooks, R. A. (1988), 'Situated Vision in a Dynamic World: Chasing Objects', in *Proceedings of the Seventh Annual Meeting of the American Association for Artificial Intelligence* (St. Paul, Minn.), 796–800.

Husbands, P., Harvey, I., and Cliff, D. (1995), 'Circle in the Round: State Space Attractors for Evolved Sighted Robots', in *Robotics and Autonomous Systems*, 15: 83–106.

Komatsu, H., and Wurtz, R. H. (1988), 'Relation of Cortical Areas MT and MST to Pursuit Eye Movements III: Interaction with Full-field Stimulation', *Journal of Neurophysiology*, 60/2: 621–44.

Maynard Smith, J. (1982), *Evolution and the Theory of Games* (Cambridge: Cambridge University Press).

Merleau-Ponty, M. (1963), *The Structure of Behaviour*, trans. A. Fisher (Boston: Beacon Press).

Meyer, J.-A., and Guillot, A. (1994), 'From SAB90 to SAB94: Four Years of Animat Research', in Cliff *et al.* (1994), 2–11.

Miller, G. F., and Freyd, J. J. (1993), 'Dynamic Mental Representations of Animate Motion: The Interplay among Evolutionary, Cognitive, and Behavioral Dynamics' (Cognitive science research paper 290, University of Sussex).

Morris, M. (1992), *The Good and the True* (Oxford: Clarendon Press).

Nilsson, N. J. (1984) (ed.), *Shakey the Robot* (SRI. AI Centre, Technical Report no. 323).

Palmer, R. (1979), *Hermeneutics* (Evanston, Ill.: Northwestern University Press).

Parker, G. A., and Maynard Smith, J. (1990), 'Optimality Theory in Evolutionary Biology', *Nature*, 348, 27–33.

Raffman, D. (1993), *Language, Music, and Mind* (Cambridge, Mass.: MIT Press/Bradford Books).

Rosenblum, R. (1975), *Modern Painting and the Northern Romantic Tradition—Friedrich to Rothko* (London: Thames and Hudson).

Smithers, T. (1992), 'Taking Eliminative Materialism Seriously: A Methodology for Autonomous Systems Research', in F. J. Varela and P. Bourgnine (eds.), *Toward a Practice of Autonomous Systems: Proceedings of the First European Conference on Artificial Life* (Cambridge, Mass.: MIT Press/Bradford Books), 31–40.

Todd, S., and Latham, W. (1992), *Evolutionary Art and Computers* (London: Academic Press).

van Gelder, T. J. (1992), 'What might Cognition be if not Computation?' (Technical report 75, Indiana University, Cognitive Sciences).

Varela, F. J., Thompson, E., and Rosch, E. (1991), *The Embodied Mind: Cognitive Science and Human Experience* (Cambridge, Mass.: MIT Press).

Webb, B. (1993), 'Modeling Biological Behaviour or "Dumb Animals and Stupid Robots"', in *Pre-Proceedings of the Second European Conference on Artificial Life*, 1090–103.

—— (1994), 'Robotic Experiments in Cricket Phonotaxis', in Cliff *et al.* (1994), 45–54.

Wheeler, M. (1994), 'From Activation to Activity: Representation, Computation, and the Dynamics of Neural Network Control Systems', *AISB Quarterly*, 87: 36–42.

Wilson, S. W. (1985), 'Knowledge Growth in an Artificial Animal', in J. J. Grefenstette (ed.), *Proceedings of an International Conference on Genetic Algorithms and their Applications* (Pittsburgh, Pa. and Hillsdale, NJ: Erlbaum), 16–23.

8

TODAY THE EARWIG, TOMORROW MAN?

DAVID KIRSH

INTRODUCTION

Is 97 per cent of human activity concept-free, driven by control mechanisms we share not only with our simian forebears but with insects? This is the challenge proposed by Rod Brooks and fellow moboticists to mainstream AI. It is not superficial. Human activities fall along a continuum. At one extreme are highly reactive, *situationally determined* activities: walking, running, avoiding collisions, juggling, tying shoelaces. At the other extreme are highly *cerebral* activities: chess, bridge-playing, mathematical problem-solving, replying to non-obvious questions, and most discursive activities found in university research laboratories. It is an open question just where to draw the line between situationally determined activity—activity that can be initiated and regulated by smart perception-action systems—and activity that requires thought, language-like conceptualization, and internal search.

Brooks's position is that if we consider precisely what sensing is required to intelligently control behaviour in specific tasks, we make the startling discovery that in most cases there is no need, or next to no need, for symbolic representation. Reasoning in the familiar sense of retrieving cases, drawing inferences, and running through possibilities ahead of time is costly and unnecessary. In fact representations often *get in the way* of behaviour control. Accordingly, efficiency and parsimony dictate using action control systems that are representation-free.

Moreover, unless we *first* understand the 97 per cent of behaviour that is non-representational, Brooks argues, we will never correctly understand the remainder. The trouble with AI so far is that it makes false abstractions. Theorists don't study the genuine requirements of intelligent behaviour. Instead of finding out exactly what vision and the rest of our sensors should deliver to permit the

Reprinted from *Artificial Intelligence*, 47 (1991), 161–84. (Special Volume: Foundations of Artificial Intelligence.) Reprinted by permission.

intelligent control of behaviour, AI researchers have cavalierly defined nicely formal models of the world—the alleged true output of the senses—and have simply assumed that somehow sensory systems can build these up. Within these false castles AI theorists have tried to solve their own versions of the planning problem, the learning problem and so on. But, of course, the assumptions of these models are false—so false, in fact, that no step-by-step relaxation of assumptions can bring them closer to reality. The models are false and so are the problems: cognitive phlogiston.

In what follows I shall question these claims. I am not yet convinced that success in duplicating insect behaviours such as wandering, avoiding obstacles, and following corridors proves that the mobotics approach is the royal path to higher-level behaviours. Insect ethologists are not cognitive scientists. There is a need for the study of representations. Nor do I think that existing research in reasoning is foundationless. Whatever the shape of robotics in the future it will have to accommodate theories of reasoning roughly as we know them. Abstractions are necessary.

My primary focus will be the claim that the majority of intelligent activity is *concept-free*. I use the term concept-free rather than representation-free, as Brooks prefers, because it seems to me that the deepest issues posed by the mobotics approach really concern the place of conceptualization in intelligent activity, rather than representation *per se*.

The concept of representation remains a sore spot in foundational studies of mind. No one is quite sure exactly what the analysis of 'state X represents the information that p is H' should be. A glance at Brooks's mobots shows that they are riddled with wires that carry messages which covary with equivalence classes of earlier signals (e.g. an edge covaries with an equivalence class of pixel configurations) and which often covary with properties in the environment (e.g. real edges, hand manipulations). If covariation is sufficient for representation then Brooks too accepts the need for representations.

It is clear that by representation, however, he means symbolic, probably conceptual, representation. Let us define a symbolic representation as one which can be combined and manipulated. This condition adds the notion of *syntax* to representation. To get systematic generation of representations it is necessary to have a notation that is sufficiently modular that individual elements of the notation can be combined to make molecular expressions. In this way, ever more complex structures can be constructed and used by a finite system. Semantic discipline is maintained on these symbol structures by enforcing Frege's requirement that however complex the symbol, its meaning is a function of the meaning of its parts and their syntactic arrangement.

If an agent has symbolic representations in the sense just defined, we may assume it has concepts.[1] But too little is understood about the nature of computation to require that all concept-imbued creatures operate with language-like internal notational elements. In principle, there could be computational architectures which implement the cognitive capacities we suppose concept-using creatures to have, but which do not pass notational elements around. These systems have the capacity for systematic representation in that they can systematically predicate property-referring states—that is *predicates*—with states that refer to individual subjects—that is, *names*. But they do not have local notational structures which we can readily identify with symbols.

This capacity to predicate is absolutely central to concept-using creatures. It means that the creature is able to identify the common property which two or more objects share and to entertain the possibility that other objects also possess that property. That is, to have a concept is, among other things, to have a capacity to find an invariance across a range of contexts, and to reify that invariance so that it can be combined with other appropriate invariances. Moreover, combinations can be considered counterfactually. Thus if an agent has the concept red then, at a minimum, the agent is able to grasp that apples can be red, paint can be red, and so on.[2] The agent knows the satisfaction conditions of the predicate. Similarly, if an agent has the capacity to make a judgement about an individual—a person, number, or an object in the visual field, for example—then the agent must be able to make other judgements about that individual too. For instance, that 5 is prime, that it comes after 4, that it is a natural number.

In the same spirit, it is because we have concepts that we can make judgements of identity, as when we decide that the person we see in the mirror is the same person we see over there. Or again, because of concepts we can reidentify an individual, recognizing that the object or person in front of us now is the same one we met on other occasions.

Animals which have such capacities clearly have extra talents, though just what these extra talents are is not entirely understood. Human newborns are largely devoid of them, but soon acquire them; dogs may have elements of them; chimps certainly do, and praying mantises certainly do not. Possession of concepts in a full-blooded form appears only some way up the evolutionary ladder.

The problem which I see Brooks posing is this: At what point in a theory of

---

[1] I am fully aware that identifying syntactic symbol manipulation with possession of concepts begs the question of symbol-grounding and the philosophical problem of reference. For the purposes of assessing Brooks's position, however, the identification is fair since one of his targets is clearly declarative representations.

[2] Providing of course that it has the other relevant concepts, apples, paint . . .

action must we advert to concepts? Which activities presuppose intelligent manipulation of concepts, and which do not? Accordingly, this is not simply a question of the role of model-based planning in intelligent activity. It is a question of the role of *thought* in action.

There are many ways of thinking that do not presuppose use of an articulated world-model, in any interesting sense, but which clearly rely on concepts. Recall of cases, analogical reasoning, taking advice, posting reminders, thoughtful preparation, mental simulation, imagination, and second guessing are a few. I do not think that those mental activities are scarce, or confined to a fraction of our lives.

Nor do I think they are slow. When a person composes a sentence, he is making a subliminal choice among dozens of words in hundreds of milliseconds. There can be no doubt that conceptual representations of some sort are involved, although how this is done remains a total mystery. As an existence proof, however, it establishes that conceptual reasoning can be deployed quickly. Yet if in language, why not elsewhere?

Brooks's own position is extreme: at what point must we advert to concepts?—almost never. Most activity is thought-free, concept-less. It is this view I shall be questioning.

My paper has two parts. In the first I spell out what I take to be the strongest reasons for extending the domain of concept-free action beyond its usual boundaries. There is in Brooks's work the outline of an alternative theory of action well worth understanding. It has clear kinship lines with associationism, ethology, the theory of J. J. Gibson, and the Society of Mind theory of Minsky. But it departs from these in interesting ways.

In the second part I consider what conceptualization buys us. More particularly, I explore the motives for postulating conceptual representations in (1) a theory of action; (2) a theory of perception; (3) a theory of learning; and (4) a theory of control.

1. ACTION AND CONCEPTUALIZATION

From a philosophical point of view the idea that concepts might not play an essential role in a theory of human action is unthinkable. According to received wisdom, what differentiates an *action* from a mere movement such as twitching or wincing is that the agent knows what he or she is doing at the time of action. The action falls under a description, understood by the agent, and partly constituting its identity. Thus the qualitative movement of raising an arm might at one moment be a communicative act such as gesturing goodbye, while at another moment be an act of stretching. Just which act is being performed is a function of at least two factors: the agent's intention, and the social context.

For an agent to have an intention, and hence to know the action performed, it is not necessary that he or she be aware of the action's description or that he or she consciously think before acting. Few agents are aware of putting their words together in sentences before they speak, or even of mapping between words in different languages when they fluently translate. This absence of conscious thought does not prevent them from saying what they mean and from translating aptly. Yet, any reasonable account of their practice must refer to their concepts, ideas, presuppositions, beliefs, etc. Introspection is misleading, then, as an indicator of when concepts and beliefs are causally involved in action.

Philosophy has bequeathed to AI this legacy of unconscious beliefs, desires, and rational explanation. AI's signal contribution to action theory, so far, has been its computational revamping. In practical terms, this has meant that an agent acts only after planning, and that in order to plan, the agent must call on vast fields of largely unconscious beliefs about its current situation, the effects of actions, their desirability, and so forth.

Brooks's rebellion, not surprisingly, stems from a dissatisfaction with this approach in dealing with real-world complexities and uncertainties. Surely children do not have to develop well-formed beliefs about liquids, however naïvely theoretical, in order to drink or go swimming. Even if we do require such implicit theories of children we cannot require them of gerbils or sea lions. The two forms of knowledge—theoretical and practical—can be divorced. But if we do not need an account of theoretical knowledge to explain the majority of animal skills and abilities, why invoke concepts, models, propositional reasoning—declarative representations more generally—to explain the majority of human action?

There are really three issues here which it is wise to distinguish. First, there is the question of what someone who wishes to explain a system—say, the designer of an intelligent system—must know in order to have proper understanding of its behaviour. Must he have an explicit theory of liquid behaviour in order to understand and design competent systems? If I am right in my interpretation of the doctrine of mobotics, pursuit of such theories is fine as an intellectual pastime but unnecessary for the business of making mobots. It is not evident what *practical* value formal theories of naïve physical, social, geometrical, and mechanical knowledge can possibly have for experienced mobot-makers.

Second, there is the question of whether declarative representations, even if these are not truly concept-based declaratives, are required for intelligent control of activity.[3] Not all declarative representations that appear in the course of a computation are conceptual. When a vision system creates intermediate representations, such as edges, texture fields, depth gradients, we need not suppose that it has concepts of these entities in the full-blooded manner in which I defined conceptual representations earlier, that is, as being subjects or objects of predication. Information is certainly being represented explicitly, but it is not the sort of information that can be used in thought; its significance is internal to the specific phase of visual processing taking place at that moment. Thus it cannot be shunted off to a long-term memory system because the representation is in the language of early vision. It fails to qualify as a predicate, since it is not predicable of anything outside its current context. The agent does not know its satisfaction conditions.

Brooks's stand on the need for these intermediate representations in a theory of intelligent action is less clear. One difficulty is that he does not explicitly distinguish representations that are *non-conceptual* declaratives from those that are *conceptual* declaratives. Consequently, much of the rhetoric that, in my opinion, is properly directed against conceptual declaratives is phrased in a manner that makes it apply to declarative representation more universally. Thus he deems it good design philosophy to avoid at all costs extracting higher visual properties such as depth maps, 3-D sketches, and, most particularly, scene parsings. Mobots are constructed by linking small-state FSMs that sample busses with tiny probes, e.g. 10 or 20 bits. The assumption is that this approach will scale up—that a mobot can gain robustness in performance by overlaying more and more specialized mechanisms, without ever having to design fairly general vision systems that might extract edges or higher visual properties. Accordingly, although some intermediate representations are inevitable—the readings of tiny probes—more general intermediate representations are outlawed even if some of these are non-conceptual.

Finally, there is the question of names and predicates. On these representations Brooks's position is unambiguous: declarative representations of individuals and properties is positively pernicious for efficient robotics. Flexible activity is possible without much (any) processing that involves drawing inferences, retrieving similar cases from memory, matching and comparing representations, and so on. In virtually all cases these computations are complex,

---

[3] A declarative is not an easy entity to define. For my purposes I will assume that if information is encoded in a state, structure, or process in a form that can be interpreted in a model-theoretic semantics, then it is declarative. Declaratives release their information upon being *read*, whereas procedures release their information upon being *run*. But clearly, there is no straightforward way of defining the difference between declaratives and procedures since in certain programming languages both can serve as first-class objects. For related discussions see Kirsh (1990).

frail, prone to bottlenecks, and they make false assumptions about the sparseness of real-world attributes.

I shall have something to say about all these forms of representation. It seems to me that there is no escaping the fact that intelligent systems often frame or pose problems to themselves in a certain way, that they search through some explicit hypothesis space at times, and that they have a memory that contains encoded propositions or frames or some other structured symbol, and that part of intelligence consists in knowing how to find the structures in memory that might be helpful in a task and putting those structures to use. Usually these processes make sense only if we assume that the creature has conceptual representations; but occasionally we can view them as involving intermediate representations alone. I believe, moreover, that there are clearly times when as designers we need an adequate domain theory to construct robots in a principled fashion. Accordingly, I shall argue that all three forms of representation are necessary for an adequate science of robotics. But equally I think we should appreciate how far we can get *without* such representations. This is the virtue of Brooks's alternative theory of action.

2. AN ALTERNATIVE THEORY OF ACTION

We may usefully itemize the core ideas underlying this alternative theory of action as follows:

1. Behaviour can be partitioned into task-oriented activities or skills, such as walking, running, navigating, collecting cans, vacuuming, chopping vegetables, each of which has its own sensing and control requirements which can be run in parallel with others.[4]

2. There is a partial ordering of the complexity of activities such that an entire creature, even one of substantial complexity, can be built incrementally by first building reliable lower-level behavioural skills and then adding more complex skills on top in a gradual manner.[5]

3. There is more information available in the world for regulating task-

---

[4] Many ethologists regard compiling an *ethogram* to be the first step in the description of a species. An ethogram is a behavioural vocabulary of a species which lists all the basic types of behaviours an organism can perform. These behaviours are unit-like in that they can be performed in sequences. Brooks's notion, it seems to me, departs from this more classical notion in being more task-oriented. Thus, an activity may be a controlled collection of simpler activities, grouped together by their common purpose of, say, grasping coke cans. Ethologists too look for the function of activities and cluster more basic behavioural units together, but their definition of function is strongly tied to the concept of evolutionary adaption. See Reynolds (1976).

[5] Cf. Gallistel (1980). Brooks diverges from Gallistel in treating the interaction of activities to be often more complex than that found in simple hierarchies.

oriented activities than previously appreciated; hence virtually no behavioural skill requires maintaining a world-model.[6] If you treat the world as external memory you can retrieve the information you require through perception.

4. Only a fraction of the world must be sampled to detect this task-relevant information. Smart perception can index into the world cleverly, extracting exactly what is needed for task-control without solving the general vision problem.[7]

5. The hardest problems of intelligent action are related to the control issues involved in coordinating the various behavioural abilities so that the world itself and a predetermined dominance or preference ordering will be sufficient to decide which activity layer has its moment in the sun.

In short, the theme of this alternative theory is that representation can be exchanged for control. If a creature knows where to look and when to look, and knows what activities to activate and deactivate, then it can approximate arbitrarily rational agents.

To take a rather simple example, consider an insect which feeds off of sugar, and lives in an environment of wily but slow predators. Such a creature must be able to sense sugars or the probability of sugars at a small distance, 'Feed' on those sugars when possible, 'Move', in a specified direction, 'Run Away' when it gets too close to certain objects—particularly predators, 'Stop Short' if it is about to hit an object directly in front of it, and be able to perform compounds of these low-level abilities such as 'Wander' so that it might improve its probability of finding food, 'Avoid Obstacles' and 'Follow Freeways' so that it may move through irregular terrain or flee predators without stumbling. Each of these activities is tuned to certain environmental conditions, such that the activity is turned on or off, amplified or diminished according to locally detectable conditions in conjunction with the internal switching circuitry. If all works well, the net effect is that as the world changes, either because the robot itself is moving through it, or because of external events, the robot will behave as if it is choosing between many goals. Sometimes it runs, sometimes it wanders, sometimes it feeds.

Obviously, the trick in making a mobot behave in a way that looks like it is choosing between many goals without it explicitly predicting the effects which the various behaviours would have on the world, is to design the right pattern of control into the circuitry. Certain pathways will carry messages which

---

[6] This idea I take to be Gibson's (1966, 1979) principal contribution to the study of sensory systems. Where Brooks departs from Gibson on this point is in viewing the process as akin to information retrieval. Gibson supposes that the information is directly picked up.

[7] Again compare Gibson (1966, 1979). In Gibson's view the senses are not passive receptors of information: they are active seeking mechanisms, searching out the information—often minimal information—required for effective action and avoidance of physical harm.

dominate the normal input to a module or which suppress the normal output. Accordingly, one goal of research is to find a way of minimizing the amount of this control. Each FSM should be tuned to the *right* stimuli so as to let the world force choice whenever possible.

Thus, for example, when the senses register a looming stimulus, the Stop Short module takes command. Stop Short was primed; it was in a state which acts on a looming stimulus and is hooked up to output so that its signal overrides any others that may also be transmitted. Similarly, if a system were on a coke can collecting mission, the Move Hand module might take over as soon as the system sensed a halt in optical flow and a streak of red. A complex cooperative behaviour might emerge, therefore, simply because each component activity becomes primed for particular changes in the state of the world that matter to it. Hence, coordination is achieved automatically without posting requests on some central blackboard or relying on some active arbitrator to pass control to slave activities because the preference relations among activities have been built into the switching network of the system.

Let us call behaviour that is controlled by the situation in this way *situation-determined behaviour*. Situation-determined behaviour can be considerably more complex than the stimulus-driven behaviour found in behaviourist theory. For instance, humans, when putting together jigsaw puzzles, may be said to be situationally determined if there is enough joint constraint in the tiles and assembled layout to ensure that they can complete the puzzle without wasted placements. No behaviourist theory can explain jigsaw performance, however, because there is no readily definable set of structural properties—i.e. stimulus conditions—that are the causes of jigsaw placements—i.e. responses. The agent is too active in perceptually questioning the world. On two confrontations with the same world the same agent might perceive different situations as present because it asked a different set of perceptual questions. These questions are a function of the state of the agent and its most recent interactions with the world.

We can say that jigsaw puzzles are perceptually hard but intellectually simple. The actions are intentional but under perceptual rather than conceptual guidance. Thus it is the eye, not the thinking centre, which must be trained to look for the salient corners that differentiate tiles and signal proper fit. It is a problem of perceptual search.

Viewing situation-determined behaviour to be a solution to a perceptual problem points out several worthwhile aspects of situationally determined tasks.

First, there is enough local constraint in the world to 'determine' successful placement despite there being several tiles that can be successfully played at any moment. In a sense each move is underdetermined, hence no deterministic behaviourist theory can explain placement behaviour. None the less, given a tile and an existing layout, the situation wholly determines whether or not the tile can be correctly placed at that time and where. There is no need to check downstream effects. In the jigsaw game, successful placements are additive. Good moves do not interact hostilely with other good moves. There are no traps, dead ends, or loops that may stymie a player. The situation contains enough information to pre-empt the need for lookahead. This is the main point of assumption three.

Second, the perceptual problem is tractable in the sense that only a fraction of the visible world state must be canvassed to determine where to move. The point of sensing is to provide enough information to permit a creature to choose between the actions it can perform next. In the case of jigsaw it is conceivable that to solve the puzzle one must identify the overall shape of all the pieces first. If this were true, a jigsaw puzzle would be a tedious game indeed, for either it would require colossal visual processing of each move, or it would require tremendous visual memory of shapes. How much easier if complete shape identification is unnecessary.

Is this possible? Is it possible to decide which tile to place next by using a strategy of visually questioning the board that does not require computing the overall shape of each tile? The question is important because if perceptual questioning can be confined to simple features there will be no need for higher-level intermediate representations.

Imagine a case where a player cannot decide which of five tiles to play in a particular opening. Each tile seems like it might be a proper fit, but it is hard to tell. An obvious aid to the problem is to have the player try to fit one of the tiles in the opening to let the world highlight the crucial feature that differentiates the proper tile from the near misses. The function of this test move is to focus the player's attention on the situationally *salient* features of the tiles. It is to identify the crucial differentiating features. Now a true expert of the game might not need this help; his perceptual system may be so tuned to the task that he can home right in on the relevant differentiating features. If so, this possibility affirms the point of assumption four: that if one knows what to look for, there is a fairly local feature which correlates with correct moves. Not only does the situation contain enough local constraint to determine good moves, these constraints are highly specific to the task and learnable.

It is worth dwelling on this issue for it emphasizes the truth of assumption five: that control is the hard problem, and the methodological importance of assumption one: that behaviour can be partitioned into task-oriented activities. These, I take it, are the backbone of this alternative approach to action.

It is standard in decision theory to treat perception as a bounded resource that must be guided in order to be used to its fullest. The problem which decision-theoretic accounts encounter, however, is that to know what question it is best to ask next, or which test it is best to perform next, the agent must know all the sources of information available now and in the future, all the decisions that might be taken now and in the future, their consequences, utilities, etc. To achieve optimality is clearly impossible in practice, for it requires knowing where you are most likely to get the information you want before you know exactly which decisions you must make. If one restricts the horizon of one's decisions to specific task-oriented activities the problem is simpler. Must I halt now? Can I proceed in that direction? Is there a predator nearby? For each of these questions there may be a straightforward test which is decisive, or nearly decisive, or indicative of what to test next. Once again the question is whether the test (or perceptual query) is computationally cheap.

In a situationally determined context such questions are necessarily cheap. The environment can be factored into a set of partial states or *indicators* which correlate well with the presence or absence of the larger environmental factors which affect task performance. Thus for a robot whose environment contains doors with right angles it may be possible to discover an invariant *microfeature* of doors which under normal conditions can be seen from all angles. Relative to door-entering activity, this invariant may be all that need be sought. Moreover, it may be simple—a top right and bottom left corner in suitable opposition, for example. This fraction of doorness is sufficient for door recognition in this environment, as long as the robot remains upright, as long as no new doors are introduced, and so forth. It correlates with all and only doors. Consequently, one of the hardest problems for mobot designers is to discover these indicators, and the perceptual queries that best identify them. For each activity the designer must determine which possible indicators correlate well with the likelihood of success or failure of the activity given the current state of the world. This is a hard problem for most activities. But the key point is that without the assumption that behaviour can be partitioned into task-oriented activities, it would be impossible to discover these indicators at all.

This introduces the third and final respect in which situationally determined tasks are illustrative of the alternative theory of action: what is most salient in the environment is usually discernible and economically detectable from the *agent's perspective*. Most task indicators are egocentrically definable. This is a crucial factor in deciding how much of activity can be intelligently controlled without concepts because concepts are often held to be non-egocentric, public, or quasi-public entities.

Developmental psychologists draw a distinction between the *egocentric space* of an agent and the *public space*, which as observers we see the agent performing in. The distinction is intuitive. In egocentric space, the agent is always at the spatio-temporal origin of its world. It sees the environment from its own perspective. Indexical terms such as beside-me, to my right, in front, on top, nearby, occluded-right-now, are all well defined, and depend essentially on the agent's location. They shift as it moves about.

In public space, by contrast, the world is understood almost as if viewed from nowhere. If the agent is included in the world at all it is included objectively as another entity in relation with objects in the world. This is done to facilitate useful generalization. Two people can see the same ball; a ball remains the same ball despite its currently being outside the agent's visual field; and it remains beside a companion ball whether partly occluded or not. Because we can count on the permanence of objects and on a consensual understanding of space-time we can usefully organize our experience of the world by appeal to public objects, public space, and public time. We can describe actions and strategies in a manner which allows people in different circumstances to use them; and we can talk about consequences of actions as if we were not there to see them. Thus, in describing the action of lifting a box five feet in the air it is usually irrelevant whether the agent approaches the box from the right or left. Where the agent was positioned in the situation is less important than what it did to make the box go up. This can be stated in terms of the lawful changes which the objects in the environment undergo.

In the classical theory of action, the beliefs that were thought causally important in determining action were stated in the language of public objects and properties. Actions were defined as situation-action rules—transformations between pre- and post-conditions, and were understood as transformations over public states.

The practice of enumerating the troubles of situation-action rules based on public concepts is by now a familiar pastime in discussions of AI planning. It is therefore regarded a virtue of the situationally determined account that the indicators which matter to situationally determined task performance are definable from an egocentric perspective.

J. J. Gibson, for example, argued at length that the genuine environment of action is not a world of objects and objective relations but a world of surfaces and textural flows as seen by the agent. Gibson, in his ecological approach to perception, emphasized that action and perception are not distinct processes. Animals and people do not passively perceive the world. They move about in it actively, picking up the information needed to guide their movement. This information is always available in an egocentric form, because as a result of the interlocking between perception and action, certain egocentric invariants emerge. Flies can find landing sites by detecting wiping of texture in the optic flow (Vicki and Green 1985: 215–18), chicks and babies can avoid precipices by detecting motion parallax and texture gradients (ibid. 234–5). These invariants can be picked up early. They do not require the level of visual processing involved in creating a full 3-D representation. The same it seems holds for most situationally determined tasks: the indicators which matter can be gleaned by relatively early attention to egocentric invariants, or properties.

The upshot is that for situationally determined activity, perception, particularly egocentric perception, rather than conceptual reasoning is the determining factor of success. This holds because there is a reliable correlation between egocentrically noticeable properties of the environment and actions that are effective.[8]

Now, from both a scientific and engineering standpoint nothing but good can come from exploring in silicon and metal how much of intelligent activity can be duplicated following the principles of this alternative theory of action. Until we construct creatures which can have hundreds of procedures turned on and waiting, we cannot know how effective the world might possibly be in deciding the sequence of the procedures to use. There may be far more indicators in the world that are able to bias performance than we would have dreamed possible prior to designing creatures to run in the real world.

Nevertheless, as with most nascent areas of AI, it is easy to see early results as compelling evidence for strong conclusions. In Brooks's case, the success of this design strategy for simple insect-like creatures is meant to justify a host of methodological directives and criticisms for design strategies of far more complex creatures and behaviours.

Accordingly, let us consider some of the limits of situationally determined actions, and the attendant reasons higher-level creatures are likely to use concepts and representations in action, perception, and control.

3. THE LIMITS OF SITUATIONALLY DETERMINED ACTION

Situationally determined activity has a real chance of success only if there are enough egocentrically perceptible cues available. There must be sufficient local constraint in the environment to determine actions that have no irreversibly bad downstream effects. Only then will it be *un*necessary for the creature to represent alternative courses of actions to determine which ones lead to dead ends, traps, loops, or idle wandering.

From this it follows that if a task requires knowledge about the world that

---

[8] The conception of situation determinedness I offer is stipulative. Others can be proposed. For instance, one could propose that a context situationally determines an action for an agent if the situation in conjunction with the inner state of the agent determines what he will do next. But to stretch the definition in that direction is to give up the distinction between situation determinedness and determinedness simpliciter. Agents are usually determined by the union of mental state and local environment. The noteworthy condition of true situation determinedness is that reasoning is not required for action.

must be obtained by reasoning or by recall, rather than by perception, it cannot be classified as situation-determined. Principal candidates for such tasks are:

- Activities which involve other agents, since these often will require making *predictions* of their behaviour.
- Activities which require response to events and actions beyond the creature's current sensory limits, such as taking precautions now for the future, avoiding future dangers, contingencies, idle wandering—the standard motive for internal lookahead.
- Activities which require understanding a situation from an objective perspective such as when a new recipe is followed, advice is assimilated, a strategy from one context is generalized or adapted to the current situation. All these require some measure of conceptualization.
- Activities which require some amount of problem-solving, such as when we wrap a package and have to determine how many sheets of paper to use, or when we rearrange items in a refrigerator to make room for a new pot.
- Activities which are creative and hence stimulus-free, such as much of language use, musical performance, mime, self-amusement.

These activities are not isolated episodes in a normal human life. Admittedly, they are all based on an underlying set of reliable control systems; but these control systems are not sufficient themselves to organize the *global* structure of the activity.

Thus, to prepare tea requires coordinating both global and local constraints. At the global level, tea-makers must be sensitive to the number of people they are serving, ensuring there is enough water, tea, cups, saucers, and biscuits. Once these items are laid out more mobot-like control systems may take over, pouring the water, stirring etc. But the initial resource-allocation problems are hard to solve. Animals are notoriously ineffective at them. Moreover, can we expect mobots intelligently to arrange plates on the tray? Arrangement or bin-packing requires attention to a number of non-local factors, such as how many items remain to be placed, how well they can be expected to stack, and how stable the overall configuration must be, given the path to the parlour. Anticipation of the future is required. Hence, whenever global considerations enter the control of action, the creature must either be pre-tuned to the future, or it must be able to call on memories, reason about contingencies, ask for advice, and so forth.

In short, the world of human action regularly falls short of total situation determinedness. Most of our life is spent managing locally constrained choice.[9]

---

[9] For an outline of the virtues and problems with local choice, see Kirsh (1989).

It is at this management level that we can best appreciate the virtue of concepts and representations.

4. THE VIRTUES OF CONCEPTS AND REPRESENTATIONS

Concepts are involved in the management of action because they serve at least three organizing functions in cognitive economies. At the *perceptual* level, concepts unify perceptions into equivalence classes. An agent possessing the concept of a dog, for instance, should be able to recognize dogs from different points of view. A dog is an invariant across images. It is also an object for the visual system in the sense that the visual field will be segmented into dog images and non-dog images, offering whatever attentional mechanisms reside in the perceptual system to be directed at specifics of dog images. Accordingly, one aspect of saying that a creature has a concept of dog is to say that he or she can identify dogs perceptually. This means that a vast array of perceptual circumstances can be simplified and reasoned about economically, and that a host of perceptual mechanisms are coordinated around the perceptual object dog.

At a more *conceptual* level, concepts license inferences. A dog is *not* identical with the set of its possible appearances. It is a spatially extended temporally enduring entity that can enter into causal relations with other objects. It is a possible subject of predication. Hence much of what is true of other objects—other possible subjects of predication—will be true of dogs. Many of these *inheritable* truths constitute the *presuppositions* which a creature able to have beliefs and thoughts about dogs will hold. In thinking about dogs, then, the creature will have in mind an entity that is alive, breathes, normally has four legs, and so on. This information is readily accessible, but of course need not be conscious. It enables the creature, however, to intelligently respond to invisible properties of dogs (Wellman and Gelman 1988). Thus a child may resist striking a dog because it knows it would hurt the dog, despite the fact that the property of being open to hurt is not a perceptually present property of dogs.[10]

At a *linguistic* level, a concept is the meaning of a term. To know the meaning of 'dog' in English is to have the concept of dog, and to know that the English word signifies that concept. The concept dog is a semantic value;

[10] Gibson argues that sentience and the like are perceivable properties of an animal. But in his system, there is almost no action-relevant property that is not perceivable. Thus, post-boxes have the perceivable property of affording letter-posting. Just how many non-obvious properties can be perceived or registered is a deep question which the alternative theory of action raises. But I think we may safely say that the line must be drawn short of *all* action-relevant properties. Default reasoning will be valuable for these.

in the Fregean system, when coupled with another appropriate semantic value it constitutes a proposition, or truth-bearer.

Now, when an agent has a concept it can do things and think thoughts it could not otherwise. As developmentalists have pointed out, once a child has the concept of an object, it can know that the same object can present different appearances. It can decide that what looks like a dog is not really a dog, but a misleading image of a bear. It can infer that your image of this dog is different than mine, but that we both know it is the same dog (Siegel 1990). And it can infer that dogs feel pain because they are alive. Concept-users understand a great deal about their environment when they conceptualize it.

There can be no doubt that the skills we identify with possession of concepts are of great value for certain forms of intelligent behaviour. But how widespread is this behaviour? Can we approximate most intelligent behaviour without concepts? This is Brooks's challenge.

One of the most important uses of concepts is to organize memory. Whether or not a system has limited memory, it has a need to index memories in a manner that facilitates recall. In action management, an effective creature will benefit from its performances in the past. It will remember dangers, failures, helpful tricks, useful sub-goals. It may recall unexpected consequences of its previous performances. These memory accesses need not be conscious. Nor need they be complete. Someone describing a particular pet dog may not have accessed all the related information he or she knows about the animal. Some information lies untouched. But this information is *primed* in the sense that retrieving that related information in the near future takes less time than had the topic never been discussed (G. Mandler 1989).

In general, if memory is deemed useful for an action it is less plausible to call that action situation-determined. The strong empirical claim Brooks makes, then, is that to access organized memories takes too long for most actions. Given the pressing exigencies of the real world, there is no time to retrieve and reason with conceptualized information.

Short of knowing the actual time a particular creature takes for accessing memory, it is impossible to argue for or against Brooks's thesis. But we can have intuitions. For instance, in tasks where the time to react is very short, recall will be costly; some recall may be possible but it must be directly applicable to tasks without much reasoning.

Yet how much of life is reactive? In driving home, for instance, I am often on autopilot, but I do come to genuine choice points, where I must decide whether to take, for example, Torrey Pines Blvd. or the highway (G. Mandler 1985). In assessing my options I have conceptualized the possibilities. My preferences are over world states, conceived sometimes as my possible future experiences, sometimes as objective states of the world. My response is not reactive, it is thoughtful. My decision depends on how I think of the future.

The point, here, is that if I wish to accommodate my present action to events, objects, or actions that are distant in time and space, I shall have to anticipate them now. A perception-driven creature can only anticipate the future if there is evidence of the future in its present. With memory, however, it can remember that Y follows X, and so coordinate its actions to a broader environment than that perceptually given.

If the future is a simple function—possibly Markovian—of the perceptually present, a system of linked FSMs might cope with simple futures. FSMs have state and so can encode information about the future. But the future they encode cannot be complicated or complexly branching. When the future is complex simple FSMs will be unreliable. For it is inevitable that one set of future states which correlates with the present will recommend action in one direction, while others, also correlating with the present, will recommend action in other directions. How is choice to be made? Prudent decision-making in such situations requires an all-things-considered approach. It requires balancing the recommendations, and setting a course of action which may involve the future coordination of a complex network of acts. It is hard to see how this could be done without the simplifications of the world which conceptualization gives us.

This capacity to accommodate the future ties in with a second ability that comes naturally to systems with concepts: to *take advice*, and to learn by imitation (J. Mandler 1988). It is characteristic of humans that if they are in the middle of a task that has several parts they can make use of hints or suggestions. These need not be linguistic clues because often it is enough if someone shows us manually what to do, or shows us a technique or move that is similar to the one we must perform. New ideas can bias performance. This implies that whatever means we have for controlling our behaviour it must be *permeable* to new information.

What makes this permeability hard to capture in models built on the alternative theory of action is that hints and advice are often offered from a non-egocentric point of view. Hence there is no reason why a hint or a suggestion should be meaningful input to the home system. This is not to say that concept-using agents have no trouble assimilating advice. Advice can be more or less ready for use. Hints phrased from an objective, perspectiveless orientation may be hard to put into practice by agents wholly immersed in their own perspective. But some form of this translation problem is solved every time we understand that other agents see the world differently.

Advice-taking also has a sensory side. Suppose I am told that a friend has been in a car accident and broken his legs. I now expect to see a person on crutches. Hence I can recognize him at a distance, and not be deceived by appearances.

This adaptation of future expectations is impossible to explain without concepts. There must be some device in an agent which functions like an indexed long-term memory of objects which keeps track of changes and which allows it to update expectations about the behaviour and appearance of objects in a controlled manner. Somehow it must be able systematically to change the attributes that an object may be assumed to inherit or possess by default.

This same idea applies to behaviour in strategic environments where the effectiveness of an action often depends on the interpretation which other agents impose on it. To take advantage of these dependencies requires knowing the interpretations of others. It presupposes that the agent can understand its opponents or colleagues as systems whose behaviour is a partial function of its current and future behaviour. It is hard to see how the effects of this recursive interpretation can be achieved without conceptual representations. First, it will require understanding other agents as agents in a common world playing in a common field, hence operating in a public domain rather than an egocentric one. Second, it will require understanding them counterfactually, in terms of how they might interpret the agent if it were to do X instead of Y.

5. THE NEED FOR REPRESENTATION IN A THEORY OF PERCEPTION

I have been describing the importance of representation, particularly conceptual representation, for a theory of action: there are limits to how subtly a system can act if it is entirely situation-determined. The ability to frame and test hypotheses about the future and about other agents' behaviour is essential for survival in human-style environments. But there are equally strong reasons to suppose that representation is important for a theory of perception.

The field of computational vision has done much to explode the myth that vision is strongly under the influence of expectations, memory, and inference *at early stages of processing*. But there are few who believe that extraction and identification of shapes can occur without at least some models of shape in memory.

Shape models are not the same as concepts. They constitute equivalence classes of perceptions, but they carry no implications of objecthood. Accordingly, it is not until *scene-parsing*, where items are identified in the visual scene and conceptualized as organized, that we are justified in claiming that a system imposes concepts.

Brooks's position on this is, I believe, much like Gibson's. Organisms detect without inference or reconstruction those properties of things which they need to achieve their goals. In general, this will not require visual processing to the point of 3-D shape recognition, and certainly never to the point of scene recognition. Brooks believes it will never require more processing than that required for a viewer-centred representation of objects; and most often the information needs of action can be fulfilled by special-purpose detectors.[11]

The trouble with this view, however, is that it does not make clear how some of the interesting visual properties that need detecting can actually be accomplished.

For instance, how can an object seen from one orientation be recognized as the same object when viewed from another orientation? This is necessary for backtracking in the world.

A key assumption of the alternative theory of action is that the world is benign: ineffective moves can be tolerated because seldom is it the case that they lead to irrecoverable states. If an ineffective move is made, the creature can either just continue from its new position, or backtrack in the world— provided, of course, the creature could remember its path. But this is the problem: how can the creature recognize where it has been if it cannot recognize the same object from both front and back?

To cope with the memory demands of search in the world humans trailblaze— they leave markers of where they have been. They can then reuse pre-existing procedures, such as go to the first visible landmark that you have not already visited. But there are obviously environments where trailblazing is impractical. In such cases, a snapshot of the relevant portion of the world state is required. This is akin to episodic memory. But the episode is not recorded as a simple snapshot. For if the creature is to use the snapshot, it must record the scene in a perspective-neutral way. Otherwise the image will be the wrong orientation to resemble what the agent sees as it backtracks. Records more abstract than agent-oriented images are required.

As a rule animals do not rely on such sophisticated perception and perceptual recall. I do not know whether they do much controlled search in the world but they can easily determine whether they have visited a spot by scent. They are locally driven machines. Such is not always the case with humans. Early in our evolution we traded olfactory prowess for visual intelligence, with the attendant advantage that we now can determine whether we have visited a spot without sniffing it at close range.

In the same way our abilities to handle complex objects without practice also feed off of our advanced visual intelligence. Funny shapes require funny grasps. Unevenly distributed masses require prudent grips, and heavy objects require

---

[11] The justification for this claim, it seems to me, is the Gibsonian theory that perception involves active exploration by an organism. Instead of asking how an organism infers the structure of its environment from the pattern of activations on its receptive field, we ask how the organism picks up what it needs to know by moving through the 'ambient optical array' containing the information. By dynamically sampling this optical array the creature is supposed to be able to get whatever information it needs about objects and layouts to fulfil its objectives.

appropriate force. We do not approach a weighty textbook the way we do a paper container.

How do we determine our approach to these objects without performing enough computation to determine (1) the centre of mass of the object, (2) a set of points or regions of opposition, and (3) the texture of the surface so that we can make a good guess about the object's material and hence its weight? One possibility is that we use a vast look-up table which associates shapes with grasps. Yet grasps vary with hardness, smoothness, and weight too. These too will have to be built into a table. The net effect would be a table of enormous complexity. Accordingly, the obvious alternative is to invoke intermediate representations and compute solutions on-line. These intermediate representations are not conceptual: they represent properties that are relevant for grasping. But they do emphasize that perception must solve big problems, and frequently in a way that is general. At the very least, the complexity of vision argues for the need to analyse the problem at a general level, if only to construct the look-up table.

6. THE NEED FOR REPRESENTATIONS IN A THEORY OF LEARNING

Skill generalization is a further area that may pose problems for the mobotics approach. One reason we currently believe that representations—of both the conceptual and non-conceptual variety—are vital to learning is that we know of no other way of *simplifying* situations so that what is similar between situations is easy to note. Obviously we want systems that can apply existing knowledge to new tasks, systems that can *transfer* expertise. Unless mobots can generalize stimuli they will have to be reprogrammed to perform what are essentially the same tasks on slightly different objects. If a mobot can pick up a coke can it should be able to pick up a coffee cup.

The trouble with coordinated FSMs is that they are each carefully tuned to the particular properties of specific tasks. If a hand-control system that regulates coke-can grasping focuses on specific coke can properties—a red streak, a shiny 'circular' surface—then it is not easy to see how that control system can be used for grasping coffee cups. The issue is not whether some of the constituent modules of the coke-grasping reflex can be used; it is, rather, that one or several FSMs depend on specific perceptual microfeatures of coke cans.

Now sometimes this task-specificness is justified. Perhaps the ability to pick up cans is different than the ability to pick up cups with handles, or to pick up flyswatters. But how are we to know this? The mobot engineering philosophy is to test out designs to see what is common across tasks. If coke-can grasping does not work on coffee cups then add extra control layers. This same process will continue until someone decides that the grasping system is too complex. At that moment, a redesigned system will be constructed that simplifies the system on the basis of what has been learned.

There is nothing objectionable in this familiar engineering approach. But it is based on two rather strong assumptions. First, that it is imprudent to pursue prior analysis because one cannot know what the natural groupings of grasping are until one knows how a grasper relying on microfeatures might work. Second, generalization of the grasping system can be achieved without extracting higher-order structural properties.

The virtue of representations, both intermediate and conceptual, is that they let us see similarity in superficial disparity. Two objects may differ in almost all their microfeatures, but be deemed relevantly similar at a more abstract level. Thus the generalization problem: is X relevantly similar to Y is easy to solve if we have characterized X and Y in a relatively sparse feature space, but hard in a dense lower-level space. The questions: 'What are the task-relevant properties common across objects?', 'What properties of objects must be made explicit to simplify control?' are what the study of representation is all about. Only in a rhetorical sense, then, can moboticists contend that they abjure representations.

7. THE NEED FOR REPRESENTATIONS IN A THEORY OF CONTROL

Any system that is to substitute control for representation for ever must be able to:

(1) cope with increasingly *complex desire systems*; and
(2) resourcefully recover from failure.

If we are ever to build the much awaited household robot, it will have to be designed with both these abilities. I think designers, however, will have an impossibly difficult time building in such abilities without using conceptual representations. Consider desire systems first.

Any household robot worth its salt must be able to make us a midnight snack. Before I rely on such a device, though, I shall want it to be able to operate with complex goal systems. I want it to be able to balance competing desiderata when it reaches the fridge. The trouble is that mobots, as we envisage them today, operate with an impoverished goal system and so are limited in their performance.

Basically, a mobot-inspired creature would work on what might be called the *refrigerator model of desire.* Open up the refrigerator, look in, and let the contents and some simple capacitor notion of wants decide what to select. This has the nice property that the creature does not have to have a fixed idea of what to select in advance; it can let the possibilities decide for it. Thus the choice problem is solved in the simplest way possible: thirst is valued more than appearance and less than gut hunger. If hunger has been largely satisfied so that the *capacitor* measuring hunger is low, then thirst prevails, and so forth.

The problem with this approach is that if the creature is to cope with many desires it is not at all clear how a ranking can be provided in so simple a fashion. Given a choice between filboid sludge for breakfast and taking a chit for a five-course lunch at Panache, I'll choose the chit. My top-level goal may be the allaying of hunger, but how I subgoal may be complex and sensitive to many desiderata, such as taste, appearance, comfort, diet, to name a few. Desires do not just compete in a simple winner-take-all fashion, because in a complex desires system it is not possible to rank desires according to a small number of lexicographically ordered dimensions. There are real limits to the capacitor concept of desire.

What this means is that when desire systems get large there must be some type of desire management, such as deliberation, weighing competing benefits and costs, and so on. This applies whether the mobot is out there in the field doing my bidding or it is an autonomous creature with its own set of desires. Without representation, desires lack the *modularity* to be reasoned about, or even flexibly assembled. If the representations are not conceptual they will not be about enduring states of the world that can be entertained and reasoned over. Conceptual representation is necessary for desire management. Without desire management, mobots will be little more than insects or lower animals.

Now consider the value of belief systems for flexible control. One of the lessons learned from first-generation expert systems is that unless an agent has some understanding of why certain if-then rules work it will be unable to respond flexibly when it finds that it has no rule that will apply in its current context or when it discovers that one of its rules fails to have the desired outcome. Models of underlying relations are important.

To take a simple example, if a radio repairman is unable to fix a broken set by standard tweaks, he will try to discover by reasoning the cause of the system's observed behaviour. The customary imputation is that experts have levels of understanding: for standard cases they operate with an abstracted representation of a device or possibly a set of precompiled procedures. But when necessary they can reflect on the rationale of those procedures, on why they work in certain cases and why they may fail in others; they may even reason from first principles.

Now in a typical mobotic system there can be no more than a small number of fixes one could try in problematic situations. In some cases this strategy will work. It achieves a type of robustness: a system that announces it does not know what to do is more resilient than a system which is determined to try something, no matter how ham-fisted.

The problem is that if one wants to do better than giving up, the fix has to be appropriate to the case. The lesson of second-generation expert systems is that such fixes require being selective about choosing what additional information to seek. This is a hard problem and requires a fairly deep understanding of the situation. But it is unclear that Rod's robots can have this kind of understanding without having the equivalent of models of the domain. How can a system whose response to failure is to try a simpler behaviour achieve this innovative resilience?

The reason this is a hard problem is that the response the system has to make varies across situations. The same behavioural failure can require different fixes. That means that at a superficial level there is not enough information to determine an action. The system must conjecture and test. Since the range of conjecture is vast, the state space of FSMs would have to be correspondingly vast. But once again this vast space would not be systematically generated, except, of course, by the designer who used concepts and compiled his answer to hide the systematicity.

8. CONCLUSION

I have been arguing that although AI can substantially benefit from greater attention to the richness of perceptual information, this richness will never replace the need for internal representations. Any plausible household robot, even one that does not have the full improvisational skills of a human, will have to rely on symbolic representations at least sometimes.

This is especially obvious if we consider how language use can accelerate evolution. No one understands how closely language is tied to vision, or how closely it is tied to reasoning. But it is widely recognized that once language is acquired certain forms of learning and reasoning become possible and certain other forms are accelerated.

For instance, with linguistic communication comes the possibility of identifying and storing very precise information. Without language it is hard to draw someone's attention to a particular perceptual fact; for it is difficult to specify *which* condition of the situation is the salient condition. The problem becomes exponentially more difficult if the condition is abstract. Imagine trying to draw someone's attention to the *bluntness* of a particular pin.

Similarly, once arbitrary amounts of knowledge can be stored and passed on from generation to generation, we can accelerate the rate at which our abilities grow by learning from the lessons of others. Cultural transmission of information is much faster than genetic transmission of information. This might explain the shockingly brief time it took for man to develop his higher mental skills when compared with the great length of time evolution took to develop sophisticated motor skills.

Thus, is 97 per cent of life concept-free? The answer depends on how you count abilities. If an ability is defined relative to an environment, then the richness of the human environment suggests that there are wildly more tasks that can be done in the human world than in environments characteristic of less language, norm-ridden creatures. Once language-like communication emerged the rate at which we could acquire new abilities rose dramatically because we could identify, create, and teach new abilities.

The magic that made this take-off possible was the ability to remember facts, rules, norms, strategies, and the like. With specific cases in mind we could avoid pitfalls, with norms and rules we could cleave to the conservative but safe path; with strategies and plans we could find our way where random search would be disastrous. And of course with the ability to communicate—which these higher-order abilities presuppose—we could also take advice.

These goods seem to flow from the ability to represent facts internally and to reason explicitly. Any theory that asserts that we can get by without conceptual representation will have to *explain away* these goods by showing that they are not necessary for intelligent activity.[12]

REFERENCES

Brooks, R. A. (1986), 'A Robust Layered Control System for a Mobile Robot', *IEEE Journal of Robotics and Automation*, 2: 14–23.
—— (1991), 'Intelligence without Representation', *Artificial Intelligence*, 47: 139–59.
Gallistel, C. R. (1980), *The Organization of Action* (Hillsdale, NJ: Erlbaum).
Gibson, J. J. (1966), *The Senses Considered as Perceptual Systems* (Boston: Houghton Mifflin).
—— (1979), *The Ecological Approach to Visual Perception* (Boston: Houghton Mifflin).
Kirsh, D. (1989), 'Managing Local Choice', in *Proceedings of the American Association for Artificial Intelligence Workshop on AI and Rational Choice*.
—— (1990), 'When is Information Explicitly Represented?', in P. Hanson (ed.), *Information, Content and Meaning* (Vancouver, BC: University of British Columbia Press).

[12] In writing this paper I have benefited considerably from insightful discussions with Peter Cudhea, Pattie Maes, Jean Mandler, Eric Saund, and Bob Stalnaker.

Mackintosh, N. J. (1983), *Conditioning and Associative Learning* (Oxford: Oxford University Press).

Mandler, G. (1985), *Cognitive Psychology* (Hillsdale, NJ: Erlbaum).

—— (1989), 'Memory: Conscious and Unconscious', in P. R. Solomon, G. R. Goethals, C. M. Kelley, and B. R. Stephens (eds.), *Memory: Interdisciplinary Approaches* (New York: Springer).

Mandler, J. (1988), 'How to Build a Baby: On the Development of an Accessible Representational System', *Cognitive Development*, 3: 113–36.

Minsky, M. (1986), *The Society of Mind* (New York: Simon and Schuster).

Reynolds, V. (1976), 'The Origins of a Behavioural Vocabulary: The Case of the Rhesus Monkey', *Journal for the Theory of Social Behaviour*, 6: 105–42.

Siegel, M. (1990), *Knowing Children: Experiments in Conversation and Cognition* (Hillsdale, NJ: Erlbaum).

Spelke, E. S. (1988), 'Where Perceiving Ends and Thinking Begins: The Apprehension of Objects in Infancy', in A. Yonas (ed.), *Perceptual Development in Infancy* (Hillsdale, NJ: Erlbaum), 197–234.

Sternberg, R. (1988) (ed.), *Advances in the Psychology of Intelligence*, 4 (Hillsdale, NJ: Erlbaum).

Vicki, B., and Green, P. (1985), *Visual Perception, Physiology, Psychology and Ecology* (Hillsdale, NJ: Erlbaum).

Wellman, H. M., and Gelman, S. A. (1988), 'Children's Understanding of the Nonobvious', in Sternberg (1988), 99–135.

9

HAPPY COUPLINGS: EMERGENCE AND EXPLANATORY INTERLOCK

ANDY CLARK

INTRODUCTION: EMERGENCE AND EXPLANATION

'Artificial Life' names a very broad church indeed. The banner encompasses work on colonies of simple simulated organisms, all kinds of 'synthetic biology', studies of real-world robots and autonomous agency, and much else besides. (For a representative sampling, see the variety of papers in volume 1 of the journal *Artificial Life*.) Underlying this surface variety, however, are a few relatively central and recurrent themes. Two such (related) themes are (1) the unfolding of patterns over time and (2) the emergence of interesting or adaptive features from clever couplings between agents and environments (including other agents).

The present chapter focuses on these key themes as they appear in work on Autonomous Agents, Dynamic Systems Theory, and systems-level neuroscientific conjecture. Attention to this range of example cases can, I believe, help us to assess the more general role of explanations of emergent phenomena in cognitive science. Such a project seems worth while for at least two reasons. First, because an emphasis on emergent phenomena is highly characteristic of much of the most recent, challenging and exciting work in Cognitive Science (from, for example, Mitchel Resnick's work on collective, decentralized behaviour (Resnick 1994*a*), to Luc Steels's work on behaviour systems (Steels 1994), to Harvey, Husbands, and Cliff's work on evolutionary robotics (Harvey *et al.* 1994)). But second, because some of the most basic questions about the explanation of emergent properties remain unresolved. Such questions include: how to define emergence itself; what general explanatory framework is best able to account for emergent features (is dynamic systems theory, for example, a better bet than classical component-based analysis?); and do such novel modes of explanation merely augment or radically displace more familiar styles of Cognitive Scientific understanding?

A longer version of this paper is under consideration by *Artificial Life*.

I shall argue that emergent phenomena do require new modes of explanation and understanding. But these modes do not displace more familiar projects such as homuncular decomposition and representational/computational description. Instead, we must use a variety of tools to understand the multiple aspects of real-time, embodied, embedded cognition. Two major explanatory projects are distinguished. One concerns the contribution of neurophysiologically real components to the psychologically characterized abilities of an agent. This project, I suggest, requires the use of some quite traditional analytic tools. And it yields a kind of understanding which is essential if we hope to explain, for example, the effects of local damage to system behaviour. The other concerns the overall dynamics of the agent/environment system. This kind of understanding is essential if we hope to explain the adaptive success of embodied, embedded agents. The task of cognitive science, I argue, is to develop and carefully *interlock* both types of explanation.

1. THREE EXPLANATORY STYLES

In this section I distinguish three styles of Cognitive Scientific explanation. The styles are quite general and cross-classify the use of particular programming styles such as connectionist vs. classicist.

1.1. Homuncular Explanation

To explain the functioning of a complex whole by detailing the individual roles and overall organization of its parts is to engage in homuncular explanation. This is the natural explanatory style to adopt when, for example, we explain the workings of a car, a television set, or a washing-machine. We explain the capacities of the overall system by adverting to the capacities and roles of its components, and the way they interrelate.

Homuncular explanation, thus construed, is the contemporary analogue to good old-fashioned *reductionistic* explanation. I avoid the vocabulary of reduction for two reasons. First, much of the philosophical discussion about reduction assumed that reduction named a relation between theories, and that theories were linguaform, law-involving constructs. But in many cases (especially biology and artificial intelligence), what we might otherwise naturally think of as reductive explanations do not take this form. Instead, they involve the development of partial *models* which specify components and their modes of interaction, and explain some high-level phenomena (e.g. being a television receiver) by adverting to a description of lower-level components and interactions. (See e.g. Bechtel and Richardson 1992.) These are reductionist explanations in a broader sense—one which 'homuncular explanation' seems to capture. And second, because to contrast emergent explanation with reductionist explanation would be to invite a common misunderstanding of the notion of emergence, that is to suggest that emergentist accounts do not explain how higher-level properties arise as a result of more basic structures and interactions. As we shall later see, recent emergentist hypotheses are by no means silent on such matters. Rather, the contrast lies in the *ways* in which the lower-level properties and features combine to yield the target phenomena. This kind of emergentist explanation is really a special case of reductionist explanation, at least as intuitively construed, since the explanations aim to render the presence of the higher-level properties unmysterious by reference to a multitude of lower-level organizational facts. (For an argument that emergence is best treated as a species of reduction, see Wimsatt (1986; forthcoming).) For these reasons, then, it will be more accurate and less confusing to contrast emergent explanation with homuncular explanation than with reductionist theorizing in general.

Modular programming methods in classical Artificial Intelligence (see e.g. Newell and Simon 1976; Haugeland 1981) lent themselves quite nicely to a homuncular form of explanation. In attempting to understand the success of such a program, it is often fruitful to isolate the various sub-routines, etc. and to display their role in dividing up the target problem into a manageable series of sub-problems (see Dennett 1978). The sub-systems which such explanations identify coordinate their activity by passing messages, and are individually understood as operating upon symbolic input encodings so as to effect some desired transformation.

Most recent 'connectionist' work, as Wheeler (1994) points out, is likewise apt for a kind of homuncular explanation. Solutions to complex problems (e.g. handwritten Zip code recognition—Le Cun *et al.* 1989) exploit highly structured, multi-layered networks (or networks of networks). In such cases it is possible to advance our understanding of how the system succeeds by asking after the roles of these gross components (layers or sub-nets). It is worth noting that homuncular explanation is most compelling when the components admit of straightforward representational interpretation, that is cases in which the target systems have 'reliably identifiable internal configurations of parts that can be usefully interpreted as representing aspects of the domain . . . and reliably identifiable internal components that can be usefully interpreted as algorithmically transforming those representations' (Beer, forthcoming: 225).

We shall return to this possible affinity between homuncular explanation and the positing of internal representations later on.

1.2. Interactive Explanation

This is less familiar and therefore merits a slightly more extended discussion. Unlike homuncular explanation, interactive explanation takes very seriously the role of the environment in promoting successful problem-solving activity. It seeks to display the ways in which crucial problem-solving moves may actively exploit the opportunities which the real world presents to embodied, mobile agents. (For a nice treatment, see Kirsh, forthcoming.) Such an explanatory strategy is not intrinsically in competition with the kind of homuncular approach reviewed above. It merely adds a new dimension of study and interest.

Work in the so-called 'Animate Vision' (also called active vision, interactive vision) paradigm provides a clean example. At the heart of this paradigm (see Ballard 1991; Churchland *et al.* 1994) lies a challenge to the traditional construction of the problem of vision itself. The traditional construction (Marr 1982) depicts the task of vision as the task of building a detailed representation of a 3-D world on the basis of what is essentially a body of 2-D data. From a certain perspective, the characterization seems obvious. Yet the problem of biological vision, Ballard suggests, is really quite different. In place of the task of 2-D to 3-D mapping he depicts the goal of vision as the production of successful actions within an environmental context, keeping computational costs as low as possible. (See Ballard 1991.) Our conception of the very task of vision, it seems, may have been distorted by an atemporal, disembodied bias.

Once we confront the problems of vision on their home turf (the acting organism in a complex world) a new set of problems and resources comes to the fore. Thus we immediately note that the human visual system exploits multiple gaze-control mechanisms so as to get the most out of the very small area of high-resolution information provided by the fovea. We must constantly saccade to various locations in visual space and do so in response to a variety of cues. Thus imagine your task is to discover the 35mm film display in a crowded drugstore. The canny cognizer, Ballard suggests, may here rely on a cheap cue detectable at the low-resolution peripheries of our vision: colour. More precisely, she will move about seeking the low-level cue of Kodak yellow and, having detected it, be in a position to reorient her gaze so as to saccade in on the fine details of the film display. (See Ballard 1991: 71.) Or suppose the task is to locate your car keys. The best strategy is to link the small object (the keys) in memory to a larger (more easily detectable) one such as a table. You can then seek the large object (the table) identifiable at low resolution and, having located it, saccade around until the keys are (hopefully) located. At this point we should note also the possibility for an active agent to alter the environment so as to increase the number of ways it may be exploited, for example deliberately placing a colourful saucer on the table and always putting the car keys on it.

Interactive explanation, as remarked above, is fully compatible with a homuncular perspective on the agent's innards. Ballard posits, for example, a 'stored model data-base' as an internal component whose role is to encode object-linking information. The contrast between the interactive approach and classical homuncular theorizing lies only in the way that close attention to environmental needs and opportunities is allowed to influence our conjectures about the components and their roles. Thus, according to Ballard, the idea of a component which encodes a full-scale model of our surroundings is misguided. Animate Vision, Ballard argues, neither needs nor can afford to create and sustain such a model. Instead, we constantly saccade around, picking up only such fragments of information as we need to support specific actions, and revisiting the scene again and again rather than relying on some internally represented surrogate.

1.3. Emergent Explanation

Emergent explanation is at once the most radical and most elusive member of our trinity. Where interactive explanation is usually just a sensitive and canny version of homuncular explanation, emergent explanation aims to offer a whole new perspective on adaptive success. At the heart of this new perspective lies the idea of organism–environment interactions which yield types of adaptive behaviour not neatly attributable to any specific inner component or system. It is, however, no easy matter to give a more precise and clearly non-trivial account of this idea of emergence. Some writers associate emergence with unexpected/unprogrammed behaviours; but this yields an overly 'observer-relative' notion of emergence. A better route, pursued by Steels (1994), is to restrict the use of emergence-talk to cases in which adaptive success is tied to the specifics of an ongoing interaction between the organism and the environment, *and* in which the patterns of results which this interaction yields require description in a vocabulary which differs from the one we use to characterize the powers and properties of the inner components themselves. Steels gives the example of emergent chemical properties such as temperature and pressure; these terms do not figure in our descriptions of the motion of individual molecules, but are needed to describe the behaviour of aggregates of such items.

The best account of emergence for our purposes, however, is one which centres on a distinction between what Steels (1994) calls *controlled* versus *uncontrolled* variables. Controlled variables track behaviours or properties which can be directly affected by the organism. Uncontrolled variables track behaviours or properties which can be affected only indirectly, for example by affecting some other gross action of the system. As Steels (1994: 90) puts it:

A controlled variable can be directly influenced by a system, for example, a robot can directly control its forward speed. . . . An uncontrolled variable changes due to actions of the system, but the system cannot directly impact it, only through a side-effect of its actions. For example, a robot cannot directly impact its distance to a wall; it can only change its direction of movement which will then indirectly change the distance.

This account applies nicely to classic examples of emergence such as Hofstadter's story about the operating system which begins to fail, to 'thrash around', once about thirty-five users are on-line. In such a case, Hofstadter notes, it would be a mistake to go to the systems programmer and ask to have the 'thrashing number' increased to, say, sixty. The reason is that the number 35 is not determined by an inner variable upon which the programmer can directly act. Instead: 'That number 35 emerges dynamically from a host of strategic decisions made by the designers of the operating system and the computer's hardware and so on. It is not available for twiddling' (Hofstadter 1985: 642).

Here we have a fully *systems-internal* version of an uncontrolled variable. In this case affecting the variable would still require an indirect route, but not via environmental action but via adjustments to a host of inner sub-systems whose collective behaviour fixes the value of the variable. Emergent phenomena, as I shall use the term, are thus any phenomena whose roots involve uncontrolled variables and are thus the products of collective activity rather than of dedicated components or control systems. Emergent phenomena, thus understood, are neither rare nor breath-taking: none the less, getting target behaviours to arise as functions of uncontrolled variables has not been a common strategy in AI, and such behaviours, when they arise, demand types of understanding and explanation which go beyond both the homuncular and the interactive models rehearsed above.

Two simple examples will help. The first is drawn from Resnick (1994*b*) and concerns a strategy for getting simulated termites to collect wood-chips and gather them into piles. One solution would be to program the termites to take chips to predesignated spots. Relative to such a solution, chip-piling would count as a controlled variable as piling behaviour would be under direct control and would be fully 'twiddle-able'. An emergentist solution, by contrast, yields the behaviour indirectly via the combined effects of two simple rules and a restricted environment. The rules were: 'If you are not carrying anything and you bump into another wood chip, pick it up; If you are carrying a wood chip and you bump into another wood chip, put down the wood chip you are carrying' (Resnick 1994*b*: 234).

It is not obvious that such a strategy will work, as it allows chips to be removed from piles as easily as they can be added! None the less, 2,000 scattered chips, after 20,000 iterations, became organized into just thirty-four piles. The reason the piling behaviour ends up overwhelming the de-piling behaviour is that whenever (by chance) the *last* chip is removed from an incipient pile, that location is effectively blocked; no *new* pile can ever begin there, given the two rules. Over time, then, the number of possible pile locations in the artificial grid diminishes, forcing the chips to congregate in the remaining locations. It is the unprogrammed feature of 'location-blocking' which enables piling activity to outrun de-piling activity! In this example, it is clear that piling behaviour is not directly controlled, but emerges as a function of the interplay between the simple rules and the restricted environment.

A second example is drawn from Hallam and Malcolm (1994). They describe a simple solution to the problem of getting a robot to follow walls. You equip the robot with an in-built bias to veer towards the right, and locate a sensor on its right-hand side which is activated by contact and which causes the device to turn a little to the left. Such a robot will, on encountering a wall on the right, first move away (thanks to the sensor) and then quickly veer back to re-encounter the wall (thanks to the bias). The cycle will repeat and the robot will follow the wall by in effect repeatedly 'bouncing off it'. The point to notice is that the behaviour of wall-following here emerges out of the interaction between the robot and its environment. It is not subserved by any internal state encoding a goal of wall-following. We, as external theorists, lay on the wall-following description as a gloss on the overall embedded behaviour of the device. But the gloss does not attach to any *agent-side* inner states.

2. DYNAMIC SYSTEMS AND EMERGENT EXPLANATION

What is the most effective explanatory framework for understanding emergent phenomena? A widely shared negative intuition is that classical homuncular explanation, at least, often fares badly in such cases (Steels 1994; Maes 1994; Wheeler 1994). There are two rather distinct reasons for such failure.

One reason turns on the fact that many (not all) emergent cognitive phenomena are rooted in factors which spread across an organism and its environment. In such cases (and we saw several examples above) we ideally require an explanatory framework which is (1) well suited to modelling both organismic and environmental parameters and (2) models them both in a uniform vocabulary and framework, thus facilitating understanding of interactions between the two. A framework which invokes computationally characterized, information-processing homunculi is not, on the face of it, ideal as a means of satisfying (1) and (2).

A second reason turns on the nature of components. When the component parts each make a distinctive special contribution to the ability of a system to display some target property, homuncular analysis is a powerful tool. But some systems are highly homogenous at the component level, with most of the interesting properties dependent solely upon the aggregate effects of simple interactions amongst the parts. An example (noted by e.g. van Gelder 1991; Bechtel and Richardson 1992) would be a simple connectionist network in which the processing units are all markedly similar and the interesting abilities are largely a function of the organization (by weighted, dense connectivity) of those component parts. A more complex case occurs when a system is highly *non*-homogenous, yet the contributions of the parts are highly inter-defined, that is, the role of a component C at time t_1 is determined by (and helps determine) the roles of the other components at t_1, and may even contribute quite differently at a time t_2, courtesy of the complex feedback and feedforward links to other sub-systems. Internal non-homogeneity and on-line functional specialization are thus no guarantee that a homuncular analysis will constitute the most revealing description.

These complexities are reflected in Wimsatt's elegant description (1986) of 'aggregate systems'. Aggregate systems are the ones for which homuncular explanation is best suited. Such systems are defined as ones in which the parts could display their explanatorily relevant behaviour even in isolation from one another, and in which the properties of a small number of sub-systems can be invoked to explain interesting systemic phenomena (see also Bechtel and Richardson 1992). As the complexities of interaction between parts increases, so the explanatory burden increasingly falls not on the parts but on their organization. At such times, we are driven to seek new kinds of explanatory frameworks. As we shall later see, it is likely that advanced biological cognition falls somewhere midway along this continuum. The systems have distinct and functionally specialized neural components. But the interactions (feedback and feedforward relations) between these components are crucial determinants of most intuitively 'psychological' phenomena. Good explanations, in such cases, require *both* a traditional homuncular explanation and something else besides. But what else?

Given our two desiderata (that we accommodate both organism/environment interactions and complex interactions between internal components) it is natural to consider the framework of Dynamical Systems Theory. Dynamical Systems Theory (Abraham and Shaw 1992) provides a set of tools for describing the evolution of system states over time. In such descriptions, the theorist specifies a set of parameters whose collective evolution is governed by a set of (usually) differential equations. One key feature of such explanations, for our purposes, is that they are easily capable of spanning organism and environment. In such cases the two sources of variance (the organism and the environment) are treated as coupled dynamical systems whose mutual evolution is described by a specific set of interlocking equations. The behaviour of a wall-mounted pendulum placed in the environmental setting of a second such pendulum provides an easy example. The behaviour of a single pendulum can be described using simple equations and theoretical constructs such as attractors and limit cycles. (We need not unpack these terms here—but see e.g. Norton (forthcoming) for a good introduction.) But two pendulums placed in physical proximity tend, surprisingly, to become swing-synchronized over time. This synchronization admits of an elegant dynamic systems explanation which treats the two pendulums as a single coupled system in which the motion equation for each pendulum includes a term which represents the influence of the other's current state (the coupling in this case is achieved via vibrations running through the wall). For a fuller account see Saltzmann (forthcoming).

Dynamical Systems explanations are thus naturally suited to spanning multiple interacting components and whole agent-environment systems. Whereas the representational/computational framework seemed geared to describing agent-side processing, the dynamical systems constructs apply as easily to environmental features (e.g. the rhythms of a dripping tap) as to internal information-processing events. It is this easy ability to describe larger integrated systems which leads theorists such as Beer and Gallagher (1992) and Wheeler (1994) to prefer Dynamical Systems Theory over classical homuncular approaches for the explanation of emergent, often environment-involving types of behaviours. Behaviours so far studied tend to be relatively basic ones such as legged locomotion and visually guided motion. But the intuition of many such theorists is that the bulk of daily, biological intelligence is rooted in canny couplings between organisms and specific task-environments, and thus that this style of explanation may extend well beyond accounts of relatively 'low level' phenomena. Indeed, Port and van Gelder (forthcoming) contains examples of Dynamical Systems Theorizing applied to such high-level tasks as planning and decision-making, language production, and event recognition.

Notice, however, that the system parameters tracked in dynamical systems style explanations can be arbitrarily far removed from facts about the real internal structure and processing of the agent. The parameters which figure in a good dynamical systems explanation can thus sometimes *target* values of uncontrolled, or emergent, variables. Thus Tim van Gelder notes that a dynamical systems style story which tracks the behaviour of a car engine over time might need to fix on a parameter such as temperature, which does not correspond to any internal component (for homuncular explanation) or to any directly controlled variable. This can occur because:

In its pure form, dynamical explanation makes no reference to the actual structure of the mechanism whose behavior it is explaining. It tells us how the values of the parameters of the system evolve over time, not what it is about the way the system itself is constituted that causes those parameters to evolve in the specified fashion. It is concerned to explore the topographical structure of the dynamics of the system, but this is a wholly different structure than that of the system itself. (van Gelder 1991: 500)

Intermediate options are clearly also available. Thus Saltzmann (forthcoming) offers a dynamical systems explanation of how we achieve multiple muscle coordination in speech production. He notes that the coordinative dynamics need to be specified in abstract informational terms which do not directly track either biomechanical or neuroanatomical structure. Instead, 'the abstract dynamics are defined in coordinates that represent the configurations of different constriction types e.g. the bilabial constrictions used in producing /b/, /p/, or /m/, the alveolar constrictions used in producing /d/, /t/, or /n/ etc.' (Saltzmann, forthcoming: 274.) These constriction types are defined in physical terms involving items such as lip aperture and lip protrusion. But the dynamical systems story is defined over the more abstract types mentioned above. This is an intermediate case in so far as it is clear how the more abstract parameters cited in the dynamical systems analysis are related to physical structures and components of the system.

Such intermediate-level analyses are of great importance. Cognitive Science, I shall next argue, cannot afford to do without *any* of the various explanatory styles just reviewed. And it is therefore crucial that we ensure that the various explanations somehow interlock and inform one another. In the second part of this chapter I develop an argument for this explanatory liberalism, and show how the requirement of explanatory interlock itself imposes powerful additional constraints on our theorizing.

3. TWO EXPLANATORY PROJECTS

Homuncular explanation and interactive explanation are both well suited to explaining adaptive behaviour by unravelling the contributions of specific agent-side components. Interactive explanation differs merely in its explicit recognition of the profound differences which attention to environmental opportunities and the demands of real-time action can make to our hypotheses concerning the information-processing organization required. The dynamical systems approach to explaining emergent phenomena, by contrast, imports a whole new perspective, one which focuses on the evolution of system parameters and is especially well suited to modelling the complex interplay between multiple agent-side parameters and environmental ones. Thus described, it seems almost *obvious* that both types of explanation (the homuncular-style analysis and the global dynamics-style analysis) are needed and should be required to interlock gracefully. Yet several recent writings suggest an alternative, more imperialist point of view. Dynamical systems theory, they suggest, is to be *preferred over* talk of homuncular decompositions and internal components which traffic in representations. Such a radical view, I shall next argue, can be sustained only by adopting an unduly impoverished vision of the *goals* of Cognitive Science.

We can begin by noticing that fans of dynamical systems theory often treat homuncular decomposition and representation-invoking explanations as somehow going together. Thus Beer declares that adaptive success often obviates any need for a 'functional de-composition into representations and modules which . . . manipulate them' (Beer, forthcoming: 25). And Wheeler (1994: 37) even defines the classical vision of homuncular decomposability (which he rejects as a framework for understanding biological cognition) as 'the view that we can compartmentalize a system into a hierarchy of specialized sub-systems that (i) solve particular sub-tasks by manipulating and/or transforming representations . . . and (ii) communicate the computed outputs to each other by passing representations'.

This intimate linking of representation-invoking stories to homuncular decomposition strikes me as problematic. It seems clear that a system *could* be interestingly modular yet not require a representation-invoking explanation (think of a car engine!), and vice versa (think of a connectionist pattern-associator). Moreover, it seems pretty clear that the brain, at least, is a system which exhibits a great deal of modularization and local specialization. (See e.g. Kandel and Schwartz 1985.) As such, it seems ill-advised to define a potential explanatory tool for biological cognition by opposition to homuncular decomposability, at least as that term would naturally be understood.

More importantly, failure to attend to the details of the modular aspects of our internal neural organization would deprive the cognitive scientist of the tools to explain a whole class of phenomena: the systematic effects of various kinds of local damage and disruption. The stress on gross system parameters which helps us understand the dynamics which obtain within whole organism/ environment systems must often obscure the details of how different inner systems contribute to that coupling, and thus how the failure of such systems would affect overall behaviour. To this end, a great deal of work in Cognitive Neuroscience aims to plot precisely the inner organization which explains patterns of breakdown following local damage (see e.g. Farah 1990, Damasio and Damasio 1994). Such explanations typically adopt both a modular/homuncular and a representation-invoking perspective. This kind of understanding *complements* any broader understanding of global dynamics. Each explanatory style helps capture a distinct range of phenomena, and helps provide different types of generalization and prediction.

To take one example, Busemeyer and Townsend (forthcoming) present an elegant application of dynamical systems style theorizing to understanding decision-making. The framework they develop, called Decision Field Theory, describes how preference states evolve over time. They describe dynamical equations which plot the interplay of various gross factors (such as the long-term and short-term anticipated value of different choices) and which also predict and explain the oscillations between likely choices which occur during the deliberation process. These are explained as effects of varying the attention which the decision-maker is currently giving to different factors. The account captures and explains several phenomena of interest, including the apparent inconsistencies between preference orderings measured by choice and those measured by selling price (Lichtenstein and Slovic 1971; Busemeyer and Townsend, forthcoming). A whole class of generalizations, explanations, and predictions thus falls out of the specific equations they use to model the evolution of the chosen parameters over time.

Other kinds of explanation and generalization, however, are not subsumed by this level of description. Thus consider the famous case of Phineas Gage. Gage was a railway construction foreman in the mid-nineteenth century who suffered a terrible injury when a tamping iron was thrust right through his face, skull and brain. Amazingly, Gage survived and regained all of his logical, spatial, and physical skills. Memory and intelligence were not affected. Yet after the accident, his life and personality changed dramatically, and for the worse. He was no longer trustworthy, or caring, or able to fulfil his duties and commitments. The damage to his brain had caused, it seemed, a very specific yet strange effect—almost as if his 'moral centres' had been destroyed. More accurately, it seemed that his ability to 'make rational decisions in personal and social matters' had been selectively compromised, leaving the rest of his intelligence and skills intact. More recently, a team of neuroscientists specializing in the use of brain-imaging techniques analysed the skull of Gage and were able, using computer-aided simulations, to identify the probable sites of neural damage (H. Damasio et al. 1994). These studies (conjoined with evidence from a group of twelve other patients, including the well-documented contemporary case of the patient EVR, A. Damasio et al. 1990) offer what A. Damasio has described as 'compelling evidence that the human brain has a specialized region for making personal and social decisions' (Blakeslee 1994; H. Damasio et al. 1994.)

Such a hypothesis needs careful elucidation since such specializations may none the less involve, in the normal case, the conjunctive activation of multiple neural sub-systems. Even so, the selective isolation of such networks of networks provides a grain of analysis not present in the more global depiction offered by Decision Field Theory.

The point, for current purposes then, is just that the account of the dynamics of decision-making offered by Decision Field Theory is quite clearly not designed either to predict or illuminate the kind of unexpectedly *selective* disturbance to the decision-making process which the neuroanatomically motivated studies address. This is not a criticism of Decision Field Theory. On the contrary, the latter likewise provides a type of understanding, prediction, and explanation which the former does not. This is because Decision Field Theory is free to treat emergent properties of the whole, intact, well-functioning system as individual abstract parameters, and hence provides a vocabulary with a level of analysis well suited to capturing patterns in the temporally evolving behaviour of well-functioning agents. Moreover, it is these more abstract parameters which will often serve us best if we seek to understand the couplings which obtain between whole systems and their environments. Uncontrolled (emergent) parameters, as we saw earlier, often play a large role in illuminating accounts of such large-scale couplings. The moral, then, is that the two styles of explanation are naturally complementary. There is no need for the kind of competition which some of the fans of dynamical systems analysis seem to encourage. Instead, we should clearly distinguish two explanatory projects, each having its own associated class of generalizations. One project aims to understand the way agents and environments are coupled, and may invoke abstract, emergent parameters in so doing. The other seeks to understand the role of various inner sub-systems in producing behaviour, and hence helps explain whole classes of phenomena (e.g. the effects of local damage) which the other does not address.

4. MICRODYNAMICS, CONVERGENCE ZONES, AND THE IMPORTANCE OF EXPLANATORY INTERLOCK

One natural way to think of the two projects just outlined is to depict the componential analysis as providing (in part) a story about the implementation of the more global and abstract dynamical systems story. Van Gelder (1991) is sceptical about the value of such implementational stories, at least as regards the understanding of complex neural networks. He notes (p. 502) that componential (or as he says, 'systematic') explanation is of little help in cases where 'the "parts" of the structure are so many and so similar, and key parameters . . . do not refer to parts of the system at all'.

While this may be true for understanding the behaviour of individual and relatively unstructured connectionist networks, it seems manifestly untrue for understanding the brains of most biological organisms. A more realistic picture, I believe, would countenance three equally important and interlocking types of explanation and description:

1. Some account of the gross couplings between the well-functioning organism and the environment. Possibly achieved via Dynamical Systems styles of description, including reference to parameters which are emergent at the level of the individual organism.

2. An account which identifies the neural components whose cooperative behaviour is tracked by the parameters mentioned in (1), and which explains (perhaps again using dynamical systems tools) how these components are *themselves* coupled (a kind of micro-level dynamic systems story).

3. At least a coarse-grained analysis of the *types of roles* played by the components identified in (2). It is this last analysis which is most likely to assign representational roles to the activities of individual neural sub-systems.

Satisfying explanations of embodied, embedded adaptive success must, I claim, touch all three bases. Moreover, each type of explanation imposes constraints and requirements on the others. There can be no legitimate agent-side parameters in (1) which lack micro-dynamic implementation detail in (2). And such detail cannot be fully understood without the gross systems level commentary on the *roles* of the various components provided by (3).

We can bring out the importance of this latter kind of systems-level commentary by considering, in a little more detail, the shape of at least one recent attempt to explain some selective deficits caused by brain damage. Note that the goal here is merely to exemplify the role of component-based, systems-level conjecture in providing such explanations; the ultimate acceptability of the precise framework reviewed is not the issue.

Consider the patient known as Boswell. Boswell (A. Damasio *et al.* 1989) is selectively impaired in the retrieval of knowledge concerning unique entities (e.g. specific individuals) and events (e.g. specific episodes of autobiography, unique places or objects). None the less, his more general categorical knowledge remains intact. He can place items as cars, houses, people, etc. Boswell shows no deficits of attention or perception, and his ability to acquire and display physical skills is unaffected.

A. Damasio and Damasio (1994) outline a framework capable of accounting for such patterns of deficits. The framework is componentially specified, but avoids the kind of simplistic homuncularism which associates each selectively impaired category of knowledge with a single internal locus. The key feature of their proposal is that the brain exploits what they term 'Convergence Zones': areas which 'direct the simultaneous activation of anatomically separate regions whose conjunction defines an entity' (A. Damasio and Damasio 1994: 65.) A Convergence Zone is then defined as a neuronal grouping in which multiple feedback and feedforward loops make contact. It is a region in which several long-range corticocortical feedback and feedforward connections converge. The function of a Convergence Zone is to allow the system to re-create, by sending signals back down to cortical areas involved in early processing, patterns of activity across widely separated neuronal groups. When we access knowledge of concepts, entities, and events, the Damasios suggest, we exploit such higher-level signals to re-create patterns of co-activations characteristic of the contents in question. If we suppose that different classes and types of knowledge require different complexes of co-activation, managed by different Convergence Zones, we can begin to see how local brain damage could selectively impair the retrieval of different types of knowledge. To explain the dissociation between knowledge of unique and non-unique events, however, we need to introduce the additional notion of a *hierarchy* of Convergence Zones. Recall that Convergence Zones, as imagined by the Damasios, project both backwards (re-activating earlier cortical representations) and forwards (to other (higher) Convergence Zones). The higher zones can economically prompt widespread lower-level activity by exploiting feedback connections to the earlier links in a Convergence Zone hierarchy. The basic hypothesis is thus that

the level at which knowledge is retrieved (e.g. supraordinate, basic object, subordinate) would depend on the scope of multiregional activation. In turn, this would depend on the level of Convergence Zone that is activated. Low level Convergence Zones bind signals relative to entity categories . . . Higher level Convergence Zones bind signals relative to more complex combinations . . . The Convergence Zones capable of binding entities into events . . . are located at the top of the hierarchical streams, in anterior-most temporal and frontal regions. (A. Damasio and Damasio 1994: 73)

The idea, then, is that retrieval of knowledge of unique entities and events requires the conjunctive activation of *more* basic loci than does knowledge of non-unique entities and events (the former subsuming the latter, but not vice versa). Similarly, knowledge of concepts would require the conjunctive activation of several areas while knowledge of features (like colour) may be restricted to a single area. Assuming a hierarchy of Convergence Zones extended in neural space, this picture would explain why damage to early visual cortices selectively impairs knowledge of features (like colour), while damage to intermediate cortices affects knowledge of non-unique entities and events and damage to anterior cortices impairs responses concerning unique individuals and events.

According to this framework, distinct but overlapping neural systems promote access to different types of knowledge. The more complex the conjunctions of information required to fix a class of knowledge, the more such coordinative activity is needed. And this in turn implicates correlatively higher sites in a hierarchy of Convergence Zones. In brain space, this corresponds to increasingly anterior loci within the temporal cortices. The authors stress that they are *not* depicting the damaged regions as the physical sites of different classes of knowledge. Rather, the damaged regions are the Control Zones which promote the conjunctive activation of several, quite distant, areas. These are typically early sensory and motor cortices which would be led to re-create their proprietary responses to certain external stimuli by the re-entrant signals. Summing up their suggestions, they comment that

the (picture) we favor implies a relative functional compartmentalization for the normal brain. One large set of systems in early sensory cortices and motor cortices would be the base for 'sense' and 'action' knowledge . . . Another set of systems in higher-order cortices would orchestrate time-locked activities in the former, that is, would promote and establish temporal correspondence among separate areas. (A. Damasio and Damasio 1994: 70)

On this account, there is functional compartmentalization for several types of sensory and motor information, and for several levels of Convergence Zone mediated control. Higher-level psychological constructs such as concepts are, however, depicted as constituted by the activity of *multiple* basic areas (in sensory and motor cortices) and mediated by the activity of *multiple* Convergence Zones, themselves linked by complex feedback and feedforward interconnections. Much of the explanatory apparatus for explaining phenomena like concept possession will thus require resources which go beyond simple homuncular analyses. We will need models which are especially well adapted to revealing the principles underlying phenomena which arise out of the complex, temporarily time-locked co-evolving activity of multiple components linked by manifold feedback and feedforward pathways. Classical homuncular analyses have not tended to fare well in such cases, and there thus looks to be a clear opening for a dynamical systems-style account of the detailed implementation of the Convergence Zone hypothesis. Yet at the same time, the explanatory power of the theory is clearly tied up with the decomposition into basic processing areas (performing identifiable representational tasks) and into a well-defined set of Convergence Zones whose different activities likewise map onto different classes of knowledge retrieval. It is only in the light of this decomposition and functional/representational commentary that the model can predict and explain the selective effects of local brain damage on, for example, retrieval of knowledge concerning unique entities and events. In this case the presence of the homuncular analysis and representational commentary seems essential as a means of bridging the phenomena to be explained (deficits affecting specific types of *knowledge*) and the models we create. Without talk of the representational functions of early sensory cortices, and talk of higher-level cortical structures as being functionally specialized to re-create complexes of representational activity, we should not understand *why* any additional descriptions of the detailed dynamics of time-locked behaviours, etc. were actually *explanatory* of the psychological phenomena.

Notice, finally, that in thus endorsing both (i) the interpretation of some basic neural areas as representation-supporting and (ii) the decomposition of the brain into specialized modules and sub-systems, we are *not* yet endorsing the vision of the brain as a rich *message-passing* device. The higher centres posited by the Damasios do not act as storehouses of knowledge 'ftp'd' from the lower-level agencies! They are instead 'merely the most distant convergence points from which divergent retroactivation can be triggered' (A. Damasio and Damasio

1994: 70). Much opposition to representational analyses is, I believe, more properly cast as opposition to a 'message-passing' vision of mind (see e.g. Brooks 1991). Thus Maes (1994: 141) notes that work on adaptive autonomous agents eschews the use of classical modules which 'rely on the "central representation" as their means of interface'. Instead, such researchers propose modules which interface via very simple messages, whose content rarely exceeds signals for activation, suppression, or inhibition. Nor do the modules share any representational format—each may encode information in highly proprietary and task-specific ways (p. 142). This vision of de-centralized control and multiple representational formats is both biologically realistic and computationally attractive. But it is, as we have seen, fully compatible with both internal modular decomposition and representation-invoking commentary. Such analyses provide essential types of understanding and explanation. Recent investigations of behavioural emergence and complex organism/environment couplings likewise provide essential insights into the nature of real-time adaptive intelligence. The goal should be to achieve a satisfying and mutually illuminating interlock between these several sources of models and analyses, not to sacrifice one on the altar of the other.

5. CONCLUSIONS: THE BRAIN BITES BACK

A full account even of embodied, embedded, and emergence-laden cognition must do justice to several kinds of data. One important body of data concerns changes in gross system parameters over time. Another concerns the specific effects of local systems damage. Complex evolved biological intelligences seem to rely on a mixture of componential specialization overlaid by increasingly complex systemic properties of feedback and feedforward modulation. These complex interrelations are probably evolution's way of pressing added utility from existing dedicated applications. The Convergence Zone hypothesis provides a neat example case, in so far as it posits a set of well-defined basic processing areas which are then orchestrated (via the Convergence Zones) into temporary ensembles which invite rather different kinds of description, for example, as supporting retrieval of a concept or of a memory of a unique event.

When evolved systems exhibit this two-sided profile (of componential specialization alongside complex internally interactive properties) the theorist should likewise be willing to exploit multiple kinds of explanatory tools, ranging from analyses which criss-cross the organism and the environment, to ones which quantify over multiple inner components and complex connectivities, to ones which isolate components and offer a functional/representational commentary on their basic roles.

Emergent properties will thus figure in this explanatory activity at two levels. First, there will be *internally* emergent features: uncontrolled parameters constituted by the interaction of multiple inner sources of variation. Second, there will be *behaviourally* emergent features: uncontrolled parameters constituted by interactions between whole functioning organisms and the environment. Both classes of emergent property need to be understood, and dynamical systems theory provides a set of tools which can help in each arena. But importantly, these multiple explanatory endeavours are not autonomous. Uncontrolled parameters must be cashed out in real (neural and environmental) sources of variance. And basic componential specialization must be identified and incorporated wherever it occurs. Failure to do so will result in explanatory failure further down the line, for example when confronted by data concerning the selective impairments caused by local brain damage. In the final analysis, the moral is simple and familiar. The recent emphasis on behavioural and internal emergence is timely and important: but it should not be seen as yet another excuse to avoid confrontation with the biological brain.

REFERENCES

Abraham, R., and Shaw, C. (1992), *Dynamics—The Geometry of Behavior* (Redwood, Calif.: Addison-Wesley).
Ballard, D. (1991), 'Animate Vision', *Artificial Intelligence*, 48: 57–86.
Bechtel, W., and Richardson, R. (1992), *Discovering Complexity: De-composition and Localization as Scientific Research Strategies* (Princeton, NJ: Princeton Univ. Press).
Beer, R. (forthcoming), 'Computational and Dynamical Languages for Autonomous Agents', in Port and van Gelder (forthcoming).
—— and Gallagher, J. C. (1992), 'Evolving Dynamical Neural Networks for Adaptive Behavior', *Adaptive Behavior*, 1: 91–122.
Blakeslee, S. (1994), 'Old Accident Points to Brain's Moral Center', *New York Times*, 24 May.
Brooks, R. (1991), 'Intelligence without Representation', *Artificial Intelligence*, 47: 139–59.
Busemeyer, J., and Townsend, J. (forthcoming), 'Decision Field Theory', in Port and van Gelder (forthcoming).
Churchland, P. S., Ramachandran, V. S., and Sejnowski, T. J. (1994), 'A Critique of Pure Vision', in Koch and Davis (1994).
Damasio, A., and Damasio, H. (1994), 'Cortical Systems for Retrieval of Concrete Knowledge: The Convergence Zone Framework', in Koch and Davis (1994).
—— Tramel, D., and Damasio, H. (1989), 'Amnesia Caused by Herpes Simplex Encephalitis, Infarctions in Basal Forebrain, Alzheimer's Disease and Anoxia', in F. Boller and J. Grafman (eds.), *Handbook of Neuropsychology*, iii, ed. L. Squire (Amsterdam: Elsevier), 149–66.

Damasio, A., Tramel, D., and Damasio, H. (1990), 'Individuals with Sociopathic Behavior Caused by Frontal Damage Fail to Respond Autonomically to Social Stimuli', *Behavioral Brain Research*, 4: 81–94.

Damasio, H., Grabowski, T., Frank, R., Galaburda, A., and Damasio, A. (1994), 'The Return of Phineas Gage: Clues About the Brain from the Skull of a Famous Patient', *Science*, 264: 1102–5.

Dennett, D. (1978), *Brainstorms* (Brighton: Harvester Press).

Farah, M. (1990), *Visual Agnosia* (Cambridge, Mass.: MIT Press).

Hallam, J. C. T., and Malcolm, C. A. (1994), 'Behaviour, Perception, Action and Intelligence—The View From Situated Robotics', *Proceedings of the Royal Society of London*, Series A, 349 (1994), 29–42.

Harvey, I., Husbands, P., and Cliff, D. (1994), 'Seeing the Light: Artificial Evolution, Real Vision', in D. Cliff, P. Husbands, J. A. Meyer, and S. Wilson (eds.), *From Animals to Animats 3* (Cambridge, Mass.: MIT Press), 392–401.

Haugeland, J. (1981), 'Semantic Engines: An Introduction to Mind Design', in J. Haugeland (ed.), *Mind Design: Philosophy, Psychology, Artificial Intelligence* (Cambridge, Mass.: MIT Press), 1–34.

Hofstadter, D. (1985), *Metamagical Themas: Questing for the Essence of Mind and Pattern* (Harmondsworth: Penguin).

Kandel, E., and Schwarz, J. (1985), *Principles of Neural Science* (Amsterdam: Elsevier).

Kirsh, D. (forthcoming), 'The Intelligent Use of Space', *Artificial Intelligence*.

Koch, C., and Davis, J. (1994) (eds.), *Large-Scale Neuronal Theories of the Brain* (Cambridge, Mass.: MIT Press).

Le Cun, Y., Boser, B., Denker, J. S., Henderson, D., Howard, R., Hubbard, W., and Jackal, L. (1989), 'Back Propagation Applied to Handwritten Zip Code Recognition', *Neural Computation*, 1/4: 541–51.

Lichtenstein, S., and Slovic, P. (1971), 'Reversals of Preference between Bids and Choices in Gambling Decisions', *Journal of Experimental Psychology*, 101: 16–20.

Maes, P. (1994), 'Modeling Adaptive Autonomous Agents', *Artificial Life*, 1: 135–62.

Marr, D. (1982), *Vision* (San Francisco, Cal.: Freeman).

Newell, A., and Simon, N. (1976), 'Computer Science as Empirical Enquiry: Symbols and Search', *Communications of the Association for Computing Machines*, repr. in M. A. Boden (ed.), *The Philosophy of Artificial Intelligence* (Oxford: Oxford University Press, 1990), 104–32.

Norton, A. (forthcoming), 'Dynamics: An Introduction', in Port and van Gelder (forthcoming).

Port, R., and van Gelder, T. (forthcoming), *Mind as Motion: Dynamics, Behavior, and Cognition* (Cambridge, Mass.: MIT Press).

Resnick, M. (1994a), *Turtles, Termites and Traffic Jams: Explorations in Massively Parallel Microworlds* (Cambridge, Mass.: MIT Press).

—— (1994b), 'Learning about Life', *Artificial Life*, 1: 229–42.

Saltzmann, E. (forthcoming), 'Dynamics and C-ordinate Systems in Skilled Sensorimotor Activity', in Port and van Gelder (forthcoming).

Steels, L. (1994), 'The Artificial Life Roots of Artificial Intelligence', *Artificial Life*, 1: 75–110.

Van Gelder, T. (1991), 'Connectionism and Dynamical Explanation', *Proceedings of the 13th Annual Conference of the Cognitive Science Society* (Chicago), 499–503.

Wheeler, M. (1994), 'From Activation to Activity', *Artificial Intelligence and the Simulation of Behaviour (AISB) Quarterly*, 87: 36–42.

Wimsatt, W. (1986), 'Forms of Aggregativity', in A. Donagan, N. Perovich, and M. Wedin (eds.), *Human Nature and Natural Knowledge* (Dordrecht: Reidel), 259–93.
—— (forthcoming), 'Emergence as Non-aggregativity and the Biases of Reductionisms', in P. Taylor and J. Haila (eds.), *Natural Conditions: Perspectives on Ecology and Change*.

10

IN PRAISE OF INTERACTIVE EMERGENCE, OR WHY EXPLANATIONS DON'T HAVE TO WAIT FOR IMPLEMENTATIONS

HORST HENDRIKS-JANSEN

1. INTRODUCTION

My interest is in explanation, not in design or engineering. The focus of this paper will therefore be on life as we know it rather than life as it could be or life as we might be able to evolve it artificially. What is more, I shall be concentrating on explanatory strategies which have a bearing on our own peculiar form of intelligent life. I believe that one of the major benefits of the branch of A-Life in which I am interested (situated robotics) is the contribution it can make to a coherent naturalistic explanation of intentional behaviour and conceptual thought as displayed by human beings.

This has become something of a heresy in A-Life circles. The anti-human bias was spelled out some years ago by Brooks (1991*b*: 140):

I, and others, believe that human level intelligence is too complex and little understood to be correctly decomposed into the right subspecies at the moment and that even if we knew the subspecies we still wouldn't know the right interfaces between them. Furthermore, we will never understand how to decompose human level intelligence until we've had a lot of practice with a simpler level intelligence.

We may call this the no-explanation-without-implementation school of thought. I shall argue in this chapter that, while it provided a necessary corrective to some of the wilder claims of classical and connectionist AI, it has now become counter-productive. Classical and connectionist models continue to dominate cognitive philosophy and are still making headway in developmental psychology. New discoveries concerning the early behaviour of human infants, made possible by the increasing precision of experimental techniques, are being interpreted in accordance with such models (see Baillargeon 1987; Diamond

Reprinted from R. A. Brooks and P. Maes (eds.), *Artificial Life IV* (Proceedings of the Fourth International Workshop on the Synthesis and Simulations of Living Systems; Cambridge, Mass.: MIT Press, 1994), 70–9.

1991; and Spelke 1991). The experiments themselves are devised from a classical perspective, which assumes that the natural kinds for a scientific explanation of human thought have to be internal representations corresponding to entities in an objective world which is somehow pre-registered into objects, properties, and relations. Development of sensory-motor skills is then conceptualized as a process of representational redescription rather than a complex process of interactive emergence involving a large number of situated activity-patterns (Karmiloff-Smith 1987).

While classical AI and connectionism thus invade the human sciences, there is a danger that Artificial Life is turning into a computational discipline specializing in slime-moulds and six-legged insects. I agree that we shall have a long time to wait for a genuine implementation of human intelligence (as opposed to systems which mimic rational choice and logical inference within some formally specified task-domain), but I believe that the new paradigm has much to tell us right now about the way in which the explanation of human behaviour should be approached. We must not allow classical AI and connectionism to have it all their own way while we spend the next few hundred years pushing our situated implementations up their evolutionary hills. The paradigm based on decomposition by activity and interactive emergence provides valuable explanatory principles as well as solidly based methods of implementation, and these principles can be applied before the implementations are achieved.

2. CLARIFICATION OF TERMS

The notion of 'emergence' may be used in different senses. Nagel (1961) distinguishes two frequently encountered meanings in scientific explanation. The first implies that properties at higher levels are not necessarily predictable from properties at lower levels. As Nagel points out, that observation can be said to hold even for phenomena whose explanations are generally considered to be reductive in the 'hard' sense, such as the atomic theory of matter. The gross properties of water, like 'wetness', cannot be deduced from the properties of molecules, for the simple reason that molecular theory does not include statements about such properties.

The second meaning picked out by Nagel (1961) is a historical one. This draws attention to the fact that simple traits and forms of organization give rise, in the course of evolution, to more complex and irreducibly novel traits and structures. As Nagel points out (p. 375), 'the question whether a property, process or mode of behaviour is a case of emergent evolution is a straightforward empirical problem and can be resolved at least in principle by recourse to historical inquiry'.

I shall discuss some of the difficulties of resolving that question in Section 4. In order to do so, I shall introduce a third type of emergence, which I have called 'interactive emergence', and which is defined more fully in that section.

The term '*Merkwelt*' derives from von Uexkull (1934) and has been used by Tinbergen (1951), and more recently by Brooks (1986). It is used to emphasize the fact that a creature's perceptual world will be species-specific and depends on the creature's sensory modalities and resolving powers, its morphology, and its patterns of movement relative to the world.

'Affordance' is a term coined by Gibson (1979). It assumes an ecological approach to the explanation of perception and behaviour, rather than the ethological approach I recommend in this chapter. I use it in the next section to bring out the fact that the features relevant to an explanation of behaviour cannot be conceptualized as abstract properties of the world. They are dynamic structures which emerge when a creature performs its species-typical activity patterns within a specific ecological niche.

'Natural kinds' may be seen as the scaffolding for scientific theory-building. Hypothetical groupings or explanatory entities, suggested by a growing theory, lead to fruitful inductions and become established as part of a new scientific paradigm. It has been suggested by Wilkes (1989) that one reason why the behavioural sciences are underdeveloped is their inability to arrive at a consensus about natural kinds. No acceptable, shared taxonomy exists in psychology. Traditional cognitive science can be seen as a (failed) attempt to establish such a consensus, proposing internal representations and computational formalisms as the natural kinds of psychology.

As Wilkes (1989) points out, the notion of natural kinds, and a recognition of their importance in scientific advance, are quite compatible with scepticism as to whether such hypothetical groupings are in any sense 'real' constituents of the world. 'Naturalness' may be glossed in terms of the likelihood that the chosen kinds can generate fruitful laws and generalizations.

3. SIX BASIC EXPLANATORY PRINCIPLES DERIVED FROM SITUATED ROBOTICS

Most of the key issues have been identified before by other authors (see Brooks 1986, 1991*a*, 1991*b*, 1992; Chapman and Agre 1987; Horswill 1992; Kirsh 1991; Smithers 1992; Steels 1991). I shall try to recapitulate the main points in a condensed form, using the engineering principles derived from situated robotics to define what I believe to be the central principles for explanations of human behaviour and thought.

1. Understanding of autonomous behaviour requires decomposition by activ-

ity rather than by function. Each component or activity module identified in this type of explanation interacts independently with the environment, and the interaction is continuous, dynamic, and unplanned. This eliminates the need for internally stored information to facilitate planning, and for the transmission of information between modules. The underlying mechanism does not depend for its operation on the manipulation of semantic tokens representing states of the world or the agent's relation to the world.

2. Behavioural emergence therefore replaces the traditional functional hierarchy. Since the activity modules do not perform tasks that are logically defined sub-tasks of the overall system, their contribution to its performance can no longer be characterized from the design perspective favoured by classical AI. An understanding of how a complex autonomous system is put together requires consideration of historical contingencies involving sensors, effectors, and neural mechanisms that evolved in response to changing environmental conditions.

3. Much of the 'knowledge' that is used by an autonomous system is 'stored' in its environment. It does not need to be retrieved from memory, or recovered from sparse perceptual data, because it is by definition available as and when it is needed, and in the form in which it is needed. The individual activity patterns work by simple indicators which cause the activities to be switched on and off and correctly oriented in the appropriate situations. In ethology such indicators are called sign stimuli and orienting stimuli. Most ethologists think of them as objective features, but interactive emergence demands a Gibsonian or Uexkullian point of view (see point 5).

4. The 'control mechanism' which makes the 'decisions' or 'choices' is thus inextricably embedded in the world. This does not mean that the system as a whole can be conceptualized as a behaviourist stimulus-response engine. Its perceptual and behavioural history will affect its responses to current stimuli, and the same stimulus may thus elicit different responses on different occasions. In the terminology of dynamical systems theory, perturbation by the environment alters the system's parameters and affects its evolution equation.

5. The creature's morphology, its sensori-motor characteristics, and the activity patterns it performs all affect its '*Merkwelt*' (von Uexkull 1934) and 'affordances' (Gibson 1979), and consequently the 'problems' it has to 'solve'. Tasks, problems, and solutions to problems cannot be characterized independently. This puts the dream of an 'implements relation' (Horswill 1992) out of reach. A three-part equation relating classes of autonomous systems to task-descriptions and environmental categories would require an objective taxonomy for each. Interactive emergence implies that no such objective classification can be made that would be relevant to the generation or explanation of autonomous behaviour.

6. The evolutionary and developmental history of the creature is important

to an understanding of how it works. Each 'layer' on the way to a complex intelligent system has to be 'debugged' in the real world, either by natural selection or by the programmer. New *Merkwelten* emerge from each successive layer. In Hendriks-Jansen (1993*a*) I argued that, in a naturally evolved creature, successive layers can confer the status of natural kind on the layers which preceded them, if it can be shown that the *Merkwelt* resulting from the earlier layer was required for the evolution of the more recent one. This gives substance to the notion of a 'historical' (Sloman 1978), or 'genetic' (Nagel 1961) explanation of autonomous behaviour resulting from interactive emergence.

4. FOUR TYPES OF SCIENTIFIC EXPLANATION

Nagel (1961) distinguishes four types of explanation that are commonly used in science:

1. Deductive explanation, in which the *explicandum* is a logically necessary consequence of the explanatory premises, which must contain a set of initial conditions and a general law.

2. Probabilistic explanation, in which the explanatory premises do not formally imply the *explicandum* but make it probable.

3. Functional or teleological explanations, in which a thing or event is explained in terms of the function it performs in some larger whole, or the role it plays in bringing something about.

4. Genetic explanations. These are different from deductive, probabilistic, or teleological explanations because the explanatory premises take the form of a historical sequence of events. An important element in this notion is that explanation depends crucially on actual occurrences. There is no central law which constrains these occurrences. It would be impossible to predict an event at time t given the events at time 0. It is not even possible to *explain*, by some general principle, how the particular form taken by E_t followed from the structure of E_0. However, given the occurrence of all stages between E_0 and E_t, it becomes clear how the latter could have issued from the former.

The classic example of this type of explanation is, of course, evolutionary biology. Like all historical explanations, it lacks a deductive or probabilistic law. Natural selection does not confer predictive power. I argue this point in detail in Hendriks-Jansen (1993*b*), and also show that functional decomposition, and hence teleological explanations by Nagel's definition of the term, do not sit well with the theory of natural selection. This has led some authors (notably Popper 1963) to question the scientific credentials of Darwin's theory, and it has led others (e.g. Gould and Lewontin 1978) to point out that a plausible adaptive story can always be found to fit any explanatory hypothesis. However, the theory has stood the test of time and proved highly successful in providing a diversity of historical explanations, not only of morphological traits, but of behavioural entities as well.

The explanatory entities or natural kinds of a genetic or historical explanation are the successive stages in the emergence of a phenomenon, trait, or event. As Nagel (1961) pointed out, one of the difficulties with this type of explanation is the problem of deciding which specific occurrences, out of a more or less continuous historical line, deserve to be singled out as particularly significant. In Hendriks-Jansen (1993a) I argued that a principled choice can in fact be made, based on a slightly modified version of Millikan's (1984) notion of 'history of use'. As an existence proof to support my contention, I referred to an autonomous, wall-following, and navigating robot developed by Mataric (Mataric 1991, 1992; Mataric and Brooks 1990).

The independent operation of four low-level reflexes in Mataric's robot, debugged in a specific office environment, results in the emergent activity of wall-following. There are no explicit instructions inside the robot which tell it to follow walls; no formal definition of walls is required to produce its behaviour. The robot is therefore unlikely to follow a particular wall in precisely the same way on different occasions. Its route will depend on its approach in a particular instance, on noise in its sensor readings, and on the numerous unspecified contingencies of a dynamic environment. But it can be relied on to spend a considerable proportion of its time following walls, as long as it remains in an environment which is roughly similar to the one by which its wall-following behaviour was 'selected'. This emergent behaviour of wall-following produces a high-level *Merkwelt* consisting of dynamic features with temporal extent which correspond only indirectly to features in the world. It allows the robot to identify 'landmarks' as reliable correlations between sonar readings averaged over time and temporal regularities in its own movements. Such a configuration, if found in a naturally occurring creature, would confer the status of natural kind on the lower level of emergent activity, since it would clearly establish a history of use for that activity in the creature's evolutionary past.

It is important to stress that the natural kinds of this type of explanation only come into existence as the result of the creature's situated activity. They are not entities which can be reduced to events in the creature's head, and neither can they be defined in terms of inputs and outputs, or by classifications of the environment. Interactive, situated behaviour cannot be explained in terms of a deductive or generative law. It requires a historical explanation because there can be no rules to predict the sorts of behaviour which might emerge. There are no short-cuts for deriving the sequence of events in a historical process.

5. BEHAVIOURAL ECOLOGY, COST-BENEFIT MODELS, AND NATURAL SELECTION

It may seem that what I have claimed in the last two sections is flatly contradicted by important work in behavioural ecology, as well as by many of the simulations done in A-Life. I am referring to 'economic' or cost-benefit studies based on such well-established notions as inclusive fitness and evolutionarily stable strategies. Clearly these theories make reference to natural selection, and clearly they also deal with classes of individuals defined in terms of abstract behavioural categories, such as 'hawks' and 'doves'. It would appear that there are obvious similarities between theories of this kind and what Nagel (1961) calls probabilistic theories, and that the effect of natural selection on behaviour may thus be characterized in those terms.

The application of cost-benefit models in behavioural ecology results in explanations of behaviour which account for observed correlations between certain environmental factors and formally defined classes of behaviour by applying a logical calculus like game-theory. Such explanations are undoubtedly of great value in their own right. Computational models may be built which incorporate and modify this logic as well as the variables which the theory has identified. But these are not explanations in the sense that they can tell us anything about the underlying mechanisms; they remain economic or actuarial models which reproduce statistical correlations. It is a category mistake to treat the programs used in such models as explanations of the mechanisms which subtend the behaviour of individual creatures.

Natural selection, writes McFarland (1985), has seen to it that there is an optimum balance between the amount of time spent by a brooding bird on incubation, and the amount of time she spends on foraging to keep up her strength. There will be a clear relation between different strategies (in this case the varying proportions of time spent on the two activities) and the bird's reproductive success. Since the two behaviours are both important to the production of offspring and compete for the bird's time during the period of incubation, there must be a measurable correlation between behavioural strategies and genetic survival.

The crucial question remains, however—namely what are the underlying mechanisms which might *explain* such a correlation? It will not do to say that they consist in a 'gene for foraging' and a 'gene for incubation', or that we are dealing with a mechanism that controls the amount of time spent on the two activities. As McFarland himself admits (1985: 456): 'such considerations are purely functional. They specify what animals ought to do to make the best decisions under particular circumstances, but they do not say anything about the mechanisms that animals might employ to attain these objectives.'

Foraging and incubation are functional categories which would need to be grounded in specific activity patterns to be linked to particular genes. The fact that cost-benefit bird (an actuarial abstraction like 'economic man') necessarily optimizes or maximizes its utility (because utility is by definition that which it optimizes) does not imply that individual birds contain choice mechanisms which work by optimization on entities like foraging and incubation. But the question which interests us as cognitive scientists is what sort of mechanism *does* subtend the bird's behaviour. We would like natural selection to help us find clues to those underlying mechanisms, and given sufficient patience and care, it can in fact be made to do so, but economic models are not the appropriate tool for the job.

6. THE ORIENTING ATTITUDES AND EXPLANATORY PRINCIPLES OF ETHOLOGY

The classic texts of ethology are often quoted in the literature on situated robotics. There is a feeling that the basic interests of the two disciplines coincide, even though their aims might be different.

Ethologists hold that behaviour should be studied in the creature's natural environment, and not under laboratory conditions that have been specifically designed to elicit certain responses. In situated robotics, there is a corresponding emphasis on producing robots which will operate in 'natural' environments, meaning, in this case, that the environments should not be altered to suit the robot's limitations. Both disciplines share an awareness of the importance of context, and of the way an autonomous creature becomes embedded in its environment, so that its activities are to a very great extent shaped by it. There is, in both disciplines, an understanding that the global behaviour of a creature may be the result of an interplay of diverse activities, each operating independently in response to action-specific stimuli, rather than a purposive succession of acts directed by a central controlling mechanism towards an internally represented goal. This leads, in autonomous agent research, to the principle of decomposition by activity, and in ethology, to an emphasis on deriving explanatory concepts from the study of simple behaviour patterns and their interdependencies, rather than imposing some overall theoretical framework on behavioural diversity.

Hinde (1982) sums up what he calls the 'orienting attitudes' of ethology as follows:

1. Start all analysis and theorizing from a secure and extensive descriptive base.

2. Study behaviour in the context of the environment by which it was selected.

3. Analyse in detail one specific type of behaviour as it is displayed by one particular species in its natural environment; then compare with other, closely related behaviours, species, and environments.

As will become clear in the next two sections, I believe it is these orienting attitudes which constitute the most important legacy of the early work in ethology, rather than the much-debated theoretical notions of fixed action pattern, sign stimulus, action-specific energy, and hierarchical organization introduced by Lorenz (1937, 1939, 1952) and Tinbergen (1951). Ethology's orienting attitudes impose their own distinctive logic on explanation. Its emphasis on detailed analysis of specific activity patterns performed by particular species in their natural environment shifts attention from generative rules and formal task-descriptions to questions of taxonomy and history. The variety of naturally occurring behaviour, and its diverse relations to the environment, rule out a single explanatory principle like the reflex arc or the negative feedback loop. Before anything like a mechanistic causal explanation can be attempted, the precise structure of each pattern of activity, and its relation to the structure of other activities and the environment, as well as its historical emergence, need to be understood.

Lorenz had an unfortunate obsession with 'innateness', which was probably a reaction against the behaviourist orthodoxy of his time. A somewhat simplistic view of ontogenesis and genetic transmission caused him to equate 'innate' with 'fixed' (both in the sense of 'totally determined by a genetic blueprint' and 'immutable in its structure'), and he was therefore forced to maintain that fixed action patterns were 'endogenously generated'. This led to a number of false starts. It tempted some ethologists to search for neurophysiological correlates of fixed action patterns and 'behaviour centres', and it tempted others to think in terms of 'software' explanations involving 'programs' or 'systems' (see Tinbergen 1951; Barlow 1968; Baerends 1976).

It can be argued (Hendriks-Jansen in press) that all these attempts are denials of ethology's most important contribution, which was to draw attention to the situated, interactive, and emergent character of naturally occurring behaviour. The best corrective to such tendencies was provided by comparative psychologists like Schneirla (1966) and Lehrman (1970), who argued that no behaviour is genetically fixed in the sense that Lorenz had decreed it to be. Species-typical activity patterns are emergent phenomena in three different senses of the word. They emerge in the species as a result of natural selection. They emerge in a maturing individual as the result of ontogenesis and learning. And they emerge every time they occur within the life of that individual as the result of interactions between the creature's low-level activities and its species-typical environment.

This means that there can be no straightforward neurophysiological correlates of complex activity patterns, just as there is no genetic blueprint for their structure. Nor can one think of units of behaviour as being 'represented' in any way inside the creature. The explanation for the recognizable structure of species-typical activity patterns must not be sought in generative mechanisms; it is a consequence of the fact that the creature evolved, matured, and acts within a particular ecological niche, ensuring that its emergent behaviour displays the structure we observe.

Lehrman's and Schneirla's critiques brought to the surface certain fundamental implications of the ethological approach. If behaviour is an emergent phenomenon in the three senses given above, it is unlikely that *any* universal laws can be discovered to describe and explain it. The problem is not just one of finding the right classifications which will point to causal generalities; it is the fact that the causal explanation is likely to be unique in each case.

There is nothing new about such a situation in science. It characterizes areas which are not susceptible to description in terms of formal rules, but only to what Marr (1982) called 'Type 2' explanations. As Marr himself explained it, in such cases the 'problem' is 'solved' by a large number of processes whose complex interaction is the simplest description of the processes involved. Marr believed that this made explanation impossibly difficult. However, that is so only if one adopts his position that behaviour is a solution to some problem set by the environment. As I have argued in this chapter, the natural environment does not set problems, and evolution does not solve any. Explanation of behaviour should not be seen as a matter of characterizing the appropriate problem space, but as a matter of describing the space of emergent phenomena by classifying and relating the actual instances produced by genetic recombination and mutation acted on by natural selection.

Computational theory does not provide an appropriate framework for this type of explanation (Hendriks-Jansen in press), but situated robotics is its natural ally. Artificially built models capable of diverse levels of situated activity within a specific environment may serve to confirm hypotheses about the interactive emergence of naturally occurring behaviour, and bring out 'family resemblances' between different kinds of behavioural dependency. Such models are models of behaviour, not attempts to model the mind or brain. There is no presumption that the computational devices used to implement the behaviour bear any resemblance to mechanisms inside the creature whose behaviour is being modelled. However, a deeper understanding of behavioural dependencies may point to fruitful investigative strategies for the neural sciences.

7. THE EMERGENCE OF MEANING IN HUMAN INFANTS

How does all this apply to an explanation of intentional behaviour as manifested by human beings, whose activities seem so clearly governed by goals,
plans, and internal representations corresponding to the objects, properties, and
relations we all take to be the basic constitutents of our world? An explanation
in terms of activity modules and interactive emergence might be adequate to
the activities of an ant or a spider, but surely *we* possess a central, directive
intelligence which traffics in concepts? Surely those concepts play a crucial
role in the generation of behaviour, and must therefore figure in any explanation as causally effective entities?

Human beings do use concepts, but the lack of progress made by classical
AI over the last thirty-five years has begun to raise some doubts as to whether
symbolic manipulation, high-level planning by a central executive, and rules of
inference working over semantic tokens are the most appropriate natural kinds
for an explanation of human behaviour and thought. Top-down analysis, both
in the sense of deriving explanatory entities from folk-psychology, and in the
sense of functional decomposition inspired by a design approach based on
classical engineering, does not seem to have got us very far. I do not intend to
rehearse all the well-known problems encountered by these strategies. Instead,
I should like to offer some evidence from recent work in developmental psychology which suggests that a historical explanation in terms of interactive
emergence might do better.

In the early 1970s investigators started to report that very young infants,
observed in their natural environment, perform activity patterns that are far
more complex and far more varied than had previously been recognized. These
investigators tended to be influenced by the orienting attitudes of ethology, as
summed up in the last section. They tried to observe infants' behaviour in the
context in which it naturally occurred, deferred analysis and theoretical specu-
lation until they had built up a solid descriptive base, and examined in great
detail one particular type of behaviour, rather than searching for evidence of a
central law that might unify diverse behavioural phenomena.

Bateson (1975) provides a good example of how such a change in emphasis
can render previously invisible (or in this case, inaudible) data perceptible to
an observer. Her research centred on the acoustic analysis of infants' vocalizations
during mother–infant interactions. It uncovered a wealth of coos and murmurs
which were clearly picked up and interpreted by the mother, but which previous
investigators appeared to have overlooked: 'The difference seems to arise from
a difference in sampling techniques, where [previous investigators] focused on
describing an acoustic phenomenon and we are concerned with describing the
acoustic aspects of an interpersonal process' (Bateson 1975: 109).

The same point is made by Trevarthen (1977) about the rich variety of facial expressions and expressive gestures displayed by very young infants, by Brazelton (1979) about the infant's species-typical responses to adult handling, and by Schaffer (1977), Kaye (1979), Tronick *et al.* (1979), and Newson (1979) about the cues and temporal patterning involved in mother–infant turn-taking.

All of these investigators made intensive use of film or video, and of the opportunities for micro-analysis which those media afford. They frequently remark that, prior to the development of such techniques, detailed investigation of activity was virtually impossible. Trevarthen (1977) writes that the actual movements of human beings—as opposed to the intentional acts in terms of which we normally describe and perceive them—were as difficult to observe before the invention of cine photography as were the planets before the invention of the telescope. He speculates that this might be one of the reasons why psychology became a science of perception and cognition, rather than a science of activity patterns, gestures, and facial expressions.

The explanatory entities of psychology have tended to be static entities like beliefs, desires, memories, and mental states, whereas these new discoveries suggested that meaning emerges in dynamic interactions. More sophisticated recording and sampling techniques, allied to the orienting attitudes of ethology, revealed the importance of temporal patterning in the establishment and maintenance of mother–infant exchanges. It began to be realized that a large number of species-typical activity patterns are either present at birth, or else mature during the first few months of life, and that the main 'function' of many of these patterns is the establishment of an interactively emergent and typically human *Merkwelt* of mother–infant 'dialogue'. Examples of such patterns are primitive reach-and-grasp (Trevarthen 1977; von Hofsten, 1984; Fischer and Bidell 1991), the early lip and tongue movements which Trevarthen called 'pre-speech' (Trevarthen 1977; Papousek and Papousek 1977), rhythmical stereotypies like supine kicking and hand-waving (Thelen 1981), and burst-pause-burst in suckling (Kaye 1982).

The existence of such well-coordinated patterns of activity at a very early age, and the way they either disappeared at a later date, or were modified into more complex types of behaviour, or served as the 'context' for the emergence of such later behaviour, prompted a reappraisal of many of the accepted views about inborn abilities and learning.

It was realized that a rigid, stage-bound picture of development, such as had been proposed by Piaget (1954), could not adequately describe the processes that were being observed. Individual activity patterns had their own developmental profiles, and though, in a particular culture, their onsets and peaks might tend to occur at roughly the same ages for all children, this could not be ascribed to a succession of rigid, unifying internal structures. Some children

follow idiosyncratic paths, and each mother–infant pair builds up its own repertoire of interactive patterns, substantially different from those of other mothers
and infants (Schaffer 1977; Bullowa 1979; Kaye 1982; Fogel and Thelen 1987).

Adult skills and concepts emerge over time through a sequence of increasingly complex activity patterns. An ability like reaching-and-grasping, as 'implemented' in human beings, cannot be explained in terms of a formally defined
competence or a specific set of internal commands contingent on appropriate
feedback signals. Only a historical explanation can make sense of the relation
between analogous but not necessarily homologous behaviours like the primitive reach-and-grasp of a two-month-old infant and the visually guided reaching of an adult human being. These behaviours are not manifestations of a
single competence, but they can be related in a situated context through history
of use (von Hofsten 1984; Fischer and Bidell 1991).

Early forms of behaviour can and usually do have their own adaptive advan-
tages, which may have little to do with the 'function' of the adult form. The
rhythmical stereotypy of supine kicking, which is almost certainly an early
manifestation of the swing-stance cycle in walking, and may serve as a preparation in the sense of strengthening the muscles, also has expressive and
communicative value. The mother tends to interpret variations in her infant's
kicking as clues to the infant's moods and desires, and as responses to her own
attempts at communication. Evolution seems to have hijacked an early form of
adult walking for other purposes.

In many cases, it can be shown to be biologically advantageous to have an
immature form of behaviour at the early stages of development, rather than the
fully developed form. The infant's inability to distinguish separate words in his
mother's vocalizations probably allows him to treat her clauses as unitary ut-
terances, equivalent to his own coos and murmurs, and thereby promotes the
process of turn-taking in early 'dialogues', and provides a 'scaffolding' for the
later parsing of clauses into meaningful sub-units (Bateson 1979; Fernald 1989;
Hirsh-Pasek et al. 1987). Limited depth of field during the first months of life
restricts the infant's resolution to objects at approximately twenty centimetres
distance, and this, coupled with early fixation patterns, produces a *Merkwelt*
consisting predominantly of his mother's face, since she appears to be biologically primed to put herself into the optimum position (Turkewitz and Kenny
1993; Johnson 1993b).

Many of these early activity patterns appear to be typical of human beings.
Burst-pause-burst in feeding does not occur even in the young of other
phylogenetically advanced primates (Kaye 1982). Human infants display a large
number of facial expressions (Charlesworth and Kreutzer 1973; Trevarthen
1977) and rhythmical stereotypies (Thelen 1981) which are absent in gorillas

and chimpanzees. Face-to-face exchanges between mothers and infants, and the complex interaction of activity patterns from which these emerge, seem also to be unique to the human species.

On the other hand, many of these species-typical activity patterns disappear, or become submerged, or disintegrate before the end of the first year. They are not functional components of adult behaviour. Often their only reason for existence seems to be that they enable other, more advanced forms of behaviour to develop within the situated context which they provide. This realization led the early researchers to formulate the notion of 'scaffolding' (Bruner 1982; Newson 1979; Kaye 1982; Fischer and Bidell 1991).

There are a number of different ways in which one can think of scaffolding. One can apply it to the supportive framework, usually provided by an adult, which enables the child to perform activities of which he may not be capable on his own until a somewhat later date. Thus, infants will demonstrate the ability to 'walk' if they are supported in the right way long before their leg muscles have developed sufficient strength to hold them up. This view of scaffolding stresses the intentional contribution of an adult. It sees the mother–infant dyad as two distinct causal entities, with the mother providing conscious support and guidance to enable her infant to learn new skills. The scaffolding continuously pushes the infant a little beyond his current capabilities, and it pushes him in the direction in which his mother wishes him to go. Scaffolding is then a pedagogical device, defined in terms of capabilities and tasks, and its nature and effect are presumed to be under the control of the adult. This is the concept of scaffolding as it was first introduced by Bruner.

A different, and for our purposes more interesting, view of scaffolding starts from the activity patterns themselves. It sees the mother–infant dyad as two tightly coupled dynamic systems (Fogel 1993). Recognizable patterns of behaviour, which, however, are not pre-planned or generated by internally represented rules within either of the participants, emerge from the continuous mutual adjustments between them, much as wall-following emerges from the continuous adjustments of Mataric's robot to its particular environment. The activity patterns, rather than the presumed intentions of the mother and the level of skill of the infant, become the natural kinds for this type of explanation. Scaffolding then takes on a meaning similar to the dynamic *Merkwelt* provided by wall-following for the emergence of landmarks and landmark navigation in Mataric's robot. Thus, the 'dialogue' between a suckling infant and the mother who jiggles him whenever he pauses in feeding (Kaye 1979, 1982) constitutes a recognizable interactive pattern which emerges from low-level reflexes and interactively generated rhythms, and which establishes a habit of turn-taking on which later, face-to-face exchanges will be built. The 'pragmatics' of meaningful communication, in this view, precede any explicit 'content', and they are best conceptualized in terms of patterns of situated activity.

This notion of scaffolding stresses the importance of species-typical activity patterns, selected for their power to attract the attention of adults, deceive them into intentional interpretations, and establish the habit of turn-taking which is essential to human learning, rather than of inborn knowledge or innate cognitive structures. Movement subtended by a central pattern generator and/or simple reflexes requires no knowledge of the world and no a priori concepts of causation, space, time, objects, or their properties. Some of the species-typical activity patterns which newborn or very young infants are capable of performing may have no place in adult behaviour. They may simply serve a 'bootstrapping' role to launch the infant into an environment of adults who think in intentional terms, communicate through language, and manipulate tools and artefacts.

8. CONCLUSION

I have argued in this chapter that an adequate understanding of intentional behaviour and conceptual thought as manifested by mature human beings will only be achieved by adopting a historical perspective which starts from early, species-typical activity patterns and conceptualizes maturation and learning as interactive emergence. Such an explanation requires an ethological approach to the collection and interpretation of behavioural data. It calls for the identification of species-typical activity patterns through intra-species and cross-species comparisons, and for the formulation of hypotheses concerning the interdependence of such patterns. Situated robotics is the only computational discipline which is currently capable of testing such hypotheses.

I am not suggesting that we will be able to construct infant robots in the near future which can enter into meaningful dialogue with human mothers. What I have argued in this chapter is that the explanatory framework of situated robotics, by providing simple existence proofs and a clear conceptual alternative to traditional explanations, can and should play a role in theories of behaviour as well as its implementation. We must not allow classical AI and connectionism to have it all their own way in cognitive science, just because we have realized that their explanations leave out all the really difficult bits, such as dynamic, context-and-activity-related perception and robust situated behaviour.[1]

---

[1] I should like to thank Margaret Boden, Dave Cliff, Inman Harvey, Maja Mataric, and Geoffrey Miller for comments related to the topics discussed in this paper.

REFERENCES

Baerends, G. P. (1976), 'The Functional Organisation of Behaviour', *Animal Behaviour*, 24: 726–38.
Baillargeon, R. (1987), 'Object Permanence in $3^{1}/_{2}$ and $4^{1}/_{2}$ Month-old Infants', *Developmental Psychology*, 23/5: 655–64.
Barlow, G. W. (1968), 'Ethological Units of Behaviour', in D. Ingle (ed.), *The Central Nervous System and Fish Behavior* (Chicago: University of Chicago Press), 217–32.
Bateson, M. C. (1975), 'Mother–infant Exchanges: The Epigenesis of Conversational Interaction', in D. Aaronson and R. W. Rieber (eds.), *Developmental Psycholinguistics and Communication Disorders* (New York: New York Academy of Sciences), 101–13.
—— (1979), 'The Epigenesis of Conversational Interaction: A Personal Account of Research Development', in Bullowa (1979), 63–78.
Brazelton, T. B. (1979), 'Evidence of Communication During Neonatal Behavioral Assessment', in Bullowa (1979), 79–88.
Brooks, R. A. (1986), 'Achieving Artificial Intelligence through Building Robots' (MIT A.I. Memo 899).
—— (1991a), 'Challenges for Complete Creature Architectures', in Meyer and Wilson (1991), 434–43.
—— (1991b), 'Intelligence without Representations', *Artificial Intelligence*, 47: 139–59.
—— (1992), 'Artificial Life and Real Robots', in Varela and Bourgine (1992), 3–10.
Bruner, J. S. (1982), 'The Organisation of Action and the Nature of Adult-Infant Transaction', in M. von Cranach and R. Harre (eds.), *The Analysis of Action* (Cambridge: Cambridge University Press), 313–28.
Bullowa, M. (1979) (ed.), *Before Speech: The Beginning of Interpersonal Communication* (Cambridge: Cambridge University Press).
Carey, S., and Gelman, R. (1991), *The Epigenesis of Mind: Essays on Biology and Cognition* (Hillsdale, NJ: Erlbaum).
Chapman, D., and Agre, P. E. (1987), 'Abstract Reasoning as Emergent from Concrete Activity', in M. P. Georgeff and A. L. Lansky (eds.), *Reasoning about Actions and Plans* (Los Angeles: Morgan-Kauffman), 411–24.
Charlesworth, W. R., and Kreutzer, M. A. (1973), 'Facial Expressions of Infants and Children', in P. Ekman (ed.), *Darwin and Facial Expression: A Century of Research in Review* (New York: Academic Press), 91–168.
Collis, G. M. (1979), 'Describing the Structure of Social Interaction in Infancy', in Bullowa (1979), 111–30.
Diamond, A. (1991), 'Neurophysiological Insights into the Meaning of Object Concept Development', in Carey and Gelman (1991), 67–110.
Fernald, A. (1989), 'Intonation and Communicative Intent in Mothers' Speech to Infants: Is the Melody the Message?', *Child Development*, 60: 1497–1510.
Fischer, K. W., and Bidell, T. (1991), 'Constraining Nativist Inferences about Cognitive Capacities', in Carey and Gelman (1991), 199–235.
Fogel, A. (1985), 'Coordinative Structures in the Development of Expressive Behavior in Early Infancy', in G. Zivin (ed.), *The Development of Expressive Behavior: Biology-Environment Interactions* (Orlando, Fla.: Academic Press).
—— (1993), 'Two Principles of Communication: Co-regulation and Framing', in Nadel and Camaioni (1993), 9–22.

Fogel, A. and Thelen, E. (1987), 'Development of Early Expressive and Communicative Action: Reinterpreting the Evidence from a Dynamic Systems Perspective', *Developmental Psychology*, 23/6: 747–761.

Gibson, J. J. (1979), *The Ecological Approach to Visual Perception* (Boston: Houghton Mifflin).

Gould, J. L., and Lewontin, R. C. (1978), 'The Spandrels of San Marco and the Panglossian Paradigm: A Critique of the Adaptionist Programme', *Proceedings of the Royal Society, London*, 205: 581–98.

Hendriks-Jansen, H. J. (1993a), 'Natural Kinds, Autonomous Robots and History of Use', in *Proceedings of the 1993 European Conference on Artificial Life, Brussels*, 440–50.

—— (1993b), 'Scientific Explanations of Behaviour: The Logic of Evolution and Learning' (Brighton, University of Sussex, Cognitive Science Research Paper No. 298).

—— (in press), *Catching Ourselves in the Act: Situated Activity, Interactive Emergence, Evolution, and Human Thought* (Cambridge, Mass.: MIT Press).

—— (forthcoming), 'Brain-Models, Mind-Models and Models of Situated Behaviour', in D. Cliff (ed.), *Evolutionary Robotics and Artificial Life* (provisional title).

Hinde, R. A. (1982), *Ethology: Its Nature and Relations with Other Sciences* (Oxford: Oxford University Press).

Hirsh-Pasek, K., Jusczyk, P. W., Wright Cassidy, K., Druss, B., and Kennedy, C. (1987), 'Clauses are Perceptual Units of Young Infants', *Cognition*, 26; 269–86.

Horswill, I. (1992), 'Characterising Adaption by Constraint', in Varela and Bourgine (1992), 58–63.

Johnson, M. H. (1993a), *Brain Development and Cognition: A Reader* (Oxford: Blackwell).

—— (1993b), 'Constraints on Cortical Plasticity', in Johnson (1993a), 703–21.

Karmiloff-Smith, A. (1987), 'Constraints on Representational Change: Evidence from Children's Drawing', *Cognition*, 34: 57–83.

Kaye, K. (1979), 'Thickening Thin Data: The Maternal Role in Developing Communication and Language', in Bullowa (1979), 191–206.

—— (1982), 'Organism, Apprentice and Person', in E. Z. Tronick (ed.), *Social Interchange in Infancy*. (Baltimore: University Park Press), 183–96.

Kirsh, D. (1991), 'Foundations of AI: The Big Issues', *Artificial Intelligence*, 47: 3–30.

Lehrman, D. S. (1970), 'Semantic and Conceptual Issues in the Nature–Nurture Problem', in L. Aronson (ed.), *Development and Evolution of Behavior* (San Francisco: Freeman), 17–52.

Lorenz, K. (1937), 'The Nature of Instinct: The Conception of Instinctive Behavior', in Schiller and Lashley (1957), 129–75.

—— (1939), 'Comparative Study of Behavior', in Schiller and Lashley (1957), 239–63.

—— (1952), 'The Past Twelve Years in the Comparative Study of Behavior', in Schiller and Lashley (1957), 288–310.

—— and Tinbergen, N. (1938), 'Taxis and Instinct: Taxis and Instinctive Action in the Egg-Retrieving Behavior of the Greylag Goose', in Schiller and Lashley (1957), 176–208.

McFarland, D. (1985), *Animal Behaviour: Psychology, Ethology and Evolution* (London: Pitman Publishing).

Marr, D. (1982), *Vision* (New York: Freeman).

Mataric, M. J. (1991), 'Navigating with a Rat Brain: A Neurobiologically Inspired Model for Robot Spatial Representation', in Meyer and Wilson (1991), 169–75.

—— (1992), 'Integration of Representation into Goal-Driven Behavior-Based Robots', *IEEE Transactions on Robotics and Automation*, 8/3: 304–12.

—— and Brooks, R. A. (1990), 'Learning a Distributed Map Representation Based on

Navigation Behaviors', in *Proceedings of the 1990 USA–Japan Symposium on Flexible Automation, Kyoto, Japan*, 499–506.

Meyer, J. A., and Wilson, S. W. (1991), *From Animals to Animats: Proceedings of the First International Conference on Simulation of Adaptive Behavior* (Cambridge, Mass.: MIT Press).

Millikan, R. (1984), *Language, Thought and Other Biological Categories: New Foundations for Realism* (Cambridge, Mass.: MIT Press).

Nagel, E. (1961), *The Structure of Science: Problems in the Logic of Scientific Explanation* (London: Routledge & Kegan Paul).

Newson, J. [1979], 'The Growth of Shared Understandings between Infant and Caregiver', in Bullowa (1979), 207–22.

Papousek, H., and Papousek, M. (1977), 'Mothering and the Cognitive Head-Start: Psychobiological Considerations', in H. R. Schaffer (1977), 63–85.

Piaget, J. (1954), *The Construction of Reality in the Child* (New York: Basic Books).

Popper, K. (1963), *Conjectures and Refutations: The Growth of Scientific Knowledge* (London: Routledge & Kegan Paul).

Schaffer, H. R. (1977), *Studies in Mother–Infant Interaction: Proceedings of Loch Lomond Symposium* (New York: Academic Press).

Schiller, C. H., and Lashley, K. S. (1957), *Instinctive Behavior: The Development of a Modern Concept* (New York: International University Press).

Schneirla, T. C. (1966), 'Behavioral Development and Comparative Psychology', *Quarterly Review of Biology*, 41: 283–302.

Sloman, A. (1978), *The Computer Revolution in Philosophy* (Hassocks, Sussex: Harvester Press).

Smithers, T. (1992), 'Taking Eliminative Materialism Seriously: A Methodology for Autonomous Systems Research', in Varela and Bourgine (1992), 31–40.

Spelke, E. S. (1991), 'Physical Knowledge in Infancy: Reflections on Piaget's Theory', in Carey and Gelman (1991), 133–69.

Steels, L. (1991), 'Towards a Theory of Emergent Functionality', in Meyer and Wilson (1991), 451–61.

Thelen, E. (1981), 'Rhythmical Behavior in Infancy: An Ethological Perspective', *Developmental Psychology*, 17/3: 237–57.

Tinbergen, N. (1951), *The Study of Instinct* (Oxford: Clarendon Press).

Trevarthen, C. (1977), 'Descriptive Analyses of Infant Communicative Behaviour', in Schaffer (1977), 227–70.

Tronick, E., Als, E., and Adamson, L. (1979), 'Structure of Early Face-to-Face Communicative Interactions', in Bullowa (1979), 349–72.

Turkewitz, G., and Kenny, P. A. (1993), 'Limitations on Input as a Basis for Neural Organisation and Perceptual Development: A Preliminary Theoretical Statement', in Johnson (1993a), 510–22.

Varela, F., and Bourgine, P. (1992), *Toward a Practice of Autonomous Systems: Proceedings of the First European Conference on Artificial Life* (Cambridge, Mass.: MIT Press).

Von Hofsten, C. (1984), 'Developmental Changes in the Organisation of Pre-reaching Movements', *Developmental Psychology*, 20/3: 378–88.

Von Uexkull, J. (1934), 'A Stroll through the Worlds of Animals and Men', in Schiller and Lashley (1957), 5–82.

Wilkes, K. (1989), 'Explanation—How not to Miss the Point', in A. Montefiore and D. Noble (eds.), *Goals, No Goals and Own Goals* (London: Unwin Hyman), 194–210.

PART IV

11

ARISTOTLE ON LIFE

GARETH B. MATTHEWS

A check of almost any standard encyclopaedia will reveal how problematic the concept of life remains for us today. Sometimes the experts try to disguise the problems; sometimes they make them completely obvious. The entry under 'Life' in a recent edition of *The World Book Encyclopedia* makes the problems obvious:

Nearly all living things share certain basic characteristics. These characteristics include (1) reproduction; (2) growth; (3) metabolism; (4) movement; (5) responsiveness; and (6) adaptation. Not every organism exhibits all these features, and even nonliving things may show some of them. However, these characteristics as a group outline the basic nature of living things.[1]

One doesn't have to be much of a Platonist to become concerned and puzzled about discussions like this. How can it be that only 'nearly all', and not simply 'all', living things share the characteristics that 'outline the basic nature of living things'? And how can a list of characteristics such that only 'nearly all' living things have those characteristics and some non-living things also have them be a list that outlines 'the basic nature of living things'? Why doesn't the admitted failure to find a set of characteristics necessary and sufficient for being alive lead to the conclusion that perhaps there really is no such thing as 'the basic nature of living things'?

Aristotle seems to have been the first thinker to try to understand what it is to be a living thing by reference to a list of characteristic 'life-functions' (or, as he called them, 'psychic powers' or 'soul-powers'—*dunameis tēs psuchēs*). The list Aristotle gives varies from place to place in his texts, but it is usually a selection from among the following: self-nutrition, growth, decay, reproduction, appetite, sensation or perception, self-motion, thinking.

© Gareth B. Matthews, 1992. Reprinted from Martha C. Nussbaum and Amélie Oksenberg Rorty (eds.), *Essays on Aristotle's* De anima (Oxford: Clarendon Press, 1992), 185–93, under the title '*De anima* 2. 2–4 and The Meaning of *Life*'. Reprinted by permission of Oxford University Press.

[1] (Chicago: World Book, 1986), xii. 242.

From our modern point of view, the strangest item on Aristotle's list of life-functions is thinking. Descartes convinced us moderns that thinking has nothing essential to do with life.[2] So it is surprising to us to find Aristotle including it. Otherwise Aristotle's list is not out of line with modern efforts to say what a living thing is by reference to a list of characteristic life-functions.

Some modern writers give a list of such functions and then say that (i) anything that can perform them all is alive; (ii) anything that cannot perform any of them is not alive; and (iii) anything that can perform some, but not all, may be alive or not. Aristotle's approach is bolder. He says it is sufficient for being living that a thing can perform *one* of these functions. 'Provided any one alone of these is found in a thing', he writes in *DA* 2. at 413ª22–5, 'we say that thing is living—viz. thinking or perception or local movement and rest, or movement in the sense of nutrition, decay and growth' (Aristotle 1984, i. 658). And at the beginning of the next chapter he makes much the same point:

Of the psychic powers above enumerated some kinds of living things, as we have said, possess all, some less then all, others one only. Those we have mentioned are the nutritive, the appetitive, the sensory, the locomotive, and the power of thinking. (414ª29–32, trans. J. A. Smith in Aristotle (1910–52))

Aristotle's claim that 'provided any one alone of these [psychic or life-functions] is found in a thing we say that thing is living' invites two different questions. First, we may ask, is it empirically true? That is, is it true as a matter of empirical fact that we count whatever, and only whatever, can perform at least one of the functions on Aristotle's list as a living thing. Let us call that question 'the Empirical Question'.

The Empirical Question asks whether a biconditional along the following lines is materially adequate as an account of what we include in the class of living things:

x is a living thing iff x can think or x can perceive something or x can move itself or . . .   (1)

By contrast, the Definitional Question asks whether a definition of the following sort is satisfactory:

x is a living thing $=_{df} x$ can think or x can perceive something or x can move itself or . . .   (2)

---

[2] '. . . because probably men in the earliest times did not distinguish in us that principle in virtue of which we are nourished, grow, and perform all those operations which are common to us with the brutes apart from any thought, from that by which we think, they called both by the single name *soul* . . . But I, perceiving that the principle by which we are nourished is wholly distinct from that by means of which we think, have declared that the name *soul* when used for both is equivocal. . . . I consider the mind not as part of the soul, but as the whole of that soul which thinks' (*Reply to Objections V* in Descrtes (1637–41), ii. 210).

Let us consider the Definitional Question first. Certainly Aristotle himself is not given to offering disjunctive definitions. His favoured form of definition belongs to the genus–differentia type. (2) can hardly be a good candidate for what Aristotle wants to say about the Greek equivalent for 'is alive', unless some special story can be told to show that its disjunctive form is accidental to the claim being made and that (2) is really equivalent to some other, non-disjunctive, way of putting things.

This sort of objection to (2) has real force. What it is for something to be alive ought to be something more unitary than the disjunctive form of (2) suggests. One wants to know what being able to think, being able to perceive something, being able to move oneself, etc., have in common that makes them *life*-functions, that is, functions such that being able to perform a single one of them qualifies a thing for the appellation 'living thing'. Thus even if (1) is correct and Aristotle's list of psychic functions is materially adequate in picking out all and only living things, (2) seems unsatisfactory.

Let's turn now to the Empirical Question. Is (1) adequate?

I have left (1) in open-ended form. A good first thing to do in evaluating (1) would be to try to get a complete list of Aristotelian psychic, or life, powers, or functions. I think this is a complete list from *DA* 2, anyway:

  (i) thinking (*nous, dianoētikon*);
  (ii) perception or sensation (*aisthēsis*);
  (iii) local (*kata topon*) movement (*kinēsis*) and rest (*stasis*);
  (iv) movement (*kinēses*) with respect to nutrition (*kata trophēn*) and decay (*phthsis*) and growth (*auxēsis*) or self-nutrition (*threptikon*);
  (v) touch (*haphē*);
  (vi) appetite (*orexis*) or desire (*epithumia*) and passion (*thumos*) and wishing (*boulēsis*);
  (vii) reproduction (*gennēsis*).

There could well be disagreement on how these powers are to be counted. Thus to some readers it may seem that growth ought to be considered a separate power in Aristotle's list; that may be correct. And perhaps the appetitive powers referred to in (vi) should be listed separately. Finally, touch is, of course, a mode of perception, or sensation. It gets discussed separately because, according to Aristotle, some animals have no other sense modality than touch (413^{b}4–9). But then, perhaps, we should list non-tactile perception as a distinct power.

In general, however, this seems to be the list of psychic powers Aristotle has in mind in *DA* 2.

Let us consider first the last item on the list, reproduction. Obviously some individual organisms, though certainly alive, are too immature to reproduce;

others are too old. Still others are sterile throughout their full lives, either because of an individual defect, or because, as is the case with mules, their very kind is sterile. So being able to reproduce is necessary neither for an individual organism to be a living thing, nor even for a kind of organism to be a kind of living thing.

Let us recall, though, that Aristotle's claim is not that every living thing has every psychic or life power; rather, it is that everything with a psychic power is alive (and, presumably, only such things). Might something be able to reproduce itself without being alive? Well, sounds reproduce themselves in echo-chambers and visual appearances reproduce themselves in mirrors, though neither sounds nor visual appearances are alive, at least not in the way, or perhaps in the sense or senses of 'alive', we are interested in. Even more troubling are viruses, which were, of course, unknown to Aristotle.

Let us dismiss worries about sounds and appearances and viruses and suppose that a suitable sense of 'reproduction' can be spelt out in an appropriate way so that everything with the power of reproduction (in *that* sense of 'reproduction') is alive. Are there difficulties with other items on Aristotle's list?

No doubt there will be similar problems with specifying the sense or senses of, say, 'appetite' and 'local movement and rest' we are interested in, so that having the power picked out by the expression in the suitable sense will definitely guarantee that the entity that has it is alive.

Suppose, however, that all such problems can be solved. Would it then be plausible to say that the Empirical Question can be answered affirmatively? Apparently so.

The Definitional Question, though, will still be difficult to handle. There are two main sorts of problem with it. The first is that in finding appropriate senses of 'reproduction', 'appetite', etc., so that the definiens will cover just the right cases, no more and no less, we may well have to make implicit or explicit appeal to the notion of life. For example, in specifying the required sense of 'reproduction' to apply to, say, the division of an amoeba but not to the echoing of a sound, we may have to make at least implicit reference to the notion of life. If this turns out to be so, the definition will be circular. Circularity is not a problem with the Empirical Question; our only demand on (1) is that it state truly necessary and sufficient conditions for something's being a living thing. But circularity is a serious problem for the Definitional Question.

The second problem, as I have already suggested, is that it is not clear what these psychic powers have in common that makes the possession of one of them sufficient for an entity to count as a living thing. This problem is one familiar to readers of Aristotle as a problem in the unity of the definition.

At this point it is worth taking into account Aristotle's ideas about how the psychic powers are related to each other. Aristotle does not suppose that a given living thing might have, say, the power of reproduction and nothing else. Rather he thinks of the psychic powers, either all of them or at least many of them, as 'nested' in an order or sequence of decreasing extension (or increasing, depending on which way you look at the sequence). The idea is that everything with power p_3 has p_2 (though not the other way around), and everything with p_2 has p_1 (though not the other way around).

Now how does this nesting idea help us deal with the Definitional Question? Well, it might be Aristotle's view that what gives the disjunctive definition, (2), its unity are supplementary connections like these:

> If x can think then x can perceive something
> (though not vice versa).   (2a)
> If x can perceive something then x has the power of touch
> (though not vice versa).   (2b)
> If x has the power of touch then x can nourish itself.   (2c)

So far the powers seem to be appropriately nested. But we have left out appetite, local motion, and reproduction. Aristotle does not seem to suppose that these powers expand the nesting by simply adding steps of increasing, or decreasing, extension; however, he does seem to think these relationships hold:

> x has appetite iff x has the power of touch.   (2d)
> x can move itself iff x has non-tactile powers of perception.   (2e)
> If x can reproduce itself, then x can nourish itself.   (2f)

If we then break up the power of perception, or sensation, into touch and non-tactile perception, we come up with the following set of relationships:

[x can think] →
  [x has non-tactile perception and x can move itself] →
    [x has touch and x has appetite] →
      x can nourish itself

                           ← [x can reproduce itself]

One implication of all this is that everything that has any one of the psychic powers has the power of self-nutrition. Should we conclude that what it means to say of something that it is alive is simply that it can nourish itself? Sometimes Aristotle talks that way. Consider this passage from *DA* 2. 4.

It follows that first of all we must treat of nutrition and reproduction, for the nutritive soul is found along with all the others and is the most primitive and widely distributed power of soul, being indeed that one in virtue of which all are said to have life (*kath' hēn huparchei to zēn hapasin*). (415ᵃ22–5, trans. Smith)

It seems to follow that the other psychic powers are not really in or of themselves life-functions; rather, they are life-*presupposing* functions, that is, functions such that nothing has them without being alive.

On this reading, Aristotle's statement, 'Provided any one alone of these [powers] is found in a thing we say that thing is living', means something like this: 'Provided any one alone of these powers is found in a thing it *will be right* to say that that thing is alive [even if "is alive" means only "can nourish and reproduce itself"].'

There are other passages, however, in which Aristotle suggests something different. Consider this passage, immediately preceding that quoted twice above:

> We resume our inquiry from a fresh starting-point by calling attention to the fact that what has soul in it differs from what has not in that the former displays life. Now this word ['life', *zēn*] has more than one sense [*pleonachōs de tou zēn legomenou*], and provided any one alone of these [powers] ... (413ª20-3, trans. Smith.)

If we take this idea seriously we might suppose that the nesting relation among 'can think', 'has non-tactile powers of perception', 'has the power of touch', and 'can nourish itself', plus the relationships given in (2a–f), are all relationships of meaning and that together they yield a series of broader and broader senses for 'is alive' or 'is a living thing'. In the narrowest sense, 'x is a living thing' would mean: 'x can think and x has power of non-tactile perception and . . . x can nourish itself.' In the broadest sense, 'x is a living thing' would mean simply 'x can nourish itself.'

Other passages in Aristotle seem to mesh with this idea. Consider this passage from book 1 of the *Nicomachean Ethics*:

> Let us exclude, therefore, the life of nutrition and growth. Next there would be a life of perception, but it also seems to be common even to the horse, the ox, and every animal. There remains, then, an active life of the element that has a rational principle ... (1098ª1–3, trans. W. D. Ross in Aristotle (1910–52))

We can understand Aristotle here to be using 'life' first in the sense of 'nutrition and growth', then in the richer sense that includes the idea of having perception, and finally in a sense that includes also the idea of having a rational principle.

There is, however, one major problem with the suggestion that, according to Aristotle, 'is a living thing' (or 'is alive') is homonymous in this way. At 415ª7 ff. Aristotle says, 'Lastly, certain living beings—a small minority—possess calculation and thought, for (among mortal beings) those which possess calculation have all the other powers above mentioned, while the converse does not hold . . .' The qualification, 'among mortal beings [*tōn phthartōn*]', makes it clear that, according to Aristotle, there can be non-mortal beings that think, and are therefore alive, but do not nourish themselves, or grow. Indeed, that seems to be Aristotle's view.

If this is right, then 'x can think' does not after all guarantee 'x can nourish itself'; at most 'x can think and x is a mortal being' provides that guarantee.

We might try saying that there is simply a further sense of 'alive' and 'living thing' such that '*x* can think and *x* is not a mortal being' yields '*x* is a living thing' in that new sense. But where, now, is the unity in these definitions? If the nesting story was supposed to avoid the unwelcome conclusion that 'living thing' is a case of mere chance homonomy and it was supposed to do so by providing some unity, some common focus, to its various senses—namely, the idea of self-nutrition—that reference point is no longer available.

I think we need to try a very different approach.

Perhaps it would be well to remind ourselves at this point that, as Aristotle supposes, individuals of a given species naturally act so as to preserve their species. Here in *DA* 2. 4, within a discussion of nutrition and reproduction, Aristotle makes that point:

... for any living thing that has reached its normal development and which is unmutilated, and whose mode of generation is not spontaneous, the most natural act is the production of another like itself, an animal producing an animal, a plant a plant, in order that, as far as its nature allows, it may partake in the eternal and the divine. That is the goal towards which all things strive, that for the sake of which they do whatsoever their nature renders possible [or 'whatever they do naturally'—*hosa prattei kata phusin*]. (415ª27–ᵇ2, trans. Smith)

Aristotle goes on to say that the soul is, among other things, 'the essence of the whole living body' (415ᵇ11). He adds that 'in everything the essence is identical with the cause of its being, and here, in the case of living things, their being is to live, and of their being and their living the soul in them is the cause or source' (415ᵇ12–14).

Now if the soul of a living thing is the cause of its living, and its living is naturally directed towards the preservation of its species, then the soul's powers (the 'psychic powers' we have been talking about) are presumably powers naturally directed toward the preservation of the species of that particular thing.

My suggestion, then, is that the list of psychic powers can be seen as a list of the general sorts of possibilities that individual organisms have to act so as to preserve, or to contribute to the preservation of, their species. For a plant this will be simply the movements of metabolism—nutrition, growth, and decay—plus, of course, reproduction. Animals, most of them, are capable of changing place. They act according to desire or appetite and perception—most rudimentarily through touch, but, in higher animal species, through non-tactile modes of perception as well. As for human beings, they need to exercise their capacity to reason and calculate to be able to act so as to preserve their species.

If we pull this point about species-preservation out of Aristotle's discussion and make it the key to our understanding of what a psychic power is supposed to be, we can offer the following as a definition of 'psychic power':

x is a psychic power $=_{df}$ there is a species s, such that, for x to be preserved, individual organisms that belong to s must, in general, exercise x.

Relativized to a species the definition would look like this:

x is a psychic power for species $s =_{df}$ for s to be preserved individual organisms that belong to s must, in general, exercise x.[3]

It is plausible to suppose that psychic powers, following this definition, will turn out to be, or at least to include, reason, sense-perception (tactile and non-tactile), local motion, appetite, metabolism (including food-intake, growth, and decay), and reproduction. It is also natural to suppose that these powers are co-exemplified in complex patterns that produce the nested sequence discussed above. Now we can say (going beyond any claim explicitly stated in Aristotle, though I think something like this is suggested by what he says) that what it means to say that an organism is alive is that it can exercise at least one psychic power; that is, at least one of the powers that organisms of its species must, in general, be able to exercise for the species to survive.

x is alive $=_{df}$ there is a species s, and a psychic power p, such that x belongs to s, p is a psychic power for species s, and x can exercise p.

Because of nesting it will turn out that any mortal organism that is alive will have the power of self-nutrition. Still, 'is alive' does not *mean* (on this reconstruction of Aristotle) 'is capable of self-nutrition'. What it does mean is 'can exercise a power such that members of the organism's species need to be able, in general, to exercise that power in order that the species may survive'.

Monsters (*terata*) might be thought to present a problem here. They are not regular members of any species, yet they can certainly be alive.

What Aristotle should do to accommodate monsters, I think, is simply to broaden the understanding of 'x belongs to [species] s' to include monsters. The idea would be that each monster is a *failed* or maimed or deformed member of one or more species. (That seems to be what Aristotle does say at, e.g. GA 769^{b}30.) So long as the monster can exercise at least one psychic power of a species it is a failed member of, it is alive.

---

[3] Fred Feldman has made clear to me how important, and how difficult, it will be to understand 'exercise' in the right way here. Perhaps many animals, such as rabbits, need to be able to exercise their power to remain motionless in the presence of predators for their species to survive. Yet such a power should not count as a psychic power lest (see the next definition) a dead rabbit count as being alive.

A first thing to say is that psychic powers are powers to act, not purely passive powers. So exercising such a power will have to be doing something, not simply failing to do something. Relevant to the rabbit case will then be the power to *keep itself* motionless, which will be part of the capacity for local movement and rest. Irrelevant will be the capacity to lie inert.

This response is only a first move, however. Much more discussion would be required to gain justified confidence that we know how to pick out the relevant powers.

This is perhaps a good point at which to address the question of circularity in the proposal I am presenting here.[4] 'Clara is alive', according to this proposal, means that there is a species, say, cat, and a psychic power, say, touch, such that Clara belongs to the species mentioned, touch is a psychic power for that species, and Clara can exercise the power. What 'touch is a psychic power for the species, cat', means is that, for the species cat to be preserved, individual cats must, in general, be able to exercise tactile perception. Although I haven't tried to say what it is for a species, such as cat, to be preserved, presumably it is, or includes, keeping in existence individual organisms, in this case individual cats. But, as Aristotle says in *DA* 2. 4, 'for living things, to be is to be alive' (415^{b}13). So keeping individual cats in existence is keeping them alive and we have, it seems, a circle.

Though, I agree, there is a certain circularity in the proposal, it is not, I think, a vicious circularity. The idea is that for Clara to be alive is for her to be able to exercise one of what is, for her species, a cluster of, so to speak, 'self-perpetuating powers'. More carefully, it is for her to be able to exercise one power in a list such that it is necessary for individuals of her species, in general, to be able to exercise those powers for there to go on being individuals in that species that can exercise one or more of those powers. If we are justified in supposing that dead cats, dead trees, and dead human beings can't exercise any powers at all, then the circularity in the proposal is not, I think, objectionable.

The account I am offering can help us reconcile these three apparently incompatible claims, each of which we seem to find in Aristotle:

(i) Being a living thing amounts to nothing more than having the power of self-nutrition.

(ii) There are (something like) distinct senses of 'living thing' to go with each of the following: (*a*) plants, (*b*) animals whose only sense modality is touch, (*c*) other non-human animals, and (*d*) human beings.

(iii) There is at least one non-mortal being that thinks and is therefore alive, even though it has no power of self-nutrition.

As for (i), it is true that among *mortal*, living things, the common and fundamental species-preserving power is self-nutrition, plus the associated power of reproduction. When Aristotle makes a claim like (i), he must be taken to be focusing on mortal beings.

Still, what exactly having species-preserving, or psychic, powers amounts to varies from species to species. And in this way something like (ii) is also true.

As for (iii), Aristotle's complicated nesting story guarantees that as long as a mortal being has at least one psychic power, it will also have the psychic

---

[4] Both the worry about monsters and the question of circularity are matters that Fred Feldman brought to my attention after he read an early draft of this paper.

powers, if any, that, so to speak, enfold it, including, of course, self-nutrition. Non-mortal beings are usually left out of Aristotle's discussion. But they can easily be included. To preserve their species they need only preserve their existence by continuing to engage in whatever activity is essentially theirs. That may just be thinking; it does not, presumably, include either self-nutrition or reproduction.

In his book, *The Selfish Gene* (Oxford, 1976), Richard Dawkins locates the origin of life in the chance formation of the first 'replicator' molecules. As Dawkins puts the matter, plants and animals, including human beings, have become the 'survival machines' for the currently successful replicator molecules, which we call 'genes'.

In many ways Dawkins's story is quite un-Aristotelian. Aristotle knew nothing of DNA and he was not what one would call an evolutionist. Still, it distorts things only a little bit to say, mimicking Dawkins, that, in Aristotle's view, individual plants and animals, including human beings, are survival machines for plant and animal *forms*. The functions that individual plants and animals need to perform to play their role in this survival process are the *dunameis tēs psuchēs*, the psychic or life functions. These functions are nested in ways that Aristotle tries to bring out. And for any given individual organism to be alive is just for it to be able to perform at least one such function (plus, of course, any functions presupposed by it in that species of organism).

Whether the notion of life that rests on the idea of life functions is really very important for modern biology I am not competent to say. But if, for whatever scientific or non-scientific reasons, we want to deal with the threats to incoherence posed by encyclopaedia entries under 'life' of the sort I began this discussion with, the best way to do so, I think, is to appeal to the picture I have constructed from *DA* 2. 2–4. According to that picture there are organisms that tend to preserve their form through the exercise of identifiable functions. For a given individual to be of the sort, living thing, is just for it to be one of these naturally species-preserving organisms. And for a given individual living thing to be actually living—that is, alive—is just for it to be able to perform one of the psychic, or living, functions appropriate to its species (though, of course, since the functions are nested in certain ways, being able to perform a given psychic function may presuppose being able to perform one or more others).[5]

[5] I wish to thank Michael Frede and Fred Feldman for their comments on an earlier version of this chapter.

REFERENCES

Aristotle (1910–52), *The Works of Aristotle Translated into English*, ed. J. A. Smith and W. D. Ross (Oxford: Clarendon Press).

Aristotle (1984), *The Complete Works of Aristotle*, ed. Jonathan Barnes, 2 vols. (Bollingen Series, 81/2; Princeton: Princeton University Press).

Descartes, R. (1637–41), *The Philosophical Works of Descartes*, ed. and trans. E. S. Haldane and G. R. T. Ross (1967) (Cambridge: Cambridge University Press).

12

SPENCER AND DEWEY ON LIFE AND MIND

PETER GODFREY-SMITH

1. INTRODUCTION

If it were possible to bring a collection of dead, famous philosophers into the present, and ask them what they thought of artificial life, I think few of them would have as much to say as Herbert Spencer and John Dewey. This chapter is an attempt to work out some of what they might say. It is also an attempt to show how some of the differences between research programmes and explanatory styles which exist in and around A-Life are manifestations of some old and basic oppositions within science and philosophy. These oppositions have to do with the general nature of causal and explanatory relations between organic systems and their environments. Thirdly, this chapter will discuss the relations between life and mind, and hence the relations between artificial life and artificial intelligence.

2. SPENCER

Herbert Spencer (1820–1903) was a wide-ranging, speculative thinker who had a great influence on the intellectual scene in Victorian Britain. He wrote large-scale works in philosophy, psychology, biology, and sociology. He also supported strongly *laissez-faire* economic and political views, and is often associated with the label 'social Darwinism' (but see Bowler 1989). Spencer first published his evolutionary approach to psychology in 1855, several years before Darwin's *Origin of Species* (1859). Although he was a major figure in the late 1800s, soon after the turn of the century Spencer's reputation fell like a stone and has barely shifted since. (See Richards 1987 for a detailed account.) In fact, one of the few places where his name has tended to come up in recent years

Reprinted (with minor revisions) from R. A. Brooks and P. Maes (eds.), *Artificial Life IV* (Proceedings of the Fourth International Workshop on the Synthesis and Simulation of Living Systems; Cambridge, Mass.: MIT Press, 1994), 80–9.

is in discussions of A-Life and complexity (Farmer and Belin 1992; McShea 1991; Lewin 1992; Levy 1992).

Spencer's work is indeed highly relevant to A-Life. In this section I shall briefly outline Spencer's overall view of the world, and then look at some of his ideas on the origins of complexity.

Spencer claimed to have found a general 'law of evolution' which applies to the evolution of solar systems, planets, species, individuals, cultural artefacts, and human social organizations. According to this law there is a universal trend of change from a state of 'indefinite, incoherent homogeneity' towards a state of 'definite, coherent, heterogeneity' (1872: 396). That is, every system tends to change from a state where the system has little differentiation of parts, little concentration of matter, and everything is much the same in structure, towards a state in which there is a variety of clearly distinguishable parts, where the individual parts differ from each other and are densely structured.

This trend appears to be 'negentropic': it tends towards increased organization. Spencer struggled with the consequences of the second law of thermodynamics, which was being formulated and investigated around the same time as his work (Kennedy 1978: 43). He accepted that the universe as a whole must run down. But though the eventual fate of the universe is 'omnipresent death', as long as the processes of organic and social evolution have the required resources there will be a growth in organization and differentiation. This process 'can end only in the establishment of the greatest perfection and the most complete happiness' (1872: 517). And once the universe has run down to death, it might start up again, produce life, and cycle this way indefinitely.

Spencer thought that a system like a galaxy will become more organized as a consequence of the fundamental properties of its constituents. However, once we reach the realms of biology and psychology, increases in complexity are the result of *external* factors. For Spencer, complexity in organic systems is explained in terms of complexity in the systems' environments.

Spencer has elsewhere been labelled an 'internalist' with respect to the explanation of biological complexity (McShea 1991; Lewin 1992). This is misleading, in my view. Spencer certainly thought that on the global scale complexity will inevitably develop by itself, but the manifestation of this trend in organic change is not 'internalist'. When he is concerned with the properties of organic systems, most of the explanatory weight is borne by the environments of these systems. Internal properties of organic systems explain why these systems are the types of things which respond to their environments so sensitively, but the *particular* changes that any system undergoes are explained in terms of the specificities of its environment.

In fact, even when Spencer is discussing physical systems, and is not making use of biological mechanisms, his explanations for the trend towards complexity often have a roughly externalist character. For example, he thought that any homogeneous system is unstable, as any new influence on the system will affect different parts of it differently. Parts on the inside of the system will experience the force differently from parts on the outside. The parts will thus respond differently and the whole system will become more heterogeneously structured.

In the remainder of this chapter, the term 'externalist' will be used specifically for explanations of internal properties of organic systems in terms of properties of their environments. Explanations of organic properties in terms of other internal or intrinsic properties of the organic system will be called 'internalist'.

Spencer's externalism is seen clearly in the specific mechanisms he used to explain biological and psychological properties. First, his biology was strongly adaptationist. He made use of both the inheritance of acquired characteristics, along the lines of Lamarck, and also Darwinian evolutionary mechanisms—the 'survival of the fittest'. He viewed these two processes as different specific ways in which organisms respond adaptively to conditions in their environments (1866: pt. 3, chs. 9–13). Spencer's psychology (1855) was associationist, in the English tradition. This is also an externalist programme of explanation; complexity in the mind is explained in terms of complexity in sensory experience. In fact, Spencer saw evolution and individual learning as basically the same type of thing: they are both modes of 'equilibration' between organism and environment.

This recognition of an underlying similarity between learning and adaptive evolution made it possible for Spencer to make an unusual move in his theory of mind, given what had gone before him. During the seventeenth and eighteenth centuries epistemological discussion was deeply concerned with the issue of whether the mind has intrinsic, innate structure, or whatever is in the mind has come in through the senses. 'Rationalists' such as Leibniz took the former view and 'empiricists' such as Locke took the latter. Spencer was basically an empiricist, but unlike empiricists before him he had no problem with the idea that the mind has rich innate structure, as rationalists claimed it did. He in fact embraced this idea. Spencer did not regard this as a concession as long as the mind's innate structure has an adaptationist evolutionary explanation. Evolution is like a population-level learning process, so the basic empiricist pattern of explanation still applies (1855: pt. 4, ch. 7).

Spencer is often compared with Lamarck (1809), and it is sometimes said that Spencer's evolutionary views are unoriginal because they are largely derived from Lamarck. It is true that Spencer learned a lot from Lamarck's ideas (which he first encountered second-hand though the criticisms of Lyell). But the relation between Spencer's ideas and Lamarck's is more interesting than mere imitation. Lamarck is remembered now for his claim that there can be evolution by the inheritance of characteristics which individuals acquire during their lifetimes in response to their environments. But this is only one of two mechanisms in Lamarck's account. The other mechanism for evolution, and the thing which explains complexity in particular, is a tendency in all living things which generates increases in the complexity of organization. This tendency is a consequence of the actions of fluids moving through the body's tissues.

The phenomenon Lamarck explains in terms of the environment and the inheritance of acquired characteristics is the fact that the pattern in nature which shows the inevitable increase in complexity is an *imperfect* pattern. Adaptation to different environments is used by Lamarck to explain departures from an orderly progression of increases in complexity. In particular, in a perfectly static and homogeneous environment Lamarck thought there would be a clear linear scale with respect to complexity (1809: 69). Spencer would predict the exact opposite: in a perfectly constant and simple environment there would be nothing that could generate increases in complexity (1866: 83). He would probably have added that if there ever was an environment like this, it would not last long. Spencer thought that environments inevitably tend to become more complex.

So Lamarck explained things other than progressive increases in complexity in terms of the environment, and had a largely internalist view of organic complexity. Spencer had an intrinsic mechanism for directional change in the environment, and an externalist account of almost all organic properties, especially complexity.

3. SPENCER ON LIFE AND MIND

The key to Spencer's conception of the organic world is his definition of life and mind. A single definition applies to both. For Spencer, life and mind are distinguished mainly by matters of degree and detail. Having a mind is an advanced mode of living. In a sense, for Spencer people are not just smarter than prawns, but also more alive than prawns.

Spencer thought that living systems are distinguished from inanimate ones by the existence of certain complex processes inside the system, and (more importantly) a special set of relations between internal processes and conditions in the systems' environments. The simplest formula he gave as an account of life was: 'the continuous adjustment of internal relations to external relations' (1855: 374; 1866: 80).

Spencer was heading, I think, towards a view of life that we now might call 'systems-theoretic' or cybernetic (Ashby 1956). Living systems are self-preserving. They maintain their organization, and the discontinuity between system and environment. They do this by responding in particular ways to environmental events which, left to themselves, would tend to disrupt the organization of the living system. Living systems actively resist disruption and decay.

All vital actions . . . have for their final purpose the balancing of certain outer processes by certain inner processes. There are unceasing external forces which tend to bring the matter of which organic bodies consist, into that state of stable equilibrium displayed by inorganic bodies; there are internal forces by which this tendency is constantly antagonized; and the perpetual changes which constitute Life, may be regarded as incidental to the maintenance of the antagonism. (1872: 82)

Here Spencer uses the term 'purpose', which is of course a suspicious one. But in my view the term 'purpose' can simply be dropped from this account, and replaced with something as simple as 'tendency', and Spencer's general intent is retained.

So Spencer anticipated a conception of life which has become quite popular during this century, a conception based upon the idea of self-preserving functional organization as fundamental to life.

In fact this general idea comes in several forms. It can appear in an externalist form, in which there is a focus on self-maintaining responses to a structured environment. And it can also appear in a more internalist form, as exemplified by the 'autopoietic' conception of life given by Maturana and Varela (1980). In this second form the focus is on self-*production* as characteristic of life, and the role of environmental structure is greatly reduced. Spencer, with his perpetual focus on the environment, exemplifies the externalist form of this view. He also anticipated some other central ideas of this account, such as the important roles played by (what we would call) negative feedback and homeostasis.

[T]o keep up the temperature at a particular point, the external process of radiation and absorption of heat by the surrounding medium, must be met by a corresponding internal process of combination, whereby more heat may be evolved; to which add, that if from atmospheric changes the loss becomes greater or less, the production must become greater or less. And similarly throughout the organic actions in general. (1872: 82–3)

In stressing this cybernetic side of Spencer I am downplaying another vocabulary he uses to talk about the basic properties of life. Spencer also says that life and mind are characterized by relations of *correspondence* between internal and external. He also defined life in terms of a correspondence between internal relations and external relations.

The talk of correspondence in Spencer is much more problematic than the discussions of (what we would call) feedback and self-preserving responses to the environment. It was also controversial in his own day, and played an interesting role in the development of some aspects of the philosophical movement known as *pragmatism*. William James (the most famous pragmatist) published his first essay in philosophy on Spencer's view of mind (1878). John Dewey also used Spencer's talk of correspondence as an illustration of the type of position he was opposed to. We shall look at Dewey's view later.

In my view, though Spencer talked a lot about correspondence as the mark of life and mind, this was actually less central to his picture than the idea that living systems are self-preserving. For Spencer, the *ways* in which living systems succeed in preserving the discontinuities between organism and environment involve relations of correspondence and 'concord' between inner and outer. That is how they succeed in responding to environmental events in a way which prevents their dissolution and disruption. For example, having inner states which correspond to the environment's structure makes possible the prediction and anticipation of environmental events.

How close is Spencer's account of life to contemporary views? There is no consensus view on what makes something alive. Many writers are very sceptical about the possibility of giving a definition of life or anything even close to a definition. Perhaps the closest thing to a consensus is the view that life is what philosophers call a 'cluster concept'. There is a list of properties that are associated with life, but to be alive a system does not have to have *all* of them. It only has to have some reasonable number of them. This is deliberately supposed to be vague, and there will be a 'grey area'. That is certainly the impression one gets from the opening pages of many biology textbooks (see e.g. Curtis and Barnes 1989, which lists seven distinct basic properties; see also Mayr 1982, ch. 2; Farmer and Belin 1992).

For many modern writers, however, there are at least two *types* of properties which are important in understanding what life is. Living systems firstly have a set of broadly 'metabolic' properties, which involve the organization of the individual living system and its relations to the environment. Homeostasis is an example of this type of property. Secondly, they have a set of properties involving reproduction, and the relations between individuals. Some take this second family of properties to be more fundamental than the first, in fact. The strongest versions of this idea claim that life can be understood in terms of the capacity to evolve (Maynard Smith 1993), or that life is a property of a population rather than an individual (Bedau and Packard 1992).

Spencer's view of life is based more on individually self-maintaining properties, but he did not neglect reproduction. His view of reproduction and how it fits into life-history properties of organisms is interesting. Spencer thought that organisms come to a 'moving equilibrium' with their environments—all evolution and development has this character. But an individual organism can go only so far in this process before it runs out of the internal properties of plasticity that are needed for further development and adaptation. Reproduction acts to jolt the organic system out of its temporary and imperfect equilibrium. It frees up each component of the system for further evolution by recombining these components into a new individual (1866: pt. 2, ch. 10). Sexual reproduction is the most effective means for this, as organic material from two dissimilar individuals is united and this union will be much more plastic and less static in its properties than the two adults are individually.

In some ways this is quite a modern idea. Reproduction plays a role similar to the role played by the injection of noise into a hill-climbing system to prevent it sticking too readily on a local maximum. (Spencer even mentions physical processes of annealing when developing this view (1866: 274).) On this account there are not two distinct types of properties involved in life, individual-level and population-level properties. Rather, a single set of organism/environment relations is attained and maintained as a consequence of *both* individual-level and population-level activities.

Spencer, as I said, had a single definition of life and mind. He wanted to see even the highest cognitive capacities of humans as continuous with the most basic forms of organic action. Spencer and Dewey both saw cognition as something which emerges out of simpler modes of interaction with the world. Dewey sometimes called this an assumption of 'continuity' (1938). In my view it is important to distinguish several different possible claims of 'continuity' between life and mind:

Weak Continuity: Anything that has a mind is alive, although not everything that is alive has a mind. Cognition is an activity of living systems.

Strong Continuity: Life and mind have a common abstract pattern or set of basic organizational properties. The functional properties characteristic of mind are an enriched version of the functional properties that are fundamental to life in general. Mind is literally life-*like*.

These are both constitutive or ontological principles, principles about what life and mind *are*. There is also a continuity principle which has a purely methodological character:

Methodological Continuity: Understanding mind requires understanding the role it plays within entire living systems. Cognition should be investigated within a 'whole organism' context.

Strong continuity, as I understand it, implies weak continuity. If the pattern of organization characteristic of mind includes the pattern characteristic of life, then anything which thinks must have a lot of what it takes to be alive. The principle of methodological continuity is supported by both weak and strong continuity, though it is not strictly implied by either of them. It is also important that methodological continuity does not imply either of the constitutive principles.

It is a consequence of weak continuity that artificial life must precede artificial intelligence (or in the limit, be simultaneous with it). The same is true under strong continuity, and in addition to this, the strong continuity principle claims that once we have artificial life we also have the raw material, or an unrefined form, of artificial intelligence. We just need to get more of the same sort of properties. Spencer is a clear example of someone who held the strong continuity thesis, and the methodological continuity thesis as well. He would have said that to build a living system you need to build a system that maintains itself in its environment, in the face of possible decay, by adjusting its internal processes and actions to deal with external events and relations. He also would have said that once you have a system that does a lot of this, and does it in a particular way, you have an intelligent system.

What is the 'particular way' characteristic of intelligence? For Spencer, the most distinctive property of intelligent internal processing is (what we would call) its *serial* nature. A transition from parallel processing to serial processing, a transition which is never complete, marks the transition from merely living activity to real intelligence (1855: pt. 4, ch. 1). The contents of thought make up a single complex series. That is not to say that intelligent systems stop dealing with problems in parallel. The point is that only the serially structured part of the system's activities is the intelligent part. In addition, adaptation to conditions in the environment that are (i) highly changeable, (ii) spatially or temporally distal, (iii) compound, (iv) hard to discriminate, and (v) abstract, involving superficially heterogeneous classes of events, all tend to demand the complex types of organic response characteristic of cognition.

So then: Spencer would have given a fairly simple recipe for artificial life, and one which is essentially the same as his recipe for artificial intelligence. I conjecture that he would have had no qualms about the idea that systems which satisfy his criteria could be realized in software. For Spencer, life and mind are patterns of interaction which systems have to their environments. He might insist that an artificial-life creature live in an environment that has the capacity to lead to the disruption and dissolution of the living system. But I do not think this would preclude environments realized inside computers.

If Spencer were to look at some current work in and around artificial life, the work which would best exemplify his conception of biology would probably be work on classifier systems, 'animats', systems constructed using genetic algorithms, and other environment-oriented work (Booker *et al.* 1989; Wilson 1991; Todd and Miller 1991). This is work which is directed at the chief focus of Spencer's biological thought—the relation between internal complexity and environmental complexity. In this work simple artificial organisms are placed in environments that have intrinsic structure or pattern. The organism's role is to adapt itself to these environmental patterns. So often, for example, an organism will have to discriminate food from poison, or devise a way to move through its world and find food while avoiding predators and obstacles. When an organism of this type is well trained, or highly evolved, it would be appropriate to describe its condition in Spencerian terms: its internal processes are adjusted to external processes. It seems to me to be a guiding idea in classifier work, animats, and in genetic algorithm work more broadly, to think that the fuel for the development of organic complexity is environmental complexity. The underlying assumption is that complex systems arise as solutions to complex environmental problems. Spencer would nod vigorously.

This family of ideas can be regarded as the externalist side of artificial-life research. My conjecture is that Spencer would certainly approve of it as a way of modelling biological phenomena. Whether or not he would regard any systems of this type as actually living might depend on which, if any, of these systems would be regarded by him as *realizations* of a pattern of organism/ environment relations, as opposed to representations of those relations. This is a familiar problem with the interpretation of many A-Life systems.

The work in A-Life which I regard as furthest from Spencer's approach is work on cellular automata (Langton 1992). This is because, as I understand it, this work is virtually environment-free. The 'environment' for a cellular automaton is just the space it is in, a lattice of cells which can be in various states. The system changes via the local interactions of cells. It can display complex dynamical behaviour in which specific patterns or structures are preserved, but it does not generate these patterns as a response to a structured environment. Neither does it respond to potentially disruptive environmental events. The environment does not contain a set of intrinsic patterns which the organic system must adapt to or contend with. Work on cellular automata is one of the more internalist domains within A-Life.

When I say that cellular automata do not contend with a structured environment, I assume that the entire cellular automaton is analogous to the organism and the space is analogous to the environment. Another way to look at these systems would be to view the system as comprising a number of individual 'organisms'. One part of the whole system can interact with other parts, with an environment of its fellows, and may succeed or fail in producing self-preserving responses. I am assuming here that this is not the appropriate way to view cellular automata.

It is also important to recognize that some research on cellular automata is not directly aimed at producing artificial life by producing a complicated cellular automaton. The stated aim in Langton (1992), for example, is to investigate the conditions under which 'a dynamics of information' will emerge and 'dominate the behavior of a physical system' (1992: 42). So we need not regard all these systems as artificial-life systems in their own right. On the other hand, cellular automata are very often intended to at least model or cast light on basic properties of the living. Langton does regard the existence of a 'dynamics of information' as a very basic property of life. For Spencer, however, the basic properties of the living are a set of organism/environment relations, not a set of complicated internal properties or processes.

So in my view Spencer would not regard cellular automata as on the road to artificial life. But he might regard them as important models for a different reason. He might see them as illustrations of some parts of his view of the *inorganic* world. Spencer held that organic complexity is a response to environmental complexity. But he also thought that environments can get more complex under their own steam. The most basic laws of matter have the consequence that homogeneous physical systems are not stable, but will constantly generate new complexities of pattern. So cellular automata specifically, and some parts of the environment-free side of A-Life work generally, might be illustrations of the possibility of heterogeneity in structure and activity arising as a consequence of local and intrinsic properties of basic elements of a physical system.

Lastly, what might Spencer think of systems like Tom Ray's 'Tierra'? Tierra is an artificial ecology in which individual organisms do contend with an 'environment', but the chief contents of this environment are other competing individuals, both of the same type or lineage and of other types. The 'abiotic' aspects of the environment are just the fixed constraints exerted by the properties of the CPU, the operating system, and the memory of the computer (see above, Ch. 3). Most environmental features are 'biotic'. Spencer would perhaps regard this as an unusual balance of biotic and abiotic, but as I understand Spencer's understanding of the concept of 'environment' this may well qualify as a simple but genuine case of lifelike interaction between organic system and environment (1891: 416). Or at least, it would be lifelike to the extent that the 'organisms' successfully interacted with these external features in a way which maintained their organization.

4. DEWEY

John Dewey (1859–1952) is, on the face of it, a philosopher with little in common with Spencer. Spencer was a science-worshipper who none the less speculated from the armchair about factual matters, and an advocate of *laissez-faire* economic libertarianism. He believed in timeless laws of nature and the inevitability of universal progress, and built one of the more elaborate systems in English-speaking philosophy.

Dewey, on the other hand, was one of the great American liberal thinkers of the early and mid-twentieth century, especially in the domains of education and the theory of democracy. He knew a lot of science but also kept science in its place. He thought that metaphysical system-building is generally a sort of pseudo-inquiry which diverts people from addressing the real, concrete problems that beset us. He rejected guarantees of universal progress as attempts to falsely promise in advance the goods that can only be gained by hard work and practical problem-solving, and which can never be guaranteed. So Spencer and Dewey differed about a lot.

It is not my goal here to say that deep down they were in agreement. But I do think the differences between them are often misunderstood, and it is possible to sharpen our understanding of the relations between them by focusing, as I am focusing here, on what they say about life, and the relation between life and mind.

Dewey is, along with Spencer, one of the very few major philosophers in the recent English-speaking tradition to think that a theory of life is of general philosophical importance—to think that our theories of knowledge and inquiry, for example, should be linked to a general theory of living organization. For Dewey, making this link between inquiry and life was a way to overcome a 'dualistic' view of the relations between mind and nature. He established a picture of the relations between organism and environment in his theory of life, and was then able to make use of these relations in his theory of thought and inquiry. He sought to use his general position on organism/environment relations to avoid the artificial separations between mind and world which so often arise in epistemology.

Thus Dewey, like Spencer, conceived of life not as an intrinsic property of a system, but as something that involves certain relations to an environment. Life is a 'transaction extending beyond the spatial limits of the organism' (1938: 25). This transaction involves an exchange of energies between the system and the environment, in which states of disturbed equilibrium in the organism are changed back into states of equilibrium. Dewey admits that there are inanimate systems in which an external change causes disequilibrium followed by a restoration to equilibrium. The distinctive properties of living systems are the *ways* in which equilibrium is restored, and the consequences of this restoration (1929a: 253–4). Living systems reach this equilibrium in a way which tends to maintain the organization of the system. The living system acts to preserve its organization and integrity in the face of disturbances.

Iron as such displays or exhibits characteristics of bias or selective reactions, but it shows no bias in favor of remaining simple iron; it had just as soon, so to speak, become iron-oxide. It shows no tendency in its interactions with water to modify the interaction so that consequences will perpetuate the characteristics of pure iron. If it did, it would have the marks of a living body, and would be called an organism. (1929a: 254. See also 1929b: 179)

So far this is not such a long way from Spencer's view, as I interpret it. It is a view of life based upon self-maintenance of organizational properties. One difference, which is especially visible in his 1938 presentation, is that Dewey is more inclined to regard the organism plus environment as constituting a single system. Organic activities tend to preserve the *pattern of interaction* between organism and environment, rather than just preserving the organism itself (1938: 26–8).

Dewey also asserted 'continuity' between life and mind, but earlier I distinguished several different continuity theses, and it is not easy to work out which ones Dewey held.

Dewey is certainly committed at least to the weak continuity thesis. He says: 'The distinction between physical, psycho-physical [living], and mental is thus one of levels of increasing complexity and intimacy of interaction among natural events' (1929a: 261). It is harder to state where he stands on strong continuity. He says the general pattern of inquiry is 'foreshadowed' by the general pattern of life (1938: 34). This suggests strong continuity. All living systems respond to environmental dangers by acting on the world; intelligent inquiry is a specific *way* of approaching this basic aspect of life. However, Dewey also says that mind has a special relationship to language and communication. Only a communicating system in a social environment can literally think, because thinking is symbolic and symbolism is social (1929a: 211, 230; 1938: 43–4). I take all views on which having a language is necessary for thought to be views which deny strong continuity between life and mind (unless a very unusual view of the nature of life is taken). According to the strong continuity thesis, life is 'proto-cognitive' or 'proto-mental'. But life is *not* proto-linguistic.

It is probably fair to say that Dewey did not accept strong continuity in a wholesale way, as Spencer did, but that he did think that *some* basic properties of cognition are formally similar to the basic properties of life. Living activity in general can be viewed as formally similar to problem-solving, although there is also more to genuine cognition than this.

In the discussion of Spencer I said that as a consequence of his holding the strong continuity thesis, Spencer would give basically the same recipe for artificial life and for artificial intelligence. To make a system which thinks, you do not need to add something wholly new to a living system; you just need to increase the magnitude of certain properties it already has. If Dewey's view is that a complex living system becomes a thinking system only in virtue of its relations to other systems in a social context, the way to create real artificial intelligence is via creating a *society* of artificial-life creatures, and having them deal with problems interactively.

I said that Dewey has a view of life which is not too far from Spencer's, and I supported this claim with the quotation above about iron. But Dewey in fact thought there was a great difference between his view and Spencer's, indeed that Spencer was part of the problem. Dewey thought this in part because he focused on a side of Spencer which I downplayed in my discussion—the side in which Spencer says that life involves a relation of 'correspondence' between the internal and the external. Dewey thought that corresponding to the external was not a good way of staying alive.

If the organism merely repeats in the series of its own self-enclosed acts the order already given from without, death speedily closes its career. Fire for instance consumes tissue; that is the sequence in the external order. Being burned to death is the order of 'inner' events which corresponds to this 'outer' order. . . . [A]ll schemes of psycho-physical parallelism, traditional theories of truth as correspondence, etc., are really elaborations of the same sort of assumptions as those made by Spencer: assumptions which first make a division [between organism and environment] where none exists, and then resort to an artifice to restore the connection which has been willfully destroyed. (1929a: 283)

Dewey's point is that Spencer's view of life enforces a false separation between organism and environment, and then invents a magical new relation of 'correspondence' to overcome this artificial problem. Dewey holds this view about the role of concepts of 'correspondence' in theories of life in general and also in theories of mind. The idea that the purpose of thought is to 'correspond' to an independent external realm is, for Dewey, a way to get around a problem which never existed. The false problem is the idea that mind and nature are completely different from one another and hence that there cannot be any straightforward, natural interactions between them.

I think Spencer is not *as* guilty of this charge as Dewey thinks. It is true that Spencer's official theory of knowledge did have a gulf between mind and nature of the sort that Dewey despised (see early chapters of Spencer 1872). It is also true that Spencer said that 'correspondence' was basic to life and mind, and was not clear about what correspondence is. But in my view, the central idea for Spencer was the idea that living systems act to preserve their organization in the face of environmental threats. The 'division' between the living system and the world on this account is the set of physical discontinuities which mark the distinction between inside and outside, and which the organism's actions maintain. Spencer's talk of correspondence is supposed to be part of an account of how this physical relation is maintained.

So what *is* the basic difference between Spencer's and Dewey's views of life?

5. ASYMMETRIC EXTERNALISM

The difference which I think is most fundamental, the one on which many of their detailed disagreements depend, concerns their relations to a perspective which I will call 'asymmetric externalism'. Spencer exhibits this attitude, and Dewey was against it.

As outlined earlier, I understand an *externalist* explanation of some property of an organic system as an explanation in terms of properties of the environment of the system. Adaptationist explanations of biological traits are often externalist, as are classical empiricist explanations of thought and knowledge. Empiricism explains what is believed or known in terms of what is experienced, in terms of what comes into the mind from outside.

An asymmetric externalist view is something stronger than this. It is a program of explanation that explains internal properties in terms of external, and also explicitly or implicitly denies that these external properties are to be explained in terms of internal properties of the organic system. So what is denied is any significant level of feedback from the organic system on its environment. The organic system has its nature or trajectory determined by the environment, but the environment goes its own way. It is dynamically self-contained, rather than 'coupled' to the organic system.

I said that classical empiricism is an externalist picture of thought. Is this also an asymmetric externalist view? It is hard to say. Most of the famous empiricists like Locke and Hume did not *deny* that the thinking agent can act on the world and hence affect the future course of experience. They just did not discuss this very much. The important point is that Dewey did think, in effect, that many orthodox epistemological views are asymmetrically externalist. He saw these views as holding that the business of thought is conforming to the world but leaving it untouched (1929b: 110). This tradition views the ideal knower as a spectator who does not interfere with the course of the game. Dewey, on the other hand, thought that effective inquiry and problem-solving do involve interfering with the world, transforming and reconstructing it. He was still basically an empiricist thinker, accepting that thought is a response to experience. To that extent Dewey had an externalist conception of mind (although a far more moderate one than Spencer's). But Dewey also held that the agent's response to experience typically involves making changes to the world, and hence changing the future course of experience.

I also said that adaptationism in biology is externalist. Is it asymmetrically externalist? Again, it is hard to say in many cases, but one of the most important recent critiques of the adaptationist programme can be understood as claiming that adaptationism *is* asymmetrically externalist. This critique is due to Lewontin (1983, 1993). Lewontin claims that orthodox adaptationist thought views organisms as the passive 'objects' of evolution, when in fact they are subjects as well as objects. Organisms impact upon their environments, and hence alter the future course of the selection pressures to which they will have to respond. I understand Lewontin's attack on adaptationism as closely analogous to Dewey's attack on orthodox empiricist epistemology. Both argue that asymmetric externalist views have to be replaced by views that recognize two-way interactions between organisms and environments.

Dewey prepares the way for his view of thought in his general view of life. And though his biological discussion is not as sophisticated as Lewontin's, the view of organism/environment relations which he develops in his view of life is designed to set up basically the same two-way or feedback-oriented picture that Lewontin supports. 'Adjustment to the environment means not passive acceptance of the latter, but acting so that the environing changes take a certain turn' (Dewey 1917: 62). Dewey's view of the 'transactions' between organism and environment which constitute life is a view based upon organic intervention in the world, as well as organic reaction to what the world does. Dewey sets up this 'interactive' picture in his view of life, and his view of inquiry follows the same pattern. Thought and inquiry are responses to environmental problems, but their goal is not to generate internal states that merely correspond or conform to external things, but rather to make a change to environmental conditions, to adapt *them* to the goals of the organism.

This is the most fundamental difference between Spencer's and Dewey's views of life, and one which extends into their views of mind also. Dewey perceives Spencer as having what I call an asymmetric externalist view of life and mind, and Dewey wants to replace this with a view based on two-way interaction. The difference between Dewey and Spencer about the role of 'correspondence' as a feature of life and mind is a consequence of this more basic difference. Dewey saw the idea of correspondence as a relation between inner and outer as a typical philosophical product of the perspective he opposed.

Is it true that Spencer had an asymmetrically externalist picture? Is this charge justified? That is not a simple question. Spencer, like the other empiricists mentioned earlier and like many adaptationists, is more guilty of *neglecting* the phenomena of organic action on the world than he is of denying them. His picture of organic action is largely one of organic *re*-action. His discussions of life generally focus on organisms taking heed of environmental facts rather than making changes to them. On the other hand, Spencer also had a very holistic view of ecological systems. He saw ecological systems as tangled webs of relationships, and his general picture of the physical world was one in which changes in one place tend to ramify through to distant places. So changes to the composition or behaviour of one species result in 'waves of influence which spread and reverberate and re-reverberate' through the flora and fauna of the area, and this will influence in turn the future of the system behind the change. Spencer also thought that organisms play an individual role in determining how complex their experience of their environment is (1866: 417–18). So there is a holistic side to Spencer, which would make it possible for him to accept some of Dewey's picture. But in general I would agree with Dewey that Spencer's picture is one in which organisms are far more the objects of external forces than they are subjects creating them. In particular, Spencer conceives of progress in the biological world as an inevitable consequence of basic laws governing all matter. Organic progress is achieved because all life is shackled to the inevitable advance of complexity in every environment. Dewey, on the other hand, views any progress that can be attained as something which we (and other living systems) must create and bring about ourselves. The universe is not going to do the work for us.

So with respect to specific projects within A-Life, I see Dewey finding an area of real agreement with Spencer, but also strongly disagreeing with him on other points. Dewey would agree with Spencer in seeking to place organism/environment relations as the central focus of research. Consequently, I think he would share with Spencer the view that cellular automata and other 'environment-free' systems are not models of basic properties of living organization. Dewey, like Spencer, opposes the idea that basic properties of organic self-maintenance can be understood in an internalist way, 'as a sort of unrolling push from within' (1917: 62).

On the other hand, while I think Spencer would regard classifier systems, animats, and the like as on just the right track, Dewey might see many systems of this type as suspiciously low in two-way interactions or feedback relations between organism and environment. Even within the environment-oriented conception of life, which is common to Spencer and Dewey, there is a major difference between views that are for the most part asymmetrically externalist and views based on two-way interactions between organism and environment. A-Life organisms can be placed in environments which are fixed or have their own autonomous principles of change, or alternatively they can be placed in their environments in such a way that their actions determine the future structure of their world. For Dewey, some of the activities of classifier systems, animats, and the like might be too close to mere 'spectating'. The form of intervention in environments that Dewey has in mind is something more than just eating when there is food and not eating when there is poison. A thoroughly Dewey-oriented A-Life system would feature rich connections in both directions between organism and environment. The environment would pose problems for the organism, and the organism would not just adjust and adapt itself to environmental events, but would intervene in the environment's course and alter its trajectory. This alteration would in turn bring about new problems and new possibilities for organic action and control. Co-evolutionary models have some of these properties (Kauffman and Johnsen 1992).

If Dewey did express a view such as this, some might reply to him: 'one step at a time!' In these early days of research it might be reasonable to idealize towards a more Spencerian picture, and neglect, for a period, the complexities of two-way interaction between organism and environment. Even Dewey admits that the simplest forms of life tend to accommodate to their environments rather than intervene in them—he regards intervention in the environment as a sign of 'higher' life (1917: 62, Dewey's scare-quotes). Perhaps there is no need to build all these properties into simple systems of the type we have now. On this view, the first problems to deal with really *are* problems like when to eat, how to keep the system intact, and how to avoid poison and predators.

Others may think that research should follow Dewey's lead from the start, and self-consciously avoid generating a picture of life in which the environment calls the shots and the organism just responds. Those who are impressed with Dewey's arguments about the conceptual quagmires and dead-ends that result from accepting an asymmetric externalist perspective should perhaps prefer this latter view.[1]

REFERENCES

Ashby, W. R. (1956), *An Introduction to Cybernetics* (New York: 1963: Wiley).

Bedau, M. A., and Packard, N. H. (1992), 'Measurement of Evolutionary Activity, Teleology, and Life', in Langton *et al.* (1992), 431–61.

Booker, L. B., Goldberg, D. E., and Holland, J. H. (1989), 'Classifier Systems and Genetic Algorithms', *Artificial Intelligence*, 40: 235–82.

Bowler, P. (1989), *Evolution: The History of an Idea*, rev. edn. (Berkeley: University of California Press).

Curtis, H., and Barnes, N. S. (1989), *Biology*, 5th edn. (New York: Worth).

Dewey, J. (1917), 'The Need for a Recovery of Philosophy', repr. in *The Philosophy of John Dewey*, ed. J. J. McDermott (Chicago: University of Chicago Press, 1981).

—— (1929a), *Experience and Nature*, rev. edn. (New York: Dover, 1958).

—— (1929b), *The Quest for Certainty*, repr. in *John Dewey: The Later Works, 1925–1953*, vol. iv: *1929*, ed. J. A. Boydston (Carbondale, Ill.: Southern Illinois University Press, 1988).

—— (1938), *Logic: The Theory of Inquiry* (New York: Henry Holt).

Farmer, J. D., and Belin, A. d'A. (1992), 'Artificial Life: The Coming Evolution', in Langton *et al.* (1992).

James, W. (1878), 'Remarks on Spencer's Definition of Mind as Correspondence', *Journal of Speculative Philosophy*, 12: 1–18. Repr. in *William James: The Essential Writings*, ed. B. Wilshire (New York: Harper and Row, 1971).

Kauffman, S. A., and Johnsen, S. (1992), 'Co-evolution to the Edge of Chaos: Coupled Fitness Landscapes, Poised States and Co-evolutionary Avalanches', in Langton *et al.* (1992).

[1] I have benefited from discussions of these matters with Tom Burke, Richard Francis, Yair Guttmann, Richard Lewontin, Greg O'Hair, and Peter Todd. This work has been supported with a grant from the Office of Technology Licensing, Stanford University.

Kennedy, J. G. (1978), *Herbert Spencer* (Boston: Twayne).

Lamarck, J. B. (1809), *Zoological Philosophy*, trans. H. Elliot (Chicago: University of Chicago Press, 1984).

Langton, C. (1989) (ed.), *Artificial Life: Proceedings of an Interdisciplinary Workshop on the Synthesis and Simulation of Living Systems* (Santa Fe Institute Studies in the Sciences of Complexity, Proceedings, 6; Redwood City, Calif.: Addison-Wesley).

—— (1992), 'Life at the Edge of Chaos', in Langton *et al.* (1992).

—— Taylor, C., Farmer, J. D., Rasmussen, S. (1992) (eds.), *Artificial Life II: Santa Fe Institute Studies in the Sciences of Complexity,* Proceedings, 10 (Redwood City, Calif.: Addison-Wesley).

Levins, R., and Lewontin, R. C. (1985), *The Dialectical Biologist* (Cambridge, Mass: Harvard University Press).

Levy, S. (1992), *Artificial Life: The Quest for a New Creation* (New York: Pantheon).

Lewin, R. (1992), *Complexity: Life at the Edge of Chaos* (New York: Macmillan).

Lewontin, R. C. (1983), 'The Organism as the Subject and Object of Evolution', repr. in Levins and Lewontin (1985).

—— (1993), *Biology as Ideology: The Doctrine of DNA* (New York: Harper Perennial).

McShea, D. (1991), 'Complexity and Evolution: What Everybody Knows', *Biology and Philosophy*, 6: 303–24.

Maturana, H., and Varela, F. J. (1980), *Autopoiesis and Cognition: The Realization of the Living* (Dordrecht: Reidel).

Maynard Smith, J. (1993), *The Theory of Evolution*, 3rd edn. (Cambridge: Cambridge University Press).

Mayr, E. (1982), *The Growth of Biological Thought* (Cambridge, Mass.: Harvard University Press).

Meyer, J.-A., and Wilson, S. W. (1991), *From Animals to Animats: Proceedings of the First International Conference on the Simulation of Adaptive Behavior* (Cambridge Mass.: MIT Press).

Richards, R. (1987), *Darwin and the Emergence of Evolutionary Theories of Mind and Behavior* (Chicago: University of Chicago Press).

Spencer, H. (1855), *Principles of Psychology* (London: Longman, Brown and Green).

—— (1866), *Principles of Biology*, i (New York: Appleton).

—— (1872), *First Principles of a New System of Philosophy*, 2nd edn. (New York: Appleton).

Todd, P. M., and Miller, G. F. (1991), 'Exploring Adaptive Agency II: Simulating the Evolution of Associative Learning', in Meyer and Wilson (1991).

Wilson, S. W. (1991), 'The Animat Path to AI', in Meyer and Wilson (1991).

13

THE NATURE OF LIFE

MARK A. BEDAU

The philosopher tries to define it [life], but no definition will cover its infinite and self-contradictory variety.

J. B. S. Haldane (1937: 64)

The idea of life, the sense of being alive, are the most familiar and the most difficult to understand of the concepts we meet.

J. Lovelock (1988: 16)

Few biologists today think it is worthwhile to pay much attention to that distinction [between life and non-life].

C. Taylor (1992: 26)

There was a time when the nature of life was a concern of philosophers—think of Aristotle and Kant—but most philosophers ignore the issue today, perhaps because it seems too 'scientific'. At the same time, while some biologists do remark on the nature of life, the field of biology has little serious and sustained discussion of the general issue, perhaps because that topic seems too 'philosophical'. But the advent of the new interdisciplinary field of artificial life has just changed this intellectual context. Combining the resources of philosophy and artificial life, I shall try to revitalize the question of the nature of life and then suggest how to answer it.

1. FACTS AND PUZZLES ABOUT LIFE

Life is amazing. It is all around us in a diversity of forms, ranging from microscopic bacteria to ancient towering trees, from almost inert lichen to transient insect blooms, from birds flocking in the sky to thriving colonies of tube worms at inky deep-sea vents. The first forms of life on earth spontaneously arose out of a pre-existing pre-biotic chemical soup. From those simple origins a diverse hierarchy of forms of life has evolved, which includes the most complex objects in the known universe. Individual living entities (organisms) maintain their self-identity and their self-organization while continually exchanging materials, energy, and information with their local environment. Different species of life flexibly and tenaciously exploit various niches in the environment. When viewed on a long enough time scale, life forms are always changing, adjusting, producing novel responses to unpredictable contingencies, adapting, and evolving through blindly opportunistic natural selection.

Not all the diversity and complexity and change in life is adaptive, of course. Random drift, architectural constraints, and other non-adaptive factors have their influence. But what is especially distinctive and striking about life in the long run is the supple, open-ended evolutionary process that perpetually produces novel adaptations. In fact, I shall contend in this chapter that supple adaptation defines life at its most general.

The concept of life raises many puzzles and ambiguities. The concrete objects ready to hand are for the most part easily classified as living or non-living. Fish and ants are alive while candles, crystals, and clouds are not. Yet many things are genuinely puzzling to classify as living or not. Viruses are one borderline case; biochemical soups of evolving RNA strings in molecular genetics laboratories are another. The Gaia hypothesis (Lovelock 1988), according to which the entire chemical and biological environment around the surface of the earth (including things like the oceans and the atmosphere) constitutes one living organism, also strains the ordinary concept of life. So does the search for extraterrestrial life. Extraterrestrial life forms, if any exist, might well not depend on DNA-encoded information or, indeed, any familiar carbon chemistry processes. How would we recognize extraterrestrial life if we found it? We have no reason to suppose it will have any of the accidental characteristics found in familiar forms of life. What, then, are the essential properties possessed by all possible forms of life? The search for extraterrestrial life needs some answer to this question, for we can search for life only if we have a prior conception of what life is.

The phenomena of life raise a variety of subtle and controversial questions. Borderline cases like viruses raise the general issue of whether life is black or white, as it might seem at first sight, or whether it comes in shades of grey. Early life-forms somehow originated from a pre-biotic chemical soup. Does this imply that there is an ineliminable continuum of things being more or less alive, as many suppose (e.g. Cairns-Smith 1985; Küppers 1985; Bagley and Farmer 1992; Emmeche 1994; Dennett 1995)? Another question concerns the different levels of living phenomena—such as cells, organs, organisms, ecosystems—and asks in what senses (if any) the concept of life applies at these various levels. Eigen and Winkler (1981) seem to be especially sensitive to this question, although they have no ready answer. Recently a third question has been receiving considerable attention (e.g. Langton 1989a; Emmeche 1992): Does the essence of life concern matter or form? On the one hand, certain distinctive carbon-based macro-molecules play a crucial role in the vital processes of all known living entities; on the other hand, life seems to be more in the nature of a process than a kind of substance. The relationship between life and mind raises a fourth question, recently reviewed by Godfrey-Smith (1994). When we consider plants, bacteria, insects, and mammals, for example, we find that different degrees of behavioural sophistication seem to correspond to different levels of intelligence. Might the various forms of life and mind be somehow connected?

To answer questions like these and make sense of the puzzling phenomena of life, we need a sound and compelling grasp of the nature of life. Can any property embrace and unify not only life's existing diversity but also all its possible forms? What is the philosophically and scientifically most plausible way to account for the characteristic lifelike features of this striking diversity of phenomena? How can we resolve the controversies about life? The concept of life as supple adaptation, explained below, is my attempt to address these issues.

Notice that our ordinary, everyday concept of life does not settle what the true nature of life is. Thus, we are not concerned here with careful delineation of the paradigms and stereotypes that we commonly associate with life. We want to know what life *is*, not what people *think* life is. Glass does not fall under the everyday concept of a liquid, even though chemists tell us that glass really is a liquid. Likewise, we should not object if the true nature of life happens to have some initially counterintuitive consequences.

2. CONCEPTIONS OF LIFE

In order to highlight some of the virtues of the particular conception of life that I wish to develop and defend, I shall first outline the three most prominent current alternative views: life as a loose cluster of properties, life as a specific set of properties, and life as metabolization. There are a number of other interesting accounts of life, such as those based on self-replication (Poundstone 1985), autopoiesis (Maturana and Varela 1973), and closed causal loops (Rosen 1991), but this is not the occasion to discuss them.

Sceptics might question whether there is any interesting single, all-inclusive account of life. The demise of vitalism taught us that no non-physical substance or force is distinctive of all instances of life. The sceptic asks what guarantees that some single property is distinctive of the diversity of life. For all we know, life might be no more unified than a collection of overlapping properties from overlapping disciplines, such as population genetics, molecular genetics, evolution, ecology, cytology, biochemistry, and physiology. Such sceptics often argue that life is characterized merely by a cluster of loosely connected properties.

The individual properties in the cluster are held to be typically but not necessarily possessed by living entities; living phenomena in their diversity are thought to bear only a Wittgensteinian family resemblance.

A number of such clusters have been proposed. Farmer and Belin (1992: 818), for example, list eight characteristics: process; self-reproduction; information storage of self-representation; metabolization; functional interactions with the environment; interdependence of parts; stability under perturbations; and the ability to evolve. What drives Farmer and Belin (1992: 818) to a cluster conception of life is despair at being unable to write down anything more precise than 'a list of properties that we associate with life' since '[t]here seems to be no single property that characterizes life. Any property that we assign to life is either too broad, so that it characterizes many nonliving systems as well, or too specific, so that we can find counter-examples that we intuitively feel to be alive, but that do not satisfy it.' Taylor provides a similar justification for characterizing life with a similarly loosely linked list of properties: 'Each property by itself, even when considered with others, is unable to clearly delineate the living from the non-living, but together they do help to characterize what makes living things unique' (1992: 26).

There is a special virtue in viewing life as a loose cluster of properties, for this provides a natural explanation of why life has vague boundaries and borderline cases. The main drawback of cluster conceptions is that they inevitably make life seem rather arbitrary or, at least, mysterious. A cluster offers no explanation of why that *particular* cluster of properties is a fundamental and ubiquitous natural phenomenon. We must acknowledge that there is no a priori guarantee of a single, unifying account of life; such are the possible hazards of philosophy and science. Still, there *might* be an account of this sort; such are the possible fruits of philosophy and science. To settle this question we must seek and evaluate more unified explanations of life. A cluster conception is a fall-back position that can be justified only after all candidate unified views have failed.

Life is sometimes characterized by a list of properties that is intended to represent not a family resemblance but something much closer to necessary and sufficient conditions. Most lists are relatively short, and most contain many of the same properties. Monod (1971) lists three defining characteristics of life: 'teleonomic' or purposeful behaviour, autonomous morphogenesis, and reproductive invariance. Crick (1981) focuses on a somewhat related set: self-reproduction, genetics and evolution, and metabolization. Crick's list is almost identical with Küppers's (1985): metabolism, self-reproduction, and mutability. In *The Problems of Biology* Maynard Smith (1986) cites two properties: metabolism and parts with functions. Ray (1992) cites two others: self-reproduction and the capacity for open-ended evolution. An especially comprehensive list is produced by Mayr (1982: 53), who thinks that '[t]he process of living . . . can be defined' by a list of 'the kinds of characteristics by which living organisms differ from inanimate matter'. It is worth while summarizing Mayr's entire list:

1. All levels of living systems have an enormously complex and adaptive organization.
2. Living organisms are composed of a chemically unique set of macro-molecules.
3. The important phenomena in living systems are predominantly qualitative, not quantitative.
4. All levels of living systems consist of highly variable groups of unique individuals.
5. All organisms possess historically evolved genetic programs which enable them to engage in 'teleonomic' processes and activities.
6. Classes of living organisms are defined by historical connections of common descent.
7. Organisms are the product of natural selection.
8. Biological processes are especially unpredictable.

Mayr's list is a quite useful compendium of the special hallmarks of living systems, and it cannot help but deepen our sense of wonder and perplexity about what could cause this striking collection of features to be present in such an indefinite diversity of natural phenomena. In this, it suffers from the same weakness that besets cluster conceptions of life. We want an account of *why* these properties all coexist. Rather than settling this question, the list raises it. Of course, as our sceptic will remind us, the list of features might have no underlying cause. The list might refer to something like a medical syndrome—a collection of symptoms with no such cause. But when doctors discover the characteristic coexistence of a list of symptoms, they *seek* an underlying cause, and they sometimes find such a cause for what previously *seemed* to be merely a syndrome. In the same way, it is appropriate always to keep one's mind open to the possibility of finding an underlying cause for any conjunction of hallmarks of life.

Schrödinger proposed that persisting in the face of the second law of thermodynamics, by means of the process of metabolization, is *the* defining feature of life. The following passages outline his position (1969: 74–5):

What is the characteristic feature of life? When is a piece of matter said to be alive? When it goes on 'doing something', moving, exchanging material with its environment, and so forth, and that for a much longer period than we would expect an inanimate piece of matter to 'keep going' under similar circumstances. . . . It is by avoiding the rapid decay into the inert state of 'equilibrium' that an organism appears so enigmatic; . . . How does the living organism avoid decay? The obvious answer is: By eating, drinking, breathing and (in the case of plants) assimilating. The technical term is metabolism.

It is compelling to think that life centrally involves the process of metabolization. For one thing, this nicely explains our intuition that a crystal is not alive (there is metabolic flux of molecules, if any, only at the crystal's edge, not inside it). But perhaps what is most compelling is that any possible form of life that persists in the face of the second law of thermodynamics apparently must have a metabolization. By this argument, metabolization is at least a necessary condition of all physical forms of life.

The main drawback of metabolization as an all-encompassing conception of life is that intuitively many metabolizing entities seem not to be alive and not to involve life in any way. Standard examples include a candle flame, a vortex, and a convection cell (Maynard Smith 1986; Bagley and Farmer 1992). These examples by themselves do not prove conclusively that metabolization is not sufficient for life. An adequate and attractive conception of life need not classify as alive all and only those things we intuitively (even confidently) classify as alive. What matters is whether metabolization is the distinctive feature that in fact explains the unified diversity of life. Any convincing defence of life as metabolization must show that metabolization accounts for life's most characteristic features; this will thereby establish that candles and the like share with all life-forms what is essential to life. Whether this is possible seems doubtful.

3. LIFE AS SUPPLE ADAPTATION

It is sometimes suggested that the central feature underlying all life is the evolutionary process of adaptation. What is emphasized is sometimes the blind operation of natural selection, sometimes the general process of evolution, and sometimes the adaptive traits produced by these means. In each case the central idea is that what distinguishes life is an underlying automatic and open-ended capacity to adapt appropriately to unpredictable changes in the environment. From this perspective, what is distinctive of life is the way in which adaptive evolution automatically fashions new and intelligent strategies for surviving and flourishing as local contexts change.

In *The Theory of Evolution* Maynard Smith (1975: 96–7) succinctly explains the justification for this view that life depends on the evolutionary process of adaptation:

We shall regard as alive any population of entities which has the properties of multiplication, heredity and variation. The justification for this definition is as follows: any population with these properties will evolve by natural selection so as to become better adapted to its environment. Given time, any degree of adaptive complexity can be generated by natural selection.

Cairns-Smith (1985: 3) also emphasizes adaptive evolution's central role in accounting for life's characteristic features:

[N]atural selection is only one component of the mechanism of evolution. Any theory that is to explain the variety and complexity of living things must also take into account the varied and varying challenges set up by a varied and varying environment. Nature, as breeder and show judge, is continually changing her mind about which types should be awarded first prize: changing selection pressures have been a key part of her inventiveness.

But nevertheless natural selection has been *the* key component, the *sine qua non*. Without it, living things could not even stay adapted to a given set of circumstances, never mind become adapted to new ones. Without natural selection the whole adventure would never have got off the ground. That kind of in-built ingenuity that we call 'life' is easily placed in the context of evolution: *life is a product of evolution.* [emphasis in original]

These remarks suggest why it is plausible that the process of adaptive evolution could explain all of life's hallmarks, including all of the entries on Mayr's list.

I endorse a specific version of this approach to life. I shall content myself with developing the general form of my view and defending it against various objections. Since the notion of adaptive evolution plays a pivotal role in my account, I shall focus most of my attention on clarifying the relevant sense of adaptation and illustrating how it can be given a precise, quantitative, empirical explication.

Evolving systems that (according to this approach) underlie living phenomena involve a specific form of adaptation. The systems are automatically evolving in an open-ended manner and thereby continually producing new adaptive traits. The essential principle that explains the unified diversity of life seems to be this *suppleness* of the adaptive processes—its unending capacity to produce novel solutions to unanticipated changes in the problems of surviving, reproducing, or, more generally, flourishing. Some forms of adaptation are rigid, such as those exemplified by artefacts like street lights or thermostats which have strictly limited options: turn on or turn off. By contrast, supple adaptation involves responding appropriately in an indefinite variety of ways to an unpredictable variety of contingencies. (The contingencies are 'unpredictable' not in some absolute sense but, rather, from the perspective of the living system itself, that is, given the limited information it can detect and its limited predictive capacities.) Phrases like 'open-ended evolution' (Lindgren 1992: 310; Ray 1992: 372) or 'perpetual novelty' (Holland 1992: 184) have also been used to refer to this same process.

One might think that natural selection will inevitably produce supple adaptation, but this is wrong. When selection is made on the basis of a fixed fitness function, the resulting adaptive dynamics eventually stabilize rather than continually produce adaptive novelty. For example, Mitchell and Forrest (1994) explain that adaptation towards a *fixed* goal is the characteristic—and desired—outcome when natural selection is implemented in a so-called 'genetic algorithm' and applied to engineering problems such as optimization (e.g. circuit design and job shop scheduling), automatic programming (evolving computer programs for specific tasks like sorting lists), and machine learning (e.g. predicting protein structure). Thus natural selection will yield supple adaptation only if the criteria for selection change as the system evolves. Changes in selection criteria can be driven by an independently changing environment, but this is not necessary. A significant aspect of the environment to which any given organism must adapt is all the other organisms with which it interacts. So, when a given organism adapts and changes, the evolutionary context of all the other organisms changes. Thus, even without an externally changing environment, adaptation can be a co-evolutionary process that internally changes the selection pressures which shape adaptation, thus making open-ended adaptive evolution an intrinsic property of the system (Packard 1989; Holland 1992). And this intrinsic form of supple adaptation probably happens even when external factors also change the environment.

There are different ways to define life in terms of supple adaptation, and I wish to emphasize two special aspects of my own approach. First, I wish to say that supple adaptation does not merely *produce* living entities. In addition, the entity that is living in the *primary* sense of that term is the supplely adapting system itself. Other entities that are living are living in a *secondary* sense by virtue of bearing an appropriate relationship to a supplely adapting system. Different kinds of living entities (organisms, cells, etc.) will stand in different kinds of relationships to the supplely adapting system from which they derive their life, although these relationships in general all involve ways in which the adapting system generates and sustains (in the 'right way') the entity. So, my conception of life can be captured by something with the form roughly of the following three definitions:

A. x is living *iff* x is living$_1$ or x is living$_2$.
B. x is living$_1$ *iff* x is a system undergoing supple adaptation.
C. x is living$_2$ *iff* there is some living$_1$ system y such that either (1) x meets condition A_1 and y meets condition B_1 and x bears relation C_1 to y or (2) x meets condition A_2 and y meets condition B_2 and x bears relation C_2 to y, or . . . or (n) x meets condition A_n and y meets condition B_n and x bears relation C_n to y.

Definitions A–C indicate only the *general* form of my approach, which I will not try here to delineate more precisely. I also will not try here to specify the content of the clauses in definition C. My intention is to show only how my approach construes supplely adapting systems as the primary living entities.

The second respect in which my view may differ from other conceptions of life as supple adaptability concerns the difference between a capacity and its exercise. Whereas some might refer only to a system's *capacity* to undergo supple adaptation, I hold that life involves the *exercise* of this capacity. For me the key is not supple adaptability but supple adaptation. I do not wish to overemphasize this difference, since the same process is implicated in both cases. Furthermore, a system that is actually undergoing supple adaptation is not *continuously* adapting; the adaptation often happens in fits and starts. A system is exhibiting supple adaptation over a given time period provided that the quiescent periods without adaptation are not permanent, that is, every quiescent period is followed by the evolution of new adaptations. If a system could undergo supple adaptation but never does, then I should be inclined to say that it could be living and could support life but is not.

With this background, we can start to see how my view of life as supple adaptation could respond to criticisms. For example, mules, the last living member of an about-to-be-extinct species, neutered, and spayed animals are all alive, but being infertile, such entities cannot play any role in the supple adaptation of their own lineage or larger population. Thus one might think that infertile organisms are counter-examples to the necessity of my account of life. However, these infertile organisms exist only because of their connections with other, fertile organisms which do play an active role in a biosphere that undergoes supple adaptation.

One might worry that it is a category mistake to think that an evolving system could be alive. This worry originates with the idea that individual organisms are the entities that are alive and concludes that life cannot be a population undergoing supple adaptation, since the whole evolving population of organisms is of a different logical category from an individual organism. However, this objection has no force for those who are seeking the fundamental explanation of the diversity of living phenomena. Supple adaptation would provide this explanation even though an individual living organism is itself only a small and transitory part of the whole adapting population.

One might worry that this approach to life would have difficulty establishing without circularity that an organism's corpse is not alive, for the corpse and the living organisms are both produced by the adapting population in the same way. However, the corpse and living organism differ in various intrinsic properties, like metabolization. These intrinsic properties would play the role of A_1 in the clause in definition C that would apply to living organisms.

The possibility of an ecology that has reached a state of stable equilibrium and altogether stopped adapting might seem to provide a more direct challenge to my view of life. After all, the organisms in such so-called 'climax' ecosystems are certainly alive, yet the ecosystem containing them is not undergoing supple adaptation, so these organisms would seem to fall outside my definition. However, this problem vanishes when one adopts a sufficiently broad perspective. Not only do climax ecosystems originate through a process of supple adaptation, they all eventually break out of their state of no adaptation. The quiescent periods of stability are transitory; in the long run supple adaptation always occurs.

Things that exhibit open-ended adaptation but seem devoid of all life might seem to be counter-examples to the sufficiency of my view. Viruses are unquestionably adapting to all our best efforts to eradicate them—the AIDS virus does this with remarkable rapidity—yet viruses are a classic borderline case. Even populations of the tiny clay crystallites that make up mud seem to have the flexibility to adapt and evolve by natural selection (Cairns-Smith 1985, Bedau 1991), and so do autocatalytic networks of chemical species (Bagley and Farmer 1992), yet to our ordinary way of thinking evolving populations of crystals or chemicals involve no life at any level. In addition, human intellectual and economic activities both seem to have a flexible, open-ended capacity to adapt to unpredictably changing circumstances; empirical support for such conjectures might be found by analysing, for example, citation patterns in the *Science Citation Index*, traffic patterns on the Internet, or patterns of transactions in stock exchanges. While intellectual and economic activities are generated by living creatures, the evolving intellectual and economic systems themselves might seem quite unlike anything that we would ordinarily want to call living. In fact, cases like these have prompted the proposal that supple adaptation is only a necessary condition of systems containing living entities (Bedau and Packard 1992). However, I am not offering supple adaptation as an explication of our everyday concept of life, so counterintuitive classifications prove nothing. My central hypothesis is that supple adaptation is the underlying explanatory factor that unifies the diverse phenomena of life. If this hypothesis is true, then, since supple adaptation plays a similar role in populations of viruses and clay crystallites, autocatalytic networks of chemicals, and even human intellectual and economic systems, these latter entities also deserve to be thought of as 'living'.

It is easy to *conceive* of circumstances that violate my account of life. The scientific fantasy of species that never evolve and adapt is 'epistemically' possible, as Kripke (1980) might say. So is the possibility that there has been and ever will be only exactly one living organism; so is the possibility that all organisms were created in seven days by an omnipotent, omniscient, and omnibenevolent deity. But I take it that these fantasies are just that—fantasies, with no bearing on the true nature of any form of life that we could discover or synthesize.

Our final evaluation of the conception of life as supple adaptation will depend on learning more about nature of supple adaptation. We need answers to at least the following questions:

1. How can supple adaptation be empirically observed and measured?
2. What minimal models exhibit supple adaptation?
3. What fundamental laws characterize supple adaptation?

In my estimation, these are among the most fundamental unresolved issues, pending whose resolution our final judgement about the scientific and philosophical utility of the conception of supple adaptation must wait.

We are not completely at a loss when it comes to answering these questions, however. For example, we noted above that metabolism is required for a physical entity to persist in the face of the second law of thermodynamics, so any physical system exhibiting supple adaptation must rely on metabolic processes to sustain itself. Similarly, some form of self-replication seems to be implicated in any evolutionary adaptation (Poundstone 1985; Bagley *et al.* 1992). Furthermore, we noted above that supple adaptation is often, and perhaps always, a co-evolutionary process that itself changes the internal selection pressures that drive adaptation. These conclusions all constrain what a minimal model of supple adaptation must be like, and thus inform the answer to Question 2.

The fundamental laws (if any) that characterize supple adaptation are much less certain. A speculative but intriguing suggestion of one such law is the hypothesis that supple adaptation depends on evolutionary dynamics being neither too simple nor too chaotic but just complex enough, poised 'at the edge of chaos' (see e.g. Langton 1992; Kaneko 1993/1994; Bedau and Bahm 1994; Bedau and Seymour 1994). Whether or not this suggestion will prove to have lasting merit, it does illustrate what an answer to Question 3 might look like and how it might be discovered.

As Question 1 implies, a crucial requirement for improving our understanding of supple adaptation—as well as our ability to assess its relevance for life in general—is to devise an empirical method for measuring supple adaptation in actual systems. In the balance of this chapter I sketch such a method and apply it to data from A-Life computer models. Contemporary philosophers might be unsure how to grasp and evaluate my explication of supple adaptation, because the field of A-Life is relatively new, unfamiliar, and—no doubt—controversial. Thus, some background about A-Life is in order. My review will be brief. A comprehensive presentation of work in the field can be found in the proceedings of recent A-Life conferences (e.g. Farmer *et al.* 1986; Langton 1989*b*; Langton *et al.* 1992; Varela and Bourgine 1992; Brooks and Maes 1994; Stonier and Yu 1994). Since A-Life promises to prompt and inform philosophical discussion on a variety of topics in a variety of ways (Bedau 1992; Dennett 1994), it is well worth while for philosophers to become better informed about the field.

4. ARTIFICIAL LIFE'S EMERGENT THOUGHT EXPERIMENTS

Artificial life is an interdisciplinary field that attempts to understand the essential nature of living systems by means of devising and studying computationally implemented models of the characteristic processes of living systems. These processes include self-organization, metabolization, self-reproduction, and adaptive evolution.

Those who work in A-Life embrace the working hypothesis that the essential nature of the fundamental processes of life can be implemented in relatively simple computer models. This working hypothesis is at odds with the conclusions often drawn from the pervasive historicity, contingency, and variety of biological systems (e.g. Mayr 1988b; Gould 1989). If true, the working hypothesis would be striking, for the complexity of living phenomena could then have a fundamentally simple explanation. A-Life involves the search for such models. In the attempt to capture the simple essence of vital processes, the models abstract away from the vast majority of the details present in natural living systems. With no pretence of accurately modelling the particular features of particular natural systems, these are 'idea' models designed to explore the consequences of certain simple premises.

Most natural systems exhibiting complex autonomous behaviour seem to be parallel, distributed networks of communicating 'agents'. These agents make decisions about how to behave based on selective information about their own local environment, and their behaviour directly affects only their own local environment. Following this lead, A-Life is exploring the dynamics of highly parallel models of simple agents in simple local environments.

These models are 'emergent' in that they generate complex macro-level dynamics from simple micro-level mechanisms. (I use 'micro' and 'macro' in a generalized sense, as relative terms. For me, an entity exists at a micro-level relative to a macro-level population of similar micro-level entities. Micro-level entities need not be literally microscopic.) This form of emergence arises in contexts in which there is a system, call it S, composed out of 'micro-level' parts. The number and identity of these parts might change over time. S has various 'macro-level' states (macrostates) and various 'micro-level' states (microstates). S's microstates are the states of its parts. S's macrostates are structural properties constituted wholly out of microstates; macrostates typically are various kinds of statistical averages over microstates. Further, there is a relatively simple and implementable microdynamic, call it D, which governs the time evolution of S's microstates. In general, the microstate of a given part of the system at a given time is a result of the microstates of 'nearby' parts of the system at preceding times. Given these assumptions, I shall say that a macrostate P of system S with microdynamic D is emergent if and only if P (of system S) can be explained from D, given complete knowledge of external conditions, but P can be predicted (with complete certainty) from D *only* by simulating D, even given complete knowledge of external conditions.

Although this is not the occasion to develop and defend this concept of emergence (see Bedau forthcoming), I should clarify three things. First, 'external conditions' are conditions affecting the system's microstates that are extraneous to the system itself and its microdynamic. One kind of external condition is the system's initial condition. If the system is open, then another kind of external condition is the contingencies of the flux of parts and states into S. If the microdynamic is non-deterministic, then each non-deterministic effect is another external condition.

Second, given the system's initial condition and other external conditions, the microdynamic completely determines each successive microstate of the system. And the macrostate P is a structural property constituted out of the system's microstates. Thus, the external conditions and the microdynamic completely determine whether or not P obtains. In this specific sense, the microdynamic plus the external conditions 'explain' P. One must not expect too much from these explanations. For one thing, the explanation depends on the massive contingencies in the initial conditions. It is awash with accidental information about S's parts. Furthermore, the explanation might be too detailed for anyone to 'survey' or 'grasp'. It might even obscure a simpler, macro-level explanation that unifies systems with different external conditions and different microdynamics. Nevertheless, since the microdynamic and external conditions determine P, they explain P.

Third, in principle we can always predict S's behaviour with complete certainty, for given the microdynamic and external conditions we can always simulate S as accurately as we want. Thus, the issue is not whether S's behaviour is predictable—it is, trivially—but whether we can predict S's behaviour only by simulating S. When trying to predict a system's emergent behaviour, in general one has no choice but simulation. This notion of predictability only through simulation is not anthropocentric; nor is it a product of some specifically human cognitive limitation. Even a Laplacian supercalculator would need to observe simulations to discover a system's emergent macrostates.

A-Life simulations explore the consequences of 'idea' models. They are in effect thought-experiments—but *emergent* thought-experiments. As with the familiar 'armchair' thought-experiments, A-Life simulations attempt to answer 'What if X?' questions. What is distinctive about emergent thought-experiments is that they uncover consequences that can be discerned only by simulation. A-Life's computational working hypothesis gives the field a characteristic and distinctive empirical character. A major part of the evidence discussed in the field is empirical evidence about the emergent properties of computer simulations, like those illustrated in the next section.

5. MEASURING SUPPLE ADAPTATION WITH USAGE STATISTICS

Before we can subject my account of life to sustained critical scrutiny, we must have some method for determining whether, and to what extent, a system exhibits supple adaptation; that is, we need an explication of supple adaptation. The explication I shall propose can be concretely illustrated in the context of A-Life models. One should not suppose that this explication applies only to computer simulations, however. Although it is especially easy to illustrate the method with computer simulations, the same method applies in the same way to data from natural systems.

Measuring supple adaptation in a computer model or even a natural system does not in itself make my account of life more plausible, of course. But my explication *does* show that the notion of supple adaptation can be made clear, coherent, and empirically verifiable—which is a necessary condition on any compelling view of life. In addition, because the explication is quantitative, it provides a measure—if my account of life is correct—that can be used in comparing the degree of 'life' in living systems. All this provides a new empirical framework for investigating the nature and implications of the conception of life as supple adaptation.

In the A-Life literature one encounters reports of people having seen supple adaptation emerging in A-Life models. For example, Tom Ray says that his Tierra model 'has generated rapidly diversifying communities of self-replicating organisms exhibiting open-ended evolution by natural selection' (Ray 1992: 373). Lindgren (1992) has made similar claims about the iterated prisoner's dilemma with noise, as has Holland (1992) about the echo class of models. There is no question that these claims help shed some light on supple adaptation, but so far they are all just informal anecdotes using unstated and undefended criteria for what supple adaptation is. Our understanding of supple adaptation would significantly increase if we had a general, objective method for empirically verifying claims of supple adaptation.

Adaptation is the process by which traits are selected for some beneficial effect or function that they perform. Such traits are called 'adaptations'. Adaptive traits do not merely provide a benefit or perform a function; they are selected *for* their functionality (Sober 1984), they persist *because* of the benefit they provide (Bedau 1992, Bedau and Packard 1992). Ultimately, the functionality of adaptive traits promotes survival, reproduction, and, more generally, flourishing of the individuals. So, if the process of adaptation is the creation of adaptive traits, then open-ended or supple adaptation consists of the continual evolution of new adaptive traits.

But how can supple adaptation of this kind be measured in actual systems, especially if we are unsure which traits in the system are adaptations at all, much less adaptations for some specific kind of functionality? The difficulty— some would say impossibility—of answering this question has been stressed in a classic paper by Gould and Lewontin (1979). I have a proposal, developed in collaboration with Norman Packard (Bedau and Packard 1992), for how to answer this question. Our proposal rests fundamentally on the idea that we can detect whether a trait is an adaptation by measuring the extent to which the trait persists in the face of selection pressures. Roughly, the argument goes as follows. Whenever a trait is 'used' or expressed, selection has an opportunity to provide feedback about the trait's adaptive value, its costs and benefits. If a trait persists and spreads through a population when it is repeatedly used, and especially if the trait accumulates significantly more use than one would expect to see if it had no adaptive value, then we have positive evidence that the trait is persisting *because of* its adaptive value. This is precisely what it is to be an adaptation. Now, since open-ended or supple adaptation is simply the continual evolution of new adaptive traits, we can convert our evidence for adaptive traits into a straightforward sign of supple adaptation, as follows: if we continually see (on a relatively long time scale) new clusters of traits that are persistently used (on a relatively short time scale) significantly more than would be expected in the absence of adaptation, then we have positive evidence for the occurrence of the process of supple adaptation.

This line of argument needs certain qualifications and amendments. In certain special circumstances, a non-adaptive or even maladaptive trait can accumulate significantly more usage than one would expect of a 'generic' non-adaptive trait. For example, the trait might be genetically linked with another trait that *is* adaptive. When a non-adaptive trait 'hitchhikes' in this way on an adaptive trait, the usage of the *pair* of traits will exceed that expected of a pair of non-adaptive traits. Thus, although we would need additional information to discern *which* trait is an adaptation, we will still have positive evidence that *at least one* of them is. So we can still interpret the continual occurrence of new traits with significantly elevated usage counts as the sign of supple adaptation. (Below I discuss another important qualification of this argument.)

To implement my proposal, one must collect statistics about traits' 'usage', that is, the extent to which their adaptive value is tested by selection. It is simple to collect and display usage data for the traits in many systems. Here I shall provide just a brief summary and two quick illustrations of the methods involved; for more details, see Bedau and Packard (1992) and Bedau (1995).

Although I shall not develop the full generality of the method, it is worth pointing out that it can measure the adaptive value of 'traits' at a variety of levels, including individual genes, clusters of genes, traits or capacities of individual organisms, or the full sets of features that define genotypes. In general, to reflect the adaptive dynamics in a population of items i, the first step is to create usage counters for the items. A usage counter $u(i,t)$ is a bookkeeping device which keeps track of the extent to which item i has been 'used' and so tested by selection during i's entire history through the course of evolution up to time t. With the help of such usage counters, one collects the usage of all the items in the whole system into one global usage distribution, $U(t,u)$, where the value at the point (t,u) in the distribution $U(t,u)$ is defined as the number (or proportion) of usage counters that are equal to u at time t, $u(i,t) = u$. This usage distribution, $U(t,u)$, is a quantitative summary of a system's adaptive dynamics.

The details of usage bookkeeping vary from case to case, depending on the kinds of items involved and the kinds of system they are in. For example, if i is a particular genetically controlled behavioural trait in an organism, then $u(i,t)$ is the 'usage' that behaviour i has accumulated up to time t. Since the usefulness of a behavioural trait i is tested by natural selection whenever that behaviour is exhibited, it would be appropriate in this case to increment $u(i,t)$ by the number of times trait i occurs at time t; Bedau and Packard (1992) illustrate one way to measure usage of such behaviours. Or, to shift to a higher level of analysis, if i is a genotype present in a population, then $u(i,t)$ is the usage of a genotype i at time t. In this case, since the viability of a genotype i is tested by natural selection to the extent to which i exists in the population (or, as we might say, i is 'used'), it would be appropriate to increment $u(i,t)$ by i's concentration in the population at t. In this case, then, a genotype's usage is just its integrated concentration, that is, the sum of its concentration throughout its history in the population.

The simplest way to observe a usage distribution $U(t,u)$ is by graphing the value of $U(t,u)$ as a function of time t and usage u, such as in Figs. 13.1 and 13.2. The most prevalent structure seen in usage distributions is 'waves': peaks of high usage that move across the $U(t,u)$ plane. In general, each significant usage wave is the sign of an adaptation. Various characteristic kinds of wave phenomenology highlight different aspects of the dynamics of adaptation. It is easy to collect usage data in A-Life models, so simulations can easily generate lots of raw data for analysis. I have measured usage waves in a half-dozen computer models, including a model of evolving sensory-motor functionality (Bedau and Packard 1992; Bedau 1995), Tierra (Ray 1992), Avida (Adami and Brown 1994), echo (Holland 1992), the iterated prisoner's dilemma with noise (Lindgren 1992), and the bar problem (Arthur 1994). The general conclusion

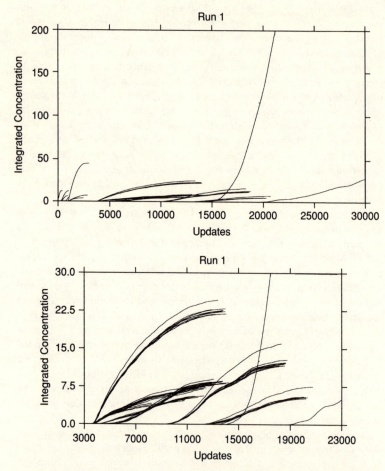

FIG. 13.1. Genotype usage waves from the Tierra model (Ray 1992). Above: a graph of the genotype usage distribution, $U(t,u)$, cropped at time 30000 and usage 200. Below: a blowup of the epoch (roughly 3500–20000) that shows threads of interwoven waves. Genotype usage is defined as the integrated concentration of the genotype, i.e. the sum of its concentration through history. Time is measured in model 'updates'. Only genotypes with concentrations above a certain (low) threshold are shown

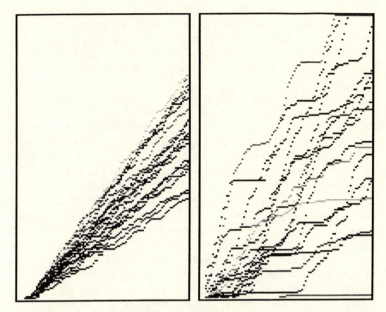

FIG. 13.2. Waves in usage distributions from the bar problem (Arthur 1994), illustrating how supple adaptation differs from a parallel random process. Left: agents randomly choose from among their predictors. Right: agents follow their most accurate predictor of recent history. All other model parameters for the two distributions are exactly the same. The axes in these usage graphs (depicted only implicitly) are just like those in Fig. 13.1; time increases horizontally to the right (100 time-steps are shown), and usage increases vertically (but is cropped above 500)

repeatedly confirmed in this work is that usage waves vividly depict the dynamics of supple adaptation. This makes usage waves a convenient empirical yardstick for comparing supple adaptation in different systems, including natural systems.

As an illustration of this technique, consider the genotype usage waves in one model—Tom Ray's Tierra (Ch. 3 above)—shown in Fig. 13.1. Tierra consists of a population of self-replicating machine language programs that 'reside' in computer memory consuming the 'resource' CPU time. A Tierran 'genotype' consists of a specific type of string of self-replicating machine code, and each Tierran 'creature' is a token of a Tierran genotype. A simulation starts when the memory is inoculated with a single self-replicating program, the 'ancestor', and then left to run on its own. At first the ancestor and its offspring repeatedly replicate until the available memory space is teeming with creatures which all share the same ancestral genotype. However, since any given machine-language creature eventually dies, and since errors (mutations) sometimes occur when a creature replicates, the population of Tierra creatures evolves. Over time the 'ecology' of Tierran genotypes becomes remarkably diverse, with the appearance of fitter and fitter genotypes, parasites, and hyper-parasites, among other things.

To collect genotype usage statistics in Tierra, we implement 'usage' counters for each genotype, as outlined above, so that the value of the usage counter $u(i,t)$ for genotype i at time t is simply the sum (more precisely, the integral) of i's concentration from its original appearance in the population up to time t. Then, the global genotype usage distribution, $U(t,u)$, of a given Tierran simulation accumulates information about the temporal changes in all the genotype usage counters. For simplicity, we can let the value of the distribution $U(t,u)$ at the point (t,u) be equal to zero unless there is at least one genotype i such that $u(i,t) = u$, in which case $U(t,u)$ is set to one. Under this scheme, as a genotype enters the population and becomes more prevalent it will trace a line (a genotype usage 'wave') moving up and to the right in the $U(t,u)$ graph. This line's slope will change as the genotype's concentration in the population changes, and when the genotype goes extinct the line will end.

With this background we can begin to appreciate the significance of the genotype usage waves the model generates. Even a cursory study of a Tierran $U(t,u)$ graph, such as Fig. 13.1, reveals a host of significant adaptive events:

1. The ancestral creature is clearly visible as the first wave in Fig. 13.1, coming out of the origin of the usage distribution.

2. The ancestral usage wave ends when the genotype goes extinct around time or 'update' 500. This coincides with the start of a new usage wave, the second one in the run. Microanalysis reveals that the second genotype is fitter than the ancestor because it is shorter and so reproduces faster. The third main event is the biggest usage wave so far, which turns out to be a still shorter genotype.

3. At around update 3,500 a new kind of wave dynamics starts. Instead of single waves we see threads consisting of interwoven waves. The bottom of Figure 1 is a blowup of $U(t,u)$ during this epoch. The separate waves in each thread are distinct genotypes, but they are acting in concert with all the other waves in the same thread. Microanalysis reveals two interesting facts: time-step 3,500 corresponds to the first introduction of a significant population of parasites, and the different genotypes in a single thread are neutral variants which differ only in unexpressed machine-language instructions.

4. At around 15,000 the biggest wave we see starts. This wave quickly dominates the entire usage distribution because this new genotype dominates the rest of the run. (The graph in Fig. 13.1 clips off the top of this wave after update 20,000.)

Without deciphering any more structure in these usage waves, we can already see how they sensitively reflect the significant adaptive events and co-evolving selection pressures that emerged in this Tierra simulation.

There is an interesting and important subtlety in this interpretation of usage waves, however. Not all usage waves reflect significant adaptations; even deleterious items can be expected to accumulate some usage. In fact, it is only because a trait *has* been used that selection has an opportunity to evaluate the trait's adaptive value. So, before we are entitled to interpret usage waves as a sign of an item's proven adaptive value, we need to discount that quantity of usage that could be expected if the item were non-adaptive. One can crudely address this concern by truncating usage below a certain threshold; in fact, this was done (at a rather arbitrarily chosen threshold) with the Tierran genotype usage shown in Fig. 13.1. A full discussion of techniques for the expected usage for non-adaptive items is beyond the scope of this chapter; Bedau and Packard (1992) and Bedau (1995) discuss this issue at greater length. Still, the idea behind these techniques can be vividly suggested by contrasting two kinds of usage distributions. For variety, and also to illustrate how usage statistics can be gathered in adaptive contexts which do not involve evolution, I shall show usage distributions from a different computer model—the bar problem, devised by Brian Arthur (1994) to illustrate a certain form of inductive reasoning.

The model for the bar problem contains a population of agents who decide each night whether to go to a certain bar. The agents' decisions are sensitive to the facts that, if the number of patrons at the bar is below a certain threshold then everyone there has a great time, but if the population exceeds the threshold the bar becomes unpleasantly overcrowded. To make a rational decision about whether to go to the bar on a given night, the agents evaluate and employ various 'predictors'. These predictors are hypotheses or heuristics about how to tell how many people will be at the bar on a given night; these hypotheses often use the recent history of the bar's population to predict the next night's population. For example, one predictor might advise that the bar population on a given night will equal the average of the population over the last five nights; another might advise that it will equal the 'inverse' (total number of agents less the population at the bar) of the last night's population; etc. Each agent considers a variety of predictors; in general, the sets of predictors considered by different agents overlap but only partially. To decide what to do on a given night, each agent evaluates all his predictors, selects the one that has most accurately predicted the bar population recently, and then follows that predictor's advice.

The agents in the bar problem are considered to be 'flourishing' to the extent that as many of them as possible have as much fun as possible, that is, to the extent that each night the bar is full but not overcrowded. The process by which they choose predictors does not involve natural selection (at least not in the simple version of the model described here). Predictors do not reproduce or die; they exist forever. What changes, however, is the extent to which a given predictor is used by the members of the population. Thus, in the context of this model, a predictor i is adaptive at a given time to the extent that i's recent predictive success is causing agents to use i to govern their behaviour and thereby flourish.

When the bar problem is simulated, one discovers that the bar population tends to fluctuate around the 'overcrowding' threshold with a mean slightly below it (Arthur 1994). This global dynamic equilibrium in the population's behaviour is achieved even though the agents as a group cannot all follow the same predictor and thereby synchronize their behaviour. (If the agents were all to follow the same predictor, they would all do the same thing and thus make the bar either packed or empty; neither leads to any fun.) Thus, the global equilibrium in the bar census emerges even though the 'ecology' of predictors actually used by the agents is continually shifting.

The process of agents adapting their behaviour in light of recent history can be visualized with a usage distribution. The basic idea is to collect data on the agents' use of the different predictors. A predictor i is 'used' whenever an agent follows i's advice because of i's recent predictive success, so it is reasonable to increment $u(i,t)$ by the number of agents that use i at t. Thus, $u(i,t)$ records the total number of times that predictor i has been used from the beginning of the run up to time t. For simplicity, we can let $U(t,u)$ be equal to zero unless there is at least one predictor i such that $u(i,t) = u$, in which case we let $U(t,u)$ be one. This predictor usage distribution $U(t,u)$ will show 'waves' which reflect the changing frequency of predictor use.

Now, if we want to determine which aspects of the predictor usage distribution $U(t,u)$ reflect predictors' adaptive value, we need some way to identify those aspects of the distribution that are *not* due to adaptation. To depict this, we can first model a parallel random process, that is, a situation with exactly the same structure as the bar model except that each agent always selects which predictor to follow simply by choosing one at random (with equal probability from all of his predictors). Figure 13.2 shows the usage waves in a pair of bar problem simulations. All the model parameters in the two simulations are the same, except that, while agents in one (on the right) select predictors on the basis of their predictive success—this is the normal bar model—in the other (on the left) agents select predictors at random. In effect, the model on the left parallels the bar model in all particulars except that the behaviour is generated randomly. In this latter 'null case' all adaptation is blocked; agents cannot rationally govern their behaviour.

When we compare the two distributions in Fig. 13.2, we see many differences.

For example we see that in the random bar model (left) all predictors are used with roughly equal frequency (depending on how equally they are distributed among the agents) and so cause roughly straight waves of roughly equal slope. In the normal bar model, when the agents' choice of predictor can adapt to recent history (right), the wave dynamics are quite different. A few perennially good predictors produce waves with unusually steep slope, but most usage waves shift between periods of steep and flat slope, often roughly in concert with other waves. This loose but coordinated zig-zagging in groups of waves is a sign of a metastable dynamic in an ecology of predictors—clear evidence of the unpredictably co-evolving selection criterion that drives supple adaptation. The distinctive pattern in the distribution from the normal bar model (right) is an empirical picture of what supple adaptation can be like in the bar problem. Even without any more detailed analysis of the usage waves in Fig. 13.2, we can sense how the difference in this pair of distributions measures the degree of adaptation in the right-hand distribution. The differences between these distributions can be characterized quantitatively (e.g. with the chi squared statistic), but it is also obvious to the eye.

The method of using usage waves to highlight supple adaptation implies many testable predictions about empirical data, including those from natural systems. The underlying form of these predictions is that usage distributions will highlight a system's adaptive dynamics. Since the details of the specific mechanisms affecting adaptation generally differ in different systems, so will much of the adaptive significance evident in usage diagrams from different systems. In Tierra, for example, what it takes for a genotype to flourish changes if dramatically shorter or parasitic genotypes arise. By contrast, in Arthur's bar model, the adaptive value of a predictor changes as its recent predictive success waxes and wanes. As the salient qualitative structures in Figs. 13.1 and 13.2 show, usage distributions in Tierra and the bar model highlight these different kinds of change in selection criteria. Still, there is rather broad applicability of some general predictions concerning the correlation between certain kinds of usage waves and certain kinds of changes in the adaptive dynamics (extinction, invasion, predator–prey interaction, cooperation, etc.). For example, the explication of supple adaptation with usage distributions predicts that the fossil record will show dramatic bursts of new usage waves only during periods of major adaptive innovation, and an analogous prediction would apply to major adaptive innovations in a wide variety of other kinds of systems. In general, usage statistics depict supple adaptation in a manner that invites empirical test.

Usage distributions can be used to define macro-properties that measure various aspects of the dynamics of supple adaptation. For example, one can quantify the rate at which new adaptations (usage waves) are entering the system and persisting (Bedau and Packard 1992), that is, the extent to which the system is exhibiting supple adaptation; call this rate a system's *vitality, V(t)*. Intuitively, a system's level of vitality $V(t)$ reflects the extent to which new significant adaptations are arising and persisting. So, if we view life as supple adaptation, we can use a system's vitality $V(t)$ to define the degree to which it is living or involves life. By this sort of means, a system's usage distribution $U(t,u)$ and vitality $V(t)$ could figure centrally in the explanation of the system's supple adaptation, and perhaps even the explanation of the extent to which the system involves life.

6. CONCLUSIONS

I suggest that we can explain and unify the diversity of life by means of the concept of supple adaptation. Furthermore, I propose that we explicate the concept of supple adaptation by means of usage statistics, as outlined above. If I am right that supple adaptation can be measured through usage statistics, then we have in hand a feasible and empirical, objective and public, repeatable and refinable method for detecting the extent to which systems exhibit life.

Even if we should not yet make final judgements, much can be said in favour of this view of life. First, it can plausibly answer the criticisms that might arise. Second, it brings explanatory order to lists of the central hallmarks of living phenomena. Third, it brings a rich set of resources to bear on the controversial questions about life. For example, if the essential feature behind life is supple adaptation, then we can attribute life's borderline cases to the indefinitely varied array of more or less supple forms that adaptation can take. Even if we do not try to settle these controversies here, we can appreciate how much more tractable are the puzzles about the different senses of life at different levels of biological organization, about the relative roles of matter and form, and even about the connection between life and mind.

The concept of supple adaptation might not map neatly on to our everyday concept of a living organism. Indeed, there might well be no scientifically and philosophically justifiable equivalent for that role. Still, the concept of life as supple adaptation, when explicated by means of usage statistics, provides a non-circular and non-arbitrary account of the essential properties underlying all forms of life. Analysis of a system's usage statistics requires no prior knowledge of whether any form of life exists at any level in the system. And since a proliferation of significant usage waves shows that clusters of traits are persisting because of their adaptive significance, usage waves allow us to see clearly and measure precisely the supple adaptation that seems to define life at its most general.

The significance of these results extends beyond our understanding of life towards a more sweeping conclusion about how practices like the pursuit of A-Life can—and, in time, will—change the face of philosophy. A-Life and philosophy are natural partners, with related goals and methods. Eschewing the accidental and the contingent, both are concerned with maximal generality and essence. In addition, A-Life's emergent thought-experiments are a natural extension of traditional philosophical methods. A-Life will affect philosophy in a variety of ways: by facilitating progress on deep and traditional philosophical questions, some of which, like the nature of life, are currently being ignored; by focusing attention on important new questions, like the nature of supple adaptation; and by bringing a new level of clarity and precision to these issues, with empirical and quantitative techniques like usage statistics. These changes will not supplant philosophy by science but will enable us to combine their resources to address fundamental questions, such as the nature of life.[1]

REFERENCES

Adami, C., and Brown, C. T. (1994), 'Evolutionary Learning in the 2D Artificial Life System "Avida"', in Brooks and Maes (1994), 377–81.

Arthur, W. B. (1994), 'Inductive Reasoning and Bounded Rationality', *American Economic Review*, 84: 406–11.

Bagley, R., and Farmer, J. D. (1992), 'Spontaneous Emergence of a Metabolism', in Langton *et al.* (1992), 93–140.

—— —— and Fontana, W. (1992), 'Evolution of a Metabolism', in Langton *et al.* (1992), 141–58.

Banzhaf, W., and Eeckman, F. (1995) (eds.), *Evolution and Biocomputation—Computational Models of Evolution* (Berlin: Springer).

Bedau, M. A. (1991), 'Can Biological Teleology Be Naturalized?', *Journal of Philosophy*, 88: 647–55.

—— (1992), 'Philosophical Aspects of Artificial Life', in Varela and Bourgine (1992), 494–503.

—— (1995), 'Three Illustrations of Artificial Life's Working Hypothesis', in Banzhaf and Eeckman (1995), 53–68.

—— (forthcoming), 'Weak Emergence', in Tomberlin (forthcoming).

—— and Bahm, A. (1994), 'Bifurcation Structure in Diversity Dynamics', in Brooks and Maes (1994), 258–68.

—— and Packard, N. (1992), 'Measurement of Evolutionary Activity, Teleology, and Life', in Langton *et al.* (1992), 431–61.

—— and Seymour, R. (1994), 'Adaptation of Mutation Rates in a Simple Model of Evolution', in Stonier and Yu (1994), 37–44.

[1] Thanks to Hugo Bedau, Maggie Boden, Clif Bowen, Mark Hinchliff, Norman Packard, David Reeve, Teresa Robertson, and anonymous reviewers for discussion and comments on the manuscript; thanks also to Titus Brown for Figure 13.1 and Robert Seymour for Figure 13.2.

Bourgine, P., and Varela, F. (1992), 'Towards a Practice of Autonomous Systems', in Varela and Bourgine (1992), pp. xi–xvii.

Brooks, R., and Maes, P. (1994) (eds.), *Artificial Life IV* (Cambridge, Mass.: MIT Press).

Cairns-Smith, A. G. (1985), *Seven Clues to the Origin of Life* (Cambridge: Cambridge University Press).

Crick, F. (1981), *Life Itself: Its Origin and Nature* (New York: Simon and Schuster).

Dennett, D. (1994), 'Artificial Life as Philosophy', *Artificial Life*, 1: 291–2.

—— (1995), *Darwin's Dangerous Idea: Evolution and the Meanings of Life* (New York: Simon and Schuster).

Eigen, M., and Winkler, R. (1981), *Laws of the Game: How the Principles of Nature Govern Chance* (New York: Knopf).

Emmeche, C. (1992), 'Life as an Abstract Phenomenon: Is Artificial Life Possible?', in Varela and Bourgine (1992), 466–74.

—— (1994), *The Garden in the Machine: The Emerging Science of Artificial Life* (Princeton: Princeton University Press).

Farmer, D., and Belin, A. (1992), 'Artificial Life: The Coming Evolution', in Langton *et al.* (1992), 815–40.

Farmer, J. D., Lapedes, A., Packard, N., and Wendroff, B. (1986) (eds.), *Evolution, Games, and Learning: Models for Adaptation for Machines and Nature* (Amsterdam: North-Holland).

Godfrey-Smith, Peter (1994), 'Spencer and Dewey on Life and Mind', in Brooks and Maes (1994), 80–9. Reprinted as Ch. 12 of this volume.

Gould, S. J. (1989), *Wonderful Life: The Burgess Shale and the Nature of History* (New York: Norton).

—— and Lewontin, R. C. (1979), 'The Spandrels of San Marco and the Panglossian Paradigm: A Critique of the Adaptationist Programme', *Proceedings of the Royal Society B*, 205, 581–98.

Haldane, J. B. S. (1937), 'What is Life?', in his *Adventures of a Biologist* (New York: Harper and Brothers), 49–64.

Holland, J. H. (1992), *Adaptation in Natural and Artificial Systems* (1975; reissued) (Cambridge, Mass.: MIT Press).

Kaneko, K. (1993/1994), 'Chaos as a Source of Complexity and Diversity in Evolution', *Artificial Life*, 1: 163–77.

Kripke, S. (1980), *Naming and Necessity* (Cambridge, Mass.: Harvard University Press).

Küppers, B.-O. (1985), *Molecular Theory of Evolution: Outline of a Physico-Chemical Theory of the Origin of Life* (Berlin: Springer).

Langton, C. (1989a), 'Artificial Life', in C. Langton (1989b), 1–47. Reprinted as Ch. 1 of this volume.

—— (1989b) (ed.), *Artificial Life: Proceedings of an Interdisciplinary Workshop on the Synthesis and Simulation of Living Systems* (Santa Fe Institute Studies in the Sciences of Complexity, Proceedings, 6; Redwood City, Calif.: Addison-Wesley).

—— (1992), 'Life at the Edge of Chaos', in Langton *et al.* (1992), 41–91.

—— Taylor, C., Farmer, J. D., and Rasmussen, S. (1992) (eds.), *Artificial Life II* (Santa Fe Institute Studies in the Sciences of Complexity, Proceedings, 10; Redwood City, Calif.: Addison-Wesley).

Lindgren, K. (1992), 'Evolutionary Phenomena in Simple Dynamics', in Langton *et al.* (1992), 295–312.

Lovelock, J. (1988), *The Ages of Gaia* (New York: Norton).

Maturana, H., and Varela, F. (1973), *Autopoiesis: The Organization of the Living* (Dordrecht: Reidel).

Maynard Smith, J. (1975), *The Theory of Evolution* (3rd edn., New York: Penguin).

—— (1986), *The Problems of Biology* (New York: Oxford University Press).

Mayr, E. (1982), *The Growth of Biological Thought* (Cambridge, Mass.: Harvard University Press).

—— (1988a), *Towards a New Philosophy of Biology: Observations of an Evolutionist* (Cambridge, Mass.: Belknap Press).

—— (1988b), 'Is Biology an Autonomous Science?', in Mayr (1988a), 8–23.

Mitchell, M., and Forrest, S. (1994), 'Genetic Algorithms and Artificial Life', *Artificial Life*, 1: 267–89.

Monod, J. (1971), *Chance and Necessity* (New York: Knopf).

Packard, N. (1989), 'Intrinsic Adaptation in a Simple Model for Evolution', in Langton (1989b), 141–55.

Poundstone, W. (1985), *The Recursive Universe* (Chicago: Contemporary Books).

Ray, T. (1992), 'An Approach to the Synthesis of Life', in Langton *et al.* (1992), 371–408. Reprinted as Ch. 3 of this volume.

Rosen, R. (1991), *Life Itself: A Comprehensive Inquiry into the Nature, Origin, and Fabrication of Life* (New York: Columbia University Press).

Ruse, M. (1989) 'Introduction', in his *Philosophy of Biology* (New York: Macmillan).

Schrödinger, E. (1969), *What is Life?* (Cambridge: Cambridge University Press).

Sober, E. (1984), *The Nature of Selection: Evolutionary Theory in Philosophical Focus* (Cambridge, Mass.: MIT Press).

Stonier, R. J., and Yu, X. H. (1994), *Complex Systems: Mechanisms of Adaptation* (Amsterdam: IOS Press).

Taylor, C. (1992), '"Fleshing Out" Artificial Life II', in Langton *et al.* (1992), 25–38.

Tomberlin, J. (forthcoming) (ed.), *Philosophical Perspectives, Metaphysics*, 10 and 11 (Altascadero, Calif.: Ridgeview).

Varela, F., and Bourgine, P. (1992) (eds.), *Towards a Practice of Autonomous Systems* (Cambridge, Mass.: MIT Press).

PART V

14

LEARNING FROM FUNCTIONALISM— PROSPECTS FOR STRONG ARTIFICIAL LIFE

ELLIOTT SOBER

I want to explore an analogy: artificial intelligence (AI) is to psychology as artificial life (AL) is to biology. Since I am interested in philosophical issues concerning both sides of this equation, I shall jump back and forth between the philosophy of psychology and the philosophy of biology.

1. TWO USES FOR COMPUTERS

There are two quite different roles that computers might play in biological theorizing. Mathematical models of biological processes are often analytically intractable. When this is so, computers can be used to get a feel for the model's dynamics. You plug in a variety of initial condition values and allow the rules of transition to apply themselves (often iteratively); then you see what the outputs are.

Computers are used here as aids to the theorist. They are like pencil and paper or a slide-rule. They help you think. The models being investigated are about life. But there is no need to view the computers that help you investigate these models as alive themselves. Computers can be applied to calculate what will happen when a bridge is stressed, but the computer is not itself a bridge.

Population geneticists have used computers in this way since the 1960s. Many participants in the Artificial Life research programme are doing the same thing. I see nothing controversial about this use of computers. By their fruits ye shall know them. This part of the AL research program will stand or fall with the interest of the models investigated. When it is obvious beforehand what the model's dynamics will be, the results provided by computer simulation will be somewhat uninteresting. When the model is very unrealistic, computer investigation of its properties may also fail to be interesting. However, when

TABLE 14.1. *Parallelism between AI and AL*

	Psychology	Biology
Computers are tools for investigating	weak AI	weak AL
Computers are part of the subject-matter of	strong AI	strong AL

a model is realistic enough and the results of computer simulation are surprising enough, no one can deny the pay-off.

I just mentioned that computers may help us understand bridges, even though a computer is not a bridge. However, the second part of the Artificial Life research programme is interested in the idea that computers are instances of biological processes. Here the computer is said to be alive, or to exemplify various properties that we think of as characteristic of life.

This second aspect of the Artificial Life research programme needs to be clearly separated from the first. It is relatively uncontroversial that computers can be tools for investigating life; in contrast, it is rather controversial to suggest that computers are or can be alive. Neither of these ideas entails the other; they are distinct.

Shifting now from AL to AI, again we can discern two possible uses of computers. First, there is the use of computers as tools for investigating psychological models that are too mathematically complicated to be analytically solved. This is the idea of computers as tools for understanding the mind. Second and separate, there is the idea that computers are minds. This latter idea, roughly, is what usually goes by the name of strong AI.

Strong AI has attracted a great deal of attention, both in the form of advocacy and in the form of attack. The idea that computers, like paper and pencil, are tools for understanding psychological models has not been criticized much, nor should it have been. Here, as in the case of AL, by their fruits ye shall know them.

So in both AI and AL, the idea that computers are tools investigating a theory is quite different from the idea that computers are part of the subject-matter of the theory. I shall have little more to say about the tool idea, although I shall occasionally harp on the importance of not confusing it with the subject-matter idea. Table 14.1 depicts the parallelism between AI and AL; it also should help keep the tool idea and the subject-matter idea properly separated.

Of course, 'strong' does not mean plausible or well defended; 'strong' means daring and 'weak' means modest.

Where did the idea that computers could be part of the subject-matter of psychological and biological theories come from? Recent philosophy has discussed the psychological issues a great deal, the biological problem almost not at all.

Is it possible to build a case for living computers that parallels the arguments for thinking computers? How far the analogy can be pushed is what I wish to determine.

2. THE PROBLEM OF MIND AND THE PROBLEM OF LIFE

The mind/body problem has witnessed a succession of vanguard theories. In the early 1950s Ryle (1949) and Wittgenstein (1953) advocated forms of logical behaviourism. This is the idea that the meaning of mentalistic terms can be specified purely in terms of behaviour. Ryle attacked the Myth of the Ghost in the Machine, which included the idea that mental states are inner causes of outward behaviour.

In the mid-1950s to mid-1960s behaviourism itself came under attack from mind/brain identity theorists. Australian materialists like Place (1956) and Smart (1959) maintained that mental states are inner causes. But more than that, they argued that mental properties would turn out to be identical with physical properties. Whereas logical behaviourists usually argued for their view in an a priori fashion, identity theorists said they were formulating an empirical thesis that would be borne out by the future development of science.

The identity theory can be divided into two claims. They claimed that each mental object is a physical thing. They also claimed that each mental property is a physical property. In the first category fall such items as minds, beliefs, memory traces, and after-images. The second category includes believing that snow is white and feeling pain. This division may seem a bit artificial—why bother to make separate claims about my belief that snow is white and the property of believing that snow is white? In a moment, the point of this division will become plain.

Beginning in the mid-1960s the identity theory was challenged by a view that philosophers called functionalism. Hilary Putnam (1967), Jerry Fodor (1968), and Daniel Dennett (1978) argued that psychological properties are multiply realizable. If this is correct, then the identity theory must be rejected.

To understand what multiple realizability means, it is useful to consider an analogy. Consider mousetraps. Each of them is a physical object. Some are made of wire, wood, and cheese. Others are made of plastic and poison. Still others are constituted by bunches of philosophers scurrying around the room armed with inverted wastepaper baskets.

What do all these mousetraps have in common? Well, they are made of matter. But more specifically, what properties do they share that are unique to them? If mousetraps are multiply realizable, then there is no physical property that all mousetraps, and only mousetraps, possess.

Each mousetrap is a physical thing, but the property of being a mousetrap is

TABLE 14.2.

	Dualism	Functionalism	Identity theory
		Are mental____physical?	
Objects	NO	YES	YES
Properties	NO	NO	YES

not a physical property. Here I am putting to work the distinction between object and property that I mentioned before.

Just as there are many physical ways to build a mousetrap, so, functionalists claimed, there are many physical ways to build a mind. Ours happens to be made of DNA and neurons. But perhaps computers could have minds. And perhaps there could be organisms in other species or in other galaxies that have minds, but whose physical organization is quite different from the one we exemplify. Each mind is a physical thing, but the property of having a mind is not a physical property.

Dualism is a theory that I have not mentioned. It claims that minds are made of an immaterial substance. Identity theorists reject dualism. So do functionalists. The relationship between these three theories can be represented by saying how each theory answers a pair of questions (see Table 14.2).

I mentioned earlier that identity theorists thought of themselves as advancing an empirical thesis about the nature of the mind. What about functionalism? Is it an empirical claim? Here one finds a division between two styles of argument. Sometimes functionalists appear to think that the meaning of mentalistic terminology guarantees that identity theory must be false. This a priori tendency within functionalism notwithstanding, I prefer the version of that theory that advances an empirical thesis. It is an empirical question how many different physical ways a thinking thing can be built. If the number is enormously large, then functionalism's critique of the identity theory will turn out to be right. If the number is very small (or even one), then the identity theory will be correct. Perhaps the design constraints dictated by psychology are satisfiable only within a very narrow range of physical systems; perhaps the constraints are so demanding that this range is reduced to a single type of physical system. This idea cannot be dismissed out of hand.

If philosophers during the same period of time had been as interested in the problem of life as they were in the problem of mind, they might have formulated biological analogues of the identity theory and functionalism. However, a biological analogue of mind/body dualism does not have to be invented—it existed in the form of vitalism. Dualists claim that beings with minds possess an immaterial ingredient. Vitalists claim that living things differ from inanimate objects because the former contain an immaterial substance—an *élan vital*.

Had the problem of life recapitulated the problem of mind, the triumphs of molecular biology might then have been interpreted as evidence for an identity theory, according to which each biological property is identical with some physical property. Finally, the progression might have been completed with an analogue of functionalism. Although each living thing is a material object, biological properties cannot be identified with physical ones.

Actually, this functionalist idea has been espoused by biologists, although not in the context of trying to recapitulate the structure of the mind/body problem. Thus, Fisher (1930) says that 'fitness, although measured by a uniform method, is qualitatively different for every different organism'. Recent philosophers of biology have made the same point by arguing that an organism's fitness is the upshot of its physical properties even though fitness is not itself a physical property. What do a fit cockroach and a fit zebra have in common? Not any physical property, any more than a wood and wire mousetrap must have something physical in common with a human mouse-catcher. Fitness is multiply realizable.

There are many other biologically interesting properties and processes that appear to have the same characteristic. Many of them involve abstracting away from physical details. For example, consider Lewontin's (1970) characterization of what it takes for a set of objects to evolve by natural selection. A necessary and sufficient condition is heritable variation in fitness. The objects must vary in their capacity to stay alive and to have offspring. If an object and its offspring resemble each other, the system will evolve, with fitter characteristics increasing in frequency and less fit traits declining.

This abstract skeleton leaves open what the objects are that participate in a selection process. Darwin thought of them as organisms within a single population. Group selectionists have thought of the objects as groups or species or communities. The objects may also be gametes or strands of DNA, as in the phenomena of meiotic drive and junk DNA.

Outside the biological hierarchy, it is quite possible that cultural objects should change in frequency because they display heritable variation in fitness. If some ideas are more contagious than others, they may spread through the population of thinkers. Evolutionary models of science exploit this idea. Another example is the economic theory of the firm; this describes businesses as prospering or going bankrupt according to their efficiency.

Other examples of biological properties that are multiply realizable are not far to seek. Predator/prey theories, for example, abstract away from the physical details that distinguish lions and antelopes from spiders and flies.

I mentioned before that functionalism in the philosophy of mind is best seen as an empirical thesis about the degree to which the psychological characteristics of a system constrain the system's physical realization. The same holds for the analogue of functionalism as a thesis about biological properties. It may be somewhat obvious that some biological properties—like the property of being a predator—place relatively few constraints on the physical characteristics a system must possess. But for others, it may be much less obvious.

Consider, for example, the fact that DNA and RNA are structures by which organisms transmit characteristics from parents to offspring. Let us call them hereditary mechanisms. It is a substantive question of biology and chemistry whether other molecules could play the role of a hereditary mechanism. Perhaps other physical mechanisms could easily do the trick; perhaps not. This cannot be judged a priori, but requires a substantive scientific argument.

3. WHAT ARE PSYCHOLOGICAL PROPERTIES, IF THEY ARE NOT PHYSICAL?

In discussing functionalism's criticism of the mind/brain identity theory, I mainly emphasized functionalism's negative thesis. This is a claim about what psychological states are not; they are not physical. But this leaves functionalism's positive proposal unstated. If psychological properties are not physical, what are they, then?

Functionalists have constructed a variety of answers to this question. One prominent idea is that psychological states are computational and representational. Of course, the interest and plausibility of this thesis depends on what 'computational' and 'representational' are said to mean. If a functionalist theory entails that desk calculators and photoelectric eyes have beliefs about the world, it presumably has given too permissive an interpretation of these concepts. On the other hand, if functionalism's critique of the identity theory is right, then we must not demand that a system be physically just like us for it to have a psychology. In other words, the problem has been to construct a positive theory that avoids, as Ned Block (1975) once put it, both chauvinism and liberalism. Chauvinistic theories are too narrow, while liberal theories are too broad, in their proposals for how the domain of psychology is to be characterized.

4. BEHAVIOURISM AND THE TURING TEST

Functionalists claim that psychological theories can be formulated by abstracting away from the physical details that distinguish one thinking system from another. The question is: how much abstracting should one indulge in?

One extreme proposal is that a system has a mind, no matter what is going on inside it, if its behaviour is indistinguishable from some other system that

TABLE 14.3. *Errors in the Turing Test*

	The subject thinks	The subject does not think
The subject passes	OK	type-1
The subject does not pass	type-2	OK

obviously has a mind. This is basically the idea behind the Turing Test. Human beings have minds, so a machine does too, if its behaviour is indistinguishable from human behaviour. In elaborating this idea, Turing was careful that 'irrel-evant' cues not provide a tip-off. Computers do not look like people, but Turing judged this fact to be irrelevant to the question of whether they think. To control for this distracting detail, Turing demands that the machine be placed behind a screen and its behaviour standardized. The behaviour is to take the form of printed messages on a tape.

Besides intentionally ignoring the fact that computers do not look like people, this procedure also assumes that thinking is quite separate from doing. If intelligence requires manipulating physical objects in the environment, then the notion of behaviour deployed in the Turing Test will be too meagre. Turing's idea is that intelligence is a property of pure cogitation, so to speak. Behaviour limited to verbal communication is enough.

So the Turing Test represents one possible solution to the functionalist's problem. Not only does thought not require a physical structure like the one our brains possess. In addition, there is no independently specifiable internal constraint of any kind. The only requirement is an external one, specified by the imitation game.

Most functionalists regard this test as too crude. Unfortunately, it seems vulnerable to both type-1 and type-2 errors. That is, a thing that does not think can be mistakenly judged to have a mind and a thinking thing can be judged to lack a mind by this procedure (see Table 14.3).

In discussions of AI, there has been little attention to type-2 errors. Yet, it seems clear that human beings with minds can imitate the behaviour of mindless computers and so fool the interrogator into thinking that they lack minds. Of perhaps more serious concern is the possibility that a machine might have a mind, but have beliefs and desires so different from those of any human being that interrogators would quickly realize that they were not talking to a human being. The machine would flunk the Turing Test, because it cannot imitate human response patterns; it is another matter to conclude that the machine, therefore, does not have a mind at all.

The possibility of type-2 error, though real, has not been the focus of attention. Rather, in order to overcome the presumption that machines can't think, researchers in AI have been concerned to construct devices that pass the Turing Test. The question this raises is whether the test is vulnerable to type-1 errors.

One example that displays the possibility of type-1 error is due to Ned Block (1975). Suppose we could write down a tree structure in which every possible conversation that is five hours or less in duration is mapped out. We might trim this tree by only recording what an 'intelligent' respondent might say to an interrogator, leaving open whether the interrogator is 'intelligent' or not. This structure would be enormously large, larger than any current computer would be able to store. But let us ignore that limitation and suppose we put this tree structure into a computer.

By following this tree structure, the machine would interact with its interrogator in a way indistinguishable from the way in which an intelligent human being would do so. Yet the fact that the machine simply makes its way through this simple tree structure strongly suggests that the machine has no mental states at all.

One might object that the machine could be made to fail the Turing Test if the conversation pressed on beyond five hours. This is right, but now suppose that the tree is augmented in size, so that it encompasses all sensible conversations that are ten hours or less in duration. In principle, the time limit on the tree might be set at any finite size—four score and ten years if you like.

Block draws the moral that thinking is not fully captured by the Turing Test. What is wrong with this branching structure is not the behaviours it produces but how it produces them. Intelligence is not just the ability to answer questions in a way indistinguishable from that of an intelligent person. To call a behaviour 'intelligent' is to comment on how it is produced. Block concludes, rightly I think, that the Turing Test is overly behaviouristic.

In saying this, I am not denying that the Turing Test is useful. Obviously, behavioural evidence can be telling. If one wants to know where the weaknesses are in a simulation, one might try to discover where the outputs mimic and where they do not. But it is one thing for the Turing Test to provide fallible evidence about intelligence, something quite different for the test to define what it is to have a mind.

A large measure of what is right about Searle's (1980) much-discussed paper 'Minds, Brains, and Programs' reduces to this very point. In Searle's Chinese room example, someone who speaks no Chinese is placed in a room, equipped with a manual, each of whose entries maps a story in Chinese (S) and a question in Chinese about that story (Q) on to an answer in Chinese to that story (A). That is, the man in the room has a set of rules, each with the form

$$S + Q \rightarrow A.$$

Chinese stories are sent into the room along with questions about those stories, also written in Chinese. The person in the room finds the $S + Q$ pairing on his list, writes down the answer on to which the pair is mapped, and sends that message out of the room. The input/output behaviour of the room is precisely what one would expect of someone who understands Chinese stories and wishes to provide intelligent answers (in Chinese) to questions about them. Although the system will pass the Turing Test, Searle concludes that the system that executes this behaviour understands nothing of Chinese.

Searle does not specify exactly how the person in the room takes an input and produces an output. The details of the answer manual are left rather vague. But Block's example suggests that this makes all the difference. If the program is just a brute-force pairing of stories and questions on the one hand and answers on the other, there is little inclination to think that executing the program has anything to do with understanding Chinese. But if the manual more closely approximates what Chinese speakers do when they answer questions about stories, our verdict might change. Understanding is not definable in terms of the ability to answer questions; in addition, how one obtains the answers must be taken into account.

Searle (1980) considers one elaboration of this suggestion in the section of his paper called 'The Brain Simulator Reply (Berkeley and MIT)'. Suppose we simulate 'the actual sequence of neuron firings at the synapses of the brain of a native Chinese speaker when he understands stories in Chinese and gives answers to them'. A system constructed in this way would not just duplicate the stimulus/response pairings exemplified by someone who understands Chinese; in addition, such a system would closely replicate the internal processes mediating the Chinese speaker's input/output connections.

I think that Searle's reply to this objection is question-begging. He says 'the problem with the brain simulator is that it is simulating the wrong things about the brain. As long as it simulates only the formal structure of the sequence of neuron firings at the synapses, it won't have simulated what matters about the brain, namely its causal properties, its ability to produce intentional states.'

Although Searle does not have much of an argument here, it is important to recognize that the denial of his thesis is far from trivial. It is a conjecture that might or might not be right that the on/off states of a neuron, plus its network of connections with other neurons, exhaust what is relevant about neurons that allows them to form intentional systems. This is a meagre list of neuronal properties, and so the conjecture that it suffices for some psychological characteristic is a very strong one. Neurons have plenty of other characteristics; the claim that they are all irrelevant as far as psychology goes may or may not be true.

There is another way in which Searle's argument recognizes something true and important, but, I think, misinterprets it. Intentionality crucially involves the relationship of 'aboutness'. Beliefs and desires are about things in the world outside the mind. How does the state of an organism end up being about one object, rather than about another? What explains why some states have intentionality whereas others do not? One plausible philosophical proposal is that intentionality involves a causal connection between the world and the organism. Crudely put, the reason my term 'cat' refers to cats is that real cats are related to my use of that term in some specific causal way. Working out what the causal path must be has been a difficult task for the causal theory of reference. But leaving that issue aside, the claim that some sort of causal relation is necessary, though perhaps not sufficient, for at least some of the concepts we possess, has some plausibility.

If this world/mind relationship is crucial for intentionality, then it is clear why the formal manipulation of symbols cannot, by itself, suffice for intentionality. Such formal manipulation is purely internal to the system, but part of what makes a system have intentionality involves how the system and its states are related to the world external to the system.

Although conceding this point may conflict with some pronouncements by exponents of strong AI, it does not show that a thinking thing must be made of neuronal material. Consistent with the idea that intentionality requires a specific causal connection with the external world is the possibility that a silicon-chip computer could be placed in an environment and acquire intentional states by way of its interactions with the environment.

It is unclear what the acquisition process must be like, if the system is to end up with intentionality. But this lack of clarity is not specific to the question of whether computers could think; it also applies to the nature of human intentionality. Suppose that human beings acquire concepts like *cat* and *house*; that is, suppose these concepts are not innate. Suppose further that people normally acquire these concepts by causally interacting with real cats and houses. The question I wish to raise is whether human beings could acquire these concepts by having a neural implant performed at birth that suitably rewired their brains. A person with an implant would grow up and feel about the world the way any of us do who acquired the concepts by more normal means. If artificial interventions in human brains can endow various states with intentionality, it is hard to see why artificial interventions into silicon computers cannot also do the trick.

I have tried to extract two lessons from Searle's argument. First, there is the idea that the Turing Test is overly behaviouristic. The ability to mimic intelligent behaviour is not sufficient for having intelligence. Second, there is the idea that intentionality—aboutness—may involve a world/mind relationship of some specifiable sort. If this is right, then the fact that a machine (or brain) executes some particular program is not sufficient for it to have intentionality. Neither of these conclusions shows that silicon computers could not have minds.

What significance do these points have for the Artificial Life research programme? Can the biological properties of an organism be defined purely in terms of environment/behaviour pairings? If a biological property has this characteristic, the Turing Test will work better for it than the test works for the psychological property that Turing intended to describe. Let us consider photosynthesis as an example of a biological process. Arguably, a system engages in photosynthesis if it can harness the sun's energy to convert water and CO_2 into simple organic compounds (principally CH_2O). Plants (usually) do this in their chloroplasts, but this is just one way to do the trick. If this is right, either for photosynthesis or for other biological properties, then the first lesson I drew about the Turing Test in the context of philosophy of mind may actually provide a disanalogy between AI and AL. Behaviourism is a mistake in psychology, but it may be the right view to take about many biological properties.

The second lesson I extracted from Searle's argument concerned intentionality as a relationship between a mental state and something outside itself. It is the relation of aboutness. I argued that the execution of a program cannot be the whole answer to the question of what intentionality is.

Many biological properties and processes involve relationships between an organism (or part of an organism) and something outside itself. An organism reproduces when it makes a baby. A plant photosynthesizes when it is related to a light source in an appropriate way. A predator eats other organisms. Although a computer might replicate aspects of such processes that occur inside the system of interest, computers will not actually reproduce or photosynthesize or eat unless they are related to things outside themselves in the right ways. These processes involve actions—interactions with the environment; the computations that go on inside the skin are only part of the story. Here, then, is an analogy between AI and AL.

5. THE DANGER OF GOING TOO FAR

Functionalism says that psychological and biological properties can be abstracted from the physical details concerning how those properties are realized. The main problem for functionalism is to say how much abstraction is permissible. A persistent danger for functionalist theories is that they err on the side of being too liberal. This danger is especially pressing when the mathematical structure of a process is confused with its empirical content. This confusion can lead one to say that a system has a mind or is alive (or has some more specific constellation of psychological or biological properties) when it does not.

A simple example of how this fallacy proceeds may be instructive. Consider the Hardy–Weinberg Law in population genetics. It says what frequencies the diploid genotypes at a locus will exhibit, when there is random mating, equal numbers of males and females, and no selection or mutation. It is, so to speak, a 'zero-force law'—it describes what happens in a population if no evolutionary forces are at work (see Sober 1984). If p is the frequency of the A allele and q is the frequency of a (where $p + q = 1$), then in the circumstances just described, the frequencies of AA, Aa, and aa are p^2, $2pq$, and q^2, respectively.

Consider another physical realization of the simple mathematical idea involved in the Hardy–Weinberg Law. A shoe manufacturer produces brown shoes and black shoes. By accident, the assembly line has not kept the shoes together in pairs, but has dumped all the left shoes into one pile and all the right shoes into another. The shoe manufacturer wants to know what the result will be if a machine randomly samples from the two piles and assembles pairs of shoes. If p is the frequency of black shoes and q is the frequency of brown ones in each pile, then the expected frequency of the three possible pairs will be p^2, $2pq$, and q^2. Many other examples of this mathematical sort could be described.

Suppose we applied the Hardy–Weinberg Law to a population of *Drosophila*. These fruit flies are biological objects; they are alive and the Hardy–Weinberg Law describes an important fact about how they reproduce. As just noted, the same mathematical structure can be applied to shoes. But shoes are not alive; the process by which the machine forms pairs by random sampling is not a biological one.

I wish to introduce a piece of terminology: the Shoe/Fly Fallacy is the mistaken piece of reasoning embodied in the following argument:

Flies are alive.
Flies are described by law L.
Shoes are described by law L.

Hence, shoes are alive.

A variant of this argument focuses on a specific biological property—like reproduction—rather than on the generic property of 'being alive'.

Functionalist theories abstract away from physical details. They go too far—confusing mathematical form with biological (or psychological) subject-matter—when they commit the Shoe/Fly Fallacy. The result is an overly liberal conception of life (or mind).

The idea of the Shoe/Fly Fallacy is a useful corrective against overhasty claims that a particular artificial system is alive or exhibits some range of biological characteristics. If one is tempted to make such claims, one should try to describe a system that has the relevant formal characteristics but is clearly not alive. The Popperian attitude of attempting to falsify is a useful one.

Consider, for example, the recent phenomenon of computer viruses. Are these alive? These cybernetic entities can make their way into a host computer and take over some of the computer's memory. They also can 'reproduce' themselves and undergo 'mutation'. Are these mere metaphors, or should we conclude that computer viruses are alive?

To use the idea of the Shoe/Fly Fallacy to help answer this question, let us consider another, similar system that is not alive. Consider a successful chain letter. Because of its characteristics, it is attractive to its 'hosts' (i.e. to the individuals who receive them). These hosts then make copies of the letters and send them to others. Copying errors occur, so the letters mutate.

I do not see any reason to say that the letters are alive. Rather, they are related to host individuals in such a way that more and more copies of the letters are produced. If computer viruses do no more than chain letters do, then computer viruses are not alive either.

Note the 'if' in the last sentence. I do not claim that computer viruses, or something like them, cannot be alive. Rather, I say that the idea of the Shoe/Fly Fallacy provides a convenient format for approaching such questions in a suitably sceptical and Popperian manner.

6. FROM HUMAN COGNITION TO AI, FROM BIOLOGY TO AL

One of the very attractive features of AI is that it capitalizes on an independently plausible thesis about human psychology. A fruitful research programme about human cognition is based on the idea that cognition involves computational manipulations of representations. Perhaps some representations obtain their intentionality via a connection between mind and world. Once in place, these representations give rise to other representations by way of processes that exploit the formal (internal) properties of the representations. To the degree that computers can be built that form and manipulate representations, to that degree will they possess cognitive states.

Of course, very simple mechanical devices form and manipulate representations. Petrol gauges in cars and thermostats are examples, but it seems entirely wrong to say that they think. Perhaps the computational view can explain why this is true by further specifying which kinds of representations and which kinds of computational manipulations are needed for cognition.

Can the analogous case be made for the artificial-life research programme? Can an independent case be made for the idea that biological processes in naturally occurring organisms involve the formation and manipulation of representations? If this point can be defended for naturally occurring organisms, then to the degree that computers can form and manipulate representations in the right ways, to that degree will the AL research programme appear plausible.

Of course, human and animal psychology is part of human and animal biology. So it is trivially true that some biological properties involve the formation and manipulation of representations. But this allows AL to be no more than AI. The question, therefore, should be whether life processes other than psychological ones involve computations on representations.

For some biological processes, the idea that they essentially involve the formation and manipulation of representations appears plausible. Thanks to our understanding of DNA, we can see ontogenesis and reproduction as processes that involve representations. It is natural to view an organism's genome as a set of instructions for constructing the organism's phenotype. This idea becomes most plausible when the phenotypic traits of interest are relatively invariant over changes in the environment. The idea that genome represents phenotype must not run afoul of the fact that phenotypes are the result of a gene/environment interaction. By the same token, blueprints of buildings do not determine the character of a building in every detail. The building materials available in the environment and the skills of workers also play a role. But this does not stop us from thinking of the blueprint as a set of instructions.

In conceding that computers could exemplify biological characteristics like development and reproduction, I am not saying that any computers now do. In particular, computers that merely manipulate theories about growth and reproduction are not themselves participants in those processes. Again, the point is that a description of a bridge is not a bridge.

What of other biological properties and processes? Are they essentially computational? What of digestion? Does it involve the formation and manipulation of representations? Arguably not. Digestion operates on food particles; its function is to extract energy from the environment that the system can use. The digestive process, *per se*, is not computational.

This is not to deny that in some systems digestion may be influenced by computational processes. In human beings, if you are in a bad mood, this can cause indigestion. If the mental state is understood computationally, then digestion in this instance is influenced by computational processes. But this effect comes from without. This example does not undermine the claim that digestion is not itself a computational process.

Although I admit that this claim about digestion may be wrong, it is important that one not refute it by trivializing the concepts of representation and computation. Digestion works by breaking down food particles into various constituents. The process can be described in terms of a set of procedures that the digestive system follows. Is it not a short step, then, to describing digestion as the execution of a program? Since the program is a representation, will one not thereby have provided a computational theory of digestion?

To see what is wrong with this argument, we need to use a distinction that

Kant once drew in a quite different connection. It is the distinction between following a rule and acting in accordance with a rule. When a system follows a rule, it consults a representation; the character of this representation guides the system's behaviour. On the other hand, when a system acts in accordance with a rule, it does not consult a representation; rather, it merely behaves as if it had consulted the rule.

The planets move in ellipses around the sun. Are they following a rule or are they just acting in accordance with a rule? Surely only the latter. No representation guides their behaviour. This is why it is not possible to provide a computational theory of planetary motion without trivializing the ideas of computation and representation. I conjecture that the same may be true of many biological processes; perhaps digestion is a plausible example.

In saying that digestion is not a computational process, I am not saying that computers cannot digest. Planetary motion is not a computational process, but this does not mean that computers cannot move in elliptical orbits. Computers can do lots of things that have nothing to do with the fact that they are computers. They can be doorstops. Maybe some of them can digest food. But this has nothing to do with whether a computational model of digestion will be correct.

I have focused on various biological processes and asked whether computers can instantiate or participate in them. But what about the umbrella question? Can computers be alive? If Turing's question was whether computers can think, should not the parallel question focus on what it is to be alive, rather than on more fine-grained concepts like reproduction, growth, selection, and digestion?

I have left this question for last because it is the fuzziest. The problem is that biology seems to have little to tell us about what it is to be alive. This is not to deny that lots of detailed knowledge is available concerning various living systems. But it is hard to see which biological theories really tell us about the nature of life. Do not be misled by the fact that biology has lots to say about the characteristics of terrestrial life. The point is that there is little in the way of a principled answer to the question of which features of terrestrial life are required for being alive and which are accidental.

Actually, the situation is not so different in cognitive science. Psychologists and others have lots to tell us about this or that psychological process. They can provide information about the psychologies of particular systems. But psychologists do not seem to take up the question 'What is the nature of mind?' where this question is understood in a suitable, non-chauvinistic way.

Perhaps you are thinking that these are the very questions a philosopher should be able to answer. If the sciences ignore questions of such generality, then it is up to philosophy to answer them. I am sceptical about this. Although philosophers may help clarify the implications of various scientific theories, I really doubt that a purely philosophical answer to these questions is possible.

So if the sciences in question do not address them, we are pretty much out of luck.

On the other hand, I cannot see that it matters much. If a machine can be built that exemplifies various biological processes and properties, why should it still be interesting to say whether it is alive? This question should not preoccupy AL any more than the parallel question should be a hang-up for AI. If a machine can perceive, remember, desire, and believe, what remains of the question of whether it has a mind? If a machine can extract energy from its environment, grow, repair damage to its body, and reproduce, what remains of the issue of whether it is 'really' alive?

Again, it is important to not lose sight of the ifs in the previous two sentences. I am not saying that it is unimportant to ask what the nature of mind or the nature of life is. Rather, I am suggesting that these general questions be approached by focusing on more specific psychological and biological properties. I believe that this strategy makes the general questions more tractable; in addition, I cannot see that the general questions retain much interest after the more specific ones are answered.

7. CONCLUDING REMARKS

Functionalism, both in the study of mind and the study of life, is a liberating doctrine. It leads us to view human cognition and terrestrial organisms as examples of mind and life. To understand mind and life, we must abstract away from physical details. The problem is to do this without going too far.

One advantage that AL has over AI is that terrestrial life is in many ways far better understood than the human mind. The AL theorist can often exploit rather detailed knowledge of the way life processes are implemented in naturally occurring organisms; even though the goal is to generalize away from these examples, real knowledge of the base cases can provide a great theoretical advantage. Theorists in AI are usually not so lucky. Human cognition is not at all well understood, so the goal of providing a (more) general theory of intelligence cannot exploit a detailed knowledge of the base cases.

An immediate corollary of the functionalist thesis of multiple realizability is that biological and psychological problems are not to be solved by considering physical theories. Existing quantum mechanics is not the answer, nor do biological and psychological phenomena show that some present physical theory is inadequate. Functionalism decouples physics and the special sciences. This does not mean that functionalism is the correct view to take for each and every biological problem; perhaps some biological problems are physical problems in disguise. The point is that, if one is a functionalist about some biological process, one should not look to physics for much theoretical help.

The Turing Test embodies a behaviouristic criterion of adequacy. It is not plausible for psychological characteristics, though it may be correct for a number of biological ones. However, for virtually all biological processes, the behaviours required must be rather different from outputs printed on a tape. A desktop computer that is running a question/answer program is not reproducing, developing, evolving, or digesting. It does none of these things, even when the program describes the processes of reproduction, development, digestion, or evolution.

It is sometimes suggested that, when a computer simulation is detailed enough, it then becomes plausible to say that the computer is an instance of the objects and processes that it simulates. A computer simulation of a bridge can be treated as a bridge, when there are simulated people on it and a simulated river flowing underneath. By now I hope it is obvious why I regard this suggestion as mistaken. The problem with computer simulations is not that they are simplified representations, but that they are representations. Even a complete description of a bridge—one faithful in every detail—would still be a very different object from a real bridge.

Perhaps any subject-matter can be provided with a computer model. This merely means that a description of the dynamics can be encoded in some computer language. It does not follow from this that all processes are computational. Reproduction is a computational process because it involves the transformation of representations. Digestion does not seem to have this characteristic. The AL research program has plenty going for it; there is no need for overstatement.

REFERENCES

Block, N. (1975), 'Troubles with Functionalism', in W. Savage (ed.), *Perception and Cognition: Issues in the Foundations of Psychology* (Minnesota Studies in the Philosophy of Science, 9; Minneapolis: University of Minnesota Press).

—— (1981), 'Psychologism and Behaviorism', *Philosophical Review*, 90: 59–43.

Dennett, D. (1978), *Brainstorms* (Cambridge, Mass.: MIT Press).

Dretske, F. (1985), 'Machines and the Mental', *Proceedings and Addresses of the American Philosophical Association*, 59 (1985), 23–33.

Fisher, R. (1930), *The Genetical Theory of Natural Selection* (Oxford: Oxford University Press, 1930, repr. New York: Dover Books, 1958).

Fodor, J. (1968), *Psychological Explanation* (New York: Random House).

Lewontin, R. (1970), 'The Units of Selection', *Annual Review of Ecology and Systematics*, 1: 1–14.

Pattee, H. (1989), 'Simulations, Realizations, and Theories of Life', in C. Langton (ed.),

Artificial Life (Santa Fe Institute Studies in the Sciences of Complexity, Proceedings, 6; Redwood City, Calif.: Addison-Wesley), 63–78. (Repr. below as Ch. 15.)

Penrose, R. (1990), *The Emperor's New Mind* (Oxford: Oxford University Press).

Place, U. T. (1956), 'Is Consciousness a Brain Process?', *British Journal of Psychology*, 47: 44–50.

Putnam, H. (1967), 'The Nature of Mental States', in *Mind, Language and Reality* (Cambridge: Cambridge University Press, 1975).

Ryle, G. (1949), *The Concept of Mind* (New York: Barnes and Noble).

Searle, J. (1980), 'Minds, Brains, and Programs'. *Behavior and Brain Sciences*, 3: 417–57; repr. in Margaret A. Boden (ed.), *The Philosophy of Artificial Intelligence* (Oxford Readings in Philosophy; Oxford: Oxford University Press), 67–88.

Smart, J. J. C. (1959), 'Sensations and Brain Processes', *Philosophical Review*, 68: 141–56.

Sober, E. (1984), *The Nature of Selection* (Cambridge, Mass.: MIT Press).

—— (1985), 'Methodological Behaviorism, Evolution, and Game Theory', in J. Fetzer (ed.), *Sociobiology and Epistemology* (Dordrecht: Reidel), 181–200.

Turing, A. M. (1950), 'Computing Machinery and Intelligence', *Mind*, 59: 433–60; repr. in Margaret A. Boden (ed.), *The Philosophy of Artificial Intelligence* (Oxford Readings in Philosophy; Oxford: Oxford University Press), 40–66.

Wittgenstein, L. (1953), *Philosophical Investigations* (Oxford: Basil Blackwell).

15

SIMULATIONS, REALIZATIONS, AND THEORIES OF LIFE

H. H. PATTEE

The phrase 'artificial life', as interpreted by participants in the first Santa Fe workshop on A-Life, includes not only 'computer simulation', but also 'computer realization'. In the area of artificial intelligence, Searle (1980) has called the simulation school 'weak AI' and the realization school 'strong AI'. The hope of 'strong' artificial life was stated by Langton (1987): 'We would like to build models that are so lifelike that they would cease to be models of life and become examples of life themselves.' Very little has been said at the workshop about how we would distinguish computer simulations from realizations of life, and virtually nothing has been said about how these relate to theories of life, that is, how the living can be distinguished from the non-living. The aim of this chapter is to begin such a discussion.

I shall present three main ideas. First, simulations and realizations belong to different categories of modelling. Simulations are metaphorical models that symbolically 'stand for' something else. Realizations are literal, material models that implement functions. Therefore, accuracy in a simulation need have no relation to quality of function in a realization. Secondly, the criteria for good simulations and realizations of a system depend on our theory of the system. The criteria for good theories depend on more than mimicry, for example, Turing Tests. Lastly, our theory of living systems must include evolvability. Evolution requires the distinction between symbolic genotypes, material phenotypes, and selective environments. Each of these categories has characteristic properties that must be represented in artificial life (AL) models.

HOW UNIVERSAL IS A COMPUTER?

It was clear from the workshop that artificial life studies have closer roots in artificial intelligence and computational modelling than in biology itself. Biology is traditionally an empirical science that has very little use for theory. A biologist may well ask why anyone would believe that a deterministic machine designed only to rewrite bit strings according to arbitrary rules could actually realize life, evolution, and thought? We know, of course, that the source of this belief is the venerable Platonic ideal that form is more fundamental than substance. This has proven to be a healthy attitude in mathematics for thousands of years, and it is easily carried over to current forms of computation, since computers are defined and designed to rewrite formal strings according to arbitrary rules without reference to the substantive properties of any particular hardware, or even to what kind of physical laws are harnessed to execute the rules.

In the field of 'traditional' artificial intelligence (AI), this Platonic ontology has carried great weight, since intelligence has historically been defined only as a quality of abstract symbol manipulation rather than as a quality of perception and sensory-motor coordination. Until very recently, it has not been conventional usage to call a bat catching an insect, or a bird landing on a twig in the wind, intelligent behaviour. The AI establishment has seen such dynamical behaviour as largely a problem for physiology or robotics. Strong AI has maintained its Platonic idealism simply by defining the domain of 'cognitive activity' as equivalent to the domain of 'universal computation' and, indeed, many detailed arguments have been made to support this view (Newell 1980; Pylyshyn 1980).

Philosophically opposed to these rule-based formalists are the Gibsonian, law-based, ecological realists who assert that sensory-motor behaviour is not only intelligent, but that all perception and cognition can be described as dynamical events that are entirely lawful, and not dependent on 'information processing' in the computationalists' sense. The ecological realist view has suffered from lack of explicit theoretical models as well as lack of empirical evidence to support it. However, recently the realists' view has been greatly strengthened by explicit models of an ecological theory of movement (Kugler and Turvey 1987), and empirical evidence that chaotic neural-net dynamics is more significant than programmed sequences (Skarda and Freeman 1987).

A third emergent AI group is loosely formed by the neural network, connectionist, and parallel, distributed processor schools. This hyperactive group is currently enjoying such highly competitive popularity that the realization vs. simulation issue has so far mainly been discussed only by philosophers (Dreyfus and Dreyfus 1988). These concurrent, distributed models are more easily associated with dynamical analogue models than with logical programmed models, and therefore are more consistent with ecological realist than with the computationalist, but they are all a long way from biological realism.

Finally, there are the more biologically knowledgeable neuroscientists who do not claim either realizations or simulations of intelligence as their primary goal, but rather a model of the brain that is empirically testable in biological systems. Their main criticism of AI is that it has 'for the most part neglected the fundamental biology of the nervous system' (Reeke and Edelman 1988). This criticism undoubtedly will be aimed at artificial life as well. The crux of the issue, of course, is who decides what is fundamental about biology. This is where a theory of life must be decisive.

REALIZATIONS, SIMULATIONS, AND THEORIES

Artificial life is too young to have established such distinguishable schools of thought, but it cannot escape these fundamental ontological and epistemological controversies. Based on the presentations of the first artificial life workshop, I see the need to distinguish between (1) computer-dependent realizations of living systems, (2) computer simulations of living-systems behaviour, (3) theories of life that derive from simulations, and (4) theories of life that are testable only by computer simulations.

We all recognize the conventional distinctions in usages of realization, simulation, and theory. Roughly speaking, a realization is judged primarily by how well it can function as an implementation of a design specification. A realization is a literal, substantive, functional device. We know what this entails for computer hardware. The problem for artificial life is to determine what operational and functional mean. What is the operation or function of living? Strong AI has some advantage over strong AL, since by embracing the classical theory of intelligence involving only symbol manipulation, they may ignore all the substantive input and output devices. But since the classical theory of life requires a symbolic genotype, a material phenotype, and an environment, I can see only two possibilities for strong AL: (1) it can include robotics to realize the phenotype–environment interactions, or (2) it can treat the symbolic domain of the computer as an artificial environment in which symbolic phenotypic properties of artificial life are realized. One might object that (2) is not a realization of life since environment is only simulated. But we do not restrict life forms to the Earth environment or to carbon environments. Why should we restrict it to non-symbolic environments?

Here we run into a fundamental question of whether a formal domain is an adequate environment for emergence and novelty in evolution or whether the essential requirement for evolution is an open-ended, physical environment. And as with the question of whether formal systems can think, I believe the issue will come down to whether we claim 'soft' simulation of emergence or 'hard' realization of emergence, and I shall return to it later.

The concept of simulation covers too much ground to give comprehensive criteria for evaluation. All I need here are some ideas on how simulation depends on theory. Simulations are not judged as functional replacements, but by how well they generate similar morphologies or parallel behaviours of some specified aspects of the system. Simulations are metaphorical, not literal. Although we give focal attention to those attributes of the system being simulated, we also have a tacit awareness that other attributes of the system are not being simulated. Furthermore, there are extra features of the simulation medium that are not to be found in the system, and as in all metaphors, these extra features are essential for the simulation to be effective. They serve as the frame setting off the painting, or the syntax that defines the language (Kelly and Keil 1987). For these reasons, there is never any doubt that the simulation, no matter how accurate, is not the same as the thing simulated. Of course, the choice of what aspects of a system are simulated depends on what is considered significant, and significance cannot be isolated from one's knowledge and theory of the system. Lacking a conceptual theory, a good simulation at least must represent the essential functions of a realization of the system (Harnad 1987).

Theories are judged by a much more comprehensive range of criteria, from the concrete test of how well they can predict specific values for the observables of the system being modelled, to abstract tests such as universality, conceptual coherence, simplicity, and elegance. As Polanyi (1964) has emphasized, the delicacy of these criteria preclude any formal test, and even evade literal definition. A theory generally must go well beyond the simulation or realization of a system in terms of its conceptual coherence and power. We accept the idea that there are many valid simulations and realizations of a given behaviour, but we think of theory more exclusively as the best we have at any given time. Early technologies often achieve functional realizations before constructing an explicit theory.

The epitome of formal theoretical structures is physics. Here we have mathematical models of great generality and formal simplicity, that often require immense computations to predict the results of measurements, but that do not have any other perceptual or behavioural similarities with the world they model. For example, the classical universe is conceived as continuous, infinite, and rate-dependent, but is represented by discrete, finite, rate-independent formalisms. In other words, it would not be normal usage to call physical theory a 'simulation' of physical events. In fact, these striking dissimilarities between the mathematical models and what they represent have puzzled philosophers since Zeno, with his paradox of motion, and still are a concern for physicists (Wigner 1960).

Historically, mathematical computation has been thought of as a tool used to give numerical results to physical theory, not as a tool for simulation. However, computers are now more frequently being used as a type of analogue model where visual images are the significant output rather than numerical solutions of equations. We now find that the study of dynamical systems by computer often blurs the distinction between theories and simulations. Cellular automata, fractals, and chaos were largely dependent on computer simulations for their rediscovery as useful theories of physical behaviour, and the role of computation in these cases might be better called 'artificial physics', rather than predictive calculation from theories. In cellular automata and relaxation networks, the computer has become an analogue of physical dynamics, even though its operation is discrete and sequential. Many of the controversies in AI result from the multiple use of computation as a conceptual theory, as an empirical tool, as simulation, and as realization of thought. AL models will have to make these distinctions.

THE LIMITATIONS OF THEORY-FREE SIMULATIONS

The field of artificial life should learn from the mistakes made in the older field of artificial intelligence, which in my view has allowed the power of computer simulation to obscure the basic requirements of a scientific theory. The computer is, indeed, the most powerful tool for simulation that man has invented. Computers, in some sense, can simulate everything except the ineffable. The fact that a universal computer can simulate any activity that we can explicitly describe seems in principle undeniable, and in the realm of recursive activities, the computer, in practice, can do more than the brain can explicitly describe, as in the case of fractal patterns and chaotic dynamics.

This remarkable property of computational universality is what led, or as I claim, misled, the strong AI school to the view that computation can realize intelligent thought because all realizations of universality must operate within this one domain. This view is expressed by Newell and Simon as the Physical Symbol System Hypothesis which, in essence, states that 'this form of symbolic behavior is all there is; in particular that it includes human symbolic behavior' (Newell 1980: 141). Now this hypothesis is in effect a theory of cognitive activity; the problem is that it has not been verified by the delicate criteria for theory, but only by coarse Turing Tests for operational simulation. In other words, the fact that human thought can be simulated by computation is treated as evidence in support of the Physical Symbol System theory. But since virtually everything can be simulated by a computer, it is not really evidence for the theory at all. One could argue as well that, since physical behaviour such as planetary motion or wave propagation can be simulated by sequential computation, it follows that rewriting strings according to rules is a realization of physics. As long as the computational theory of cognition was the 'only straw afloat', a working simulation did appear as evidence in favour of the theory, but now with the evidence that concurrent, distributed networks can also simulate cognitive behaviour, we have a promising alternative theory of cognition. It is now clear that deciding between these theories will take more than benchmark or Turing Test comparisons of their operation. Both simulations and realizations must be evaluated in terms of a theory of the brain, and the empirical evidence for that theory.

Artificial life modellers should not fall into this trap of arguing that working simulations are by themselves evidence for or against theories of life. Computer users, of all people, should find it evident that there are many alternative ways to successfully simulate any behaviour. It should also be evident, especially to computer manufacturers, that while there are many hardware realizations that are equivalent for executing formal rules, there are strong artificial and natural selection processes that determine survival of a computer species.

This illustrates what I see as a real danger in the popular view of the computer as a universal simulator. Indeed, it is symbolically universal, but as in the case of AI, this universal power to simulate will produce more formal models that can be selectively eliminated by empirical evidence alone. As a consequence, too much energy can be wasted arguing over the relative merits of models without any decision criteria. This is where theory must play an essential role in evaluating all our intellectual models. At the same time, when we are modelling life as a scientific enterprise, we must be careful not explicitly or tacitly to impose our rational theories and other cultural constraints on how life attains its characteristic structures and behaviours. In particular, whether we use natural or artificial environments, we must allow only universal physical laws and the theory of natural selection to restrict the evolution of artificial life. This means that simulations that are dependent on *ad hoc* and special-purpose rules and constraints for their mimicry cannot be used to support theories of life.

SIMULATIONS DO NOT BECOME REALIZATIONS

There is a further epistemological danger in the belief that a high-quality simulation can become a realization—that we can perfect our computer simulations of life to the point that they come alive. The problem, as we stated, is that there is a categorical difference between the concept of a realization that is a literal, substantial replacement, and the concept of simulation that is a metaphorical representation of specific structure or behaviour, but that also requires specific differences which allow us to recognize it as 'standing for' but not realizing the system. In these terms, a simulation that becomes more and more 'lifelike' does not at some degree of perfection become a realization of life. Simulations, in other words, are in the category of symbolic forms, not material substances. For example, in physics the simulation of trajectories by more and more accurate computation never results in realization of motion. We are not warmed by the simulation of thermal motions, or as Aristotle said, 'That which moves does not move by counting.'[1]

Simulation of any system implies a mapping from observable aspects of the system to corresponding symbolic elements of the simulation. This mapping is called measurement in physics and in most other sciences. Since measurement can never be made with absolute accuracy, the quality of simulations must be judged by additional criteria based on a theory of the system. Measurement presents a serious conceptual problem in physics, since it bridges the domains of known laws and unknown states of the system (Wigner 1967). Even in classical physics there is no theory of this bridge, and in quantum theory the measurement problem is presently incomprehensible (Wheeler and Zurek 1983). The practical situation is that measurement can be directly realized in physics, but it cannot presently be simulated by physical laws alone. By contrast, although a measurement might be simulated by computer, it can never be realized by computation alone. The process of measurement in cognitive systems begins with the sensory transducers, but how deeply the process penetrates into the brain before it is completed is not understood. At one extreme, we have computationalists who say that measurement is completed at the sensory transducers, and that all the rest is explicit symbol manipulation (Pylyshyn 1980). At the other extreme are physicists who consider the consciousness of the observer as the ultimate termination of a measurement (von Neumann 1955; Wigner 1967). A more common view is that neural cell assemblies that are large enough to be feature detectors may be said to measure events, but we are still a long way from a consensus on a theory of perception or a theory of measurement.

THE SYMBOL–MATTER PROBLEM

The molecular facts of the genetic code, protein synthesis, and enzymatic control form an impressive empirical base, but they do not constitute a theory of how symbolic forms and material structures must interact in order to evolve. That is, the facts do not distinguish the essential rules and structures from the frozen accidents. The only type of theory that can help us make this distinction for artificial life is the theory of evolution, and in its present state it is by no means adequate.

[1] *Physics*, Bk, viii, ch. 8, quoted in H. Weyl, *Philosophy, Mathematics, and Natural Science* (Princeton: Princeton University Press, 1949), 54.

Von Neumann's (1966) kinematic description of the logical requirements for evolvable self-replication should be a paradigm for artificial-life study. He chose the evolution of complexity as the essential characteristic of life that distinguishes it from non-life, and then argued that symbolic instructions and universal construction were necessary for heritable, open-ended evolution. He did not pursue this theory by attempting a realization, but instead turned to formalization by cellular automata. This attempt to formalize self-replication should also serve as a warning to AL research. Von Neumann issued the warning himself quite clearly: 'By axiomatizing automata in this manner, one has thrown half the problem out the window and it may be the more important half' (1966: 77). By 'half the problem' von Neumann meant the theory of the molecular phenotype. I am even more sceptical than von Neumann. I would say that by formalization of life, one may be throwing out the whole problem, that is, the problem of the relation of symbol and matter. This is one issue that AL must address. To what extent can a formal system clarify the symbol–matter relation? To what extent is the evolutionary nature of life dependent on measurements of a material environment?

The Physical Symbol System Hypothesis is, in my view, an empirically obvious half-truth. We, indeed, can construct symbol systems from matter, the computer and brain being impressive examples. The converse is not true, that matter can be constructed from symbols, since this would violate physical laws. However, we must also give full recognition to the Evolutionary Hypothesis that under the symbolic control of genotypes, material phenotypes in an environment can realize endless varieties of structures and behaviours. We, therefore, can summarize the following three symbol–matter possibilities: (1) we can simulate everything by universal symbol systems, (2) we can realize universal symbol systems with material constructions, and (3) we can realize endless types of structures and behaviours by symbolic constraints on matter. But we must also accept the fundamental impossibility: we cannot realize material systems with symbols alone. Evolving genes of natural living systems have harnessed matter to realize an enormous variety of structures and behaviours. What we need to learn from artificial-life studies is the extent to which a simulated environment can provide artificial organisms with the potential for realizing emergent evolution.

WEAK OR STRONG ARTIFICIAL EVOLUTION?

This brings us to the central question that is bound to be raised in AL studies. How should we respond to the claim that a computer system is a new form of life and not a mere simulation? According to what is known to be universal in present-day life and evolution, I would require the AL realization to include the genotype-phenotype-environment distinctions as well as the corresponding mutability, heritability, and natural selection of neo-Darwinian theory. I would further require, with von Neumann and others, that a realization of life should have the emergent or novel evolutionary behaviour that goes beyond adaptation to an environment. I do not believe we presently have a theory of evolution that is explicit enough to decide the question of whether a formal environment like a computer can realize evolutionary novelty, or merely simulate it; however, let us reconsider the question for physics models.

We need to return to the distinctions between simulations, realizations, and theories to clarify what aspects of theory are necessary to evaluate computational simulations and realizations. In particular, we need to look more closely at the relation of computation to physical theory. We saw that the property of universality in computation theory has been claimed as a central argument for strong AI (Newell 1980). I believe that computational universality can only be used to claim that computers can simulate everything that can be represented in a symbolic domain, that is, in some language. Physical theories also claim universality within their domains, but these two usages of universality are completely different since they refer to different domains. The domain of physical theory is the observable world in which measurements define the state of the system. To achieve universality in physical theories, the form of the laws must satisfy so-called conservation, invariance, or symmetry principles. These theoretical principles of universality place exceedingly powerful restrictions on the forms of physical theories. By contrast, universality in computation corresponds to unrestricted forms of symbolic rewriting rules, and has nothing whatsoever to do with the laws of physics. Indeed, to achieve symbolic universality, even the hardware must not reflect the laws of physics, but only the rules imposed by the artificial constraints of its logic elements. It is only by constructing a program of additional rules reflecting the physical theory that a computer can be said to simulate physics. The point is that the quality of this type of simulation of physics clearly depends on the quality of the theory of physics that is simulated. Precisely because the computer is symbolically universal, it can simulate Ptolemaic epicycles, Newton's laws, or relativistic laws with equal precision. In fact, we know that even without laws, we can find a statistical program that simply 'simulates' behaviour from the raw observational data.

Why should this situation be fundamentally different for a computer simulating life? I do not think it is different for simulations of this type that are based on explicit theories. Large parts of what is called theoretical biology are simulations of physical laws under particular biological constraints. Although this type of reduction of life to physical laws is challenging, there is very little doubt that with enough empirical knowledge of the biological constraints, and a big enough computer, such a simulation is always possible, although not with Laplacean determinism. No one doubts that life obeys physical laws.

However, in the cases of cellular automata and chaotic dynamics, we have seen other forms of modelling that are not based on numerical solutions of equations, or derived from natural laws of motion. The artificial 'laws' of these models are the computer's local rules, although the behaviour of the model is an analogue of the physical behaviour of the natural environment. As I said earlier, these simulations are appropriately called artificial physics. There is no reason why we cannot create a population of artificial cells evolving in such an artificial environment. I proposed this type of model some twenty years ago, and Conrad (Conrad and Pattee 1970) simulated an entire artificial ecosystem to study the evolution of artificial organisms. Even though the artificial environment of his ecological simulation was almost trivially simple, the populational behaviour of the biota appeared to be chaotic, although we did not know the significance of chaos at that time. However, in spite of biotic behaviour that was unendingly novel in the chaotic sense, it was also clear that the environment was too simple to produce interesting emergent behaviour. The 'reality' of the organism, therefore, is intrinsically dependent on the 'reality' of its environment. In other words, the emergence of chaotic behaviour is not an adequate model of evolutionary emergence.

THREE LEVELS OF EMERGENT BEHAVIOUR

Emergence as a classical philosophical doctrine was the belief that there will arise in complex systems new categories of behaviour that cannot be derived from the system elements. The disputes arise over what 'derived from' must entail. It has not been a popular philosophical doctrine, since it suggests a vitalistic or metaphysical component to explanation which is not scientifically acceptable. However, with the popularization of mathematical models of complex morphogeneses, such as Thom's (1975) catastrophe theory, Prigogine's (1970) dissipative structures, Mandelbrot's (1977) fractals, and the more profound recognition of the generality of symmetry-breaking instabilities and chaotic dynamics, the concept of emergence has become scientifically respectable.

In spite of the richness of these formal concepts, I do not believe they convey the full biological essence of emergence. They are certainly a good start. Symmetry-breaking is crucial for models of the origin of the genetic code (Eigen 1971), and for many levels of morphogenesis (Kauffman 1986). Many biological structures and behaviours that are called frozen accidents fall into this category, that is, a chance event that persists because it is stabilized by its environment (e.g. driving on the right side of the road).

However, the counter-claim can be made that frozen accidents are not fully emergent, since the frozen behaviour is one of the known possible configurations of the formal domain, and therefore not an entirely novel structure. In the normal course of these arguments, the sceptical emergentist proposes a higher level of functional complexity, and the optimistic modeller proposes a more complex formal domain or artificial environment to try to simulate it.

The concept of emergence in AL presents the same type of ultimate complexity as does the concept of consciousness in AI. Critics of AI have often used the concept of strong consciousness as the acid test for a realization of thought as distinguished from a simulation of thought (Reeke and Edelman 1988), but no consensus or decidable theory exists on what a test of strong consciousness might entail. Similarly, the concept of strong emergence might be used as the acid test for a realization of life as distinguished from a simulation, but again, no consensus exists on how to recognize strong emergent behaviour. If one takes an optimistic modeller's view, both consciousness and emergence can be treated as inherently weak concepts, that is, as currently perceived illusions resulting from our ignorance of how things really work, that is, lack of data or incomplete theories. The history of science in one sense supports this view as more and more of these mysteries yield to empirical exploration and theoretical description. One, therefore, could claim that consciousness and emergence are just our names for those areas of awareness that are presently outside the domain of scientific theory.

However, more critical scientists will point out that physical theory is bounded, if not in fact largely formed, by impotency principles which define the epistemological limits of any theory, and that mathematical formalisms also have their incompleteness and undecidability theorems. There is, therefore, plenty of room for entirely unknown and fundamentally unpredictable types of emergence.

In any case, there are at least two other levels of emergence beyond symmetry-breaking and chaos that AL workers need to distinguish. The first is best known at the cognitive level, but could also occur at the genetic level. It is usually called creativity when it is associated with high-level symbolic activity. I shall call the more general concept semantic emergence. We all have a rough idea of what this means, but what AL needs to consider is the simplest level of evolution where such a concept is important. We must distinguish the syntactical emergence of symmetry-breaking and chaotic dynamics from the semantic emergence of non-dynamical symbol systems which stand for a referent. I distinguish dynamical from non-dynamical systems by the rate-dependence and continuity of the former. By contrast, symbol systems are intrinsically rate-independent, and discrete (Pattee 1985). That is, the meaning of a gene, a sentence or a computation does not depend on how fast it is processed, and the processing is in discrete steps. At the cognitive level, we have many heuristic processes that produce semantic emergence, from simple estimation, extrapolation, and averaging, to abstraction, generalization, and induction. The important point is that semantic emergence operates on existing data structures that are the result of completed measurements or observations. No amount of classification or reclassification of these data can realize a new measurement.

This leads to the third type of emergence, which I believe is the most important for evolution. I will simply call it measurement itself, but this does not help much because, as I indicated, measurement presents a fundamental problem in physics as well as biology (Pattee 1985). In classical physics, measurement is a primitive act—a pure realization that has no relation to the theory or to laws except to determine the initial conditions. However, in quantum theory measurement is an intrinsic part of the theory, so where the system being measured stops and the measuring device begins is crucial.

Here again, von Neumann (1955) was one of the first to discuss measurement as a fundamental problem in quantum theory, and to propose a consistent mathematical framework for addressing it. The problem is determining when measurement occurs. That is, when, in the process of measuring a physical system, does the description of a system by physical laws cease to be useful, and the result of the measurement become information? Von Neumann pointed out that the laws are reversible in time, and that measurement is intrinsically irreversible. But since all measuring devices, including the senses, are physical systems, in principle they can be described by physical laws, and therefore as long as the system is following the reversible laws, no measurement occurs. Von Neumann proposed, and many physicists agreed at the time, that the ultimate limit of this lawful description may be the consciousness of the observer (Wigner 1967). Presently, there seems to be more of a consensus that any form of irreversible 'record' can complete a measurement, but the problem of establishing objective criteria for records remains a problem (Wheeler and Zurek 1983).

CAN WE ARTIFICIALLY EVOLVE NEW MEASUREMENTS?

I wish to suggest that new measurements be considered as one of the more fundamental test cases for emergent behaviour in artificial-life models. For this purpose, we may define a generalized measurement as a record stored in the organism of some type of classification of the environment. This classification must be realized by a measuring device constructed by the organism (Pattee 1985). The survival of the organism depends on the choice and quality of these classifications, and the evolution of the organism will depend on its continuing invention of new devices that realize new classifications.

Now the issue of emergence becomes a question of what constitutes a measurement. Several of the simulations at the first AL workshop have produced autonomous classifications of their artificial environments. Hogeweg (1988) has made this non-goal-directed classification her primary aim. Autonomous classification is also demonstrated by Pearson's model of cortical mapping (Pearson *et al.* 1987). However, from the point of view of measurement theory, these models do not begin with measurement, but only with the results of measurements, that is, with symbolic data structures. I therefore would call these realizations of semantic emergence in artificial environments. It is clear, however, that none of these reclassifications, in themselves, can result in a new measurement, since that would require the construction of a new measuring device, that is, a realization of measurement.

Biological evolution is not limited to reclassification of the results of existing measurements, since one of the primary processes of evolution is the construction of new measuring devices. The primitive concept of measurement should not be limited to mapping patterns to symbols, but should include the mapping of patterns to specific actions, as in the case of enzymatic catalysis (Pattee 1985). The essential condition for this measurement mapping is that it be arbitrarily assignable, and not merely a consequence of physical or chemical laws. We therefore can see that the ability of a single cell to construct a new enzyme enables it to recognize a new aspect of its environment that could not have been 'induced' or otherwise discovered from its previously recognized patterns. In the same way, human intelligence has found new attributes of the environment by constructing artificial measuring devices like microscopes, X-ray films, and particle accelerators and detectors. This type of substantive emergence is entirely out of the domain of symbolic emergence, so we cannot expect to realize this natural type of evolutionary emergence with computers alone. The question that should motivate AL research is how usefully we can simulate the process of measurement in artificial environments. As I have argued, the answer to this question will require a theory of measurement.

CONCLUSIONS

The field of artificial life has begun with a high public profile, but if it is to maintain scientific respectability, it should adopt the highest critical standards of the established sciences. This means that it must evaluate its models by the strength of its theories of living systems, and not by technological mimicry alone. The high quality of computer simulations and graphics displays can provide a new form of artificial empiricism to test theories more efficiently, but this same quality also creates illusions. The question is one of the claims we make. The history of artificial intelligence should serve as a warning. There is nothing wrong with a good illusion as long as one does not claim it is reality. A simulation of life can be very instructive both empirically and theoretically, but we must be explicit about what claims we make for it.

Again, learning from the mistakes of AI, and using our natural common sense that is so difficult to even simulate, the field of AL should pay attention to the enormous knowledge base of biology. In particular, AL should not ignore the universals of cell structure, behaviour, and evolution without explicit reasons for doing so. At present these include the genotype, phenotype, environment relations, the mutability of the gene, the constructability of the phenotype under genetic constraints, and the natural selection of populations by the environment.

I have proposed the process of measurement as a test case for the distinction between simulation and realization of evolutionary behaviour. This is not because we know how to describe measurements precisely, but because new measurements are one requirement for emergent evolution. We know at least that measurement requires the memory-controlled construction of measuring devices by the organism, but this is obviously not an adequate criterion to distinguish a simulated measurement from a realization of a measurement. To make such a distinction will require a much clearer theory of measurement. The study of artificial life may lead, therefore, to new insight to the epistemological problem of measurement as well as to a sharper distinction between the living and the non-living.

REFERENCES

Conrad, M., and Pattee, H. (1970), 'Evolution Experiments with an Artificial Ecosystem', *Journal of Theoretical Biology*, 28: 393–409.

Dreyfus, H. L., and Dreyfus, S. E. (1988), 'Making a Mind versus Modelling a Brain', *Daedalus*, 117: 15–44.

Eigen, M. (1971), 'Self-Organization of Matter and Evolution of Biological Macromolecules', *Naturwissenschaften*, 58: 465–522.

Harnad, S. (1987), 'Minds, Machines, and Searle', in id. (ed.), *Categorical Perception: The Groundwork of Cognition* (Cambridge: Cambridge University Press), 1–14.

Hogeweg, P. (1988), 'MIRROR beyond MIRROR, Puddles of LIFE', in C. Langton (ed.), *Artificial Life* (Santa Fe Institute Studies in the Sciences of Complexity, Proceedings, 6; Redwood City, Calif.: Addison-Wesley), 297–316.

Kauffman, S. (1986), 'Autocatalytic Sets of Proteins', *Journal of Theoretical Biology*, 119: 1–24.

Kelly, M. H., and Keil, F. C. (1987), 'Metaphor Comprehension and Knowledge of Semantic Domains', *Metaphor and Symbolic Activity*, 2: 33–55.

Kugler, P., and Turvey, M. (1987), *Information, Natural Law, and the Self-Assembly of Rhythmic Movement* (Hillsdale, NJ: Erlbaum).

Langton, C. (1987), 'Studying Artificial Life with Cellular Automata', *Physica D*, 22: 120–49.

Mandelbrot, B. (1977), *Fractals: Form, Chance, and Dimensions* (San Francisco: W. H. Freeman).

Newell, A. (1980), 'Physical Symbol Systems', *Cognitive Science*, 4: 135–83.

Pattee, H. (1985), 'Universal Principles of Measurement and Language Functions in Evolving Systems', in John Casti and Anders Karlqvist (eds.), *Complexity, Language, and Life: Mathematical Approaches* (Berlin: Springer-Verlag), 168–281.

—— (1988), 'Instabilities and Information in Biological Self-Organization', in F. E. Yates (ed.), *Self-Organizing Systems: The Emergence of Order* (New York: Plenum).

Pearson, J., Finkel, L., and Edelman, G. (1987), 'Plasticity in the Organization of Adult Cerebral Cortical Maps: A Computer Simulation Based on Neuronal Group Selection', *Journal of Neuroscience*, 7/12: 4209–23.

Polanyi, M. (1964), *Personal Knowledge* (New York: Harper-Row).

Prigogine, I. (1970), *From Being to Becoming* (San Francisco: W. H. Freeman).

Pylyshyn, Z. (1980), 'Computation and Cognition: Issues in the Foundations of Cognitive Science', *Behavioral and Brain Sciences*, 3: 111–69.

Reeke, G., and Edelman, G. (1988), 'Real Brains and Artificial Intelligence', *Daedalus*, 17: 143–74.

Searle, J. (1980), 'Minds, Brains, and Programs', *Behavior and Brain Sciences*, 3: 417–57; repr. in Margaret A. Boden (ed.), *The Philosophy of Artificial Intelligence* (Oxford Readings in Philosophy; Oxford: Oxford University Press, 67–88).

Skarda, C. A., and Freeman, W. J. (1987), 'How Brains Make Chaos in Order to Make Sense of the World', *Behavioral and Brain Sciences*, 10: 161–95.

Thom, R. (1975), *Structural Stability and Morphogenesis* (Reading, Mass.: W. A. Benjamin).

von Neumann, J. (1955), *The Mathematical Foundations of Quantum Mechanics* (Princeton: Princeton University Press).

—— (1966), *The Theory of Self-Reproducing Automata*, ed. A. W. Burks (Urbana, Ill.: University of Illinois Press).

Wheeler, J. A., and Zurek, W. H. (1983), *Quantum Theory and Measurement* (Princeton: Princeton University Press).

Wigner, E. P. (1960), 'The Unreasonable Effectiveness of Mathematics in the Natural Sciences', *Communications in Pure and Applied Mathematics*, 13: 1–14.

—— (1964), 'Events, Laws of Nature, and Invariance Principles', *Science*, 145: 995–9.

—— (1967), 'The Problem of Measurement', *Symmetries and Reflections* (Bloomington, Ind.: Indiana University Press).

NOTES ON THE CONTRIBUTORS

MARK A. BEDAU is Associate Professor of Philosophy at Reed College.

MARGARET A. BODEN is Professor of Philosophy and Psychology at the University of Sussex (School of Cognitive and Computing Sciences).

RICHARD M. BURIAN is Director of the Center for the Study of Science in Society and Professor of Science Studies and Philosophy at Virginia Polytechnic Institute and State University.

ANDY J. CLARK is Reader in Philosophy in the School of Cognitive and Computing Sciences, University of Sussex. Until summer 1996 he is Visiting Professor in the Philosophy/Neuroscience/Psychology Research Program at Washington University in St. Louis, USA.

PETER GODFREY-SMITH is Assistant Professor of Philosophy in the Department of Philosophy, Stanford University.

HORST HENDRIKS-JANSEN's book *Catching Ourselves in the Act*: *Situated Activity, Interactive Emergence, and Human Thought* will be published in 1996 by MIT Press. His address is: 2 Burlesbridge Cottages, Dippenhall, Farnham, Surrey, GU10 5DN, England.

DAVID KIRSH is Associate Professor in the Department of Cognitive Science at the University of California at San Diego.

CHRIS LANGTON is Research Professor and director of the Artificial Life Program at the Santa Fe Institute, New Mexico.

DAVID MCFARLAND is Reader in Animal Behaviour and Fellow of Balliol College, University of Oxford.

GARETH B. MATTHEWS is Professor of Philosophy at the University of Massachusetts, Amherst.

JOHN MAYNARD SMITH is Emeritus Professor of Biology at the University of Sussex.

HOWARD H. PATTEE is Professor of Systems Science in the Department of Systems Science and Industrial Engineering, T. J. Watson School of Engineering and Applied Science, State University of New York at Binghamton.

THOMAS S. RAY is Associate Professor of Tropical Ecology at the School of Life and Health Sciences, and Associate Professor of Digital Biology at the Department of Computer and Information Science, University of Delaware.

ROBERT C. RICHARDSON is Professor of Philosophy at the University of Cincinnati.

ELLIOTT SOBER is Hans Reichenbach Professor of Philosophy at the University of Wisconsin, Madison.

MICHAEL WHEELER is a Research Fellow at Christ Church, Oxford.

SELECTED BIBLIOGRAPHY

BOOKS

Introductory texts are asterisked.

BEDAU, M. A. (in press), *Evolution, Life, and Mind: The Emerging Implications of Artificial Life* (Cambridge, Mass.: MIT Press).

* BRAITENBERG, V. (1984), *Vehicles: Experiments in Synthetic Psychology* (Cambridge, Mass.: MIT Press).

* CLARK, A. (forthcoming), *Being There: Putting Mind, Body, and World Together Again.*

* CLIFF, D. (in press), *Artificial Intelligence or Artificial Insects?* (provisional title) (Cambridge, Mass.: MIT Press).

—— HARVEY, I., and HUSBANDS, P. (in preparation), *Evolutionary and Adaptive Systems* (provisional title) (Cambridge, Mass.: MIT Press).

* COHEN, J., and STEWART, I. (1994), *The Collapse of Chaos: Discovering Simplicity in a Complex World* (London: Penguin).

* DAWKINS, R. (1986), *The Blind Watchmaker* (Harlow: Longman).

* —— (1995), *River Out of Eden* (London: Weidenfeld and Nicolson).

DENNETT, D. C. (1995), *Darwin's Dangerous Idea: Evolution and the Meaning of Life* (New York: Simon and Schuster; London: Allen Lane, The Penguin Press).

DEPEW, D. J., and WEBER, B. H. (1994), *Darwinism Evolving: Systems Dynamics and the Genealogy of Natural Selection* (Cambridge, Mass.: MIT Press).

DYSON, F. (1985), *The Origins of Life* (Cambridge: Cambridge University Press).

* EMMECHE, C. (1994), *The Garden in the Machine* (Princeton: Princeton University Press).

FRAZER, J. (1995), *An Evolutionary Architecture* (London: Architectural Association).

* GARDNER, M. (1982), *Wheels, Life, and Other Mathematical Amusements* (San Francisco: W. H. Freeman).

* GELL-MANN, M. (1994), *The Quark and the Jaguar: Adventures in the Simple and the Complex* (London: Little Brown).

GIBSON, J. J. (1979), *The Ecological Approach to Visual Perception* (Boston: Houghton Mifflin).

HENDRIKS-JANSEN, H. (in press), *Catching Ourselves in the Act: Situated Activity, Interactive Emergence, and Human Thought* (Cambridge, Mass.: MIT Press).

HOLLAND, J. H., HOLYOAK, K. J., NISBETT, R. E., and THAGARD, P. R. (1986) (eds.), *Induction: Processes of Inference, Learning, and Discovery* (Cambridge, Mass.: MIT Press).

KAUFFMAN, S. A. (1993), *The Origins of Order: Self-Organization and Selection in Evolution* (Oxford: Oxford University Press).

* KELLY, K. (1994), *Out of Control: The Rise of Neo-biological Civilization* (Reading, Mass.: Addison-Wesley).

* LEVY, S. (1992), *Artificial Life: The Quest for a New Creation* (New York: Random House).

MATURANA, H. R., and VARELA, F. J. (1980), *Autopoiesis and Cognition: The Realization of the Living* (Boston: Reidel).

MATURANA, H. R., and VARELA, F. J. (1987), *The Tree of Knowledge: The Biological Roots of Human Understanding* (Boston: New Science Library).

* MAZLISH, B. (1993), *The Fourth Discontinuity: The Co-evolution of Humans and Machines* (New Haven: Yale University Press).

MINSKY, M. L. (1985), *The Society of Mind* (New York: Simon and Schuster).

* MORAVEC, H. (1988), *Mind Children: The Future of Robot and Human Intelligence* (Cambridge, Mass.: Harvard University Press).

SIMON, H. A. (1969), *The Sciences of the Artificial* (Cambridge, Mass.: MIT Press).

SOBER, E. (1993), *Philosophy of Biology* (Oxford: Oxford University Press).

THOMPSON, D. W. (1961), *On Growth and Form*, abridged edn., ed. J. T. Bonner (first publ. 1917) (Cambridge: Cambridge University Press).

TODD, S., and LATHAM, W. (1992), *Evolutionary Art and Computers* (London: Academic Press).

VARELA, F. J., THOMPSON, E., and ROSCH, E. (1991), *The Embodied Mind: Cognitive Science and Human Experience* (Cambridge, Mass.: MIT Press).

* WALDROP, M. M. (1992), *Complexity: The Emerging Science at the Edge of Order and Chaos* (New York: Simon and Schuster).

EDITED COLLECTIONS

BARLOW, C. (1994) (ed.), *Evolution Extended: Biological Debates on the Meaning of Life* (Cambridge, Mass.: MIT Press).

BROOKS, R. A., and MAES, P. (1994) (eds.), *Artificial Life IV* (Proceedings of the Fourth International Workshop on the Synthesis and Simulation of Living Systems; Cambridge, Mass.: MIT Press).

BURKS, A. W. (1970) (ed.), *Essays on Cellular Automata* (Champaign-Urbana: University of Illinois Press).

CLIFF, D. (1994) (ed.), *AISB Quarterly*, no. 87, 15–54 (Special Theme: AI and Artificial Life).

CLIFF, D., HUSBANDS, P., MEYER, J.-A., and WILSON, S. W. (1994) (eds.), *From Animals to Animats 3* (Proceedings of the Third International Conference on Simulation of Adaptive Behavior; Cambridge, Mass.: MIT Press).

COWAN, G. A., PINES, D., and METZGER, D. (1995) (eds.), *Complexity: Metaphor and Reality* (Reading, Mass.: Addison-Wesley).

FORREST, S. (1991) (ed.), *Emergent Computation: Self-organizing, Collective, and Cooperative Phenomena in Natural and Artificial Computing Networks* (Cambridge, Mass.: MIT Press).

LANGTON, C. G. (1989) (ed.), *Artificial Life* (Santa Fe Institute Studies in the Sciences of Complexity, 6: Proceedings of the Interdisciplinary Workshop on the Synthesis and Simulation of Living Systems held September 1987, Los Alamos; Redwood City, Calif.: Addison-Wesley).

—— (1994) (ed.), *Artificial Life III* (Santa Fe Institute Studies on the Sciences of Complexity, Proceedings, 17; Redwood City, Calif.: Addison-Wesley).

—— (1995) (ed.), *Artificial Life: An Overview* (Cambridge, Mass.: MIT Press).

—— TAYLOR, C., FARMER, J. D., and RASMUSSEN, S. (1992) (eds.), *Artificial Life II* (Redwood City, Calif.: Addison-Wesley).

MAES, P. (1990) (ed.), *Designing Autonomous Agents* (Cambridge, Mass.: MIT Press).

MEYER, J.-A., and WILSON, S. W. (1991) (eds.), *From Animals to Animats* (Proceedings of the First International Conference on Simulation of Adaptive Behavior; Cambridge, Mass.: MIT Press).

——ROITBLAT, H., and WILSON, S. W. (1993) (eds.), *From Animals to Animats 2* (Proceedings of the Second International Conference on Simulation of Adaptive Behavior; Cambridge, Mass.: MIT Press).

MORAN, F., MORENO, A., MERELO, J. J., and CHACON, P. (1995) (eds.), *Advances in Artificial Life* (Proceedings of the Third European Conference on Artificial Life, Granada, 1995; Berlin: Springer-Verlag).

PORT, R., and VAN GELDER, T. (1995) (eds.), *Mind as Motion: Dynamics, Behavior, and Cognition* (Cambridge, Mass.: MIT Press).

ROITBLAT, H., and MEYER, J.-A. (1995) (eds.), *Comparative Approaches to Cognitive Science* (Cambridge, Mass.: MIT Press).

SOBER, E. (1994) (ed.), *Conceptual Issues in Evolutionary Biology*, 2nd edn. (Cambridge, Mass.: MIT Press).

STEELS, L. (1995) (ed.), *The Biology and Technology of Intelligent Autonomous Agents* (Berlin: Springer-Verlag).

—— and BROOKS, R. (1995) (eds.), *The A-Life Route to AI* (Hillsdale, NJ: Erlbaum).

THELEN, E., and SMITH, L. B. (1993) (eds.), *A Dynamic Systems Approach to the Development of Cognition and Action* (Cambridge, Mass.: MIT Press).

VARELA, F. J., and BOURGINE P. (1992) (eds.), *Toward a Practice of Autonomous Systems* (Proceedings of the First European Conference on Artificial Life; Cambridge, Mass.: MIT Press).

PAPERS

Articles included in the collections recommended above are not itemized here.

ARBIB, M. (1969), 'Self-producing Automata—Some Implications for Theoretical Biology', in C. H. Waddington (ed.), *Trends Towards a Theoretical Biology*, ii: *Sketches* (Edinburgh: Edinburgh University Press), 204–26.

—— (1993), Review of Allen Newell, 'Unified Theories of Cognition', in *Artificial Intelligence*, 59: 265–83.

BALLARD, D. (1991), 'Animate Vision', *Artificial Intelligence*, 48: 57–86.

BEER, R., and GALLAGHER, J. C. (1992), 'Evolving Dynamical Neural Networks for Adaptive Behavior', *Adaptive Behavior*, 1: 91–122.

BODEN, M. A. (1980), 'The Case for a Cognitive Biology', *Proceedings of the Aristotelian Society*, Supp. vol. liv, 25–49. (For an extended version, see M. A. Boden, *Minds and Mechanisms: Philosophical Psychology and Computational Models* (Ithaca, NY: Cornell University Press, 1981), 89–112.

BROOKS, R. A. (1991), 'Intelligence Without Representation', *Artificial Intelligence*, 47: 139–59.

CLIFF, D., HARVEY, I., and HUSBANDS, P. (1993), 'Explorations in Evolutionary Robotics', *Adaptive Behavior*, 2: 71–108.

DENNETT, D. C. (1978), 'Why not the Whole Iguana?', *Behavioral and Brain Sciences*, 1: 103–4.

—— (1994a), 'Artificial Life as Philosophy', *Artificial Life*, 1: 291–2.

—— (1994b), 'The Practical Requirements for Making a Conscious Robot', *Philosophical Transactions of the Royal Society, Series A*, 349: 133–46. (Special Issue on 'Artificial

Intelligence and the Mind: New Breakthroughs or Dead-Ends?', ed. M. A. Boden, A. Bundy, and R. M. Needham.)

DE SOUSA, R. (1995), 'Individualism and Local Control', *Canadian Journal of Philosophy*, Supp. vol. 20: 165–85.

DIETRICH, E. (1994), 'AI and the Tyranny of Galen, or Why Evolutionary Psychology and Cognitive Ethology are Important to Artificial Intelligence', *Journal of Experimental and Theoretical Artificial Intelligence*, 6: 325–30.

FLEISCHAKER, G. R. (1988), 'Autopoiesis: The Status of its System Logic', *BioSystems*, 22: 37–9.

GARDNER, M. (1970), 'The Fantastic Combinations of John Conway's New Solitaire Game "Life"', *Scientific American*, 223/4: 120–3.

GOUDGE, T. A. (1967), 'Emergent Evolutionism', in P. Edwards (ed.), *The Encyclopedia of Philosophy* (New York: Macmillan), ii. 474–7.

HARNAD, S. (1994), 'Levels of Functional Equivalence in Reverse Bioengineering', *Artificial Life*, 1: 293–301.

HOLLAND, J. H. and GOLDBERG, D. E. (1988), 'Genetic Algorithms and Machine Learning: Introduction to the Special Issue on Genetic Algorithms', *Machine Learning*, 3: 95.

HUSBANDS, P., HARVEY, I., and CLIFF, D. (1995), 'Circle in the Round: State Space Attractors for Evolved Sighted Robots', *Journal of Robotics and Autonomous Systems*, in press. (Special Issue on the Biology and Technology of Intelligent Autonomous Agents, ed. L. Steels.)

KAUFFMAN, S. A. (1991), 'Antichaos and Adaptation', *Scientific American* (Aug.), 78–84.

LANGTON, C. G. (1984), 'Self-Reproduction in Cellular Automata', *Physica D*, 10: 135–44.

MINGERS, J. (1989), 'An Introduction to Autopoeisis—Implications and Applications', *Systems Practice*, 2: 159–80.

RAY, T. S. (1994), 'An Evolutionary Approach to Synthetic Biology: Zen and the Art of Creating Life', *Artificial Life*, 1: 179–210.

REYNOLDS, C. W. (1987), 'Flocks, Herds, and Schools: A Distributed Behavioral Model', *Computer Graphics*, 21: 25–34.

SIMS, K. (1991), 'Artificial Evolution for Computer Graphics', *Computer Graphics*, 25: 319–28.

SPAFFORD, E. (1994), 'Computer Viruses as Artificial Life', *Artificial Life*, 1: 249–65.

STEELS, L. (1994), 'The Artificial Life Roots of Artificial Intelligence', *Artificial Life*, 1: 75–110.

TURING, A. M. (1952), 'The Chemical Basis of Morphogenesis', *Philosophical Transactions of the Royal Society (London), Series B*, 237: 37–72.

VAN GELDER, T. (1995), 'What Might Cognition Be, if not Computation?', *Journal of Philosophy*, 92: 345–81.

VARELA, F. J., MATURANA, H. R., and URIBE, R. (1974), 'Autopoiesis: The Organization of Living Systems', *Bio-Systems*, 5: 187–96.

VERA, H. A., and SIMON, H. A. (1993), 'Situated Action: A Symbolic Interpretation', *Cognitive Science*, 17: 117–33.

Future progress in the field can be followed in the journals *Adaptive Behavior* and *Artificial Life* (founded in 1993/1994), and in the regular published proceedings of the International Conference on A-Life, the European Conference on A-Life, and the International Conference on Simulation of Adaptive Behavior.

INDEX OF NAMES